MED Essence
YOUR PERSONALISED STUDY GUIDE

NEET (UG)

Handwritten Notes

Chemistry

ENRICHED WITH

PYQ Punch • NEET Concentrate

NEET (UG)

Handwritten Notes

Chemistry

ENRICHED WITH

PYQ Punch • NEET Concentrate

SANJAY SHARMA
M.Sc. B.Ed.

ARIHANT PRAKASHAN (Series), MEERUT

卐 Administrative & Production Offices

Regd. Office

'Ramchhaya' 4577/15, Agarwal Road, Darya Ganj, New Delhi -110002
Tele: 011- 47630600, 43518550

卐 Head Office

Kalindi, TP Nagar, Meerut (UP) - 250002
Tel: 0121-7156203, 7156204

卐 Sales & Support Offices

Agra, Ahmedabad, Bengaluru, Bareilly, Chennai, Delhi, Guwahati, Hyderabad, Jaipur, Jhansi, Kolkata, Lucknow, Nagpur & Pune.

卐 **PRICE** ₹350.00

卐 **PO No :** TXT-59-T065266-05-25

Published by Arihant Publications (India) Ltd.

For further information about the books published by Arihant, log on to www.arihantbooks.com or e-mail at info@arihantbooks.com

Follow us on    

Preface...

A Word for Aspiring NEET Scholars

First of all, congratulations on starting one of the most challenging and rewarding journeys of your life—the preparation for **NEET (National Eligibility cum Entrance Test)**. The path ahead may seem difficult, but remember, it is also full of chances for learning and personal growth..

These **handwritten notes** have been crafted with the aim to guide you through the vast and intricate landscape of **Chemistry**, one of the most fundamental yet challenging subjects in the NEET syllabus. As someone who has been through the rigorous grind of IIT preparation, I understand the importance of clarity, simplicity, and conceptual depth when it comes to mastering **Chemistry**. This is exactly what I've tried to bring into these notes.

The notes are designed to help you develop a deep understanding of core concepts, which is crucial for tackling the application-based questions often found in NEET. I have tried a different approach by dividing each topic into digestible segments that you can easily comprehend and retain.

The Features like **NEET Concentrate**, will help you build a strong foundation while keeping the subject engaging.

The NEET exam demands not only knowledge but also the ability to apply that knowledge efficiently under time constraints. With Features like **MCQ Punch** and **PYQ Punch** will help you strike the right balance between theory and questions. They will not only clarify your concepts but also give you the confidence to approach any problem, no matter how tricky it seems at first.

Remember, success in NEET is not about rote learning or memorizing facts. It's about developing a clear understanding and applying it in innovative ways. These notes are not just a tool to help you study; they are meant to be a companion in your journey, designed to build your problem-solving skills and foster a deeper connection with the subject.

I encourage you to go through these notes with patience, consistency, and an open mind. Don't hesitate to revisit any topic as many times as necessary. Believe in yourself, stay focused, and keep pushing forward. With the right approach, hard work, and these notes in hand, you are well on your way to achieving your NEET goals.

Best wishes for your preparation. May you achieve all the success you aim for!

SANJAY SHARMA
M.Sc., B.Ed.

Key Features

MCQ Punch

MCQ Punch

Conceptual/Numerical solved MCQs helpful for better conceptual understanding

Q.1 According to Bohr's theory, which of the following in Hydrogen atom will give rise to least energetic

(a) $n=6$ to $n=1$ (b) $n=5$ to $n=4$

(c) $n=6$ to $n=5$ (d) $n=5$ to $n=3$

Sol $\Delta E \propto \left[\frac{1}{n_1^2}-\frac{1}{n_2^2}\right]$ where $n_2>n_1$; Remember! energy between orbits decreases as you move away from

PYQ Punch

Q.1. Select the correct statement of the following – NEET 2023

A. Atoms of all elements are composed of 2 fundamental particles.

B. The mass of e⁻ is 9.10939×10^{-31} kg

C. All the isotopes of a given element show same chemical properties

D. Protons and electrons are collectively known as nucleons

E. Dalton's atomic theory, regarded the atom as ultimate particle of matter.

Choose the correct answer from the options given below –

(a) C, D & E only (b) A & E only (c) B, C & E only (d) A, B & C only

Sol Factual

PYQ Punch

Selective PYQs helpful in Theory-PyQ syncing along with learning enhancement.

NEET concentrate

- The energy associated with Threshold frequency is called Work Function (fn) of metal. It is denoted by w
- Li < Na < K < Rb < Cs ⟶ Work Function for different metals

Related curves

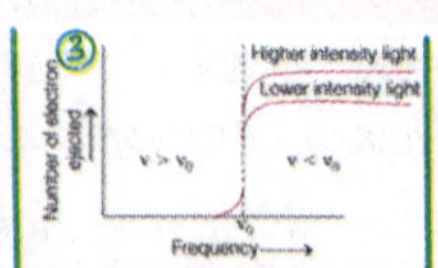

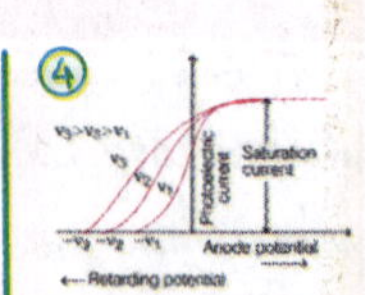

NEET Concentrate

Specialised Tips. Tricks & conceptual Info, most Important from NEET preparation prospective

Contents

1. Some Basic Concepts of Chemistry

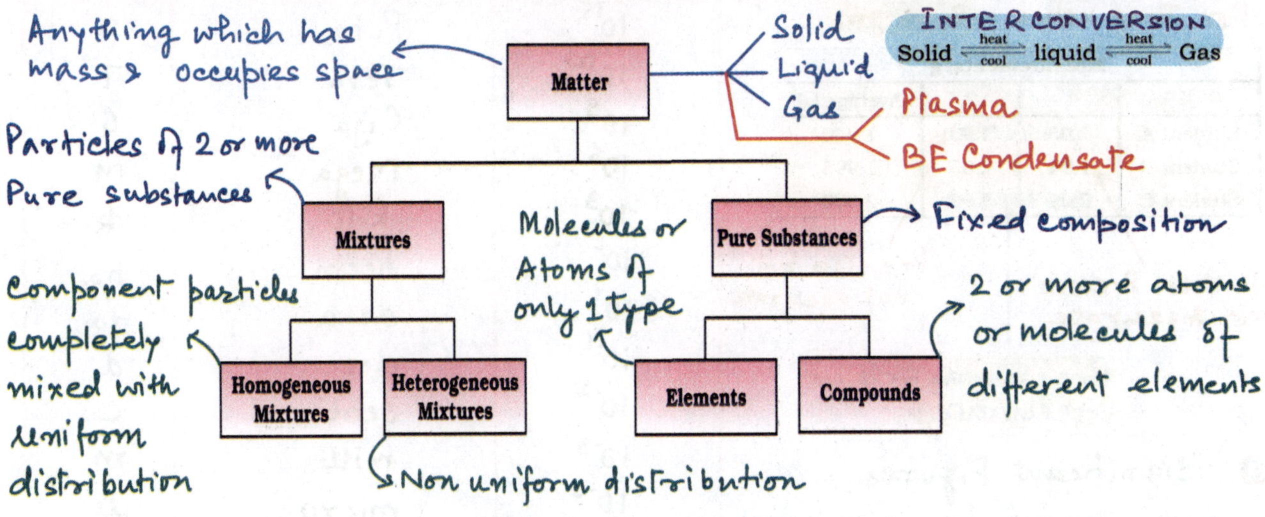

Physical ⟵ **Properties of Matter** ⟶ Chemical

Physical: Measured / Observed without changing the identity or composition of substance
e.g., colour, odour, M.P., B.P., Density etc.

Chemical: Measured / observed after changing the identity or composition of substance i.e., after chemical change.
e.g., composition, combustibility etc.

- Measurement of Physical Quantities – Earlier by English & Metric system but after 1960 by SI (International System) with
  - 7 Fundamental Units i.e., Meter (Length), Kilogram (Mass), second (Time), ampere (Electric current), Kelvin (Temperature) candela (Luminous Intensity) & Mole (Amount of substance)
  - 2 Supplementary units i.e., Plane angle & Solid Angle
- Mass ⟶ Amount of matter present in an object

  Weight ⟶ Force exerted by gravity on that object.

  Volume ⟶ Amount of space occupied by an object, measured as $(length)^3$ or $(m)^3$ or cm^3 or dm^3

  $1\ L = 1000\ mL = 1000\ cm^3 = 1\ dm^3$

  Density ⟶ Mass / volume $= kg/m^3$; It can be relative or absolute

  Temperature ⟶ $°F = \frac{9}{5}(°C) + 32$; $K = °C + 273.15$

Prefixes used in SI →

Number	Prefix	Symbol
10^{18}	Exo	E
10^{15}	Peta	P
10^{12}	Tera	T
10^{9}	Giga	G
10^{6}	Mega	M
10^{3}	kilo	k
10^{2}	hecta	ha
10^{1}	deka	da
10^{-1}	deci	d
10^{-2}	centi	c
10^{-3}	milli	m
10^{-6}	micro	μ
10^{-9}	nano	n
10^{-10}	Angstrom	Å
10^{-12}	pico	p
10^{-15}	fermi / femto	f
10^{-18}	atto	a

Precision & Accuracy

For True value = 2.00 gm

	Measurements/g		
	1	2	Average (g)
Student A	1.95	1.93	1.940
Student B	1.94	2.05	1.995
Student C	2.01	1.99	2.000

Student A: Precise but not accurate

Student B: Neither Precise Nor Accurate

Student C: Precise as well as Accurate.

- Significant Figures are meaningful figures which are known by certainty plus one which is estimated or uncertain.
- Method used to convert units from 1 system to other → unit factor method or Factor label method or Dimensional analysis.

Laws of Chemical combination

1. Law of conservation of Mass

By Antoine Lavoisier in 1789

No net change in mass occur during a physical or chemical process.

2. Law of Definite composition or Law of Definite Proportions

By Joseph Proust

A given compound always contains exactly the same proportion of elements by wt.

3. Law of Multiple Proportion

By Dalton in 1803

If 2 elements can combine to form more than 1 compound then the masses of 1 element that combined with a fixed mass of other element, are in the ratio of small whole numbers

4. Gay Lussac's law of Gaseous Volumes

By Gay Lussac in 1808

Gases combine or produced in chemical reactions in simpler ratios provided all of them are at STP.

- **Avogadro's Law** – By Avogadro in 1811, Equal volumes of all gases should contain equal number of molecules at same temperature and pressure. He gave this Number also as 6.022×10^{23} (N_A)
- **Dalton's Atomic Theory** – By John Dalton, 1808
  1. Matter consists of indivisible atoms
  2. Atoms of same element → identical mass & other properties
     Atoms of different elements → Different mass & other properties
  3. compounds → atoms of different elements combine in fixed ratio
  4. Chemical Reactions → reorganisation of atoms; Atoms are neither created nor destroyed in a chemical reaction
- A mass exactly equal to $1/12^{th}$ of the mass of 1 C–12 atom → amu (atomic mass unit) or u (unified mass)

Isotope	Relative Abundance	Atomic Mass
^{12}C	98.892	12
^{13}C	1.108	13.00335
^{14}C	2×10^{-10}	14.00317

Used in Periodic Table and normal Calculations

Average Atomic Mass

$(0.98892 \times 12) + (0.01108 \times 13.00335) + [(2 \times 10^{-12}) \times 14.00317] = 12.011\, u$

- Sum of atomic masses in covalent compounds → Molecular Mass
  Sum of atomic masses in ionic compounds → Formula Mass

Molar Mass →
- Atomic mass of an element in gms.
- Molecular mass of a covalent compound in gms.
- Formula mass of an ionic compound in gms.

Mole →
- Formula mass
- Number of particles = $N_A = 6.02214076 \times 10^{23}$
- 22.4 L (exactly 22.7) of any gas at STP

PYQ Punch

Q. The highest no. of helium atoms is in — NEET 2024

(a) 4 mol of He, (b) 4 u of He (c) 4 g of He (d) 2.271098 L He at STP

Sol optionwise atoms are (a) $4 \times N_A$ (b) 1 (c) N_A (d) $0.1 N_A$

- Mass percent of any element in a compound →

$$\frac{\text{Mass of element in gm}}{\text{Molar mass of substance in gm}} \times 100$$

- Simplest whole number ratio of various atoms present in a compound → Empirical formula.

- Exact number of various atoms present in a compound ⟶ Molecular Formula.

Stepwise approach to get Molecular & Empirical formula from percentage composition

- **Step 1** Convert given Mass percent to grams (Element wise)
- **Step 2** Calculate no. of moles from mass (gms) obtained
- **Step 3** Divide each of the mole values obtained in step 2 by the smallest number amongst them. This division gives the simplest ratio of all elements.
- **Step 4** Write the empirical formula by mentioning the numbers after writing the symbol of respective elements.
- **Step 5** Write molecular formula after comparing empirical formula mass with molar mass

PYQ Punch

Q. A compound X contains 32% of A, 20% of B and remaining percentage of C. Then the empirical formula of X is (Given, Atomic masses A = 64; B = 40 & C = 32 u) **NEET 2024**

(a) A_2BC_2 (b) ABC_3 ✓ (c) AB_2C_2 (d) ABC_4

Sol Step 1 ⟶ $A = 32/64 = 0.5$; $B = 20/40 = 0.5$; $C = 48/32 = 1.5$

Step 2 ⟶ $A - 0.5/0.5 = 1$; $B - 0.5/0.5 = 1$; $C - 1.5/0.5 = 3$

So Empirical formula = ABC_3

- Stoichiometry (Gr Stoicheron = element; metron = measure) deals with the calculation of masses or volumes of reactants & products involved in a chemical Reaction.
- The stoichiometric interpretation can be visible as –

$$CaCO_3 \xrightarrow{\Delta} CaO + CO_2$$

Interpretation

	$CaCO_3$	CaO	CO_2
In terms of Moles ①	1 mole	1 mole	1 mole
Mass ②	100 gms	56 gms	44 gms
Volume ③	22.4 L	22.4 L	22.4 L
No. of atoms ④	(i) 6.022×10^{23} Ca (ii) 6.022×10^{23} C (iii) $3\times6.022\times10^{23}$ O	(i) 6.022×10^{23} Ca (ii) 6.022×10^{23} O	(i) 6.022×10^{23} C (ii) $2\times6.022\times10^{23}$ O

- These interpretations are used in solving problems related to

a. Mass – Mass relationship
b. Mole – Mass relationship
c. Mass – volume relationship
d. Mole – volume relationship

- In general, the reactant which is consumed first, usually limits the amount of product formed → Limiting reagent

Dhyan Rakhna! Limiting reagent related problems mein final product quantity limiting reagent pr dependent hoti hai, Bache hue Excess reagent pr nahi.

Concentration Terms

Molarity (M)

$$\frac{\text{No. of Moles of solute}}{\text{Volume of solution in litres}}$$

Mass percent (% w/w)

$$\frac{\text{Mass of solute}}{\text{Mass of solution}} \times 100$$

Molality (m)

$$\frac{\text{No. of Moles of solute}}{\text{Mass of solvent in kg}}$$

Mole fraction (x)

$$\frac{\text{Moles of solute/solvent}}{\text{Moles of solute + Moles of solvent}}$$

PYQ Punch

Q. 1 gm of NaOH was treated with 25 mL of 0.75 M HCl solution, the mass of NaOH left unreacted is equal to — NEET 2024
(a) 750 mg ✓(b) 250 mg (c) Zero mg (d) 200 mg

Sol Given mass of NaOH = 1 g; Mole of NaOH = $1/40 = 0.025$; Mole of HCl $= \frac{0.75 \times 25}{1000} = 0.01875$; Limiting Reagent is HCl $\left(\text{as } \frac{0.025}{1} > \frac{0.01875}{1}\right)$

So Moles unreacted = $0.025 - 0.01875 = 0.00625$
Mass unreacted = $0.00625 \times 40 = 0.25$ gm = 250 mg.

- Out of the concentration terms written above –
  a. Molality & % w/w are temperature independent while rest are temperature dependent
  b. Molality is used in most of the calculations of labs (as it remains unchanged in temperature variations)

NEET concentrate

- The mass of a substance that can combine with or replace a fixed amount of another substance ⟶ Equivalent Mass.

  In General $\text{Eq. Mass} = \dfrac{\text{Molecular Mass}}{n\text{-factor}}$

  - Basicity of an acid or Acidity of a base
  - Total (+)ve or (−)ve charge for a salt
  - No. of e^- lost or gained for redox reactions

- Normality (N) ⟶ $\dfrac{\text{No. of equivalents of solute}}{\text{Volume of solution (in L)}}$

  $= \text{Molarity} \times n\text{-factor}$

2. Atomic Structure

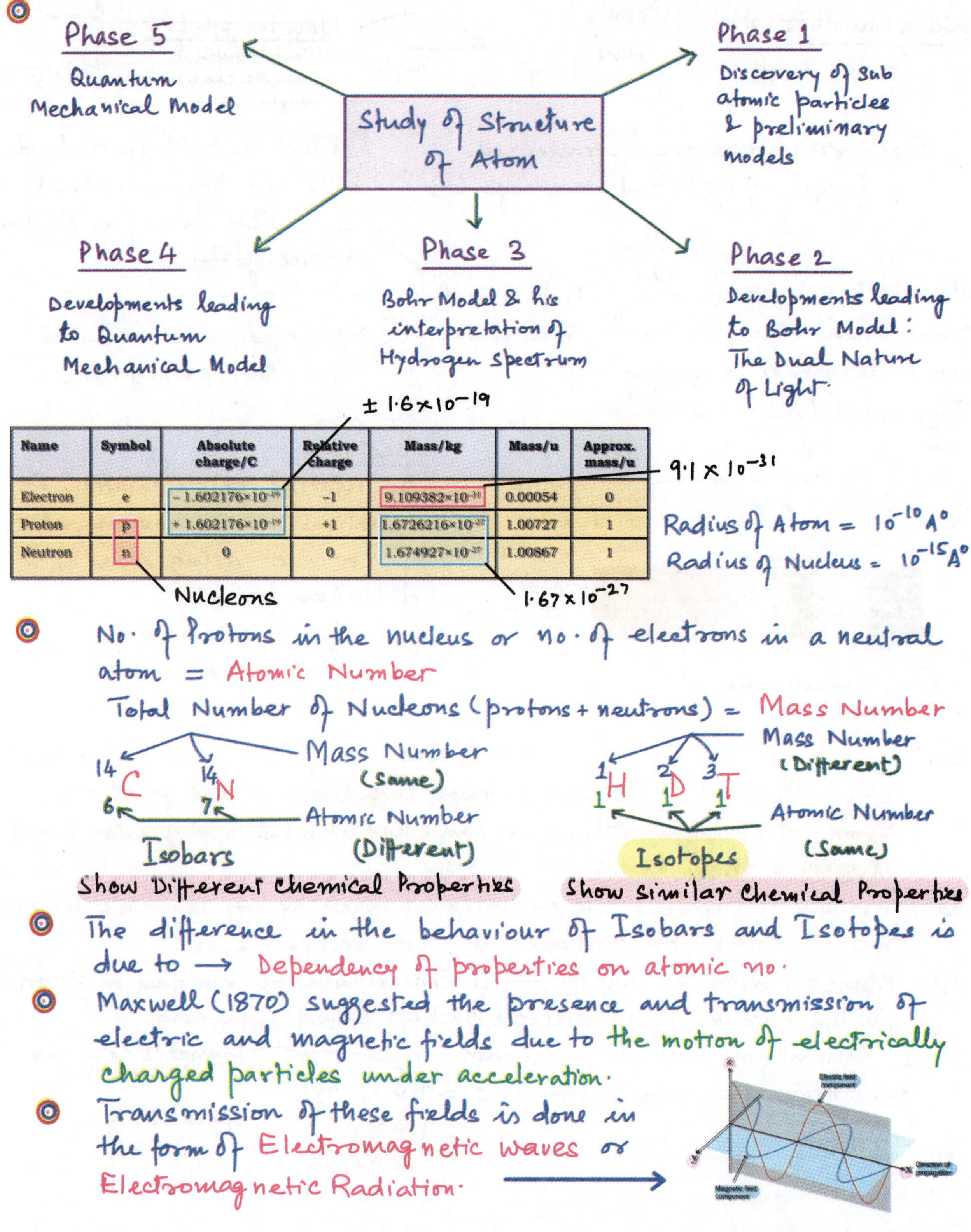

Name	Symbol	Absolute charge/C	Relative charge	Mass/kg	Mass/u	Approx. mass/u
Electron	e	-1.602176×10^{-19}	-1	9.109382×10^{-31}	0.00054	0
Proton	p	$+1.602176\times10^{-19}$	+1	1.6726216×10^{-27}	1.00727	1
Neutron	n	0	0	1.674927×10^{-27}	1.00867	1

$\pm 1.6\times10^{-19}$

9.1×10^{-31}

1.67×10^{-27}

p, n: Nucleons

Radius of Atom = 10^{-10} A°

Radius of Nucleus = 10^{-15} A°

- No. of Protons in the nucleus or no. of electrons in a neutral atom = Atomic Number

  Total Number of Nucleons (protons + neutrons) = Mass Number

  $^{14}_{6}C$, $^{14}_{7}N$ — Mass Number (Same), Atomic Number (Different) — **Isobars**: Show Different Chemical Properties

  $^{1}_{1}H$, $^{2}_{1}D$, $^{3}_{1}T$ — Mass Number (Different), Atomic Number (Same) — **Isotopes**: Show similar Chemical Properties

- The difference in the behaviour of Isobars and Isotopes is due to → Dependency of properties on atomic no.
- Maxwell (1870) suggested the presence and transmission of electric and magnetic fields due to the motion of electrically charged particles under acceleration.
- Transmission of these fields is done in the form of Electromagnetic waves or Electromagnetic Radiation. →

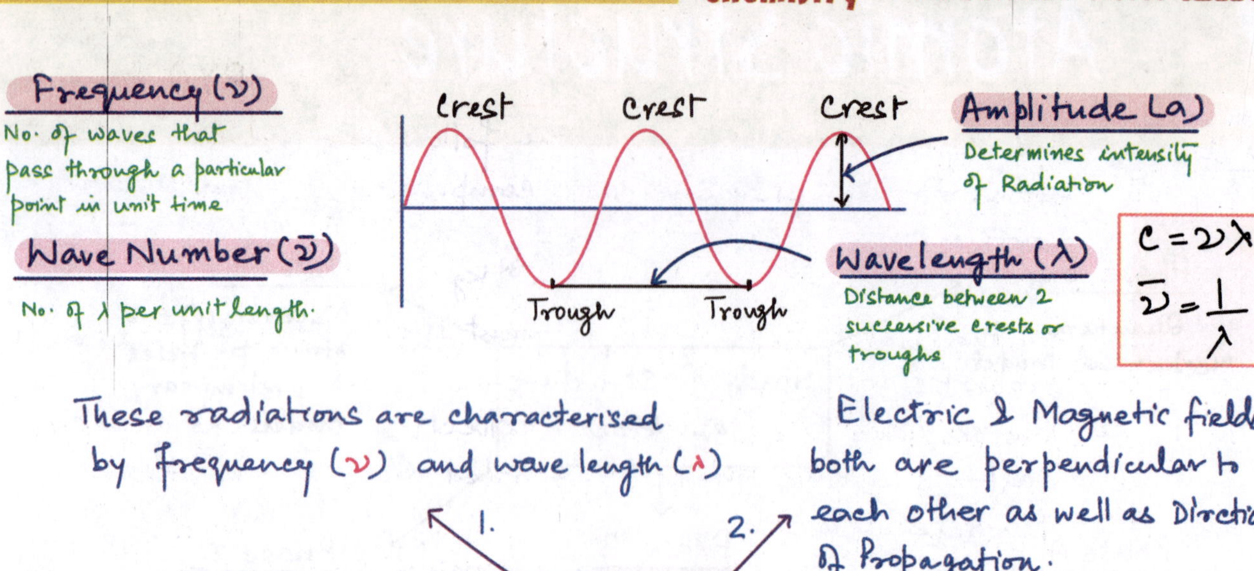

Frequency (ν)
No. of waves that pass through a particular point in unit time

Wave Number ($\bar{\nu}$)
No. of λ per unit length.

Amplitude (a)
Determines intensity of Radiation

Wavelength (λ)
Distance between 2 successive crests or troughs

$c = \nu\lambda$

$\bar{\nu} = \frac{1}{\lambda}$

Properties of EM Waves

1. These radiations are characterised by frequency (ν) and wave length (λ)
2. Electric & Magnetic fields both are perpendicular to each other as well as Direction of Propagation.
3. No Medium is required for their propagation
4. Different EM waves differ from each other in wave length or frequency. This constitute EM spectrum

γ rays | X rays | UV | IR | Microwave | FM | AM | Long radio waves (Radio waves)

10^{-16} 10^{-14} 10^{-12} 10^{-10} 10^{-8} 10^{-6} 10^{-4} 10^{-2} 10^{0} 10^{2} 10^{4} 10^{6} 10^{8} λ(m)

Visible spectrum ← Visible light spectrum

400 500 600 700 750
Wavelength λ (nanometers)

V I B G Y O R

Spectrum

- Pictorial representation of radiations in increasing order of λ or decreasing order of ν.
- It can be –
  a. Emission or Absorption
  b. Continuous or Band
  c. Discontinuous or Line.

- Presence of visible light in EM spectrum justifies its wave nature
  Dhyan Rakhna! γ, X and UV rays have lesser λ and greater ν from violet light. IR, Micro and Radio waves have greater λ and lesser ν than Red light.
- Particle nature of EM Radiation proven by → Planck's Quantum theory, Black Body radiation & Photo electric effect.
- Planck's Quantum theory → 1. Radiant energy emitted or absorbed in the form of small discrete packets called Quantum.
  2. Quantum of Light = Photon.
  3. Energy of 1 Quantum → $E = h\nu = hc/\lambda$

  $= \frac{12400}{\lambda(\text{Å})}$ eV

  h = Planck's constant 6.626×10^{-34} Js
  c = Speed of light 3×10^{8} m/s

PYQ Punch

Q.1. Select the correct statement of the following – NEET 2023

A. Atoms of all elements are composed of 2 fundamental particles.

B. The mass of e^- is 9.10939×10^{-31} kg

C. All the isotopes of a given element show same chemical properties

D. Protons and electrons are collectively known as nucleons

E. Dalton's atomic theory, regarded the atom as ultimate particle of matter.

Choose the correct answer from the options given below –

(a) C, D & E only (b) A & E only ✓(c) B, C & E only (d) A, B & C only

Sol Factual

Q.2. Calculate the energy in joule corresponding to light of λ 45 nm (Planck's constant $h = 6.63 \times 10^{-34}$ Js; Speed of light $c = 3 \times 10^8$ m/s) NEET 2014

(a) 6.67×10^{15} (b) 6.67×10^{11} (c) 4.42×10^{-15} ✓(d) 4.42×10^{-18}

Sol $E = hc/\lambda = 6.63 \times 10^{-34} \times 3 \times 10^8 / 45 \times 10^{-9} = 4.42 \times 10^{-18}$

Photo electric effect

◎ Certain metals (eg. K, Rb, Cs etc.) eject e^- when exposed to beam of light.

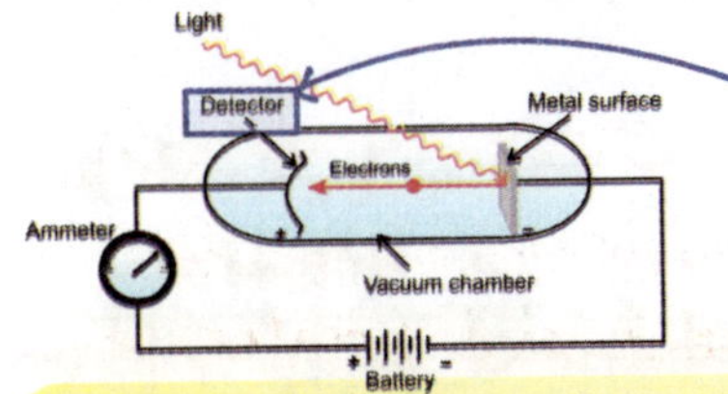

Measures K.E. of ejected Photo electrons

Experimental setup of Hertz

Observations

a. No time lag between striking of light beam & ejection of e^-.

b. The no. of e^- ejected $\propto$ Intensity or Brightness of light

c. (i) A minimum characteristic frequency ν_0 is there for each metal.

(ii) With light less than ν_0 → No photoelectric effect seen.

(iii) Above which ⟶ Photoelectrons ejected with certain K.E.

(iv) This KE of photoelectrons $\propto$ Frequency of light used. ↑ Concluded & confirmed by Einstein in 1905

Explanation For light $E = h\nu = hc/\lambda$

For Photo electron $K.E. = h(\nu - \nu_0) = hc\left(\frac{1}{\lambda} - \frac{1}{\lambda_0}\right)$

Threshold Frequency (ν_0), Threshold wavelength (λ_0)

NEET concentrate

- The energy associated with Threshold frequency is called Work function ($h\nu_0$) of metal. It is denoted by w
- Li < Na < K < Rb < Cs ⟶ Work function for different metals

Related curves

① KE of ejected electron vs Frequency of light (ν) ⟶ ; ν_0 = Threshold frequency

② KE of ejected electron vs Intensity of light (Frequency constant); $\nu > \nu_0$

③ Number of electron ejected vs Frequency ⟶ ; Higher intensity light; Lower intensity light; $\nu > \nu_0$; $\nu < \nu_0$

④ Photoelectric current vs Anode potential; ⟵ Retarding potential; $\nu_3 > \nu_2 > \nu_1$; Saturation current; $-V_3$ $-V_2$ $-V_1$

- At a given frequency, increase in intensity of light increases the number of Photons of same frequency ⟶ So, when light intensity is increased, more e^- are ejected but no change is visible in their energy.

◉ **Black Body** ⟶ An ideal body which is a perfect emitter and perfect absorber of radiations.

Black Body radiation ⟶ Term used to describe the relationship between an objects temperature & λ of EM radiations it emit.

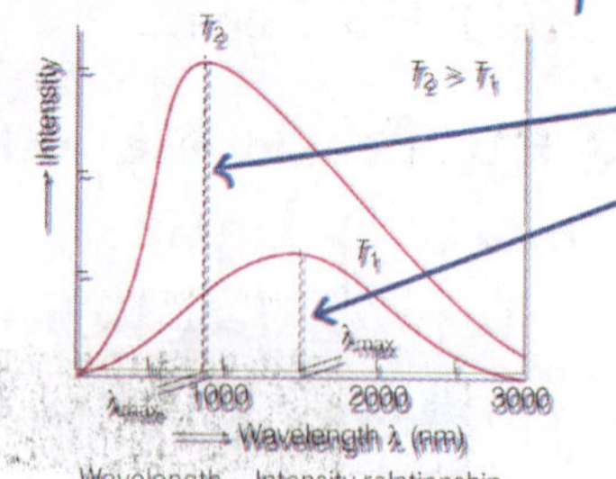

Wavelength = Intensity relationship

Different λ peaks at different temperatures suggests $E \propto \nu$ (Frequency dependence of Energy emitted)

Dhyan Rakhna | Stars bhi Black bodies ki tarah hi behave karte hain Aur stars ka different colour bhi Black Body radiations se hi explain kiya jaata Hai

Bohr's Model

◉ Electron revolves around the nucleus in fixed circular orbits of definite energy ⟶ Energy of an electron is quantised with angular momentum

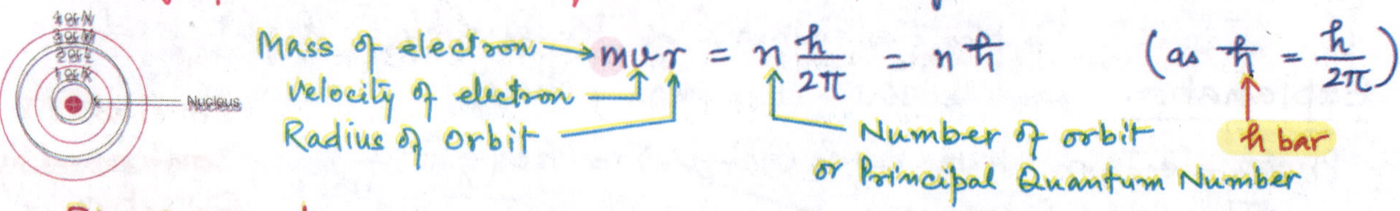

$$mvr = n\frac{h}{2\pi} = n\hbar \quad \left(\text{as } \hbar = \frac{h}{2\pi}\right)$$

Fixed circular orbits of definite energy = Stationary Energy levels.

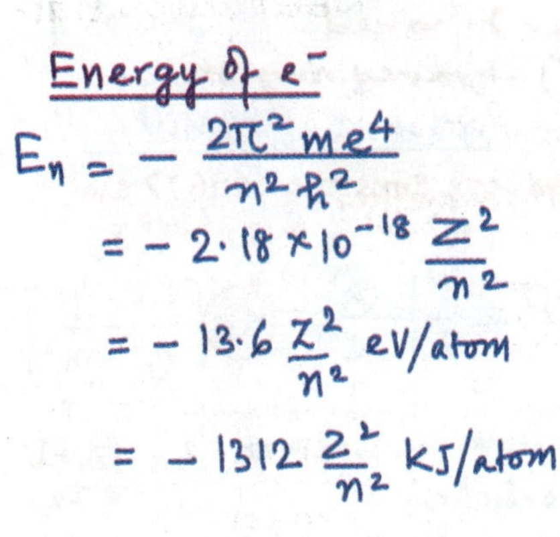

Energy of e^-

$$E_n = -\frac{2\pi^2 me^4}{n^2h^2}$$
$$= -2.18\times10^{-18}\frac{Z^2}{n^2}$$
$$= -13.6\frac{Z^2}{n^2}\ \text{eV/atom}$$
$$= -1312\frac{Z^2}{n^2}\ \text{kJ/atom}$$

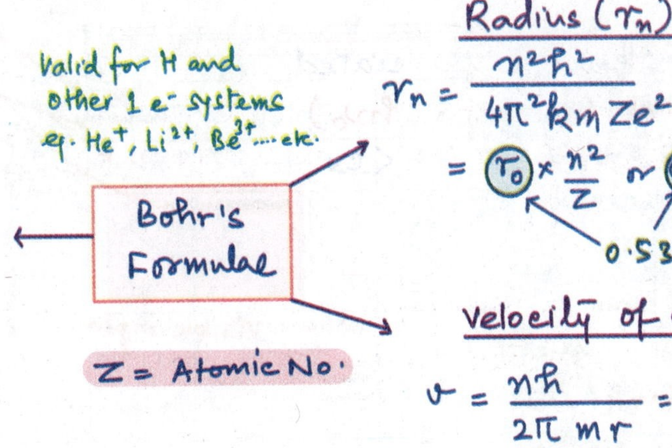

Valid for H and other 1 e^- systems eg. He^+, Li^{2+}, Be^{3+}.... etc.

Bohr's Formulae

Z = Atomic No.

Radius (r_n)

$$r_n = \frac{n^2h^2}{4\pi^2 kmZe^2}$$
$$= r_0 \times \frac{n^2}{Z} \text{ or } a_0 \times \frac{n^2}{Z}\ \text{Å}$$

r_0, a_0 = 0.53 Å

Velocity of e^-

$$v = \frac{nh}{2\pi mr} = \frac{2\pi Ze^2k}{nh}$$
$$= 2.188\times10^6\times\frac{Z}{n}\ \text{m/s}$$

PYQ Punch

Q.1. The energy of an e^- in ground state (n=1) for He^+ ion is $-x$ J, then that for an e^- in n=2 state for Be^{3+} ion in J is

(a) $-x$ (b) $-x/9$ (c) $-4x$ (d) $-4/9x$ NEET 2024

Sol. $E \propto Z^2/n^2$; $\frac{E_1}{E_2} = \frac{2^2}{1^2}\times\frac{2^2}{4^2} = 1$; $E_1 = E_2$

Q.2 If the radius of second Bohr orbit of He^+ ion is 105.8 pm, what is the radius of third Bohr orbit of Li^{2+} ion NEET 2022

(a) 15.87 pm (b) 1.587 pm (c) 158.7 Å (d) 158.7 pm

Sol $r = n^2/Z$; $\frac{(r_3)_{Li^{2+}}}{(r_2)_{He^+}} = \frac{n_1^2\times Z_2}{n_2^2\times Z_1} = \frac{3^2\times2}{2^2\times3}\times 105.8\ \text{pm} = 158.7\ \text{pm}$.

Line Spectrum of Hydrogen

- According to stationary energy level concept although e- revolves in fixed energy orbits but it can transit from 1 orbit to other by simply absorbing or emitting energy.
- The frequency of radiation absorbed or emitted (ν) = $\frac{E_2 - E_1}{h}$ ← Energies of orbits
- This is the basis of line emission or atomic emission spectra of H. It is obtained when an electric discharge is passed through Hydrogen gas at low pressure → seen as bluish light which contain several isolated sharp lines, visible when seen through Prism.

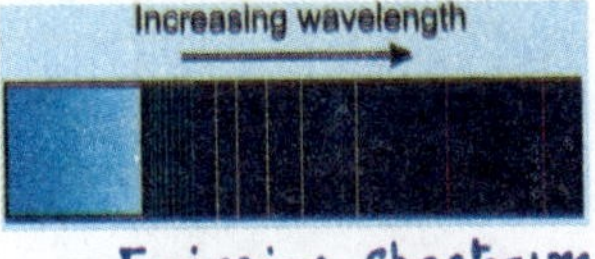

Emission spectrum

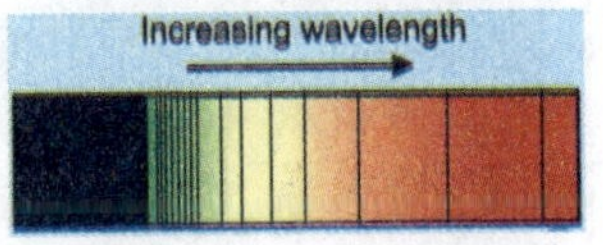

Absorption spectrum

6 series of lines named after scientists who discovered them.

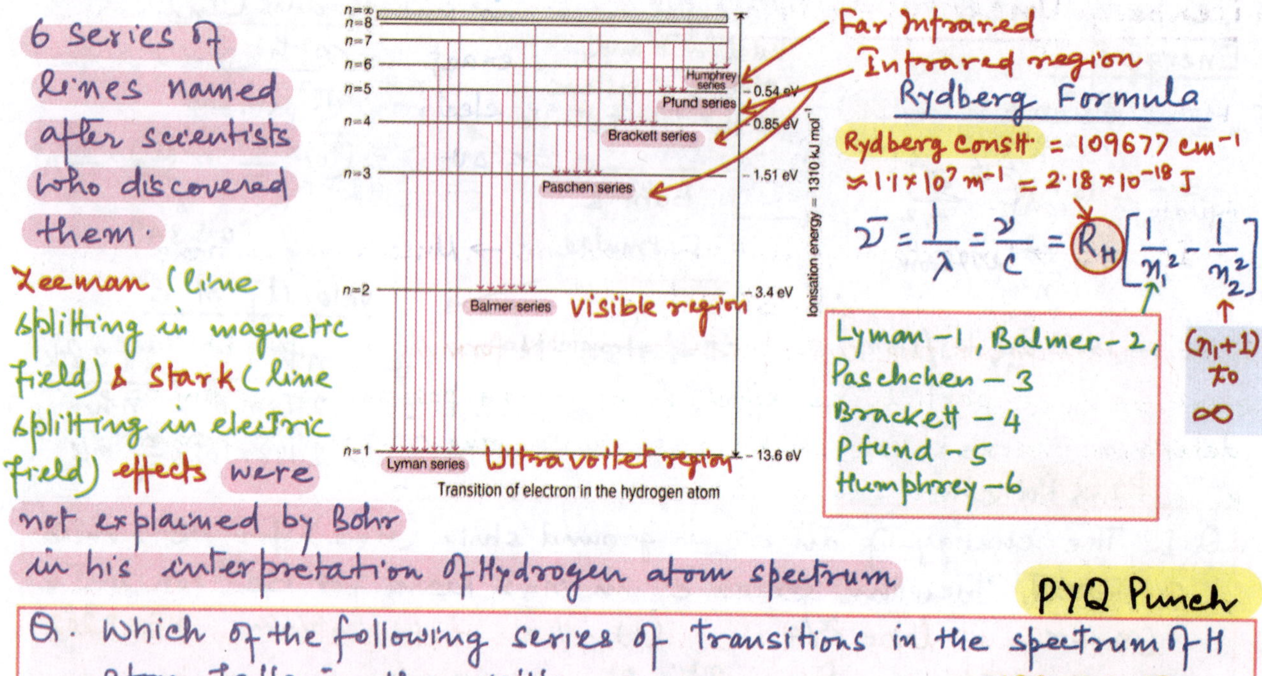

Transition of electron in the hydrogen atom

Zeeman (line splitting in magnetic field) & Stark (line splitting in electric field) effects were not explained by Bohr in his interpretation of Hydrogen atom spectrum

Rydberg Formula

Rydberg const = 109677 cm^{-1} $\approx 1.1 \times 10^7\ m^{-1}$ $= 2.18 \times 10^{-18}$ J

$$\bar{\nu} = \frac{1}{\lambda} = \frac{\nu}{c} = R_H\left[\frac{1}{n_1^2} - \frac{1}{n_2^2}\right]$$

n_2: (n_1+1) to ∞

Lyman – 1, Balmer – 2, Paschen – 3, Brackett – 4, Pfund – 5, Humphrey – 6

PYQ Punch

Q. Which of the following series of transitions in the spectrum of H atom falls in the visible region **NEET 2019**

(a) Brackett Series (b) Lyman Series ~~(c)~~ Balmer Series (d) Paschen Series

Sol Factual

Limitations of Bohr's Model
- Unable to explain the spectrum of multielectron system
- Didn't gave any clue, how chemical bonds are formed
- No explanation of zeeman & stark effect.
- Discuss 2D (circular) atom, no clue about 3D existence of atom.
- Unable to explain the dual nature of matter.

MCQ Punch

Q.1 According to Bohr's theory, which of the following transitions in Hydrogen atom will give rise to least energetic Photon.

(a) n = 6 to n = 1 (b) n = 5 to n = 4 ~~(c)~~ n = 6 to n = 5 (d) n = 5 to n = 3

Sol $\Delta E \propto \left[\frac{1}{n_1^2} - \frac{1}{n_2^2}\right]$ where $n_2 > n_1$; Remember! energy difference between orbits decreases as you move away from nucleus.

Q.2 In H atom, the energy of first excited state is –3.4 eV Then, KE of same orbit of H atom is

~~(a)~~ +3.4 eV, (b) +6.8 eV, (c) –13.6 eV (d) +13.6 eV

Sol $E_T = K.E + P.E = \frac{1}{2}\frac{Ze^2}{r} - \frac{Ze^2}{r}$ or $-3.4\,eV = -\frac{1}{2}\frac{Ze^2}{r} = +3.4\,eV$

Heisenberg Uncertainty Principle

◎ It is impossible to determine the exact position (x) and exact momentum (or velocity) of any particle like electron.

$$\Delta x \cdot \Delta p \geq \frac{h}{4\pi} \text{ or } \frac{\hbar}{2} \text{ or } \Delta x \cdot \Delta v \geq \frac{h}{4\pi m} \leftarrow 0.52 \times 10^{-34}$$

Equals to $m\Delta v$ → (Δp)

If ΔE → Uncertainty in Energy and Δt → Uncertainty in time then

$$\Delta E \cdot \Delta t \geq h/4\pi$$

Always remember the interpretation of this formula as "Jab bhi hum electron jaise particle ke exact momentum + position ko simultaneously determine karne ki koshish karenge toh always 0.52×10^{-34} magnitude ki minimum error aayegi hi"

NEET concentrate

- The explanation behind such uncertainty is → extremly small size of e^- like particles which loose their position and change their momentum after collision with much-2 bigger particles of light (Photons) whenever we try to locate them or focus light on them.
- Uncertainty principle also serves as the basis for the development of electron microscope.

de Broglie's Equation

◎ By de-Broglie (1924), proposed Dual nature of matter just like dual matter of light & gave the relationship equation between a particle in motion and a wave i.e.,

$$\lambda = \frac{h}{p} = \frac{h}{mv} = \frac{h}{\sqrt{2meV}} = \frac{h}{\sqrt{2mKE}} \simeq \frac{12.25}{\sqrt{V}} = \sqrt{\frac{150}{V}} \text{ Å}$$

◎ Bohr theory can be proven with de-Broglie equation as

$2\pi r = n\lambda$ leading to $mvr = nh/2\pi$ (as $\lambda = h/mv$)

(n →) no. of waves made in 1 revolution

NEET concentrate

de-Broglie suggested that every object in motion has a wave character but as it is inversely proportional to mass of that body hence macroscopic bodies (with larger mass) give undetected λ.

PYQ Punch

Q. In H atom, the de-Broglie λ of an electron in the second orbit of Bohr, is (given that Bohr radius $a_0 = 52.9$ pm) NEET 2019

(a) 211.6 pm (b) ✓ 211.6π pm (c) 52.9π pm (d) 105.8 pm

Sol $\lambda = \frac{2\pi n a_0}{Z} = 2\pi \times 2 \times 52.9 = 211.6\pi$ pm (n=2, Z=1)

Quantum Mechanical Model

◎ By Schrödinger, suggested 3D existence of an atom and gave

Distribution of ψ along the cartesian coordinates x, y & z

$$\frac{\partial^2 \psi}{\partial x^2} + \frac{\partial^2 \psi}{\partial y^2} + \frac{\partial^2 \psi}{\partial z^2} + \frac{8\pi^2 m}{h^2}(E - V)\psi = 0$$

E → Total Energy; V → Potential Energy; ψ → psi, wave function (Basically amplitude of 3D e⁻ wave)

Basically tells us about the 3D existence of atom.

◎ Solutions of this equation, for different values of psi were called as Eigen Functions. These were portrayed in the form of numbers ⟶ Quantum Numbers (l, m especially in sync with n which was taken from Bohr's Model)

◎ According to this model atoms consists of Orbitals of definite shape which combine to form subshells. These orbitals are defined through $|\psi^2|$ i.e., probability of finding an e⁻ & their shapes + sizes depends upon ψ. These are —

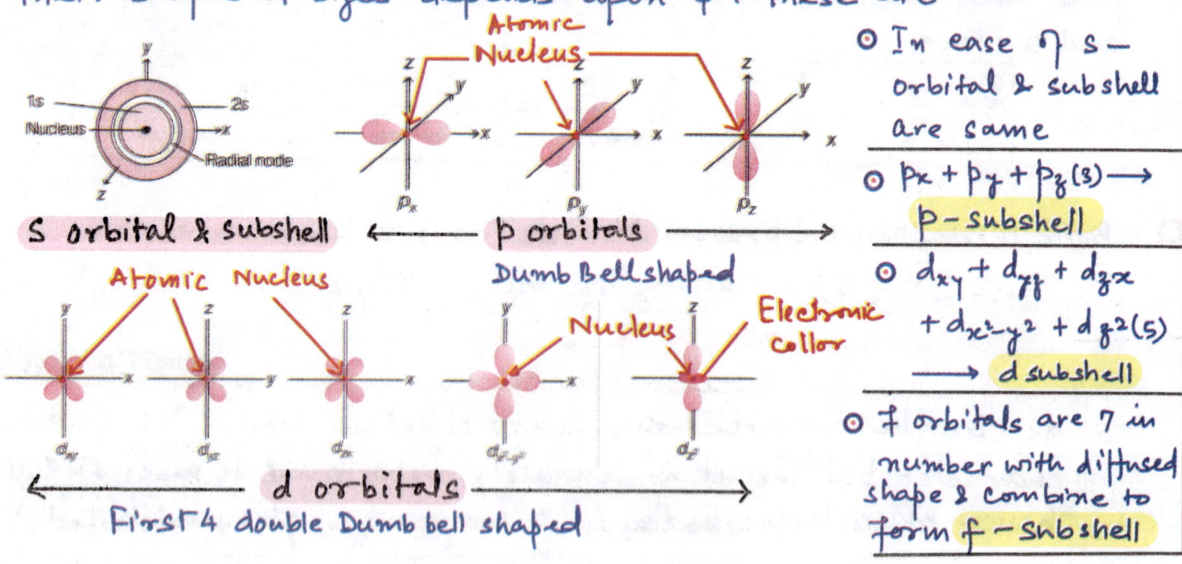

⊙ In case of s-orbital & subshell are same

⊙ $p_x + p_y + p_z$ (3) ⟶ p-subshell

⊙ $d_{xy} + d_{yz} + d_{zx} + d_{x^2-y^2} + d_{z^2}$ (5) ⟶ d subshell

⊙ f orbitals are 7 in number with diffused shape & combine to form f-subshell

- An orbital can accommodate a maximum of 2 e^-. Thus the no. of e^- which s, p, d, f subshells can accommodate are 2, 6, 10 and 14 respectively.

Quantum Numbers

1. Principal Q. No. (n)

- Proposed by Bohr, denotes hypothetical energy boundary (orbit or shell) with in atom.
- $n = 1, 2, 3, 4 \ldots\ldots$
  K, L, M, N ……
- Total orbitals → n^2
  Total e^- → $2n^2$

2. Azimuthal Q. No. (l)

- Also called Angular Q. No. proposed by Sommerfield.
- Tells the energy and shapes of subshells
  s < p < d < f – Energy
- Value – s → 0
  p → 1
  d → 2
  f → 3
- Maximum no. of e^- in subshell → $2(2l + 1)$
- Orbital angular momentum → $\frac{h}{2\pi}\sqrt{l(l+1)}$

3. Magnetic Q. No. (m)

- Proposed by Zeeman.
- Tells the no. of orbitals & their orientation in a subshell
- Values $-l$ to $+l$ through 0.
- Total number of values of $m = (2l + 1)$
- All orbitals of a subshell with same energy → Degenerate orbitals.

4. Spin Q. No. (s)

- Proposed by Goldsmith & Ulen Back.
- Signifies the spin of 2 e^- present with in the orbital
- Values → $+\frac{1}{2}$ & $-\frac{1}{2}$ signify clockwise & anticlockwise spin respectively.
- Arbitary value, Not the solution of wave equation
- Spin angular momentum → $\frac{h}{2\pi}\sqrt{s(s+1)}$

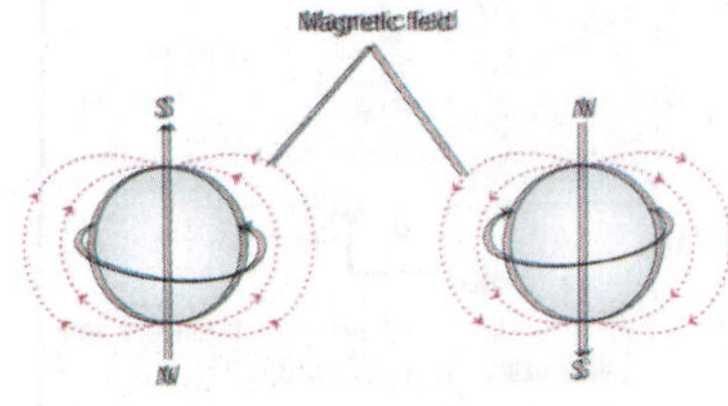

Electrons with opposite spin with in an orbital showing magnetic fields produced by their motion. Attraction between these fields supports their presence with in an orbital inspite similar charges

PYQ Punch

Q1. Match list I with list II — NEET 2024

List I (Quantum Number)	List II (Information Provided)
A. m_l	I. Shape of orbital
B. m_s	II. Size of orbital
C. l	III. Orientation of orbital
D. n	IV. Orientation of spin of e^-

Choose the correct answer from the options given below

(a) A-I, B-III, C-II, D-IV
(b) A-III, B-IV, C-I, D-II ✓
(c) A-III, B-IV, C-II, D-I
(d) A-II, B-I, C-IV, D-III

Sol Factual

Q.2 The relation between n_m (n_m = the number of permissible values of magnetic Q. No. m) for a given value of l i.e., azimuthal Q. No., is — NEET 2023

(a) $l = 2n_m + 1$ (b) $n_m = 2l^2 + 1$ (c) $n_m = l + 2$ (d) $l = \frac{n_m - 1}{2}$ ✓

Sol $n_m = 2l + 1$ or $l = (n_m - 1)/2$

Dhyan Rakho | NEET mein every year Quantum Numbers se question expected Hota Hai; clarity ke liye neeche di gayi values ko yaad rakho –

$l = 0$ ⟶ for s subshell having 1 orbital & 2 e^- only

$l = 1$; $m = -1, 0, +1$ signifying p subshell, with p_x, p_y, p_z orbitals and 6 e^- only.

$l = 2$; $m = -2, -1, 0, +1, +2$ signifying d subshell with $d_{xy}, d_{yz}, d_{zx}, d_{x^2-y^2}, d_{z^2}$ orbitals & 10 e^- only

$l = 3$; $m = -3, -2, -1, 0, +1, +2, +3$ signifying f subshell with 7 diffused orbitals & 14 e^- only.

Important Curves

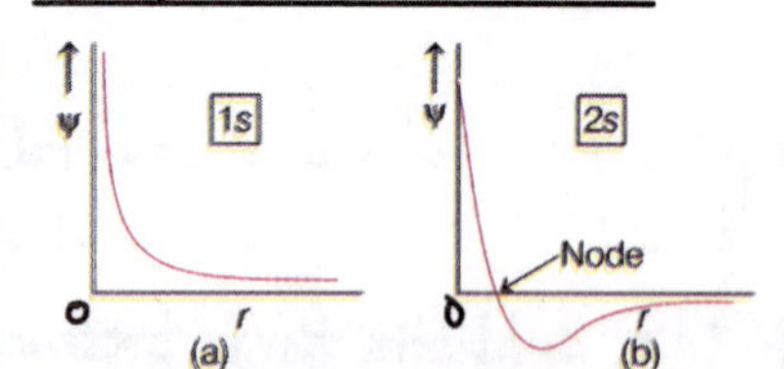

(a) and (b) Plot of wave function ψ with distance r from the nucleus for (a) 1s and (b) 2s orbitals.

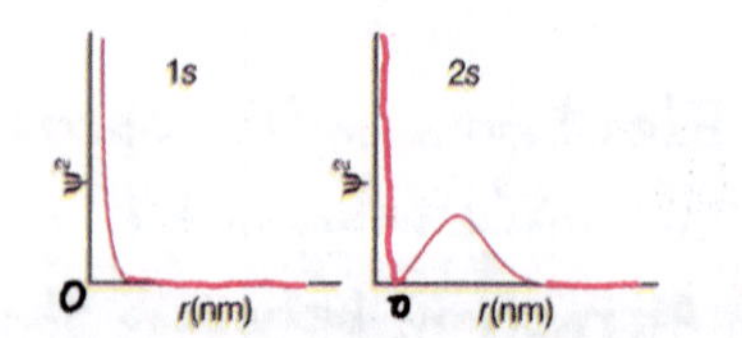

(b) Variation of probability density (ψ^2) with distance r from the nucleus for (a) 1s and (b) 2s orbitals.

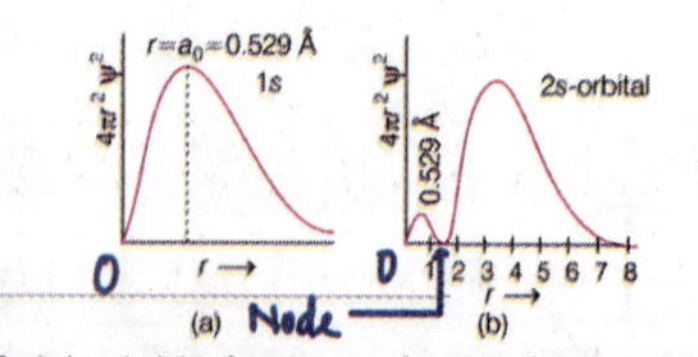

Radial probability function as a function of distance, r from the nucleus for (a) 1s and (b) 2s

NEET concentrate

Nodes ⟶ The only space with in an orbital (except nucleus) where probability of finding e^- is zero.

For a given subshell

Total Nodes in an orbital = $n-1$

Radial or spherical nodes = $n-l-1$

Nodal planes or Angular Nodes = l

Electronic Configuration

Shell ⟶ $n l^{x}$ ⟵ subshell; x ⟵ no. of electron

Rules ⟶ A. Aufbau Principle (Building up) ⟶ Orbitals & subshells are filled up in increasing order of their energy.

1s < 2s < 2p < 3s < 3p < 4s < 3d < 4p < 5s < 4d < 5p < 6s < 4f < 5d < 6p < 7s < 5f < 6d < 7s

1s, 2s, 2p, 3s, 3p, 3d, 4s, 4p, 4d, 4f, 5s, 5p, 5d, 5f, 6s, 6p, 6d, 7s, 7p

Increasing order of energy

Always Remember | ① Orbit change occur after p

② d orbital is filled in $(n+1)$ mode i.e., 3d after 4s, 4d after 5s, 5d after 6s & 6d after 7s

③ f orbital is filled in $(n+2)$ mode i.e., 4f after 6s and 5s after 7s

B. Hund's rule of maximum multiplicity ⟶ (i) Degenerate orbitals first filled singly and pairing occurs only when all orbitals of a subshell filled first.

(ii) Half filled and completely filled orbitals are extra stable (due to more no. of exchange energies)

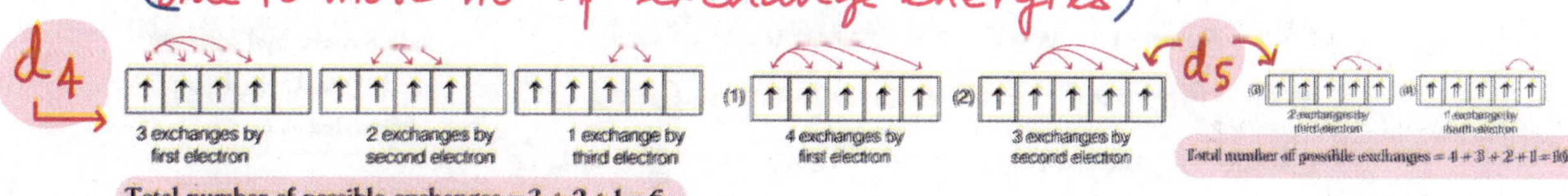

Pauli's Exclusion Principle

Dhyan Rakho | yeh rule e^- ki filling se related Nahi Hai.

No 2 e^- in an atom can have same set of 4 Quantum Nos.

even the same orbital have e^- with opposite spin

⥮ ⥮ Correct ⇈ ⇊ Incorrect

3. Classification of Elements & Periodicity in Properties

Genesis of Periodic Classification

1. Dobereiner's Triads (1829)

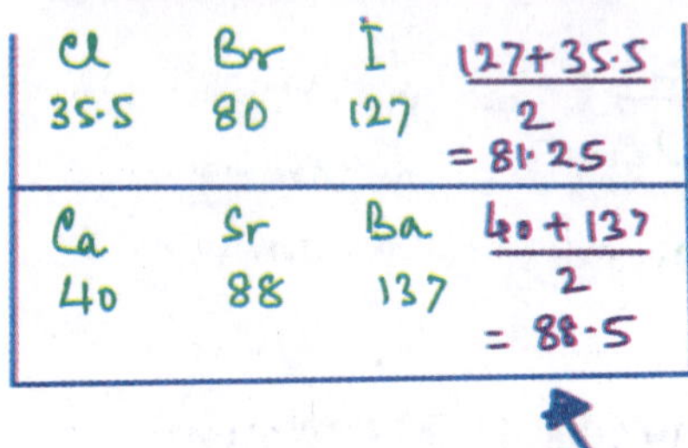

Cl	Br	I	
35.5	80	127	$\frac{127+35.5}{2} = 81.25$
Ca	Sr	Ba	
40	88	137	$\frac{40+137}{2} = 88.5$

2. Newland's law of Octaves (1865)

Newlands' Octaves with Musical Octave

Musical scale	Sa	Re	Ga	Ma	Pa	Dha	Ne
Element	Li	Be	B	C	N	O	F
Atomic weight	7	9	11	12	14	16	19
Element	Na	Mg	Al	Si	P	S	Cl
Atomic weight	23	24	27	29	31	32	35.5
Element	K	Ca					
Atomic weight	39	40					

3. Lothar Mayer's Atomic Volume Curve

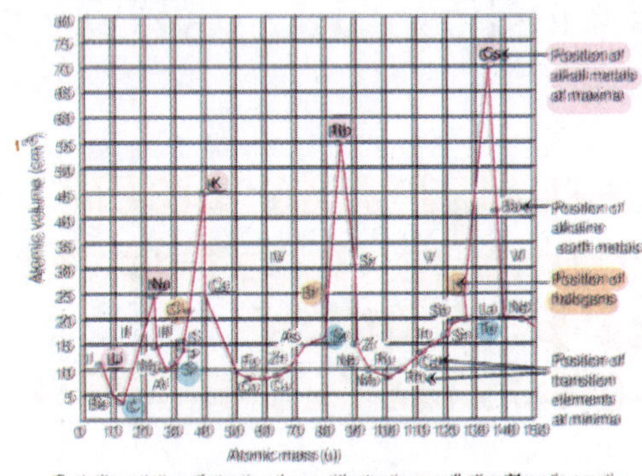

Periodic variation of atomic volume with atomic mass (Lothar Meyer's curve)

4. Mendleev's Periodic Table

Physical & chemical properties of elements are periodic functions of their atomic masses ⟶ Periodic Law

63 elements in 8 vertical columns (Groups) and 6 rows (Periods)
← with sub groups A & B

NEET concentrate

- In Periodic Table of Mendeleev Group VIII had 9 elements arranged as Triads in 3 rows.
- eka silicon ⟶ silicon like properties ⟶ Scandium (Sc)
  eka aluminium ⟶ Gallium (Ga)
  eka Boron ⟶ Germanium (Ge)
  eka Manganese ⟶ Technetium (Tc)

Elements not known but Predicted by Mendeleev

Mendeleev's Periodic Table

Merits ⟵ | ⟶ **Demerits**

Merits	Demerits
1. Prediction of new elements	1. Position of H & isotopes
2. Correction of doubtful atomic weights	2. Anomalous pairs
	3. Like elements placed in different groups & Unlike in same

Findings of Moseley

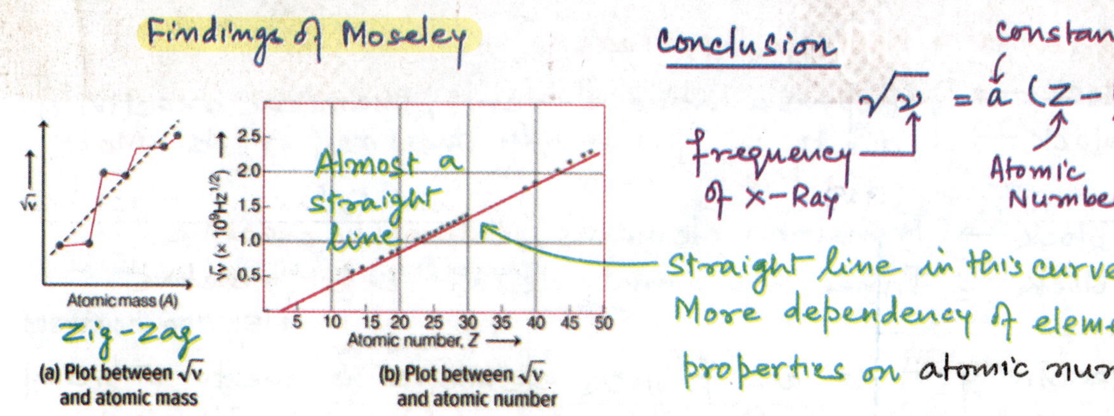

(a) Plot between $\sqrt{\nu}$ and atomic mass

(b) Plot between $\sqrt{\nu}$ and atomic number

Straight line in this curve suggested More dependency of elemental properties on atomic number.

Conclusion

$$\sqrt{\nu} = a(Z - b)$$

- $\sqrt{\nu}$ → frequency of X-Ray
- a → constant
- Z → Atomic Number
- b → screening constant

- **Modern Periodic Law (Moseley)** → The physical & chemical properties of elements are periodic function of their atomic numbers.

Largest group of Periodic Table (32 elements) → IIIB (3)

s-block Representative elements; d-block Transition elements; p-block Representative elements; f-block

Key: 1 ← Atomic number; H ← Symbol; 1.00794 ← Atomic weight

Groups according to Modern Periodic Table	IA	IIA	IIIB		IVB	VB	VIB	VIIB	VIII			IB	IIB	IIIA	IVA	VA	VIA	VIIA	0
Groups according to Long form of Periodic Table	(1)	(2)	(3)		(4)	(5)	(6)	(7)	(8)	(9)	(10)	(11)	(12)	(13)	(14)	(15)	(16)	(17)	(18)
	s^1	s^2	d^1s^2	f-block	d^2s^2	d^3s^2	d^5s^1	d^5s^2	d^6s^2	d^7s^2	d^8s^2	$d^{10}s^1$	$d^{10}s^2$	s^2p^1	s^2p^2	s^2p^3	s^2p^4	s^2p^5	s^2p^6
*n = 1																			2 He (s^2)
n = 2	3 Li	4 Be												5 B	6 C	7 N	8 O	9 F	10 Ne
n = 3	11 Na	12 Mg												13 Al	14 Si	15 P	16 S	17 Cl	18 Ar
n = 4	19 K	20 Ca	21 Sc		22 Ti	23 V	24 Cr	25 Mn	26 Fe	27 Co	28 Ni	29 Cu	30 Zn	31 Ga	32 Ge	33 As	34 Se	35 Br	36 Kr
n = 5	37 Rb	38 Sr	39 Y		40 Zr	41 Nb d^4s^1	42 Mo	43 Tc	44 Ru d^7s^1	45 Rh d^8s^1	46 Pd	47 Ag	48 Cd	49 In	50 Sn	51 Sb	52 Te	53 I	54 Xe
n = 6	55 Cs	56 Ba	57 La	58 Ce → 71 Lu	72 Hf	73 Ta	74 W d^4s^2	75 Re	76 Os	77 Ir	78 Pt d^9s^1	79 Au	80 Hg	81 Tl	82 Pb	83 Bi	84 Po	85 At	86 Rn
n = 7	87 Fr	88 Ra	89 Ac	90 Th → 103 Lr	104 Rf	105 Db	106 Sg	107 Bh	108 Hs	109 Mt	110 Ds	111 Rg	112 Cn	113 Nh	114 Fl	115 Mc	116 Lv	117 Ts	118 Og

f-block Inner-transition elements

n = 6	Lanthanide series $4f^{2-14}5d^{0-1}6s^2$	58 Ce	59 Pr	60 Nd	61 Pm	62 Sm	63 Eu	64 Gd	65 Tb	66 Dy	67 Ho	68 Er	69 Tm	70 Yb	71 Lu	4f-subshell being filled
n = 7	Actinide series $5f^{2-14}6d^{0-1}7s^2$	90 Th	91 Pa	92 U	93 Np	94 Pu	95 Am	96 Cm	97 Bk	98 Cf	99 Es	100 Fm	101 Md	102 No	103 Lr	5f-subshell being filled

*n is the principal quantum number. The d^1s^2, d^2s^2... designations represent electronic configurations. They refer to $(n-1)$ d and ns-orbital.

- Modern Periodic Table was proposed by Moseley → Table with 0 – VIII groups all except 0 were divided into subgroups A & B.
  Long form of Periodic Table was proposed by 20+ scientists including Bohr, Bury, Werner etc. → Table with 18 groups

divided in to 4 Blocks & 7 periods.

Blocks
- s-block → } Representative elements; chemical reactivity due to e^- present in outermost orbits. Most Reactive.
- p-block → }
- d-block → Transition elements, Moderatily reactive
- f-block → Inner Transitonal elements, Least reactive

NEET concentrate

- Reactivity of d and f block elements is due to e^- present in their outer 2 (d) and outer 3 (f) orbits respectively.
- Except p-block, the elements of all other blocks are metals
  - p-block ← Metals + Metalloids + Non Metals

Notation For IUPAC Nomenclature of Elements

Digit	0	1	2	3	4	5	6	7	8	9
Root name	nil	un	bi	tri	quad	pent	hex	sept	oct	enn
Abbreviation	n	u	b	t	q	p	h	s	o	e

Elements having Z > 100 with their Names and Symbols

Atomic number	IUPAC name	Symbol	Elemental name	IUPAC symbol
101	Unnilunium	Unu	Mendelevium	Md
102	Unnilbium	Unb	Nobelium	No
103	Unniltrium	Unt	Lawrencium	Lr
104	Unnilquadium	Unq	Rutherfordium	Rf
105	Unnilpentium	Unp	Dubnium	Db
106	Unnilhexium	Unh	Seaborgium	Sg
107	Unnilseptium	Uns	Bohrium	Bh
108	Unniloctium	Uno	Hassnium	Hs
109	Unnilennium	Une	Meitnerium	Mt
110	Ununnilium	Uun	Darmstadtium	Ds
111	Unununilium	Uuu	Rontgenium	Rg
112	Ununbium	Uub	Copernicium	Cn
113	Ununtrium	Uut	Nihonium	Nh
114	Ununquadium	Uuq	Flerovium	Fl
115	Ununpentium	Uup	Mosovium	Mc
116	Ununhexium	Uuh	Livermorium	Lv
117	Ununseptium	Uus	Tennessine	Ts
118	Ununoctium	Uuo	Oganesson	Og

Periodic Properties

1. Atomic Radius → Avg. distance of valence shell electron from the centre of nucleus. This can be measured as –

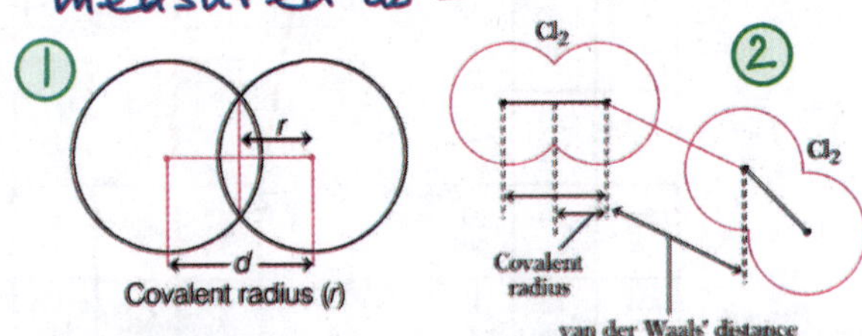

③ Metallic radius – ½ of the internuclear distance between the 2 adjacent metal atoms in the metallic crystal.

④ Ionic Radius – This can be either cationic or anionic

$Mg > Mg^+ > Mg^{2+}$ $\quad$ $O^{2-} > O^- > O$

Dhyan Rakho | vander Waal's radius = 2 × covalent radius.

secondly, Atomic Radius ∝ 1/nuclear charge ∝ Screening effect

vander Waal's radius > Metallic Radius > Covalent Radius

Measurment of Radius ⟶ X-Ray or Spectroscopy

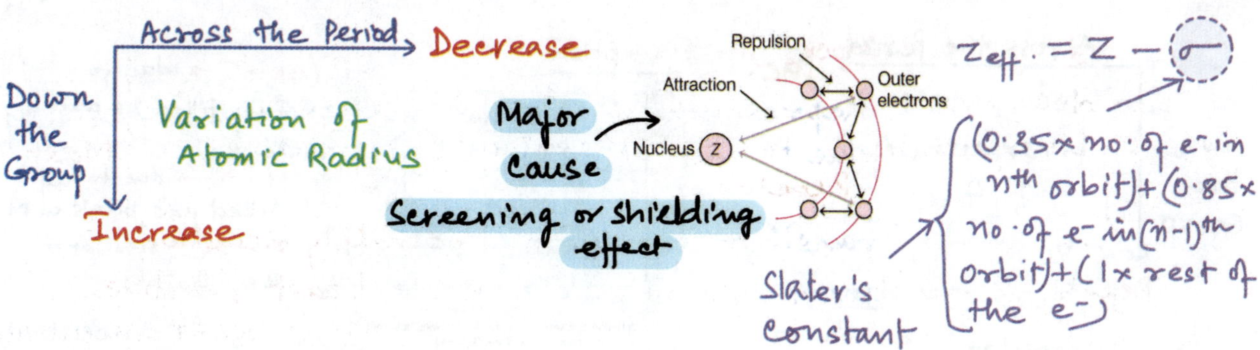

Exceptions ⟶ The atomic radius values of 18th (0) group elements increases abruptly in a period (as in their case vander Waal's radii are considered while for rest of the elements covalent radii are considered)

2. Ionisation Enthalpy — Enthalpy change when an e^- is removed from the outermost orbit of an isolated gaseous atom, also called Ionisation Energy (kJ/mol) or Ionisation Potential (volts/atom or eV/atom)

◎ For an atom –

(i) No· of I.E. = No· of e^- present

(ii) $I.E_1 < I.E_2 < I.E_3$ ..... $I.E_N$

Factors affecting Ionisation Enthalpy

1. Atomic Size — Inverse Relation
2. Effective Nuclear charge — Direct Relation
3. Screening Effect — Inverse Relation
4. Penetration power of sub-shells — Direct Relation
   - Attraction of subshells towards nucleus i.e; s > p > d > f
5. Electronic configuration — Removal of e^- from half filled & completely filled orbitals is most difficult
6. Oxidation state
   - (+)ve O.S. ↑ I.E.
   - (−)ve O.S. ↓ I.E

Dhyan Rakho! s-subshell is nearest to nucleus hence more energy will be required to remove an e^- from it.

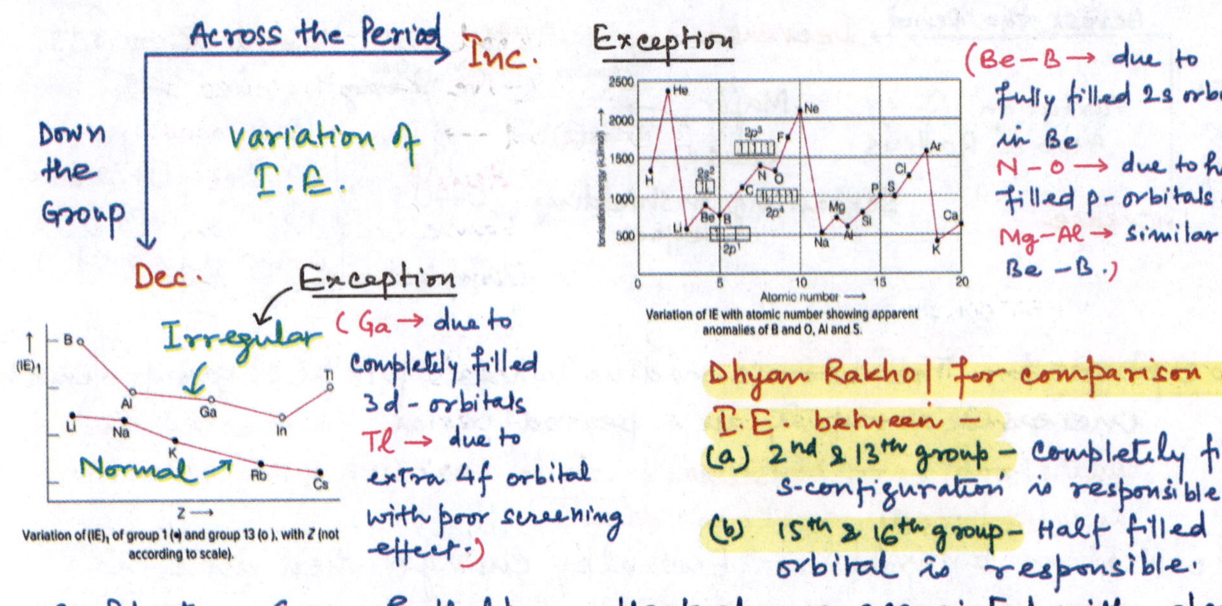

3. Electron Gain Enthalpy – Heat change associated with electron gain. It is also called Electron affinity in terms of energy absorbed or released when an e^- is added to an isolated gaseous atom.

- Measure of the ease with which an e^- is added to an atom to form anion.
- Just like I.E. an atom can have more than 1 values of $\Delta_{eg}H$

→ For successive e^- addition in Anion the $\Delta_{eg}H$ is always High (+) ve value.

Dhyan Rakho | Enthalpy ke terms mein high (+)ve value but Energy ke terms mein energy absorbed (Endothermic)

Thus $O \xrightarrow{+2e^-} O^{--}$ (Endothermic process)

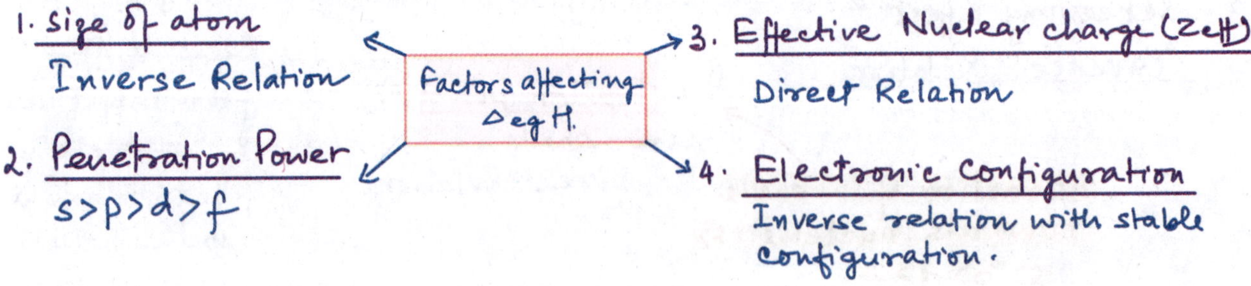

Enthalpies of gaseous atoms must be measured in their ground state (as it is the most stable state for gaseous atoms)

Across the Period → Inc.

Down the Group ↓ Dec.

Variation of $\Delta_{eg}H$

But in General 2nd Period elements have less (−)ve $\Delta_{eg}H$ values than those of 3rd Period → Due to very small size and high e^- density of second period elements (Same reason can be given for comparison between F & Cl)

NEET concentrate

> $\Delta_{eg}H$ for Metals → Low, Non-metals → High; Halogens → Highest
> $\Delta_{eg}H$ for Cl → most (−)ve value in periodic table = −349 kJ/mol
> $\Delta_{eg}H$ for F = −328 kJ/mol; S = −200 kJ/mol; O = −141 kJ/mol
> Reason — small size, high e^- density so high interelectronic repulsions in smaller atoms.

4. Electronegativity (E_N) → Tendency of an element to attract shared pair of e^- towards itself.

Dhyan Rakho! Being Tendency, E_N can not be measured like I.E and $\Delta_{eg}H$ & it does not has units as well. However, we can scale up E_N to get an idea of Electronegativities of different elements.

Scales

- Pauling = Approximate scale, most widely used; E_N of F → 4 (arbitrary max. value) rest can be calculated through

$$\chi_A - \chi_B = 0.1017\sqrt{\Delta}, \quad \Delta = E_{A-B} - \sqrt{E_{A-A} \times E_{B-B}} \text{ kJ/mole}$$

Bond Energies (E_{A-B}, E_{A-A}, E_{B-B})

- Mulliken–Jaffe = Almost obsolete; Based on $\Delta_{eg}H$ & I.E. values
- Allred–Rochow = Most accurate & most recent; based on covalent radius

---

Factors affecting E_N

1. Atomic Size — Inverse Relation
2. Zeff — Direct Relation
3. Hybridisation state — Direct relation with s character; E_N of C ≈ 2.5 (sp^3), ≈ 2.1 (sp)
4. oxidation state
   - for cation — Direct relation with (+)ve charge
   - for anion — Inverse relation with (−)ve charge

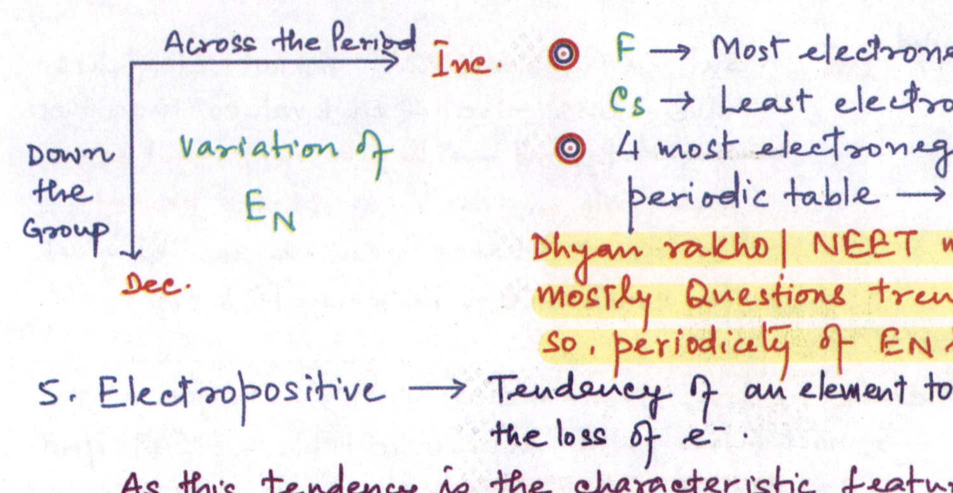

- F → Most electronegative element
  Cs → Least electronegative element
- 4 most electronegative elements of periodic table → F > O > N ≈ Cl

Dhyan rakho | NEET mein E_N se related mostly Questions trend waale aate haim so, periodicity of E_N is very important.

5. Electropositive → Tendency of an element to form the cation by the loss of e^-.

As this tendency is the characteristic feature of metals hence it is also called → Metallic character

Across the Period → Dec.

Down the Group → Inc.

Variation of Metallic Character

NEET concentrate

Always remember → (i) Metals are good reducing agents as they have tendency to loose e^- i.e., oxidise easily.
(ii) Metallic character has inverse relation with I.E. & E_N of an element.

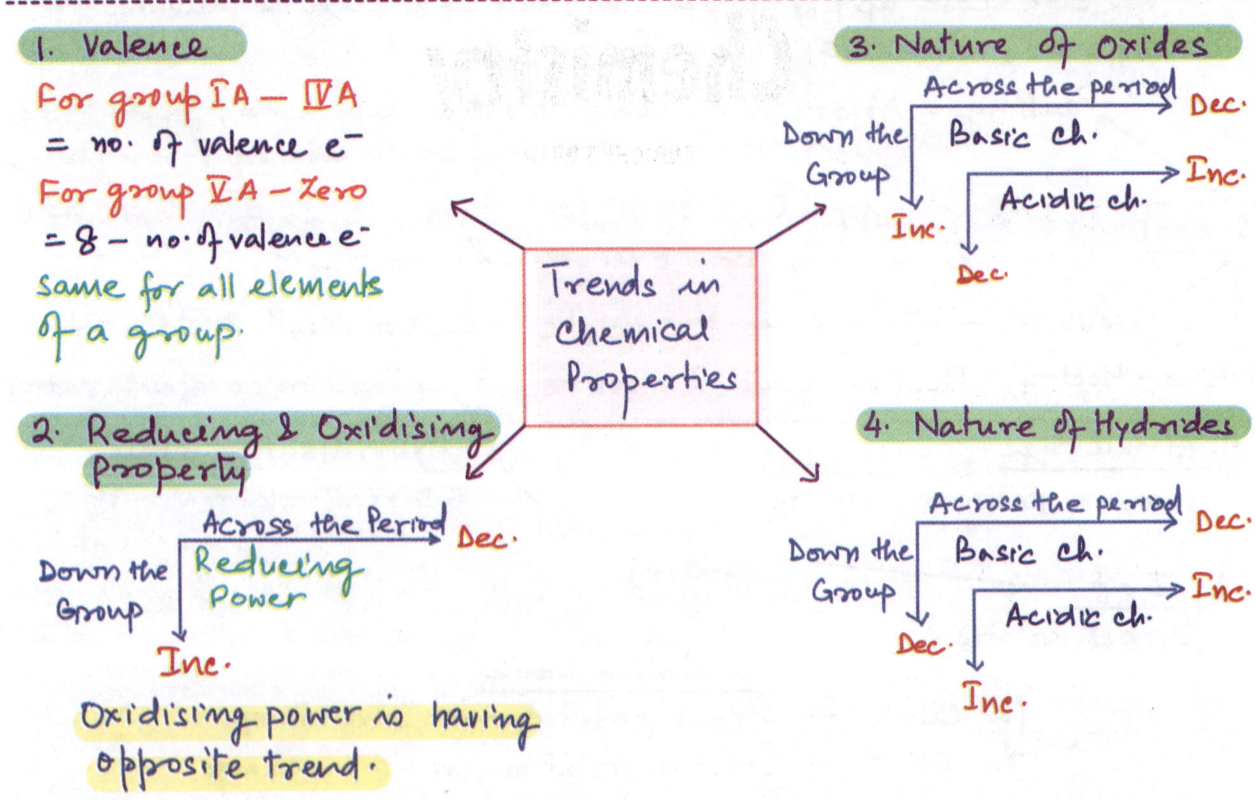

NEET concentrate

- CO, N_2O, NO & H_2O → Neutral oxides
- The acidic or basic nature of oxides depends upon the nature of bond present within the oxide.

  Ionic Oxides → Basic

  Covalent oxides → Acidic

  Partly ionic & partly covalent oxides → Amphoteric or Amphiprotic in nature (i.e., have the ability to react with acid and base both)
- The acidic character of Non metal oxide ↑ with increase in no. of Oxygen in it (i.e., $N_2O_3 < N_2O_5$; $SO_2 < SO_3$ etc.)

  Non metal Oxide + H_2O → Oxy acids

  ↳ Basicity = No. of –OH groups present.

  Acidic Strength ↑ with increase of Oxygen e.g.

  $H_2SO_3 < H_2SO_4$

  $HClO < HClO_2 < HClO_3 < HClO_4$

  Exception $H_3PO_4 < H_3PO_3 < H_3PO_2$
- Reasons for Anomalous behaviour of IInd Period Elements
  - a. Small size
  - b. Large charge/Radius Ratio
  - c. High EN
  - d. Absence of vacant d-orbitals

4. Chemical Bonding & Molecular Structure

- The attractive force that holds various atoms, ions & molecules together in different chemical species ⟶ Chemical Bond
  (Bond = Agreement = invisible attractive forces)
- Valence (outermost) shell e^- play most significant role in bonding. Valence shell is called Octet and every element of periodic table always try to acquire the valence shell configuration of nearest inert gas ⟶ Octet rule
- Atoms can combine (i) either by loosing or gaining the e^- OR (ii) by sharing the e^- of valence shell
  - (i) ↑ Ionic Bond
  - (ii) ↑ Covalent bond

Dhyan Rakhna | as an atom contains only nucleus & e^- (i.e., 2 charged bodies) hence attractive forces between 2 atoms can be electrostatic forces only, means nature wise bond mein sirf aur sirf ek hi type ki forces hoti hain aur woh **electrostatic force of attraction** hi ho sakti hain.

- **Octet rule Violations**

1. Incomplete Octet of central atom
   e.g., BeF_2, BX_3, AlX_3 etc.
2. Odd e^- molecules
   e.g., N = O
   7e⁻ 8e⁻
3. Expanded octet
   PCl_5 — 10 electrons around the P atom; SF_6 — 12 electrons around the S atom; H_2SO_4 (H–O–S(=O)(=O)–O–H) — 12 electrons around the S atom
4. Noble gas compounds
   e.g., XeF_2, XeF_4, $XeOF_4$, $XeOF_2$, KrF_2

- Formal charge of an atom in Lewis's structure = [Total No. of valence e^- in free atom] − [Total no. of Non bonding (lone pair) e^-] − (1/2) [Total no. of Bonding e^-]

NEET concentrate

- Formal charge do not indicate real charge separation within the molecule.
- Formal charge helps in the selection of lowest energy structure from many possible structures given for a species (the one with smallest formal charges provided e^- pairs are shared equally)

- Electrostatic force of attraction that hold 2 or more ions with opposite charges → Ionic Bonds or Electrovalent Bond

No. of unit charges present on ions = Electrovalence of that ion.

Factors affecting Ionic Bond formation →
1. Ionisation Enthalpy
2. Electron Gain Enthalpy
3. Lattice Enthalpy.

Ionic Compound Characteristics

Without Molecular Formula

Higher lattice Enthalpy

1. Crystalline
2. Hard & brittle
3. High mp & bp
4. Non rigid (specific), Non directional
5. Soluble in polar but insoluble in Non polar solvents.
6. Show isomorphism (with similar no. of valence e^- e.g., NaF & MgO)
7. Electricity conduction in fused or molten state ; No such conduction in solid state

- Polarisability Vs Polarisation

Polarisability: Development of covalent ch. in an ionic compound

Polarisation: Development of Ionic ch. in a covalent compound.

Cation Anion → Unpolarised anion, Polarised anion

Polarisation of an anion by a cation

In both the cases the resulting mol. seems as same i.e., partly ionic and partly covalent.

- Extent of covalent character decided by set of rules called

Fajan's rule →
1. Smaller size of cation e.g., LiCl > NaCl
2. Larger size of anion e.g., LiI > LiBr > LiCl > LiF
3. High charge density on cation or anion e.g., NaCl < $MgCl_2$

All of them are collectively responsible for ↑ in covalent character

However, Covalent ch. of CuCl > NaCl (due to pseudo inert gas conf. of Cu)

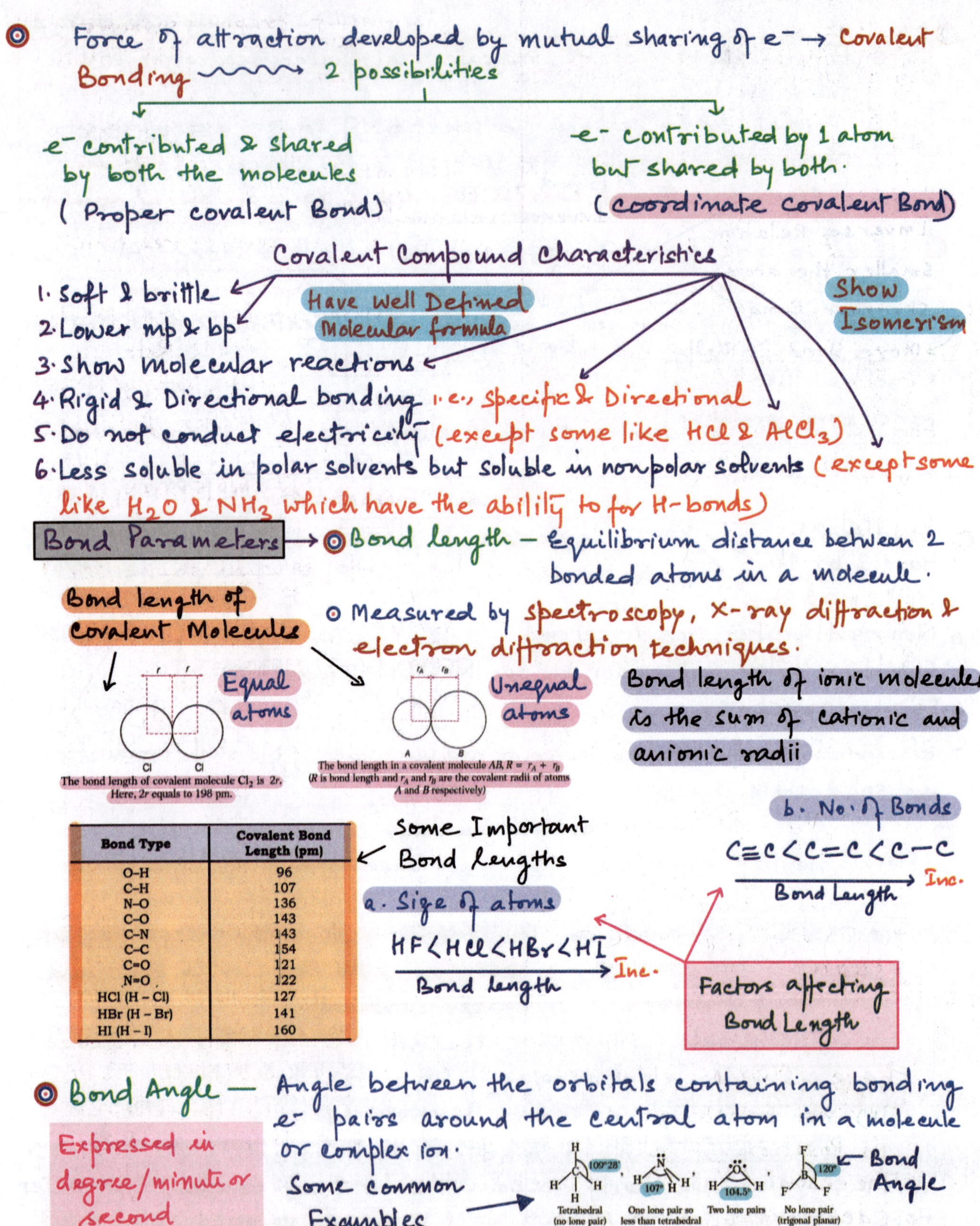

Force of attraction developed by mutual sharing of e^- → Covalent Bonding ⟿ 2 possibilities

- e^- contributed & shared by both the molecules (Proper covalent Bond)
- e^- contributed by 1 atom but shared by both. (coordinate covalent Bond)

Covalent Compound Characteristics

1. Soft & brittle
2. Lower mp & bp
3. Show molecular reactions
4. Rigid & Directional bonding i.e., specific & Directional
5. Do not conduct electricity (except some like HCl & $AlCl_3$)
6. Less soluble in polar solvents but soluble in nonpolar solvents (except some like H_2O & NH_3 which have the ability to for H-bonds)

Have Well Defined Molecular formula

Show Isomerism

Bond Parameters → Bond length – Equilibrium distance between 2 bonded atoms in a molecule.

Measured by spectroscopy, X-ray diffraction & electron diffraction techniques.

Bond length of Covalent Molecules

Equal atoms

The bond length of covalent molecule Cl_2 is $2r$. Here, $2r$ equals to 198 pm.

Unequal atoms

The bond length in a covalent molecule AB, $R = r_A + r_B$ (R is bond length and r_A and r_B are the covalent radii of atoms A and B respectively)

Bond length of ionic molecules is the sum of cationic and anionic radii

Bond Type	Covalent Bond Length (pm)
O–H	96
C–H	107
N–O	136
C–O	143
C–N	143
C–C	154
C=O	121
N=O	122
HCl (H – Cl)	127
HBr (H – Br)	141
HI (H – I)	160

← Some Important Bond Lengths

Factors affecting Bond Length

a. Size of atoms

HF < HCl < HBr < HI → Inc. Bond length

b. No. of Bonds

C≡C < C=C < C–C → Inc. Bond Length

Bond Angle – Angle between the orbitals containing bonding e^- pairs around the central atom in a molecule or complex ion.

Expressed in degree/minute or second

Some common Examples →

Bond Enthalpy — Heat change in breaking one mole bonds of a particular type (formed between 2 atoms in gaseous state).
Units — kJ/mol

NEET concentrate

Factors affecting Bond Enthalpy

1. Atomic Size
Inverse Relation
smaller the atom → stronger Bond → More Bond Enthalpy

2. Bond length
Inverse relation

3. Lone pair No.
Inverse relation

4. Number of Bonds
Direct Relation.
H−H < O=O < N≡N

For Polyatomic molecules term Average or Mean Bond Enthalpy is used.

Bond Order — No. of Bonds formed between two atoms

Dhyan Rakho! Isoelectronic molecules & ions have identical Bond orders. e.g., F_2 & O_2^{2-} → 1; N_2, CO, NO^+ → 3. Aur

$$\text{Bond order} \propto \text{Bond Enthalpy} \propto \frac{1}{\text{Bond Length}}$$

Resonance — When single lewis structure is inadequate for the representation of a molecule to explain all of its properties. The we draw 2, 3 or more structures → Resonating structures or Canonical forms → Each of these explain some of the properties.

- The actual structure is considered as the hybrid of resonating forms → Resonance Hybrid.

NEET concentrate

Remember! All resonating structures of a compound have similar (i) Energy (ii) Position of nuclei (iii) bonding (iv) non bonding e^- pairs. However they may differ in (i) Position of e^- (ii) Position of bonds.
The canonical forms are always represented with ⟷ (double headed arrows).

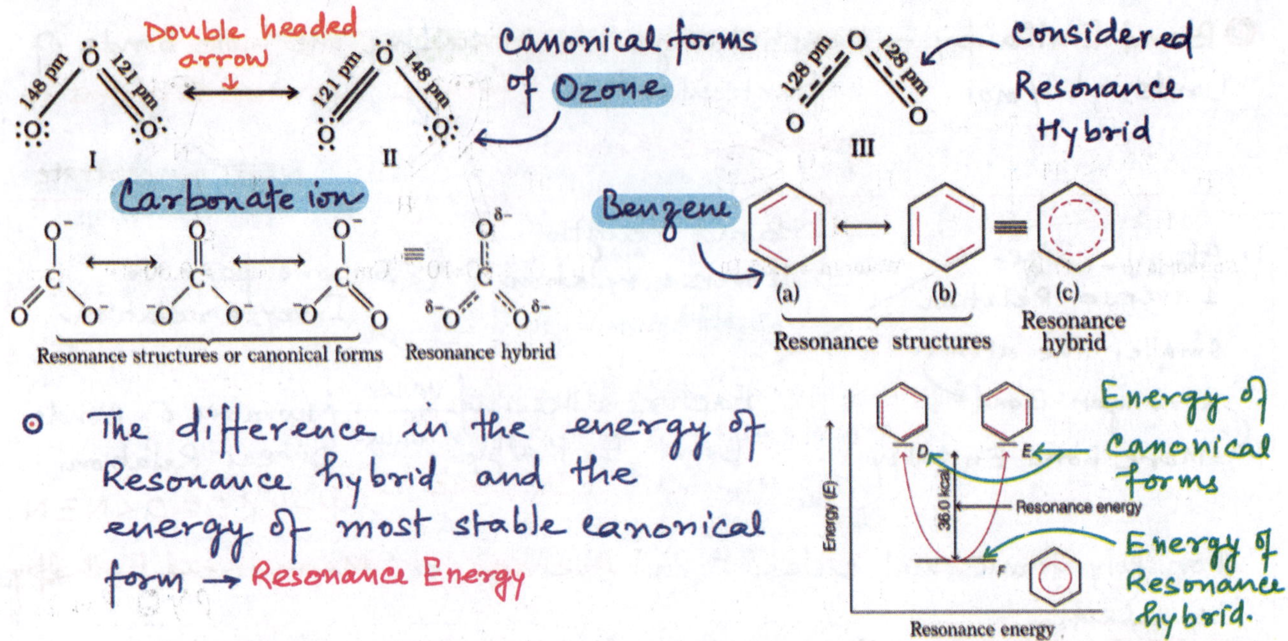

- The difference in the energy of Resonance hybrid and the energy of most stable canonical form → Resonance Energy

Always Remember | ① The phenomenon of Resonance is completely hypothetical i.e., canonical forms do not have any real existence.

② The molecules have a single structure which is nearly explainable via Resonance hybrid i.e., molecules does not exist for a certain fraction of time in one canonical form & for other fractions of time in other canonical forms.

③ The participation of canonical forms in hybrid may or may not be equal.

- **Dipole Moment** – Product of magnitude of charge and the distance between the centres of (+)ve and (–)ve charges.

Units – Debye (D)

Mathematically Dipole Moment (μ) = Charge (q) × Distance of charges (d)

vector quantity — Magnitude of charge → $^{\delta+}H \longrightarrow Cl^{\delta-}$ ← Direction

- Symmetrical molecules have $\mu = 0$

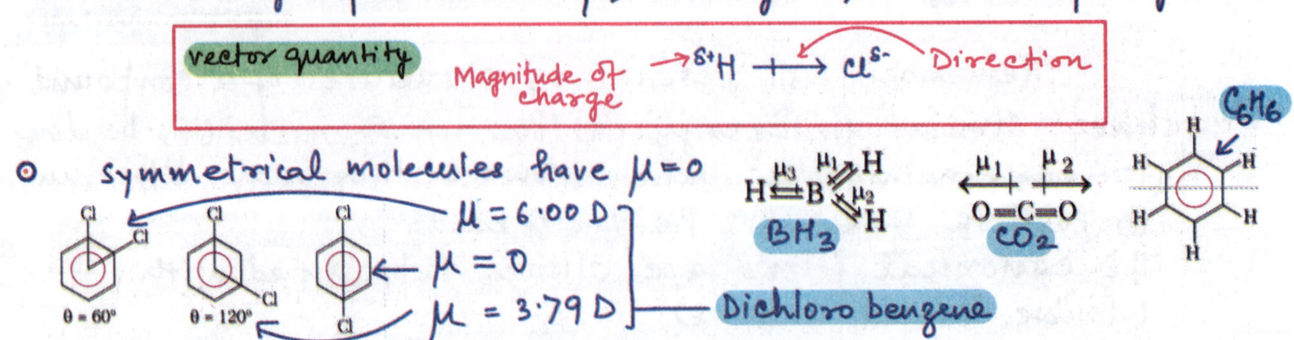

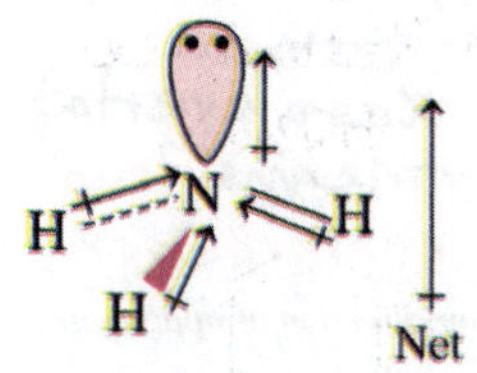

Ammonia (μ = 1.47 D)

Net
O
H
H

Water (μ = 1.85 D)

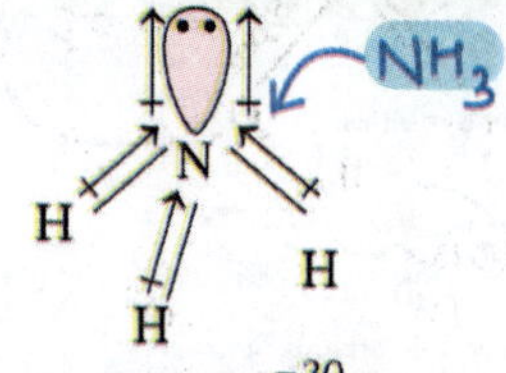

$\mu_{net} = 4.90 \times 10^{-30}$ Cm

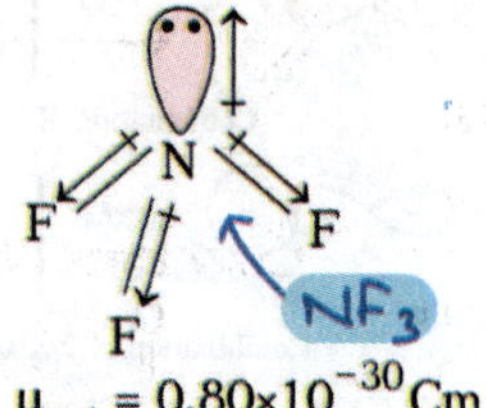

$\mu_{net} = 0.80 \times 10^{-30}$ Cm

NEET concentrate

$$\%\ \text{ionic character in a molecule} = \frac{\text{Observed value of } \mu}{\text{Theoritical value of } \mu} \times 100$$

HF > HCl > HBr > HI (% ionic character)
39.4% 16.0% 10.8% 4.7%

PYQ Punch

Q. The dipole moments of diatomic molecules AB & CD are 10.41 D and 10.27 D while their bond distances are 2.82 & 2.67 A° respectively, This indicates that **NEET 2023**

(a) Bonding is 100% ionic in both the molecules
(b) AB has more ionic character than CD
(c) ✓ AB has lesser ionic character than CD
(d) Bonding is nearly covalent in both the molecules.

Sol DM of AB = $4.8 \times 10^{-10} \times 2.82 \times 10^{-8} = 13.53$ D; DM of CD = $4.8 \times 10^{-10} \times 2.57 \times 10^{-8} = 12.81$ D

% ionic ch. AB = (10.41/13.53) × 100 = 76.94%; % ionic ch. CD = (10.27/12.81) × 100 = 80.23%

Valence Bond Theory (Heitler & London 1927, Extended by Pauling & Slater in 1931)

Postulates

1. Overlapping of 2 distinct Atomic orbitals → Covalent bond
2. Energy released in the process → Bond Energy
3. The electrostatic attraction between the nuclei of atoms & overlapped e^- cloud → Major binding force of bond.
4. Neutralisation of spin magnetic moments adds up to bonding
5. Strength of bond ∝ Extent of overlapping.
6. Overlapping with directional e^- cloud (like p-orbital) results in stronger bond.

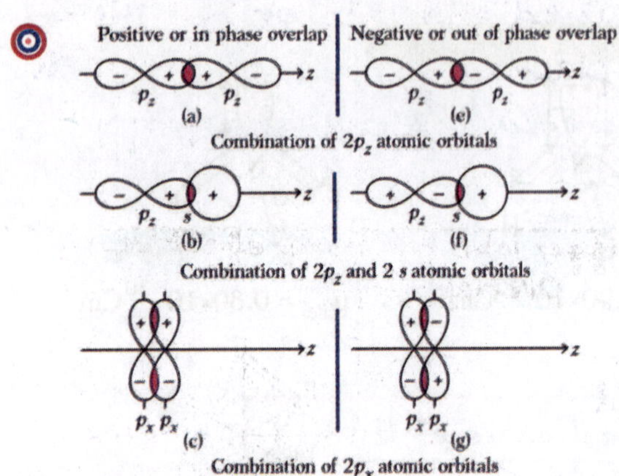

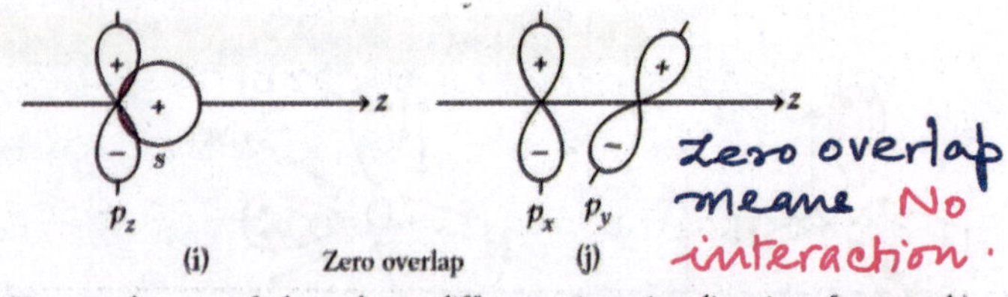

(Zero overlap, out of phase due to different orientation direction of approach)

Zero overlap means No interaction.

Positive overlap of orbitals results to attractive interactions

Negative overlap of orbitals results to repulsive interactions.

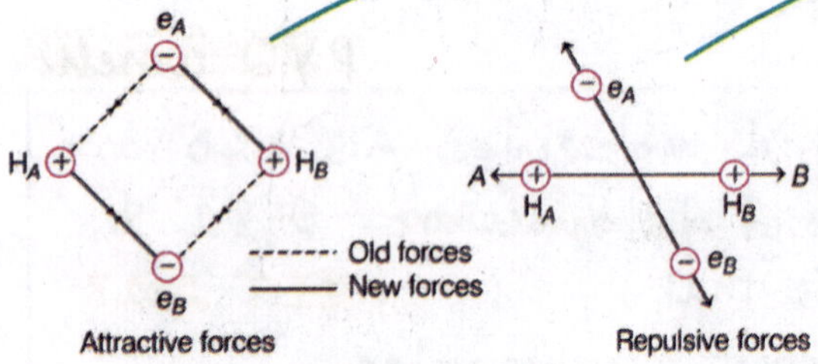

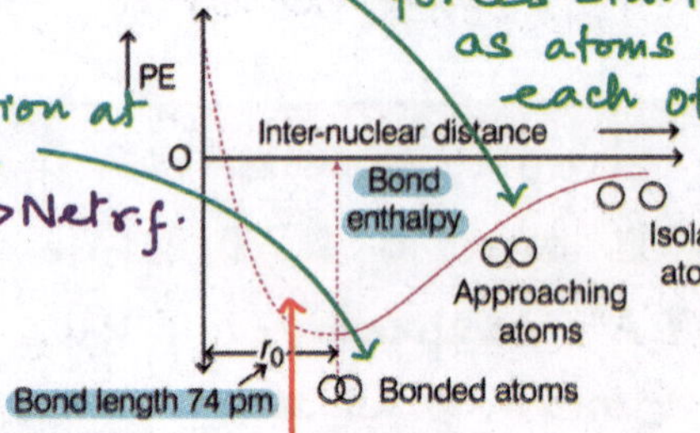

Attractive forces

Old forces

New forces

Repulsive forces

PE

Inter-nuclear distance

Bond enthalpy

Isolated atoms

Approaching atoms

Bonded atoms

Bond length 74 pm

Both attractive & repulsive forces start increasing as atoms approach each other.

Condition at which Net a.f > Net r.f.

Repulsive forces become too high after this.

Structure of H_2 molecule as per VBT

Bond Enthalpy = 435.8 KJ/mol.

Sigma (σ) bond ← Covalent Bonds → Pi (π) bond

Head on or end to end overlap along the internuclear axis.

σ bond

s-orbital + s-orbital → s-s overlapping

s-orbital + p-orbital → s-p overlapping

p-orbital + p-orbital → p-p overlapping

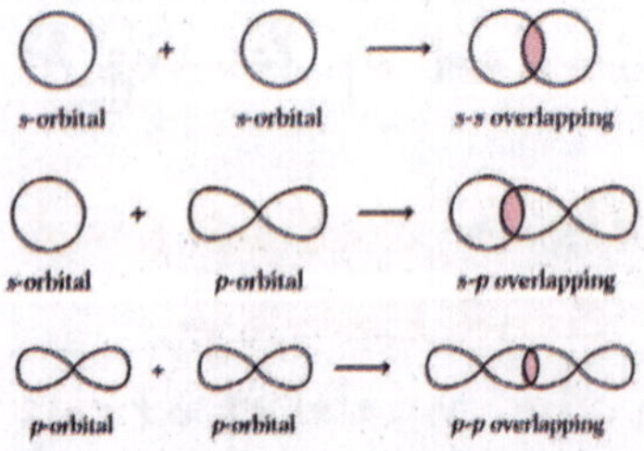

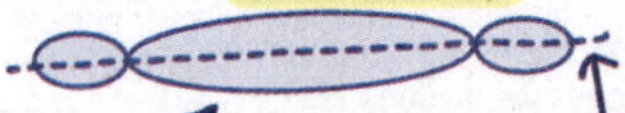

Resulting cloud

Internuclear axis

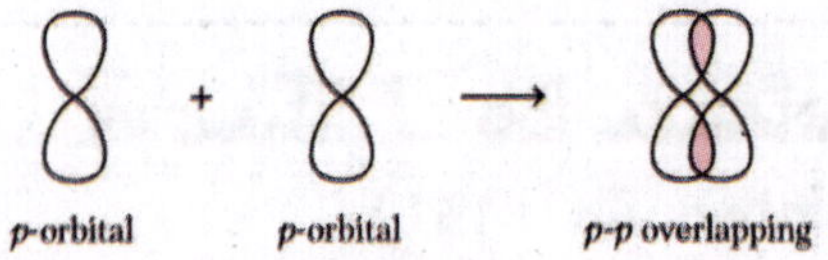

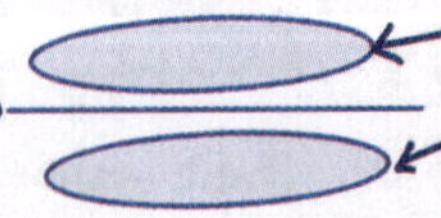

Sidewise overlap or lateral overlap.

p-orbital + p-orbital → p-p overlapping

Resulting cloud

π bond.

H—H (σ)

O=O (σ, π)

N≡N (σ, 2π)

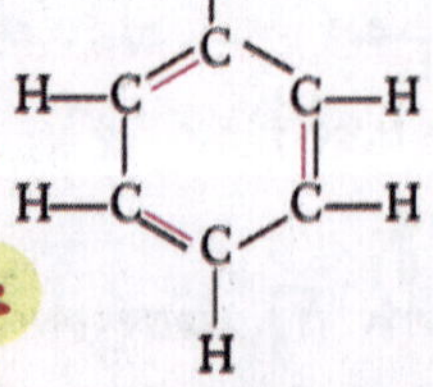

Benzene (3π, 12σ)

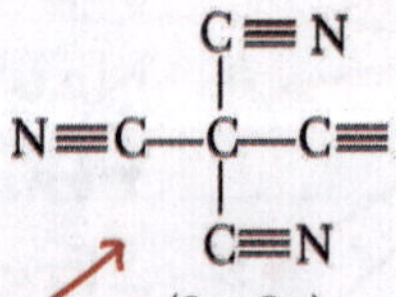

Tetracyanoethylene-type structure $C(C\equiv N)_4$ (8π, 8σ)

Dhyan Rakhna | usually between 2 atoms 1st bond is σ and rest π as shown

- Overlapping of orbitals was unexplained without their equivalence. This equivalence of orbitals was explained by Pauling through Hybridisation i.e., mixing of orbitals of almost equal energy to form same no. of orbitals of exactly equal energy.

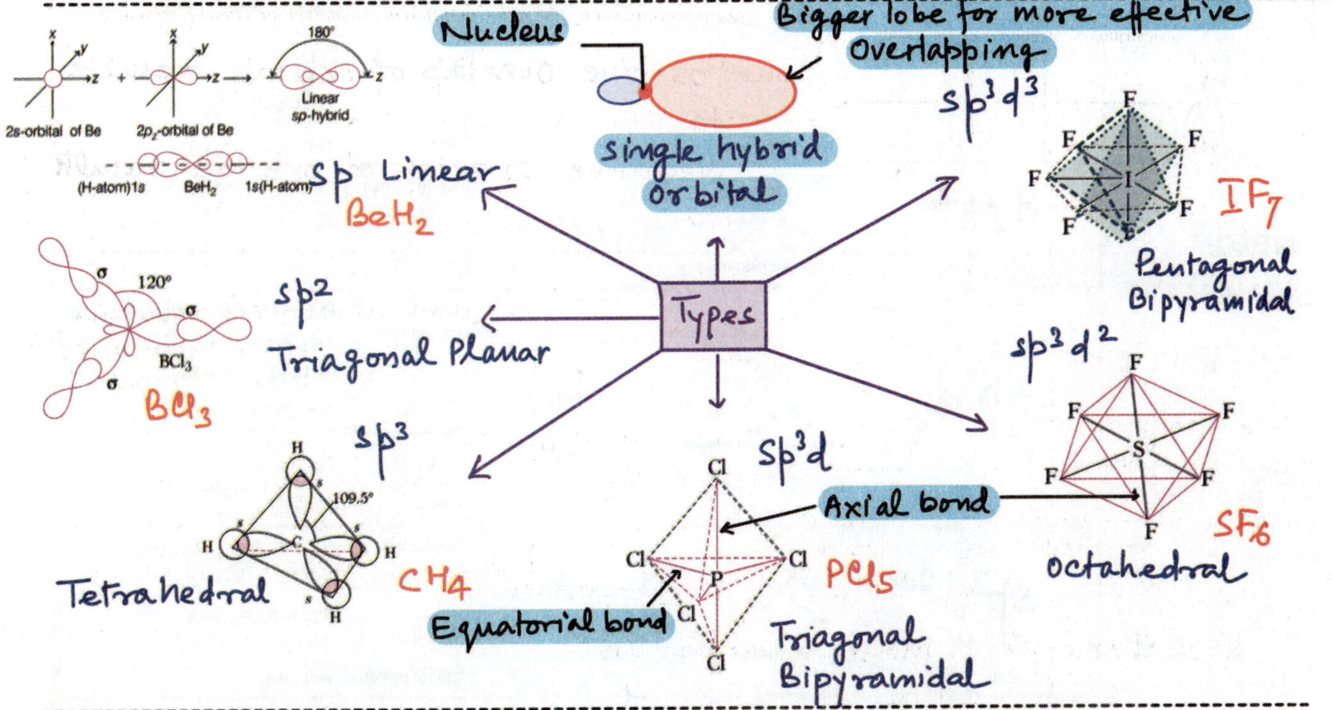

- **Valence Shell electron pair repulsion (VSEPR) Theory** (Powell & Sidgwick, 1940; Gillespie & Nyholm 1957)

  Shape of covalent molecules depends upon the number of valence shell electrons pairs (bonded as well as non bonded) and repulsion among them. This repulsion follows –

  Lone pair → lp – lp > lp – bp > bp – bp ← Bond pair

	Hybridisation	Geometry of molecules as per Hybridisation	No. of bonded atoms	No. of lone pairs	Actual shape of molecules due to VSEPR	Example
NEET concentrate	sp	180° A Linear	2	0	Linear	CO_2, $HgCl_2$, BeF_2, $ZnCl_2$, $MgCl_2$, C_2H_2, HCN, BeH_2, CS_2, N_2O, Hg_2Cl_2, $[Ag(NH_3)_2]^+$
	sp^2	A 120° Trigonal planar, 120°	3	0	Trigonal planar	BF_3, $AlCl_3$, C_2H_4, NO_3^-, CO_3^{2-}, HCHO, C_6H_6, CH_3^+; graphite, C_2Cl_4, $C_2H_2Cl_2$, $[HgI_3]^-$, $[Cu(PMe_3)_3]^+$
			2	1	V-shape (bent)	NO_2^-, SO_2, $SnCl_2$

NEET concentrate

Hybridisation	Geometry of molecules as per Hybridisation	No. of bonded atoms	No. of lone pairs	Actual shape of molecules due to VSEPR	Example
sp^3	Tetrahedral, 109.5°	4	0	Tetrahedral	CH_4, SiH_4, SO_4^{2-}, $SnCl_4$, $POCl_3$ ClO_4^-, BF_4^-, NH_4^+, CCl_4, SiF_4, $[BF_4]^-$, XeO_4 $[AlCl_4]^-$ $SnCl_4$, PH_4^+ Diamond silica, $Ni(CO)_4$, $Si(CH_3)_4$, SiC, $[NiCl_4]^{2-}$
	< 109.5°	3	1	Trigonal pyramidal	PCl_3 H_3^+O, XeO_3
	104.5°	2	2	Bent	H_2O, SF_2
dsp^2	90° Square planar	4	0	Square planar	$[Ni(CN)_4]^{2-}$, $[Pt(NH_3)_4]^{2+}$
sp^3d	90° 120° Trigonal bipyramidal	5	0	Trigonal bipyramidal	PCl_5, $SbCl_5$, XeO_3F_2, PF_5 AsF_5, $[Cu(Cl)_5]^{3-}$ $[Ni(CN)_5]^{3-}$, $[Fe(CO)_5]$
		4	1	Irregular tetrahedral	$TeCl_4$, SF_4
		3	2	T-shaped	ClF_3, IF_3
		2	3	Linear	I_3^-, XeF_2
sp^3d^2	Octahedral	6	0	Octahedral	SF_6, PF_6^-, $SnCl_6^-$, MoF_6, $(PF_6)^-$, $[Fe(CN)_6]^{4-}$, $[FeH_2O)_6]^{3+}$
		5	1	Square pyramidal	ICl_5, BrF_5, IF_5, $XeOF_4$
		4	2	Square planar	XeF_4, ICl_4^-
sp^3d^3	90° 72 Pentagonal bipyramidal	7	0	Pentagonal bipyramidal	IF_7, $[ZrF_7]^{3-}$ $[UF_7]^{3-}$ $[UO_2F_5]^{3-}$
		6	1	Distorted octahedral	XeF_6

Dhyan Rakhna | Isoelectronic (with same no. of e^-) species have similar shape or Geometry.

Molecular Orbital Theory (F. Hund & R S Mulliken, 1932)

2 or more Atomic Orbitals —combine→ Molecular Orbitals

Bonding M.O. (ψ_b)

Lower Energy, More stable
Also called HOMOs (Highly occupied M.O.) as these are preferred by e^- while filling

Antibonding M.O. (ψ_{ab})

Higher Energy, less stable
Also called LUMOs (Lowly or Unoccupied M.O.) as these are not pref. by e^- while filling

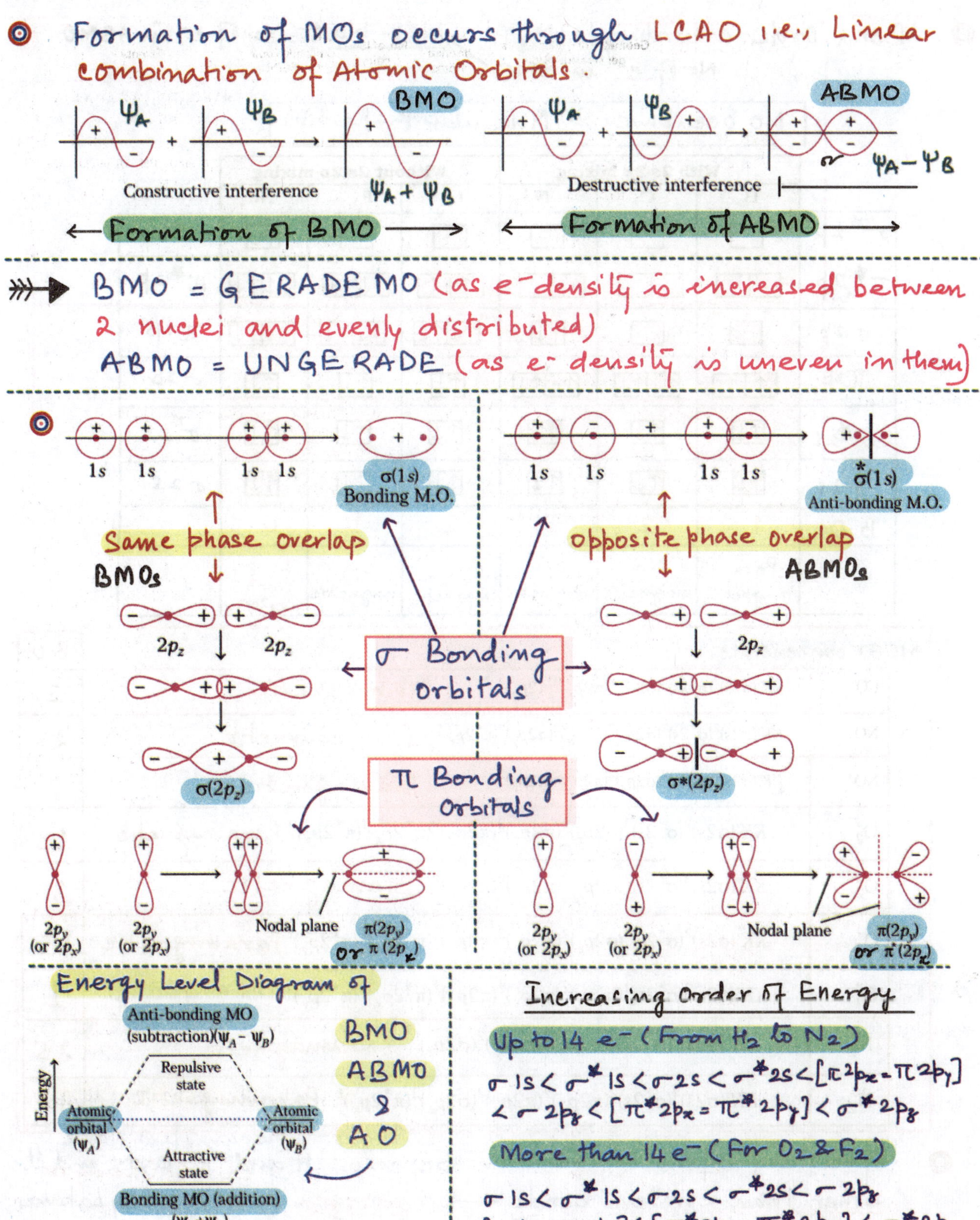
Formation of MOs occurs through LCAO i.e., Linear combination of Atomic Orbitals.
ψ_A
ψ_B
BMO
Constructive interference
$\psi_A + \psi_B$
ABMO
Destructive interference
or $\psi_A - \psi_B$
Formation of BMO
Formation of ABMO
BMO = GERADE MO (as e⁻ density is increased between 2 nuclei and evenly distributed)
ABMO = UNGERADE (as e⁻ density is uneven in them)
1s
1s
σ(1s)
Bonding M.O.
$\overset{*}{\sigma}(1s)$
Anti-bonding M.O.
Same phase overlap
BMOs
Opposite phase overlap
ABMOs
$2p_z$
σ($2p_z$)
σ*($2p_z$)
σ Bonding orbitals
π Bonding Orbitals
$2p_y$ (or $2p_x$)
Nodal plane
π($2p_y$) or π ($2p_x$)
π($2p_y$) or π*($2p_x$)
Energy Level Diagram of
Anti-bonding MO (subtraction)($\psi_A - \psi_B$)
Repulsive state
Energy
Atomic orbital (ψ_A)
Atomic orbital (ψ_B)
Attractive state
Bonding MO (addition) ($\psi_A + \psi_B$)
BMO
ABMO
&
AO
Increasing Order of Energy
Up to 14 e⁻ (From H_2 to N_2)
$\sigma 1s < \sigma^* 1s < \sigma 2s < \sigma^* 2s < [\pi 2p_x = \pi 2p_y] < \sigma 2p_z < [\pi^* 2p_x = \pi^* 2p_y] < \sigma^* 2p_z$
More than 14 e⁻ (For O_2 & F_2)
$\sigma 1s < \sigma^* 1s < \sigma 2s < \sigma^* 2s < \sigma 2p_z < [\pi 2p_x = \pi 2p_y] < [\pi^* 2p_x = \pi^* 2p_y] < \sigma^* 2p_z$

◎ Bond order according to MOT $= \frac{N_b - N_a}{2}$

N_b ← No. of e^- in BMO; N_a ← No. of e^- in ABMO

MO occupancy & Molecular Properties

	With 2s-2p mixing			Without 2s-2p mixing			
	B_2	C_2	N_2	O_2	F_2	Ne_2	
$\sigma^* 2p$	□	□	□	□	□	↑↓	$\sigma^* 2p$
$\pi^* 2p$	□□	□□	□□	↑ ↑	↑↓ ↑↓	↑↓ ↑↓	$\pi^* 2p$
$\sigma 2p$	□	□	↑↓	↑↓ ↑↓	↑↓ ↑↓	↑↓ ↑↓	$\pi 2p$
$\pi 2p$	↑ ↑	↑↓ ↑↓	↑↓ ↑↓	↑↓	↑↓	↑↓	$\sigma 2p$
$\sigma^* 2s$	↑↓	↑↓	↑↓	↑↓	↑↓	↑↓	$\sigma^* 2s$
$\sigma 2s$	↑↓	↑↓	↑↓	↑↓	↑↓	↑↓	$\sigma 2s$
B.O.	1	2	3	2	1	0	
	Para magnetic	Dia magnetic	Dia magnetic	Para magnetic	Dia magnetic	Does not exist	

NEET concentrate

			B.O.
CO	$KK'(\sigma 2s)^2(\sigma^* 2s)^2(\sigma 2p_z)^2(\pi 2p_x)^2(\pi 2p_y)^2$	Diamagnetic	3
NO	$KK'(\sigma 2s)^2(\sigma^* 2s)^2(\sigma 2p_z)^2(\pi 2p_x)^2(\pi 2p_y)^2(\pi^* 2p_x)^1$	Paramagnetic	2.5
NO^+	$KK'(\sigma 2s)^2(\sigma^* 2s)^2(\sigma 2p_z)^2(\pi 2p_x)^2(\pi 2p_y)^2$	Diamagnetic	3
O_2^+	$KK'(\sigma 2s)^2(\sigma^* 2s)^2(\sigma 2p_z)^2(\pi 2p_x)^2(\pi 2p_y)^2(\pi^* 2p_x)^1(\pi^* 2p_y)^0$	Paramagnetic	2.5
O_2^{2+}	$KK'(\sigma 2s)^2(\sigma^* 2s)^2(\sigma 2p_z)^2(\pi 2p_x)^2(\pi 2p_y)^2$	Diamagnetic	3
O_2^-	$KK'(\sigma 2s)^2(\sigma^* 2s)^2(\sigma 2p_z)^2(\pi 2p_x)^2(\pi 2p_y)^2(\pi^* 2p_x)^2(\pi^* 2p_y)^1$	Paramagnetic	1.5
O_2^{2-}	$KK'(\sigma 2s)^2(\sigma^* 2s)^2(\sigma 2p_z)^2(\pi 2p_x)^2(\pi 2p_y)^2(\pi^* 2p_x)^2(\pi^* 2p_y)^2$	Diamagnetic	1
N_2^+	$KK'(\sigma 2s)^2(\sigma^* 2s)^2(\pi 2p_x)^2(\pi 2p_y)^2(\sigma 2p_z)^1$	Paramagnetic	2.5
N_2^-	$KK'(\sigma 2s)^2(\sigma^* 2s)^2(\pi 2p_x)^2(\pi 2p_y)^2(\sigma 2p_z)^2(\pi^* 2p_x)^1$	Paramagnetic	2.5

◎ Specialised Dipole attractions between H and F, O, N and Cl other than covalent bonds ⟶ Hydrogen Bonding (By Latimer and Rodebush in 1920)

Conditions for H- bonding

(i) Hydrogen is bonded covalently to either of F, O, N or Cl to acquire a certain degree (+)ve charge.

(ii) Any of F, O, N or Cl is in neighbourhood of this H with certain degree of (-)ve charge.

Types

Intermolecular

Water

HF

Carboxylic Acid

Responsible for elevation in b.p. & unexpected phase change from gas to liquid or liquid to solid. Decreases volatile nature & increases solubility

Intramolecular

o-hydroxybenzaldehyde

o-nitrophenol

Nickel dimethyl glyoximate (a chelate)

Anti-form

Syn-form

Pyridine-2-carboxyl dioxime

Responsible for depression in b.p. & unexpected phase change from solid to liquid or liquid to gas. Increases volatile nature & decreases solubility.

5. Thermodynamics

- Deals with different forms of energy changes and interrelates them from quantitative view point.
- It is the only chapter of physical sciences which does not has any definite law (as it is completely based on human experiences which varies from person to person)

Thermodynamic Terms

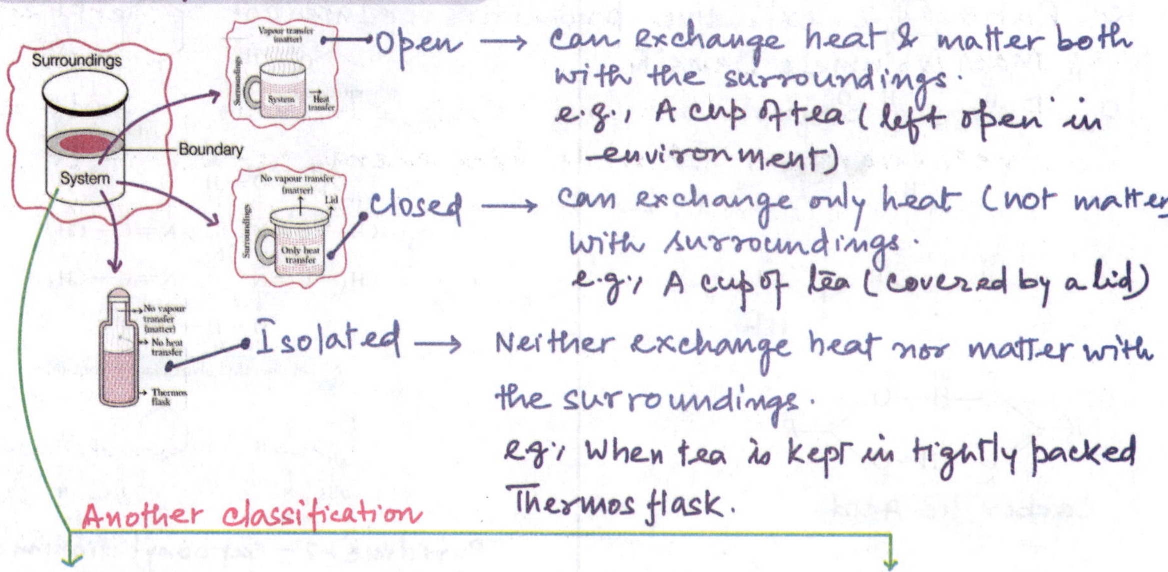

Homogeneous

System composed uniformly in a single phase

e.g.,

$$2NH_3(g) \rightleftharpoons 3H_2(g) + N_2(g)$$

Heterogeneous

System composed of 2 or more phases

e.g.,

Phase 1 solid → $CaCO_3(s) \rightleftharpoons CaO(s) + CO_2(g)$ ← Phase 2 gas

NEET concentrate

- Mixture of liquids can be considered homogeneous only if all the liquids present in it are completely miscible with each other
- Gaseous mixture is always one phase system
- Every solid is always considered as different phase system.

Thermodynamic Properties

→ **Intensive** i.e., whose values does not change on division of substances e.g., Molar volume, Density, Refractive index, surface tension, viscosity, free energy per mole, pressure, temperature bp & freezing point.

↓ **Extensive** i.e., whose values change on division of substances e.g., volume, No. of moles, Mass Free energy, Entropy, Enthalpy Heat capacity.

NEET concentrate

- Ratio of 2 extensive properties = Intensive property e.g., Mass/volume = Density
- Extensive property per unit volume = Intensive property e.g., Free energy → EP while free energy per mole → IP.
- Extensive properties → Additive; Intensive properties → Non additive.

Thermodynamic Processes

Always Remember
$W_{irr} < W_{rev}$

1. **Isothermal**
   At constant temperature i.e., $\partial T = 0$
2. **Isobaric**
   At constant Pressure i.e., $\partial P = 0$
3. **Isochoric**
   At constant volume i.e., $\partial V = 0$
4. **Adiabatic**
   No Heat exchange with the system i.e., ∂H or $\partial Q = 0$
5. **Irreversible**
   Unidirectional system i.e., moving in one direction only, no come back to initial state.
6. **Reversible**
   Bidirectional, i.e., come back to initial state.
7. **Cyclic**
   Reversible process which reaches to its initial state after more than 1 steps.

- The set of conditions in which physical & chemical properties of a system are fixed & specific → system or state variables

State Function
Depends only on Initial & Final state

Path Function
Depends only upon the path followed

PYQ Punch

Q. Match list I with list II NEET 2024

List I (Process)	List II (Conditions)
A. Isothermal process	I. No Heat exchange
B. Isochoric process	II. Carried out at constant temperature
C. Isobaric process	III. Carried out at constant volume
D. Adiabatic process	IV. Carried out at constant pressure

Choose the correct answer from the options given below

(a) A−IV, B−III, C−II, D−I
(b) A−IV, B−II, C−III, D−I
(c) A−I, B−II, C−III, D−IV
(d) A−II, B−III, C−IV, D−I

Sol Factual II for A is given in d option only ← Time saver

- The sum of all possible kinds of energies associate with a system ⟶ Internal Energy (E or U) of that system

  Dhyan Rakhna | As thermodynamics is based on human perception and the observation + expression power of every person are different, hence, in thermodynamics we always calculate & use the difference between initial or final values of any function and denote it by Δ (delta). So this Δ is very oftenly seen in this chapter.

- Like others internal energy of the system is measured as

  $\boxed{\Delta U} = U_{initial} \sim U_{final}$

  ↑ This change may occur by

  1. Work is done on or by the system
  2. Heat movement in or out of the system
  3. Movement of matter (in or out of the system)

NEET concentrate

Sign Convention in Thermodynamics

WORK
- Compression or work done on the system ⟶ (+)ve
- Expansion or work done by the system ⟶ (−)ve

Heat
- Heat is transferred from surroundings to system ⟶ (+)ve
- Heat is transferred from system to surroundings ⟶ (−)ve

- Work = Intensity factor × Capacity factors

  SI unit of Work: Joule

  Intensity factor: Factors that are responsible for work e.g., Force, pressure, surface tension.

  Capacity factors: Factors that are measure of extent of work done e.g., Displacement, change in vol. change in length etc.

- For any system when change in pressure results to change in volume then work done → Pressure – Volume work OR Expansion or compression work $= -p_{ex} \times \Delta V$

For any gaseous sys.

$p_{ex} < p_{int}$. $W = -p\Delta V$ is (–)ve (+ +)
Expansion of gas will occur

$W = -p\Delta V$ is (+)ve (+ –) $p_{ex} > p_{int}$.
Compression of gas will occur

Expansion ← Initial system → Compression

A' B' V_i V_f p_{ex} | A B p_{ex} | Pressure, p A A B B p_{ex} V_i

NEET concentrate

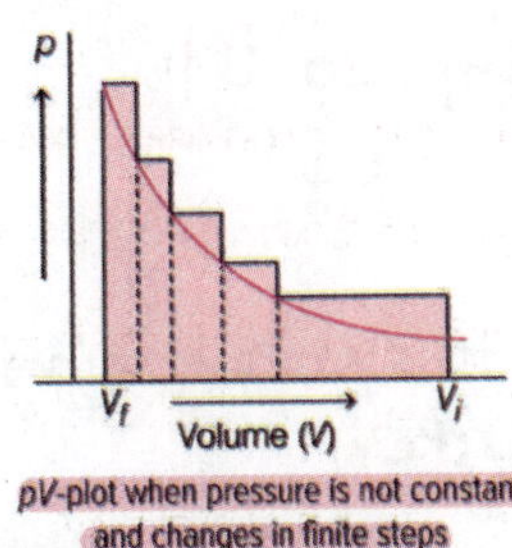

pV-plot when pressure is not constant and changes in finite steps

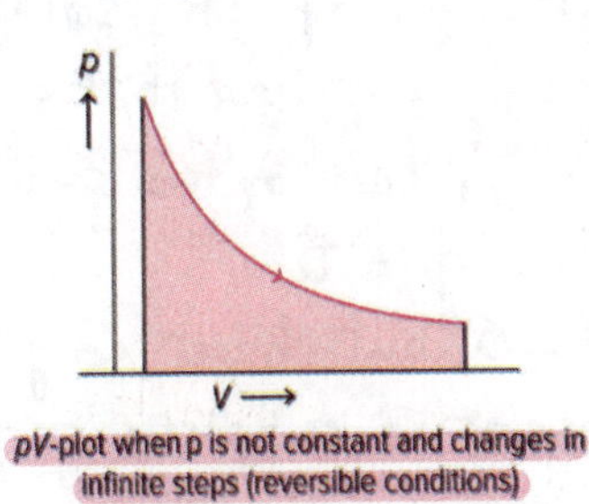

pV-plot when p is not constant and changes in infinite steps (reversible conditions)

1. Work done in isothermal irreversible expansion
$W = -p_{ex}(V_2 - V_1)$
2. Work done in isothermal reversible expansion
$W = -2.303\, nRT \log \frac{p_1}{p_2}$

Dhyan Rakhna | In free expansion W = 0

PYQ Punch

Q. The work done during reversible isothermal expansion of one mole of Hydrogen gas at 25°C from pressure of 20 Atm. to 10 Atm. is (Given R = 2.0 cal K^{-1} mol^{-1}) NEET 2024
(a) 0 calorie (b) –413.14 calories (c) 413.14 calories (d) 100 calories

Sol $W = -2.303\, nRT \log p_1/p_2 = -2.303 \times 1 \times 2 \times 298 \log 20/10 = -413.14$ cal

- Form of energy that is transferred from one body to another as a result of temperature difference between them → Heat (SI unit Joule) → Its gain raises the temperature of any system & its loss lowers the temperature of any system.

- Heat capacity $q = C \cdot \Delta T$
  - → Heat quantity that raises the temperature of any system by 1°
  - → C_s i.e., specific heat capacity → when temp. is raised of unit mass
  - → C_m i.e., Molar heat capacity → when temp. is raised of 1 mole.

Molar heat capacity → At constant pressure (C_p) ; At constant volume (C_v)

$C_p - C_v = R; \frac{C_p}{C_v} = \gamma$

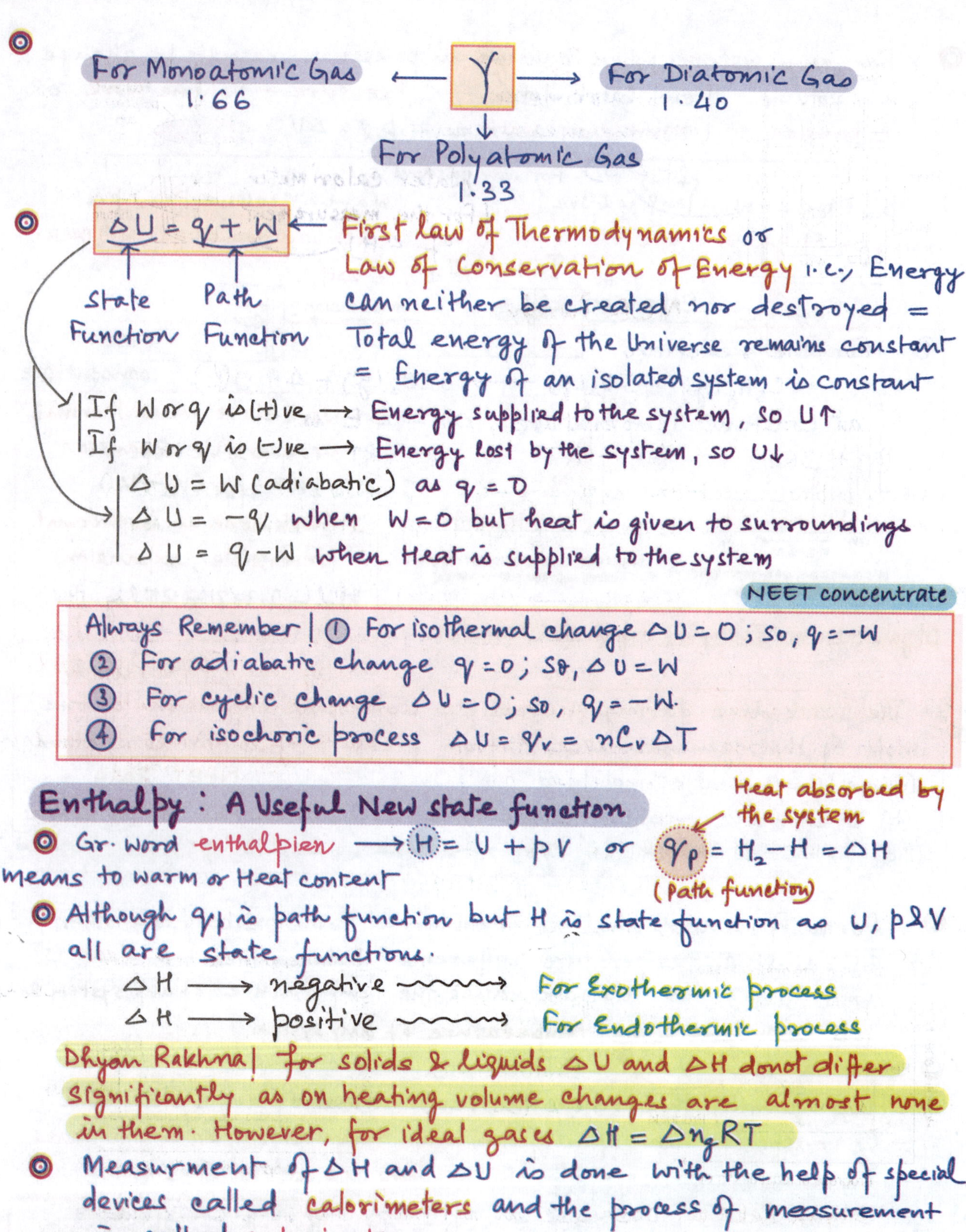

- For Monoatomic Gas 1.66 ← γ → For Diatomic Gas 1.40
  ↓ For Polyatomic Gas 1.33

- $\Delta U = q + W$ ← **First law of Thermodynamics** or **Law of Conservation of Energy** i.e., Energy can neither be created nor destroyed = Total energy of the Universe remains constant = Energy of an isolated system is constant

  ΔU → State Function; $q + W$ → Path Function

  - If W or q is (+)ve → Energy supplied to the system, so U↑
  - If W or q is (−)ve → Energy lost by the system, so U↓

  - $\Delta U = W$ (adiabatic) as $q = 0$
  - $\Delta U = -q$ when $W = 0$ but heat is given to surroundings
  - $\Delta U = q - W$ when Heat is supplied to the system

NEET concentrate

Always Remember
1. For isothermal change $\Delta U = 0$; so, $q = -W$
2. For adiabatic change $q = 0$; so, $\Delta U = W$
3. For cyclic change $\Delta U = 0$; so, $q = -W$.
4. For isochoric process $\Delta U = q_v = nC_v\Delta T$

Enthalpy : A Useful New state function

- Gr. word **enthalpien** → $H = U + pV$ or $q_p = H_2 - H = \Delta H$ means to warm or Heat content

  q_p → Heat absorbed by the system (path function)

- Although q_p is path function but H is state function as U, p & V all are state functions.

  ΔH ⟶ negative ⟿ For Exothermic process

  ΔH ⟶ positive ⟿ For Endothermic process

Dhyan Rakhna! for solids & liquids ΔU and ΔH donot differ significantly as on heating volume changes are almost none in them. However, for ideal gases $\Delta H = \Delta n_g RT$

- Measurment of ΔH and ΔU is done with the help of special devices called **calorimeters** and the process of measurement is called **calorimetry**.

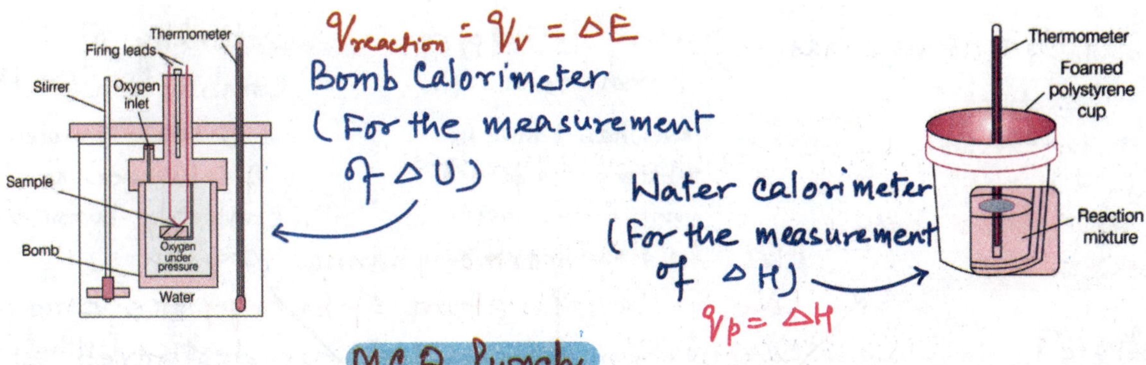

MCQ Punch

Q. For the reaction

$$C_3H_8(g) + 5O_2(g) \longrightarrow 3CO_2(g) + 4H_2O(l)$$

at constant temperature, $\Delta H - \Delta E$ is

(a) $+3RT$ (b) $-RT$ (c) $+RT$ (d) $-3RT$ ✓

Sol As per reaction $\Delta n_g = 3 - 6 = -3$; Now by the equation

$\Delta H = \Delta E + n_g RT$ or $\Delta H - \Delta E = -3RT$

- $CH_4(g) + Cl_2(g) \longrightarrow CH_3Cl(g) + HCl(g)$; $\Delta H = -115$ kJ/mol

  $C_2H_5OH(l) + 3O_2(g) \longrightarrow 2CO_2(g) + 3H_2O(l)$; $\Delta H = -1367$ kJ/mol

  Thermochemical Equations

  ΔH: Enthalpy change with specified no. of moles of reactants & products (Here Heat released in both the equations)

  Heat absorbed ⟶ (+)ve sign.

Imp: When equation is reversed then sign of ΔH is also reversed but its magnitude remains same.

$2H_2(g) + O_2(g) \longrightarrow 2H_2O(l)$; $\Delta H = +136.8$ kcal

$2H_2O(l) \longrightarrow 2H_2(g) + O_2(g)$; $\Delta H = -136.8$ kcal

- Thermochemical Reactions can be

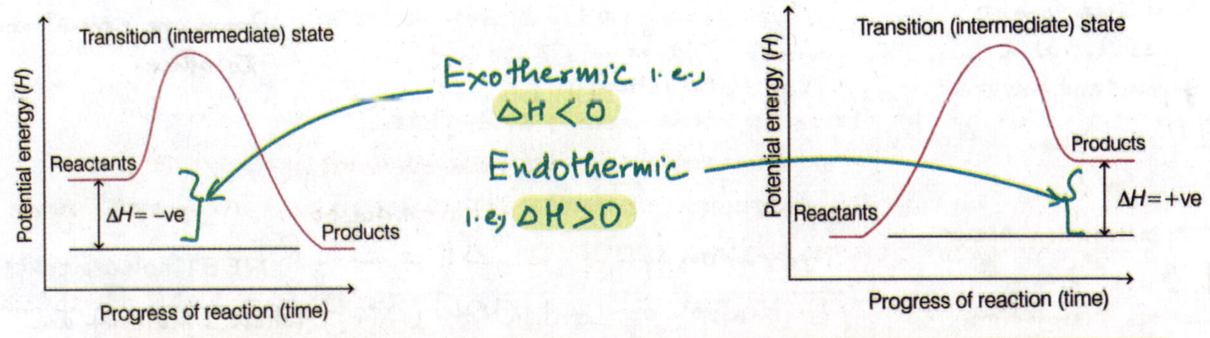

Dhyan Rakhna | Decrease in enthalpy may be a contributory factor for spontaneity but it is not true for all cases.

Reaction Enthalpy ($\Delta_r H$)

Enthalpy change when the reacting species, as represented by a balanced chemical equation are completely reacted.

$\Delta_r H$ = Sum of H_p – Sum of H_R

(Enthalpy of Products; Enthalpy of Reactants)

If $H_P = H_R$ then $\Delta H = 0$

If $H_P > H_R$ then $\Delta H = (+)ve$ Endothermic

If $H_P < H_R$ then $\Delta H = (-)ve$ Exothermic

Standard Enthalpy of Reaction (ΔH°)

i.e., under thermodynamical standard state (Purest form for solid & liquid; Gases at 1 bar & 298K)

Standard Enthalpy of Formation ($\Delta_f H$)

i.e., when 1 mole of substance is formed from its elements in standard state

Enthalpy of Combustion ($\Delta_c H$)

i.e., when 1 mole of substance is completely burnt in oxygen.

Enthalpy of Atomisation ($\Delta_a H$)

i.e., when 1 mole of a given substance dissociate in to gaseous atoms

Lattice Enthalpy

$\Delta_{lattice} H$

when 1 mole of crystal of an ionic compound is completely converted in to respective gaseous ions at standard conditions.

Enthalpies of phase Transition –

(a) Enthalpy of Fusion ($\Delta_{fus} H$)

(b) Enthalpy of vaporisation ($\Delta_{vap} H$)

(c) Enthalpy of sublimation ($\Delta_{sub} H$)

Enthalpy of Hydration ($\Delta_{hyd} H$)

when 1 mole of salt combines with specific moles of water to form a specific hydrate

Enthalpy of Solution ($\Delta_{sol} H$)

when 1 mole of substance is dissolved in a specified quantity of solvent at a given temperature

$\Delta_{sol} H^\circ = -\Delta_{lattice} H^\circ + \Delta_{hyd} H^\circ$

- If $\Delta_{lattice} H^\circ < \Delta_{hyd} H^\circ$
  → Dissolution occur
- If $\Delta_{lattice} H^\circ > \Delta_{hyd} H^\circ$
  → No Dissolution
- If $\Delta_{lattice} H^\circ = \Delta_{hyd} H^\circ$
  → Solute & Solvent in Equilibrium

Enthalpy of Neutralisation ($\Delta_n H$)

i.e., when 1 equivalent of acid is neutralised by 1 equivalent of base

- $\Delta_n H$ of strong acid & strong base → –57.3 or –13.7 kJ/mol (constant)
- $\Delta_n H$ of weak acid + strong base or vice versa → less than –57.3 kJ/mol
- $\Delta_n H$ of HF = –68.6 kJ/mol (due to Hydration of F^-)

Enthalpy of Dilution ($\Delta_{dil} H$)

when any solution containing 1 mole of solute is diluted from one concentration to other.

NEET concentrate

Enthalpy of Ionisation ($\Delta_{ion} H$) when 1 mole of an electrolyte is completely ionised into its constituents

This can be obtained by subtracting heat of neutralisation of weak acid/base with that of strong acid/base

Bond Enthalpies ($\Delta_{bond} H^\circ$)

Enthalpy change associated with making or breaking of Bonds.

$\Delta_r H$ = Sum of $BE_{Reactants}$ − Sum of $BE_{products}$

Bond Dissociation ← Bond Enthalpies → **Mean or Average**

Bond Dissociation: when all bonds of one type are broken in 1 mole gaseous covalent substance to form products in gaseous state.

For Diatomic molecules $\Delta_a H = \Delta_{BD} H^\circ$

Mean or Average: In Polyatomic molecules where bond dissociation enthalpies of all the bonds is not equal, BE is expressed in the terms of Mean or Average BE

◎ A —ΔH→ B; A —ΔH₁→ C —ΔH₂→ D —ΔH₃→ B

$\Delta H = \Delta H_1 + \Delta H_2 + \Delta H_3$

Hess's Law of constant Summation

The total heat change for any reaction is independent of path (i.e., single step or multiple step)

Its best interpretation is when chemical reactions are added, subtracted or multiplied, heat changes associated with them are also added subtracted & multiplied accordingly

Applications

Helpful in finding

- $\Delta_f H^\circ$, Bond, Transition, Resonance & Lattice Enthalpies
- Enthalpies of Extremely slow reactions.

PYQ Punch

Q. At standard conditions, if the change in enthalpy for the following reaction is −109 kJ/mol

$$H_2(g) + Br_2(g) \longrightarrow 2HBr(g)$$ NEET 2020

Given that, Bond energy of H_2 and Br_2 is 435 and 192 kJ/mol respectively then what is the bond energy of HBr in kJ/mol

(a) 368 ✓ (b) 736 (c) 518 (d) 259

Sol $\Delta_r H$ = Sum of $BE_{Reactants}$ − Sum of $BE_{Products}$ or

$-109 = [BE_{H_2} + BE_{Br_2}] - BE_{HBr} \times 2 = (435+192) + BE_{HBr} \times 2$

or BE_{HBr} = 368 kJ/mol

Dhyan Rakhna | Thermochemical calculations usually depends upon the way you write their equations & if your way of writing the equation is correct you can obtain the result correctly

(i) Either by adding, subtracting or multiplying them

(ii) or by BE of Reaction = Σ Enthalpies of Products − Σ Enthalpies of Reactants

◎ Max Born and Fritz Haber developed the Born Haber cycle based upon the Hess's law of constant summation.

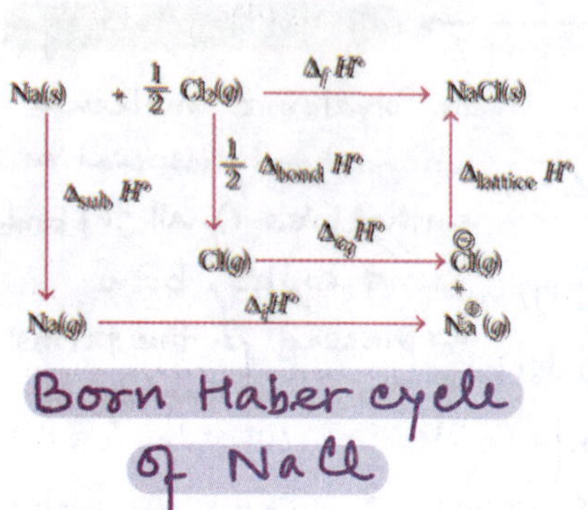

Born Haber cycle of NaCl

(i) $Na(s) \longrightarrow Na(g); \Delta_{sub}H^\circ = 108.4\,kJ/mol$

$\downarrow$

$Na^+(g) + e^-(g); \Delta_iH^\circ = 496\,kJ/mol$

(ii) $\frac{1}{2}Cl_2 \longrightarrow Cl(g); \Delta_aH^\circ = 121\,kJ/mol$

$+e^- \downarrow$

$Cl^-(g); \Delta_{eg}H^\circ = -348.6\,kJ/mol$

(iii) $Na^+(g) + Cl^-(g) \longrightarrow Na^+Cl^-(s); \Delta_{lattice}H^\circ = U$

$Na(s) + \frac{1}{2}Cl_2(g) \longrightarrow Na^+Cl^-(s); \Delta_fH^\circ = 411.2\,kJ/mol$

- The process will be spontaneous only if

  Sum of Energies Required $\leq$ Sum of Energies Released

NEET concentrate

- Hess's law is in agreement with I[st] law of Thermodynamics
- The numerical value of Enthalpy of decomposition of a compound = Numerical value of enthalpy of formation of that compound with opposite sign ⟶ Lavoiser & Laplace Law
- $$\Delta_nH = \frac{Q}{100} \times 1000 \times \frac{1}{X}$$

  X ← Normality of Acid or Base

  Q: Heat change in Reaction = mass of the solution × Specific Heat $(T_2 - T_1)$
- Δ_rH° (Ionisation Enthalpy) $= E_0$ (I.E) $+ 5/2\,RT$

  Δ_rH° (Electron Gain Enthalpy) $= -A$ (electron affinity) $- 5/2\,RT$

- Physical or Chemical changes which has the potential to proceed without the assistance of any external agency ⟶ spontaneous processes and this phenomenon ⟶ spontaneity

Entropy

- 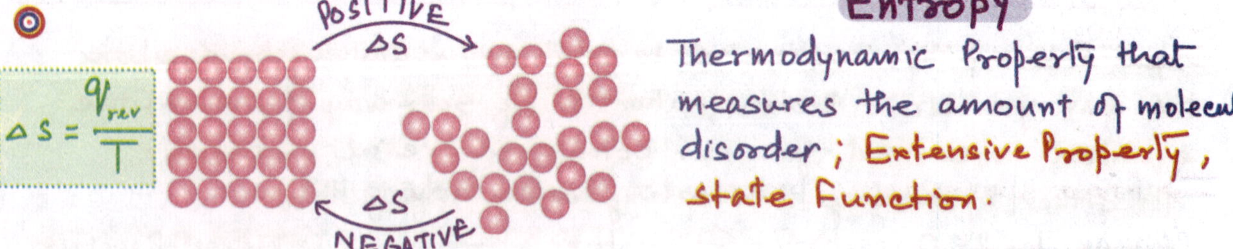

  Thermodynamic Property that measures the amount of molecular disorder; Extensive Property, state function.

- At absolute zero, entropy of pure crystal ⟶ Zero

  Third Law of Thermodynamics

NEET concentrate

- $S_{solid} < S_{Liquid} < S_{gas}$
- On increasing the no. of molecules ⟶ Entropy ↑
- On increasing temperature ⟶ Entropy usually increases
- S° ⟶ Entropy of 1 mole of a pure substance at 1 atm pressure and specified temperature (usually 25°C)
- Boiling of Egg ⟶ ΔS = (−)ve as inside content of eggs become liquid ⟶ solid

Entropy w.r.t. Boiling & freezing point

Change	Temperature	Sign of (a) ΔS_{sys}	Sign of (b) ΔS_{surr}	Comparison of (a) and (b)	ΔS_{univ}	Spontaneity
Melting (solid → liquid)	(i) > melting point	+	−	>	>0	Spontaneous
	(ii) = melting point	+	−	=	=0	Equilibrium
	(iii) < melting point	+	−	<	<0	Non-spontaneous
Freezing (liquid → solid)	(i) > freezing point	−	+	>	<0	Non-spontaneous
	(ii) = freezing point	−	+	=	=0	Equilibrium
	(iii) < freezing point	−	+	<	>0	Spontaneous

Conclusion
- Spontaneous: $S_{total} > 0$
- Equilibrium: $S_{total} = 0$
- Non-spontaneous: $S_{total} < 0$

- So, we can say "Whenever a spontaneous process takes place, an increase in the S_{total} of Universe is visible." ⟵ statement of 2nd Law of Thermodynamics

"It is impossible to convert the taken heat into work by a cyclic process without transferring a part of heat to a cool reservoir." ⟵ Kelvin statement of 2nd Law

"It is impossible for a cyclic process to transfer heat from a body at lower temperature to one at higher temperature without same work input". ⟵ Clausius statement of 2nd law

⟹ For a spontaneous process (In Isolated system) ΔS = (+)ve.

- Change in Gibb's free energy ⟶ $\Delta G = \Delta H - T\Delta S$

  G, state Function

  Free energy ⟵ A Hypothetical Infinite energy which is always used up in a spontaneous process.

PYQ Punch

Q1. If for a certain reaction $\Delta_r H$ is 30 kJ/mol at 450 K, the value of $\Delta_r S$ (in kJ/mol) for which the same reaction is spontaneous at same temperature is NEET 2020

(a) 70 (b) −33 (c) 33 (d) −70

Sol From $\Delta G = \Delta H - T\Delta S$; for a spontaneous reaction $\Delta G < 0$
i.e., $T\Delta S > \Delta H$; at 450 K $\Delta S > \frac{30 \times 1000 \text{ J/mol}}{450 \text{ K}} = 66.67$ J/mol K

So $S > 66.67$ i.e., 70 J/mol K is the correct answer.

Imp. tip → ΔS can not be (−)ve for any spontaneous process hence option (b) and (d) are already omitted.

Q2. For irreversible expansion of an ideal gas under isothermal condition the correct option is NEET 2021

(a) $\Delta U = 0$, $\Delta S_{total} = 0$ (b) $\Delta U \neq 0$, $\Delta S_{total} \neq 0$
(c) $\Delta U = 0$, $\Delta S_{total} \neq 0$ (d) $\Delta U \neq 0$, $\Delta S_{total} = 0$

Sol For Isothermal process $\Delta T = 0$ so, $\Delta U = 0$
On Gas expansion entropy increases so $\Delta S \neq 0$

	ΔH	ΔS	ΔG	Reaction spontaineity
Exothermic	−	+	−	spontaneous at all temp.
	−	−	−	Spontaneous at low temp.
	−	−	+	Non-Spontaneous at high temp.
Endothermic	+	+	+	Non-spontaneous at low temp.
	+	+	−	Spontaneous at high temp.
	+	−	+	Non-Spontaneous at all temp.
	$T\Delta S = \Delta H$		0	Equilibrium

6. Equilibrium

- Irreversible changes ⟶ Proceed in one direction only & always reach to completion

  Reversible changes ⟶ Proceed in 2 opposite direction & never reach to completion.

- The state of a change at which the rate of forward and backward changes become equal ⟶ Equilibrium state

  Forward change $\rightleftharpoons$ Backward change

  ($\rightleftharpoons$) Indicates process in both the directions going on simultaneously

- Equilibrium is seen in physical as well as chemical processes.

  Physical: The one that is seen between different Physical states of a substance.
  - Solid $\rightleftharpoons$ Liquid
  - Liquid $\rightleftharpoons$ Gas
  - Solid $\rightleftharpoons$ Gas

  Chemical: The one that is seen in reversible reactions.

- Ice and water kept in a perfectly insulated thermal flask at 0°c (or 273k) under pressure ⟶ In equilibrium

  i.e., Solid $\rightleftharpoons$ Liquid equilibrium appears only at a particular temperature & pressure.

  temperature ⟵ Normal melting point (For ice at 1 atm = 273k) or Normal Freezing point (For water at 1atm = 273k)

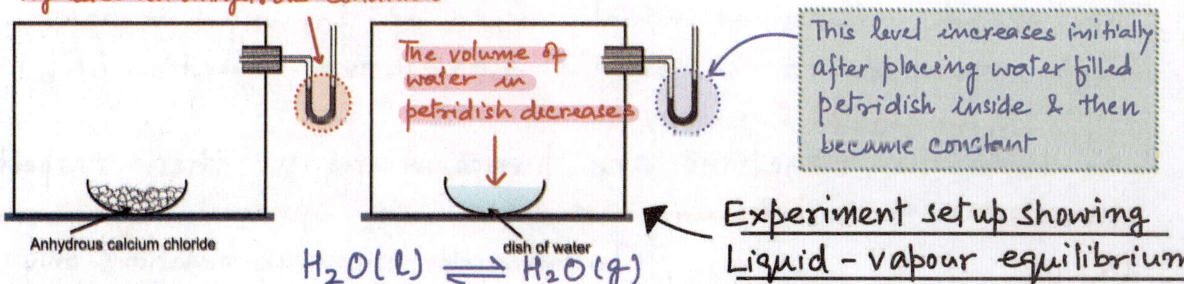

$H_2O(l) \rightleftharpoons H_2O(g)$

Experiment setup showing Liquid - vapour equilibrium

- Vapour ⟶ Gaseous state of any liquid in contact with its liquid phase

- Temperature at which vapour pressure of a liquid equals to the atmospheric pressure ⟶ Boiling Point.

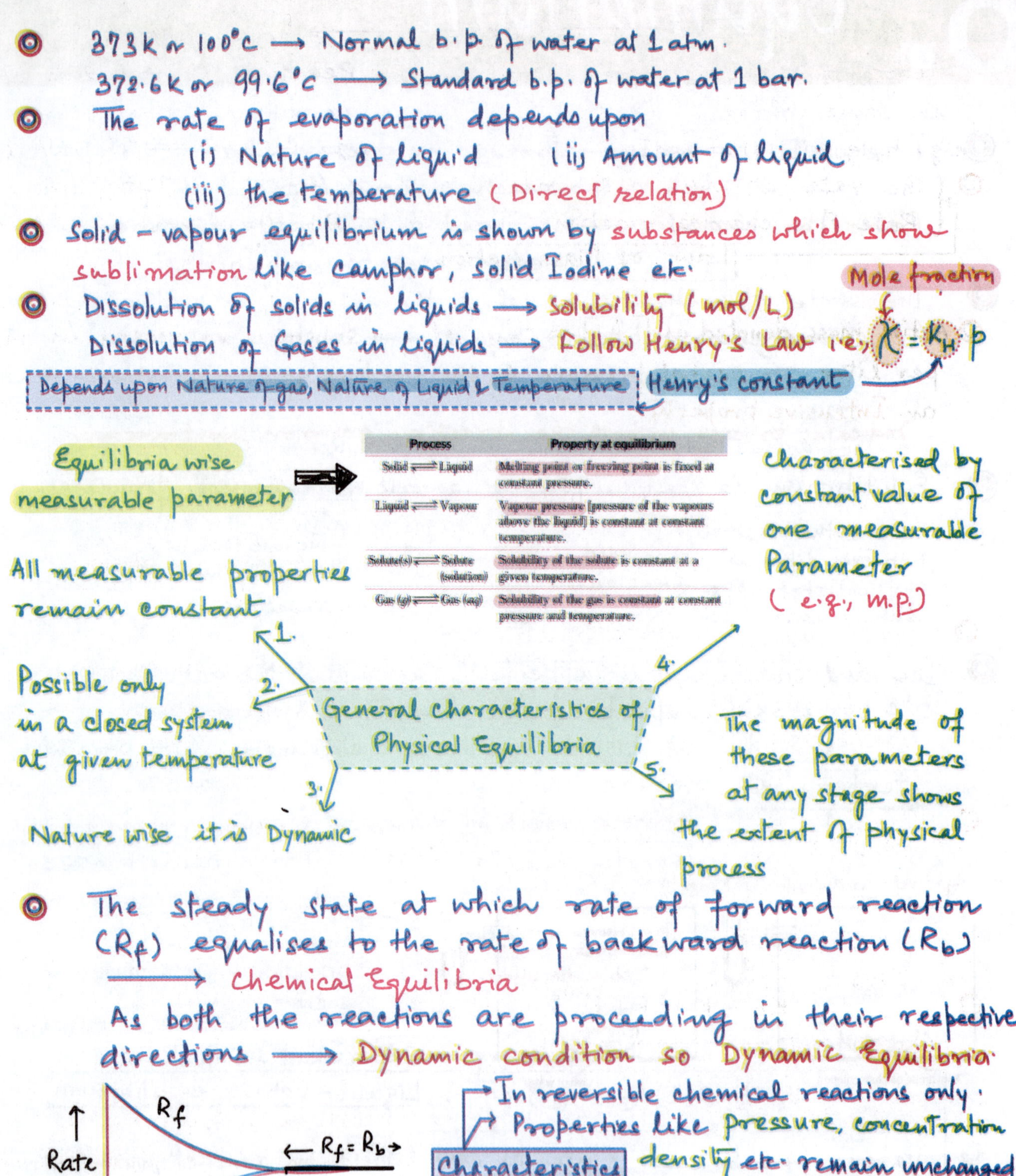

- 373 K or 100°C ⟶ Normal b.p. of water at 1 atm.
  372.6 K or 99.6°C ⟶ Standard b.p. of water at 1 bar.
- The rate of evaporation depends upon
  (i) Nature of liquid (ii) Amount of liquid
  (iii) the temperature (Direct relation)
- Solid – vapour equilibrium is shown by substances which show sublimation like camphor, solid Iodine etc.
- Dissolution of solids in liquids ⟶ Solubility (mol/L)
  Dissolution of Gases in liquids ⟶ Follow Henry's Law i.e., $\chi = K_H \, p$
  (χ → Mole fraction; K_H → Henry's constant: Depends upon Nature of gas, Nature of Liquid & Temperature)

Equilibria wise measurable parameter ⟹

Process	Property at equilibrium
Solid ⇌ Liquid	Melting point or freezing point is fixed at constant pressure.
Liquid ⇌ Vapour	Vapour pressure [pressure of the vapours above the liquid] is constant at constant temperature.
Solute(s) ⇌ Solute (solution)	Solubility of the solute is constant at a given temperature.
Gas (g) ⇌ Gas (aq)	Solubility of the gas is constant at constant pressure and temperature.

General characteristics of Physical Equilibria

1. All measurable properties remain constant
2. Possible only in a closed system at given temperature
3. Nature wise it is Dynamic
4. Characterised by constant value of one measurable Parameter (e.g., m.p.)
5. The magnitude of these parameters at any stage shows the extent of physical process

- The steady state at which rate of forward reaction (R_f) equalises to the rate of backward reaction (R_b) ⟶ Chemical Equilibria
  As both the reactions are proceeding in their respective directions ⟶ Dynamic condition so Dynamic Equilibria

Rate of Reaction ↑ vs Time ⟶ (R_f, R_b; $R_f = R_b$ at Equilibrium)

Characteristics
- In reversible chemical reactions only.
- Properties like pressure, concentration density etc. remain unchanged
- Can be attained from either side
- No effect of catalyst
- ΔG = zero.

Types

Homogeneous: Reactants & Products are in same phase
e.g., $H_2(g) + I_2(g) \rightleftharpoons HI(g)$

Heterogeneous: Reactants & Products are in different phases
e.g., $CaCO_3(s) \rightleftharpoons CaO(s) + CO_2(g)$

- The rate at which a substance reacts ∝ Active Mass of that subs.
  Rate of a chemical reaction ∝ The multiples of active masses of Reactants
  → **Law of Mass Action**

- Active mass denoted as [A] = Conc. of any substance expressed in moles per litre OR partial pressure of the reacting gaseous substance. It is an Intensive property.

NEET concentrate

> The active mass of pure solids & liquids → 1 (unity)
>
> $$\text{Active mass} = \frac{\text{Density of a substance (g/L)}}{\text{Molecular mass of the substance}}$$
>
> The concept of active mass was given by Guldberg & Waage

- For $aA + bB \rightleftharpoons cC + dD$

$$\frac{[C]^c [D]^d}{[A]^a [B]^b} = \text{constant } (K_c)$$

Law of chemical equilibrium
where K_c = Equilibrium constant
i.e., Ratio of conc. of products & reactants raised to the power of their stoichiometric coefficients.

- If reactants & products are in gaseous phase

$$\frac{p_C^c \cdot p_D^d}{p_A^a \cdot p_B^b} = \text{Constant } (K_p)$$

Here p_A, p_B, p_C and p_D are partial pressures of gases A, B, C & D respectively.

- $K_p = K_c (RT)^{\Delta n_g}$

R = Gas constant; T = Temp.
Δn_g = Difference of no. of moles of gaseous Products & Reactants in a balanced chemical reaction

Δn	K_p Vs K_c	Units K_p	Units K_c
0	$K_p = K_c$	—	—
>0	$K_p > K_c$	$(atm)^{\Delta n}$	$(mol\ L^{-1})^{\Delta n}$
<0	$K_p < K_c$	$(atm)^{\Delta n}$	$(mol\ L^{-1})^{\Delta n}$

Dhyan Rakhna! number of moles (Δn_g) calculate karte samay solid aur liquid components ke moles consider nahi karne hain.

PYQ Punch

Q. In which of the following equilibria K_p and K_c are not equal — NEET 2024

✓(a) $PCl_5(g) \rightleftharpoons PCl_3(g) + Cl_2(g)$

(b) $H_2(g) + I_2(g) \rightleftharpoons 2HI(g)$

(c) $CO(g) + H_2O(g) \rightleftharpoons CO_2(g) + H_2(g)$

(d) $2BrCl(g) \rightleftharpoons Br_2(g) + Cl_2(g)$

Sol $K_p = K_c$ if $\Delta n_g = 0$; this condition is not applicable only in equation of option (a).

	Equilibrium	Δn_g	$K_p = K_C(RT)^{\Delta n_g}$
1.	$H_2(g) + I_2(g) \rightleftharpoons 2HI$	0	$K_p = K_C$
2.	$N_2O_4(g) \rightleftharpoons 2NO_2(g)$	1	$K_p = K_C(RT)$
3.	$2SO_2(g) + O_2(g) \rightleftharpoons 2SO_3(g)$	-1	$K_C = K_p(RT)$
4.	$N_2(g) + 3H_2(g) \rightleftharpoons 2NH_3(g)$	-2	$K_C = K_p(RT)^2$
5.	$C(s) + O_2(g) \rightleftharpoons CO_2(g)$	0	$K_p = K_C$
6.	$NH_4HS(s) \rightleftharpoons NH_3(g) + H_2S(g)$	2	$K_p = K_C(RT)^2$
7.	$NH_3(g) + H_2O(l) \rightleftharpoons NH_4OH(l)$	- 1	$K_C = K_p(RT)$

Some Important Reactions and Relation between their K_c and K_p

Especially memorise the reactions in which $K_p = K_c$

Characteristics of Equilibrium Constant

1. If reaction is reversed then $K_c' = \frac{1}{K_c}$
2. If equation is multiplied by n then $K_c' = (K_c)^n$
3. If equation is divided by n, then $K_c' = \sqrt{K_c}$
4. If two equations are subtracted, then $K_c' = K_{c_1}/K_{c_2}$
5. If two equations are added, then $K_c' = K_{c_1} \times K_{c_2}$

For a particular reaction the value of K_c is
- always constant
- temperature dependent
- catalyst & initial concentration independent.

Most of the questions of last 5 year NEET were based on these relations

PYQ Punch

Q. The equilibrium constants of the following are

$$N_2 + 3H_2 \rightleftharpoons 2NH_3 ;\ K_1$$

$$N_2 + O_2 \rightleftharpoons 2NO ;\ K_2$$

$$H_2 + \frac{1}{2}O_2 \rightleftharpoons H_2O ;\ K_3$$

The equilibrium constant (K) of the reaction

$$2NH_3 + \frac{5}{2}O_2 \rightleftharpoons 2NO + 3H_2O$$ will be

NEET 2017, AIPMT 2007, 2003

(a) $K_2K_3^3/K_1$ ✓ (b) K_2K_3/K_1 (c) $K_2^3K_3/K_1$ (d) $K_1K_3^3/K_2$

Sol Reversing eq. 1, multiplying eq. 3 with 3 and then adding them with 2 to get final equation.

Applications of Equilibrium Constant

a. Predicting the direction of Reaction

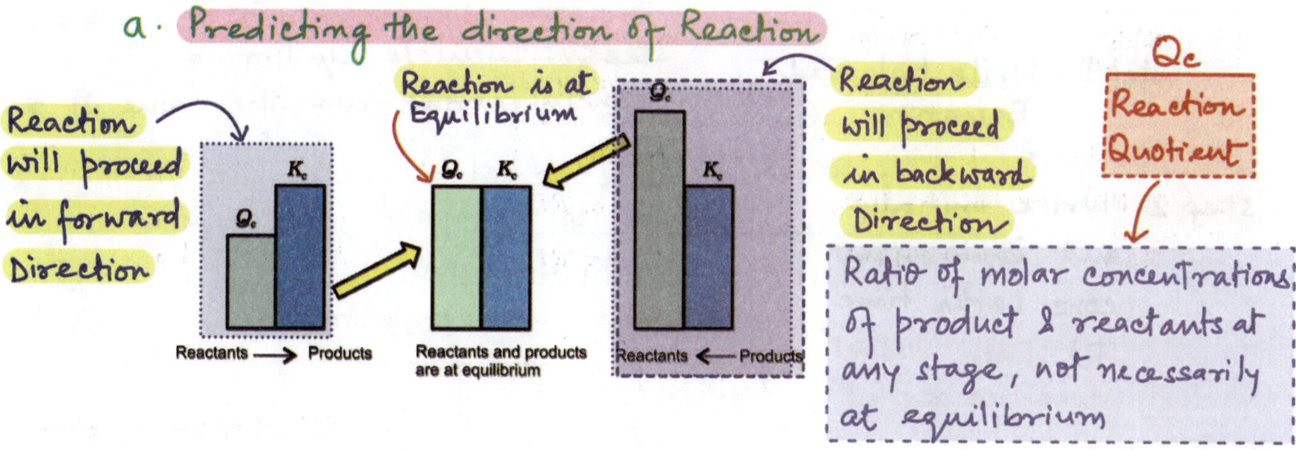

Dhyan Rakhna! if partial pressures are taken in the place of molar concentrations than $Q_c = Q_p$

b. Predicting the extent of a reaction

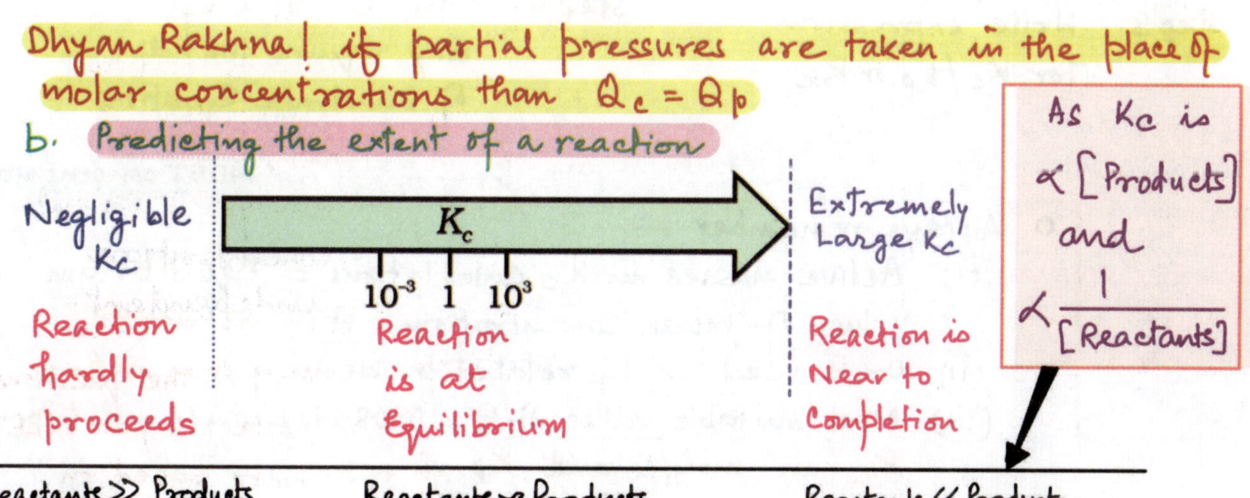

PYQ Punch

Q. For the reaction $2A \rightleftharpoons B + C$; the value of K_c is 4×10^{-3}. At a given time the composition of reaction mixture is $[A] = [B] = [C] = 2 \times 10^{-3}$ M. Then which of the following is correct NEET 2024

(a) Reaction is at equilibrium
(b) Reaction has a tendency to go in forward direction
(c) Reaction has a tendency to go in backward direction
(d) Reaction has gone to completion in forward direction

Sol $Q_c = \frac{[B][C]}{[A]^2} = 1$ & as $Q_c > K_c$ so reaction has the tendency to go in backward direction

Stepwise Approach to Calculate Equilibrium concentrations

Step 1. Write balanced Equation

Step 2. Write initial, and equilibrium conc. (after time t) Take product conc. as x

Step 3. Write expression for K_c / K_p or K_x

Step 4. Solve it for x (It may require the help of Quadratic Equation)

Step 5. Calculate Equilibrium concentrations from the value of x

NEET concentrate

- Always remember —
  (i) Active masses in K_c calculations = Equilibrium values of molar concentration (without units)
  (ii) Units used in K_p related problems → Atm or Bar
  (iii) Most suitable value of R = 0.08211 L atm/K mol (If K_c in mol/L and K_p in atm.

- The value of K_c is independent of reaction rate. However, it is connected with thermodynamics as

$$\Delta G = \Delta G^\circ + 2.303\, RT \log Q_c$$

or $\Delta G^\circ = -2.303\, RT \log K_c$ (as at equilibrium $\Delta G = 0$)

Case 1. If $\Delta G^\circ < 0$, Reaction is spontaneous in forward direction
Case 2. If $\Delta G^\circ > 0$, Reaction is non spontaneous or proceeds in forward direction to a very small extent
Case 3. If $\Delta G^\circ = 0$, Reaction is at equilibrium
Case 4. If ΔG° = Large (−)ve number i.e., $K_c >> 1$, then the forward reaction is nearly complete.
Case 5. If ΔG° = very small (+)ve number, then backward reaction is nearly complete.

PYQ Punch

Q. The equilibrium concentrations of the species in the reaction
$$A + B \rightleftharpoons C + D$$
are 2, 3, 10 and 6 mol/L respectively at 300K. ΔG° for the reaction is (R = 2 cal/mol K) NEET 2023

(a) −137.26 cal (b) −1381.80 cal (c) −13.73 cal (d) 1372.60 cal

Sol $K_c = \frac{10 \times 6}{2 \times 3} = 10$; $\Delta G^\circ = -2.303 \times 2 \times 300 \times \log(10) = -1381.80$ cal

- For any system at equilibrium if a disturbance is created by changing the – (i) Concentration of any one component
(ii) Temperature
(iii) Pressure

then the system will move in such a way, so as to oppose the effect created by such a change ⟶ Le-Chatelier's Principle

Means If a stress is applied to any system at equilibrium ⟶ The reaction will proceed in such a direction to relieve that stress.

Factors affecting Equilibrium:
- Change in conc. of either Reactant or Product
- Change in volume & Pressure
- Change in temperature
- Addition of Catalyst
- Addition of Inert Gas

For the reaction $aA + bB \rightleftharpoons cC + dD$
where, $\Delta n_g = (c+d) - (a+b)$

	Changes Imposed	Reaction favored	Eq. Position	Eq. constant
1.	A or B added	Forward	To right	No change
2.	C or D added	Backward	To left	No change
3.	Pressure ↑	Forward (if c+d > a+b) Backward (if c+d < a+b) No change (if c+d = a+b)	To right To Left No change	No change No change No change
4.	Pressure ↓	Opposite to above under similar conditions		No change
5.	Temperature ↑	Backward (For Exothermic Rxn.) Forward (For Endothermic Rxn.)	To left To Right	Value decreases Value increases
6.	Addition of catalyst	No change	No change	Eq. reached faster
7.	Addition of Inert gas (i) At constant pressure	To the direction of increasing gaseous mol.	No Change	No change.
	(ii) At constant volume	No effect	No change	No change

Favorable Conditions for some Imp. Reactions.

NEET concentrate

Equilibrium reaction		Direction on changing p			Direction on changing T		Direction on changing conc.		Favourable condition for forward direction
Exothermic ↓	Δn_g	P↑	P↓	ΔH	T↑	T↓	Reactant ↑	Product ↑	Most Imp.
$N_2(g) + 3H_2(g) \rightleftharpoons 2NH_3(g) + Q$	–2	Forward	Backward	–ve	Backward	Forward	Forward	Backward	High p, low T and isolation of NH_3 by liquefaction
$PCl_5(g) \rightleftharpoons PCl_3(g) + Cl_2(g)$	+1	Backward	Forward	+ve	Forward	Backward	Forward	Backward	Low p high T, and isolation of PCl_3 and Cl_2
$2HI(g) \rightleftharpoons H_2(g) + I_2(g)$	0	No effect	No effect	+ve	Forward	Backward	Forward	Backward	High T and isolation of product formed
$H_2O(l) \rightleftharpoons H_2O(g)$	+1	Backward	Forward	+ve	Forward	Backward	Forward	Backward	Increase in p cause liquefaction of $H_2O(g)$ hence, b.p. of $H_2O(l)$ is increased
$NH_3(g) + H_2O(l) - Q \rightleftharpoons NH_4OH(l)$	–1	Forward	Backward	–ve	Backward	Forward	Forward	Backward	Any gas is dissolved in water under height p.

↑ Endothermic

- Substances which dissociate into their ions while dissolving in polar solvents like water ⟶ **Electrolytes**

Strong	Weak
Almost completely dissociated	Never completely dissociated
e.g., NaCl, H_2SO_4, HNO_3 etc.	e.g. CH_3COOH, NH_4OH, H_3PO_4 etc.

- The dissociation of electrolyte is a reversible process and after some time an equilibrium is established between dissociated ions and undissociated molecules ⟶ Arrhenius theory of electrolytic ionisation or dissociation

> The sum or total fraction of molecules that undergo ionisation in its solution ⟶ Degree of Ionisation or Dissociation (α)
>
> $$= \frac{\text{No. of molecules ionised into ions}}{\text{Total no. of molecules of electrolyte dissolved}}$$
>
> = Amount of electrolyte ionised / Initial amount

- For strong electrolyte $\alpha \simeq 1$
  For weak electrolyte α is less than 1 but on infinite dilution it reaches to unity (1)

Factors affecting Ionisation
- Extent of Solvation of Ions
- Strength of Bond

- For weak electrolytes $K_a = \frac{C\alpha^2}{(1-\alpha)}$ (C → Initial Concentration)
  $= C\alpha^2$ (as $1-\alpha \simeq 1$ because $\alpha \ll 1$)

  Ostwald Dilution Law — Applicable to weak electrolyte only

- For the reaction $2H_2O(l) \rightleftharpoons H_3O^+(aq) + \bar{O}H(aq)$

  Ionic Product of water OR Auto ionisation constant OR Auto-protolysis constant

  $K_w = K_c[H_2O]^2 = [H_3O^+][OH^-] = 1 \times 10^{-14}\ mol^2 L^{-2}$ at 298 K

NEET concentrate

- Nature → Neutral; $[H^+] = [\bar{O}H] = 10^{-7}M$; pH = pOH = 7 all at 25°C
  No. of moles in 1 litre H_2O or Molar conc. ⟶ 1000/18 = 55.5 mole
  No. of H_2O molecules in 1 litre = $55.5\ N_A$

Acids & Bases

a. Arrhenius Concept – Acids → Proton donors
Base → Hydroxyl ion donors

b. Bronsted Lowry concept – { Acids → Proton donors
Bases → Proton acceptors }

Both will work in conjugate pairing →
{ Strong Acid —Give Rise to→ Weak conjugate base
Weak Base —Give Rise to→ Strong conjugate acid } & vice versa

NEET concentrate

Strongest	Acid	Conjugate base	Weakest
↓	$HClO_4$	ClO_4^-	↓
	HI	I^-	
	HBr	Br^-	
	HCl	Cl^-	
	H_2SO_4	HSO_4^-	
	HNO_3	NO_3^-	
	H_3O^+	H_2O	
	HSO_4^-	SO_4^{2-}	
	HF	F^-	
	HNO_2	NO_2^-	
	$HCOOH$	$HCOO^-$	
	CH_3COOH	CH_3COO^-	
	HCN	CN^-	
	H_2O	OH^-	
Weakest			Strongest

	Base	Conjugate acid	
Strongest	CH_3NH_2	$CH_3NH_3^+$	Weakest
↓	NH_3	NH_4^+	↑
	N_2H_4	$N_2H_5^+$	
	NH_2OH	NH_3OH^+	
Weakest	H_2O	H_3O^+	Strongest

Some Imp. Acids/Bases with conjugate partners

Dhyan Rakhna | $HClO_4$ is a stronger acid than HF as its conjugate base (ClO_4^-) is much more stable.
Means kisi acid/base ki strength uske conjugate pair pr bhi depend karti hai

c. Lewis Concept – Acids → e^- pair acceptor (e^- deficient)
Base → e^- pair donor (usually with lone e^- pairs)

Examples [BX_3, AlX_3, PF_3, $SnCl_4$, SF_4 etc.] → Acids

Examples [$H_2\ddot{O}$, NH_3, $R\ddot{O}H$, X^-, F^-, $\bar{O}H$] → Base

d. Pearson Concept – **Imp.**
Hard acid – Small, carry high charge H^+, Na^+, Cr^{3+} etc.
Soft acid – Large, carry low charge Pd^{2+}, Cu^+, Hg^{2+} etc.
Hard base – Lewis base that hold e^- strongly H_2O, NH_3
Soft base – Lewis base from which e^- can be removed easily I^-, CN^-, RS^- etc.

Ionisation Constants of weak acids & bases

$$K_a = \frac{[A^-][H^+]}{[HA]}$$ larger the value of K_a (Acid Ionisation constant), stronger the acid.

$$K_b = \frac{[B^+][\bar{O}H]}{[BOH]}$$ larger the value of K_b (Base ionisation constant), stronger the base.

- $\frac{\alpha_1}{\alpha_2} = \sqrt{\frac{K_1}{K_2}}$ ← K_1 can be K_{a_1} or K_{b_1}; K_2 can be K_{a_2} or K_{b_2}

Relative strength of 2 weak acids/bases in terms of degree of dissociation

PYQ Punch

Q. Consider the following reaction in a sealed vessel at equilibrium with conc. of $N_2 = 3.0 \times 10^{-3}$ M, $O_2 = 4.2 \times 10^{-3}$ M, $NO = 2.8 \times 10^{-3}$ M

$$2NO(g) \rightleftharpoons N_2(g) + O_2(g)$$ NEET 2024

If 0.1 mol L^{-1} of NO(g) is taken into a closed vessel, what will be the degree of dissociation (α) of NO(g) at equilibrium.

(a) 0.00889 (b) 0.0889 (c) 0.889 (d) 0.717 ✓

sol $K_c = \frac{3 \times 10^{-3} \times 4.2 \times 10^{-3}}{(2.8 \times 10^{-3})^2} = 1.60$; $K_c = \frac{C\alpha^2}{4C^2(1-\alpha)^2}$ so $\left(\frac{\alpha}{1-\alpha}\right)^2 = 4 \times 1.6$

or $\frac{\alpha}{1-\alpha} = 2 \times 1.26$ or $\alpha = 0.717$

Dhyan Rakho! $K_a \times K_b = K_w$ means for any conjugate acid-base pair the product of K_a & K_b is always equal to Ionic product of water. ⟶ $pK_a + pK_b = 14 = pK_w$ (as $pK_a = -\log K_a$; $pK_b = -\log K_b$) (all at 298 K)

- $HA \rightleftharpoons H^+ + A^-$
  $HCl \rightleftharpoons H^+ + Cl^-$
  Common ion (H^+)

  The decrease in the ionisation of a weak electrolyte by the presence of a common ion from a strong electrolyte → Common Ion effect

- Significant applications of common ion effect are visible in analytical chemistry especially in the qualitative analysis of basic radicals where limited quantity of a particular ion is required e.g., $NH_4OH \rightleftharpoons NH_4^+ + {}^-OH$
  $NH_4Cl \rightleftharpoons NH_4^+ + Cl^-$
  (NH_4^+: common ion for limited precipitation)

- 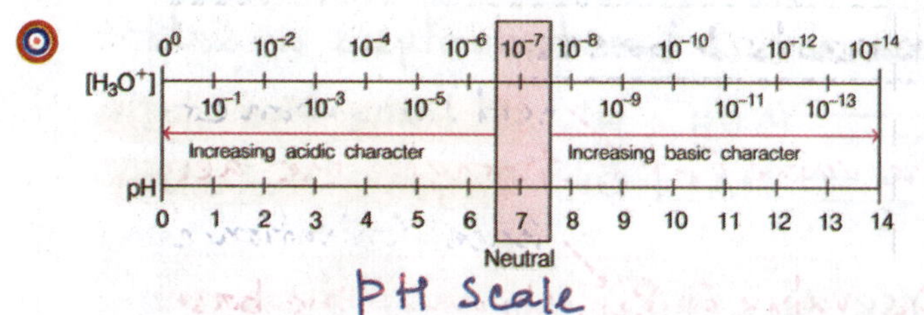

pH Scale

$pH = -\log_{10}[H^+]$

Most common interpretation ⟶ $[H^+] = 1 \times 10^{-pH}$

Similar is the case with pOH

- $pk_w = pH + pOH = 14$ Dhyan Rakhna | pH and pOH are always in inverse relationship.

Special cases related to pH

- **pH of weak acid**: $\frac{1}{2}[pk_a - \log C]$
- **pH of weak base**: $\frac{1}{2}[pk_b - \log C]$
- **pH of mixture of acids or base**: $\frac{\sum NV}{\sum V}$ (where N = conc. in Normality, V = volume)
- **pH of mixture of acids & bases**

Mixture of strong acid + strong base

case 1. If N_1V_1 (acid) = N_2V_2 (base) ⟶ pH = 7 (Neutral)

case 2. If N_1V_1 (acid) > N_2V_2 (base) ⟶ pH < 7 (acidic)

$$N_{H^+} \text{(Mixture)} = \frac{N_1V_1 - N_2V_2}{(V_1 + V_2)}$$

case 3. If N_2V_2 (Base) > N_1V_1 (acid) ⟶ pH > 7 (basic)

$$N_{\bar{O}H} \text{(Mixture)} = \frac{N_2V_2 - N_1V_1}{(V_1 + V_2)}$$

case 4. If $N_1V_1 = N_2V_2$ & acid is weak ⟶ pH > 7 mixture alkaline (due to hydrolysis of anions)

case 5. If $N_1V_1 = N_2V_2$ & base is weak ⟶ pH < 7 mixture acidic (due to hydrolysis of cation)

- For polyprotic acids $Ka_1 > Ka_2 > Ka_3$ (as it is always difficult to remove H^+ from any (–)vely charged ion)

Salts
- Strong acid + strong base e.g., NaCl, KCl etc.
- Strong acid + weak base e.g., $CH_3COO^-Na^+$
- Weak acid + strong base e.g., NH_4Cl
- Weak acid + weak base e.g., $CH_3COO^-NH_4^+$

- The process of interaction of cation or anion with water which involves cleavage of O–H bond as well ⟶ Hydrolysis or salt Hydrolysis.

$$B^+ + H_2O \rightleftharpoons BOH + H^+ \quad \text{Cationic Hydrolysis}$$

$$A^- + H_2O \rightleftharpoons HA + \bar{O}H \quad \text{Anionic Hydrolysis}$$

NEET concentrate

⟶ Salt hydrolysis is the reverse of Neutralisation reaction

- Degree of Hydrolysis → $h = \dfrac{\text{No. of moles of salt Hydrolysed}}{\text{Total no. of moles of salt taken}}$

- For Generalised reaction $BA + H_2O \rightleftharpoons BOH + HA$

$$K \times [H_2O] = \frac{[HA][BOH]}{[BA]} = K_h \leftarrow \text{Hydrolysis constant}$$

Types of Salt Hydrolysis

a. Hydrolysis of strong acid + strong base salt → Resulting solution Neutral (pH=7) (as both cation and anions are stronger in this case)

b. Hydrolysis of strong acid & weak base salt → Only cationic hydrolysis seen (as anion is weak) Resulting solution acidic (pH < 7)

Important Formulae:

1. $K_h = \dfrac{K_w}{K_b}$

2. $h = \sqrt{\dfrac{K_h}{C}} = \sqrt{K_h \times V} = \sqrt{\dfrac{K_w}{K_b \times C}}$

3. $pH = 7 - \frac{1}{2} pK_b - \frac{1}{2} \log C$

c. Hydrolysis of weak acid & strong base salt → Only anionic hydrolysis seen (as cation is weak) Resulting solution basic (pH > 7)

Important Formulae:

1. $K_h = \dfrac{K_w}{K_a}$

2. $h = \sqrt{\dfrac{K_h}{C}} = \sqrt{K_h \times V}$

3. $pH = 7 + \frac{1}{2} pK_a + \log C$

d. Hydrolysis of weak acid + weak base salt → No significant hydrolysis of any ion (as cation & anion both are weak) Solution may be neutral, acidic or basic

Important Formulae:

1. $K_h = \dfrac{K_w}{K_a \cdot K_b}$

2. $h = \sqrt{K_h} = \sqrt{\dfrac{K_w}{K_a \cdot K_b}}$ (If $h << 1$)

3. $pH = 7 + \frac{1}{2} pK_a - \frac{1}{2} pK_b$

- If $pK_a = pK_b$ → pH = 7
- If $pK_a > pK_b$ → pH > 7
- If $pK_b > pK_a$ → pH < 7

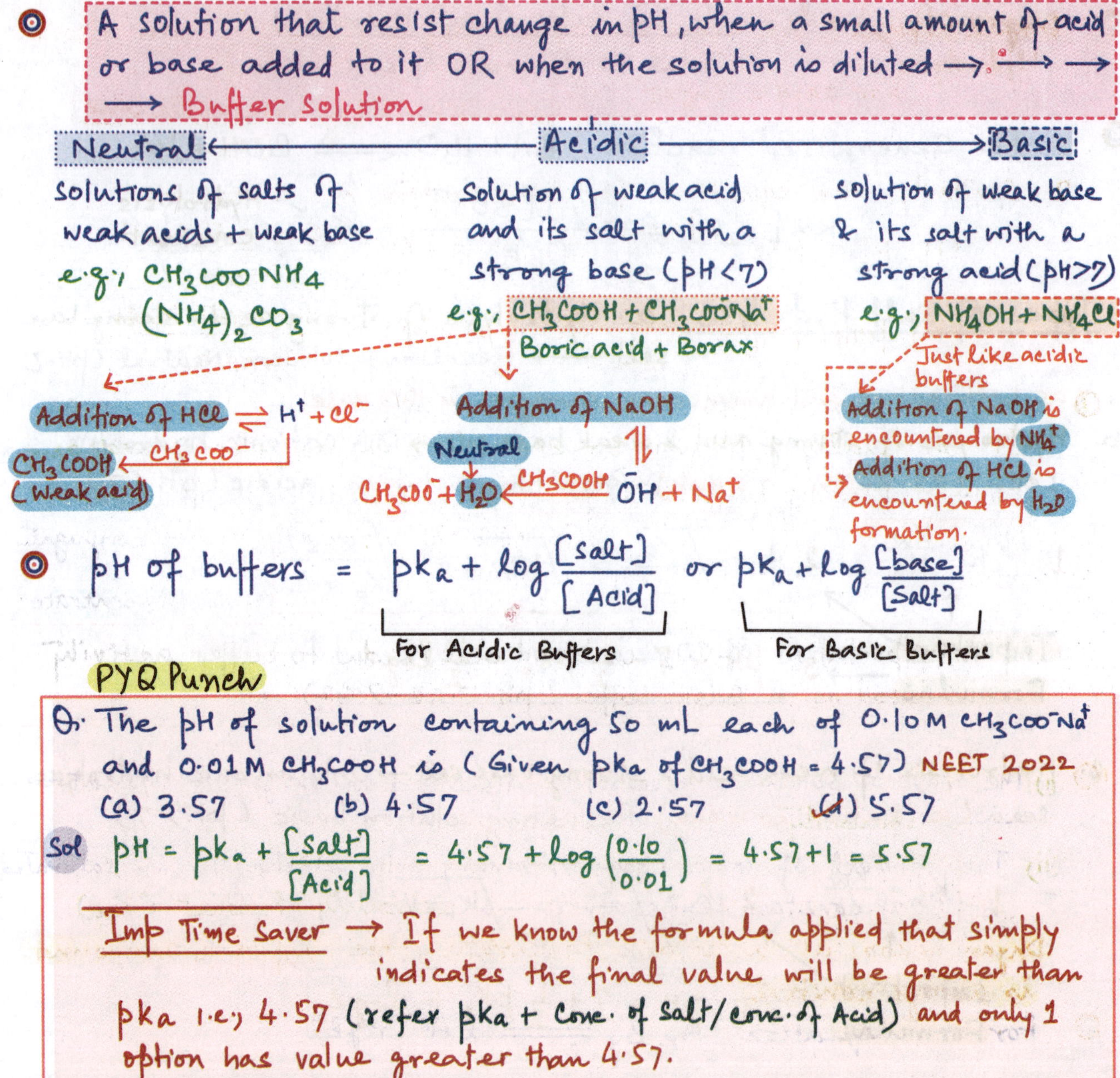

A solution that resist change in pH, when a small amount of acid or base added to it OR when the solution is diluted → → → Buffer solution

Neutral ← **Acidic** → **Basic**

- **Neutral:** solutions of salts of weak acids + weak base
  e.g., CH_3COONH_4, $(NH_4)_2CO_3$
- **Acidic:** Solution of weak acid and its salt with a strong base (pH < 7)
  e.g., $CH_3COOH + CH_3COO^-Na^+$; Boric acid + Borax
- **Basic:** solution of weak base & its salt with a strong acid (pH > 7)
  e.g., $NH_4OH + NH_4Cl$

Addition of HCl $\rightleftharpoons H^+ + Cl^-$; $H^+ \xrightarrow{CH_3COO^-}$ CH_3COOH (weak acid)

Addition of NaOH $\rightleftharpoons \bar{O}H + Na^+$; $\bar{O}H \xrightarrow{CH_3COOH} CH_3COO^- + H_2O$ (Neutral)

Just like acidic buffers: Addition of NaOH is encountered by NH_4^+. Addition of HCl is encountered by H_2O formation.

pH of buffers $= pK_a + \log \dfrac{[Salt]}{[Acid]}$ (For Acidic Buffers) or $pK_a + \log \dfrac{[base]}{[Salt]}$ (For Basic Buffers)

PYQ Punch

Q. The pH of solution containing 50 mL each of 0.10 M $CH_3COO^-Na^+$ and 0.01 M CH_3COOH is (Given pK_a of $CH_3COOH = 4.57$) NEET 2022

(a) 3.57 (b) 4.57 (c) 2.57 (d) 5.57

Sol. $pH = pK_a + \dfrac{[Salt]}{[Acid]} = 4.57 + \log\left(\dfrac{0.10}{0.01}\right) = 4.57 + 1 = 5.57$

Imp Time Saver → If we know the formula applied that simply indicates the final value will be greater than pKa i.e., 4.57 (refer pKa + Conc. of Salt/conc. of Acid) and only 1 option has value greater than 4.57.

No. of moles of acid or base added in 1 litre of a buffer solution to change its pH by 1 unit → Buffer capacity (ϕ)

It is the measure of effectiveness of a buffer → Larger the Buffer capacity stronger is the buffer.

$$\text{Buffer capacity } (\phi) = \frac{\text{No. of moles of acid/base added per litre}}{\text{Change in pH of Buffer solution}}$$

Dhyan Rakhna 1 the equation $\left\{ pH = pKa + \log \frac{[Salt]}{[Acid]} \right.$ can also be

For Acidic Buffer

Handerson – Hasselbalch Equ. → $pH = pKa + \log \frac{[Conjugate\ base]}{[Acid]}$

2 Similarly, the equation for basic buffer has 4 variants

(i) $pH = pKa + \frac{[Salt]}{[base]}$ (ii) $pH = pKa + \frac{[conjugate\ Acid]}{[base]}$

(iii) $pOH = pK_b + \frac{[Salt]}{[base]}$ (iv) $pOH = pK_b + \frac{[conjugate\ Acid]}{[base]}$

- The pH range in which a buffer is effective → Buffer Range
  It is usually 1 pH unit on either side of pKa value of weak acid
  Factors affecting Buffer Range → pKa of weak acid in buffer
  ↙ Buffer capacity ↘ conc. of weak acid & its conjugate base.

NEET concentrate

Transportation of CO_2 in blood occurs due to buffer activity as blood is a Basic buffer (pH 7.26–7.42)

- (i) The mass of solute or electrolyte dissolved in 100 gm of solvent → → solubility
  (ii) The product of ionic conc. of binary solid electrolyte in saturated state at constant temperature → Solubility Product (K_{sp})
  Dhyan Rakho! at a certain temperature the K_{sp} of a compound is always constant.
- For the equation $A_x B_y \rightleftharpoons xA^{y+} + yB^{x-}$

$K_{sp} = [A^{y+}]^x [B^{x-}]^y = x^x \cdot y^y (S)^{x+y}$ (where S = Solubility in moles per litre)

case I: for 1:1 or AB type of salts ($AgCl$, $BaSO_4$, $PbSO_4$ etc.)

$K_{sp} = S^2$ or $S = \sqrt{K_{sp}}$

case II. for 1:2 or 2:1 type of salts means A_2B or AB_2 (Ag_2CrO_4, $CaCl_2$ etc)

$K_{sp} = 4S^3$ or $S = (K_{sp}/4)^{1/3}$

case III. for 1:3 type of salts means AB_3 or A_3B ($FeCl_3$, AlX_3, $Fe(OH)_3$ etc.)

$K_{sp} = 27S^4$

- In the presence of common ion $K'_{sp} < K_{sp}$ thus solubility decreases.

◎ For $AB(s) \rightleftharpoons A^+(aq) + B^-(aq)$; $[A^+][B^-] = Q_{sp}$ ← Ionic Product

case 1. If $Q_{sp} = K_{sp}$ ⟶ saturated solution, Rxn. at equilibrium

case 2. If $Q_{sp} > K_{sp}$ ⟶ supersaturated solution, precipitation occur

case 3. If $Q_{sp} < K_{sp}$ ⟶ Unsaturated solution, precipitation will not occur

PYQ Punch

Q. Find out the solubility of $Ni(OH)_2$ in 0.1 M NaOH. Given that ionic product of $Ni(OH)_2$ is 2×10^{-15} NEET 2020

(a) 2×10^{-8} M (b) 1×10^{-13} M (c) 1×10^{8} M ✓(d) 2×10^{-13} M

Sol $NaOH(aq) \rightleftharpoons \underset{0.1\,M}{Na^+(aq)} + \underset{0.1\,M}{\bar{O}H(aq)}$; $Ni(OH)_2(s) \rightleftharpoons \underset{s'}{Ni^{+}(aq)} + \underset{0.1+2s'}{2\bar{O}H(aq)}$

$Q_{sp} = (s')(0.1+2s')^2$ or $2\times10^{-15} = s'(0.1)^2$ (as $2s'$ is very small)

so $2\times10^{-13} = s'$

Remember ! pH of a mixture of 2 weak acids $= \sqrt{K_{a_1}\times C_1 + K_{a_2}\times C_2}$

NEET concentrate

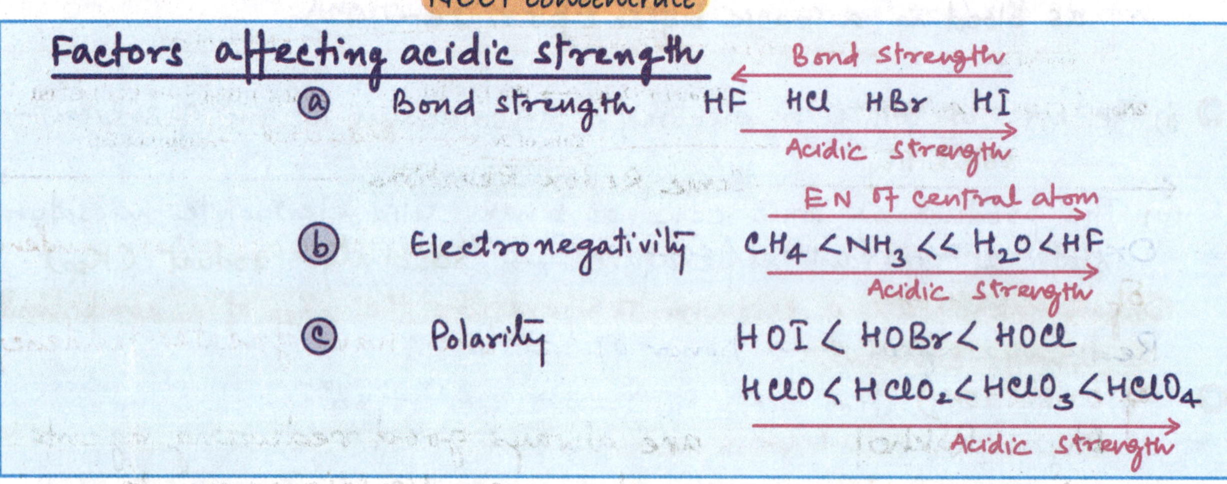

7. Redox Reactions

- **Oxidation** → (i) Addition of Oxygen OR electronegative element
  (ii) Removal of Hydrogen OR electropositive element
  (classical concept: (i), (ii))
  (iii) Loss of electron ← Modern concept

- **Reduction** → (i) Addition of Hydrogen or electropositive element
  (ii) Loss of Oxygen OR electronegative element
  (classical concept: (i), (ii))
  (iii) Gain of electron ← Modern concept

NEET concentrate

> Term **Loss** is best to remember both Oxidation & Reduction
> LOSS — O signifies oxidation i.e., loss of e⁻ opposite to which is reduction

- Oxidation and reduction always occur simultaneously hence the word "Redox" is coined for such reactions.

Some Redox Reactions

- Oxidising agent → Acceptor of e^- (i.e., have greater tendency of Reduction)
  Reducing agent → Donor of e^- (i.e., have greater tendency of oxidation)

Dhyan Rakho! Metals are always good reducing agents while Non Metals are always good oxidising agents.

Competitive electron transfer reactions

- In such reactions where a weak and a strong metal is present → Weak metal preferred to be in elemental state while strong metal always remain in Ionic state. e.g., Redox reaction between Zn and $Cu(NO_3)_2$ (aq.)

Oxidation

$Cu(s) \longrightarrow Cu^{2+}(aq) + 2e^-$

Reduction

$2Ag^+(aq) + 2e^- \longrightarrow Ag(s)$

Reaction between $Cu(s)$ and $AgNO_3(aq)$

- Above 2 experiments suggest reactivity order of Cu, Ag & Zn as $\longrightarrow$ Zn > Cu > Ag (least reactive)

- release of $2e^-$

  $Co(s) + Ni^{2+}(aq) \rightleftharpoons Co^{2+}(aq) + Ni(s)$

  gain of $2e^-$

  This reaction suggests that both Ni and Co have almost equal tendency to loose e^-

Oxidation Number (O.N.) – The actual number of e^- that an atom can give / take or share with another atom $\longrightarrow$ Oxidation Number of that atom.

- Technical Definition $\rightarrow$ Oxidation Number denotes the oxidation state of an element in a compound ascertained according to a set of rules formulated on the basis that e^- pair in a covalent bond belongs entirely to more electronegative atom.

  It basically denotes the Oxidation state of an element in a compound.

Rule 1 Elemental / free / uncombined state $\longrightarrow$ Zero O.N.
e.g., Each atom in H_2, O_2, Cl_2; O_3, P_4 etc. $\rightarrow$ Zero O.N.

Rule 2 Ions with single atom $\longrightarrow$ O.N. = Charge on ion
e.g., $Mg^{2+} \rightarrow +2$; $O^{2-} \rightarrow -2$; $Cl^- \rightarrow -1$; $Fe^{3+} \rightarrow +3$ etc.

Rule 3 Oxygen $\longrightarrow$ -2 in oxides; -1 in peroxide (H_2O_2); $-\frac{1}{2}$ in superoxides (KO_2) and (+)ve oxidation state only with F.
e.g., $OF_2 \rightarrow +2$; $O_2F_2 \rightarrow +1$

Rule 4 Hydrogen $\longrightarrow$ +1 O.N. in all compounds except Hydrides where it has $\rightarrow$ -1 O.N. e.g., $\overset{+}{Li}\overset{-}{H}$, $\overset{+}{Na}\overset{-}{H}$, $\overset{2+}{Ca}H_2$

Rule 5 Halogens $\longrightarrow$ usual O.N. -1; F $\rightarrow$ only -1; Rest halogens usually -1 but may have (+)ve O.N. also. e.g., Cl has +1 in HClO; $CaOCl_2 \rightarrow$ Both +1 and -1 for Cl,

Rule 6 (i) The algebraic sum of the O.N. of all the atoms in a compound is zero. e.g., $CaOCl_2 \rightarrow Ca(OCl)Cl = +2 + (-2+1) - 1 = 0$

(ii) In polyatomic ion, the algebraic sum of all the O.N. of participating atoms equals to the charge on ion

e.g., $CO_3^{--} \longrightarrow +4 + (-2 \times 3) = -2$

Group	1	2	13	14
Element	Na	Mg	Al	Si
Compound	NaCl	$MgSO_4$	AlF_3	$SiCl_4$
Highest oxidation number state of the group element	+1	+2	+3	+4

Group wise Highest possible (+)ve oxidation states/Number

- When O.N. is written in Romans after metal with in the parentheses (Bracket) ⟶ Stock Notation. e.g., Au(I)Cl; Au(III)Cl_3; Sn(II)Cl_2; Sn(IV)Cl_4 etc.

NEET concentrate

Fractional O.N. ⟶ C_3O_2 = $\overset{-2}{O}=\overset{+2}{C}=\overset{0}{C}=\overset{+2}{C}=\overset{-2}{O}$ (Avg. 4/3)

Br_3O_8 ⟶ $O=\overset{+6}{Br}(=O)_2-\overset{+4}{Br}(=O)_2-\overset{+6}{Br}(=O)_2=O$ (avg. 16/3)

$S_4O_6^{--}$ ⟶ $^-O-\overset{+5}{S}(=O)_2-\overset{0}{S}-\overset{0}{S}-\overset{+5}{S}(=O)_2-O^-$ (avg. 2.5)

Similar cases – $Pb_3O_4 \rightarrow PbO.Pb_2O_3$; $Fe_3O_4 - FeO.Fe_2O_3$

Redox in purview of Oxidation Number

1. Increase in O.N. ⟶ Oxidation
2. Decrease in O.N. ⟶ Reduction
3. Reagent with ability to increase O.N. of an element ⟶ Oxidant or Oxidising agent
4. Reagent with ability to reduce O.N. of an element ⟶ Reductant or Reducing agent.
5. Reactions which involve change in O.N. ⟶ Redox Reaction

- Redox Reactions
  - ⟶ Combination ⟶ A + B → C
  - ⟶ Decomposition ⟶ C ⟶ A + B
  - ⟶ Displacement ⟶ X + YZ → XZ + Y
  - ⟶ Disproportionation ⟶ 2A ⟶ $A^- + A^+$

NEET concentrate

- For combination reactions any of the reactants must be in elemental form.
- All Combustion reactions involving O_2 are combination Reactions.
- In Decomposition Reactions atleast one of the products must be in elemental form.
- The displacement can be metal displacement e.g.,
  $CuSO_4(aq.) + Zn(s) \longrightarrow ZnSO_4(aq) + Cu(s)$
  or Non Metal Displacement e.g.,
  $2Na(s) + 2H_2O(l) \longrightarrow 2NaOH(aq) + H_2(g)\uparrow$
- The disproportionation reactions are shown by those elements which show variable Oxidation states.

Balancing of Redox Reactions

Oxidation Number method

Step 1 Assign O.N. to all atoms after writing correct formula of Reactants & Products + Identify atoms with change in O.N.

e.g., For a reaction of $K_2Cr_2O_7$ with Na_2SO_3 to give Chromium (III) and sulphate ion in acidic medium

$$\overset{+6\ -2}{Cr_2O_7^{2-}}(aq) + \overset{+4\ -2}{SO_3^{2-}}(aq) \longrightarrow \overset{+3}{Cr^{3+}}(aq) + \overset{+6\ -2}{SO_4^{2-}}(aq)$$

(Oxidation: S; Reduction: Cr)

Step 2 Calculate the increase or decrease in O.N. per atom & for entire molecule/ion (in which it occurs) and balance it

Cr ⟶ decrease of +3 O.N.

S ⟶ increase of +2 O.N. So,

$$\overset{+6\ -2}{Cr_2O_7^{2-}}(aq) + \overset{+4\ -2}{SO_3^{2-}}(aq) \longrightarrow 2\overset{+3}{Cr^{3+}}(aq) + 3\overset{+6\ -2}{SO_4^{2-}}(aq)$$

Half Reaction Method

Step 1 Write given unbalanced reaction in ionic form.

e.g., An equation showing oxidation ($Fe^{2+} \longrightarrow Fe^{3+}$) by $Cr_2O_7^{2-}$ in acidic medium.

$$Fe^{2+}(aq) + Cr_2O_7^{2-}(aq) \rightarrow Fe^{3+}(aq) + Cr^{3+}(aq)$$

Step 2 Separate the equation into half reactions

e.g., For above reaction

$Fe^{2+} \longrightarrow Fe^{3+}$ (oxidation half)

$Cr_2O_7^{2-} \longrightarrow Cr^{3+}$ (Reduction half)

Step 3 Balance the atoms other than O & H in each half reaction individually.

e.g., Oxidation half is already balanced in above case and for reduction half add 2 on product side

$$Cr_2O_7^{2-} \longrightarrow 2Cr^{3+}$$

Oxidation Number Method

Step 3 Now equalise Cr & S atoms of both the side

$\overset{+6\ -2}{Cr_2O_7^{2-}}(aq) + 3\overset{+4-2}{SO_3^{2-}}(aq) \longrightarrow 2\overset{+3}{Cr^{3+}}(aq) + 3\overset{+6-2}{SO_4^{2-}}(aq)$

Step 4 Now equalise the total ionic charges of reactants & products by adding H^+ or $\bar{O}H$ on appropriate side ($H^+ \rightarrow$ Acidic; $\bar{O}H \rightarrow$ Basic)

Add $8H^+$ on reactant side to make the charges of both the side equal

$Cr_2O_7^{2-} + 3SO_4^{2-} + 8H^+ \longrightarrow 2Cr^{3+} + 3SO_4^{2-}$

$\leftarrow -2+(-6)+8=0 \rightarrow$ $\leftarrow +3\times2+(-2\times3)=0 \rightarrow$

Step 5 Make the numbers of H atom equal by adding H_2O molecules to reactants or products.

Add $4H_2O$ molecules to the product side

$Cr_2O_7^{2-} + 3SO_3^{2-} + 8H^+ \longrightarrow 2Cr^{3+} + 3SO_4^{2-} + 4H_2O$

Step 6 Count & equalise the number of oxygen atoms

$Cr_2O_7^{2-} + 3SO_3^{2-} + 8H^+ \longrightarrow 2Cr^{3+} + 3SO_4^{2-} + 4H_2O$

$\longleftarrow$ 12 atoms $\longrightarrow$ $\longleftarrow$ 12 atoms $\longrightarrow$

So the equation is balanced.

NEET concentrate

> O.N. Balancing is used only upto step 2 of this reaction after which it follow normal hit and trial Method.

Half Reaction Method

Step 4 For reactions occurring in acidic medium add H_2O to balance O atoms and then add H^+ on the opposite side to balance H.

In above given reaction add $7H_2O$ to product side and then $14H^+$ to reactant side in reduction half (Oxidation half does not contains oxygen)

$Cr_2O_7^{2-} + 14H^+ \longrightarrow 2Cr^{3+} + 7H_2O$

Step 5 (i) Add e^- to one side of the half reaction to balance the charges & then,

(ii) If needed equalise the number of e^- by multiplying 1 or both the half reactions by appropriate number.

So in the above half reactions

(i) $Fe^{2+} \longrightarrow Fe^{3+} + e^-$

$Cr_2O_7^{2-} + 14H^+ + 6e^- \longrightarrow 2Cr^{3+} + 7H_2O$

Then multiply oxidation half with 6 to make the e^- count equal.

(ii) $[Fe^{2+} \longrightarrow Fe^{3+} + e^-] \times 6$

Step 6 Now add both half reactions and cancel e^- of the sides to get final balanced equation

$6Fe^{2+} + Cr_2O_7^{2-} + 14H^+ + \cancel{6e^-} \longrightarrow 2Cr^{3+} + 6Fe^{3+} + 7H_2O + \cancel{6e^-}$

Redox Reactions & Electrode Process

- Oxidised & Reduced forms of a substance taking part in an oxidation or Reduction half reaction $\longrightarrow$ Redox couple

- Redox couple is represented as separating the oxidised form from the reduced form by a slash or vertical line representing an interface.

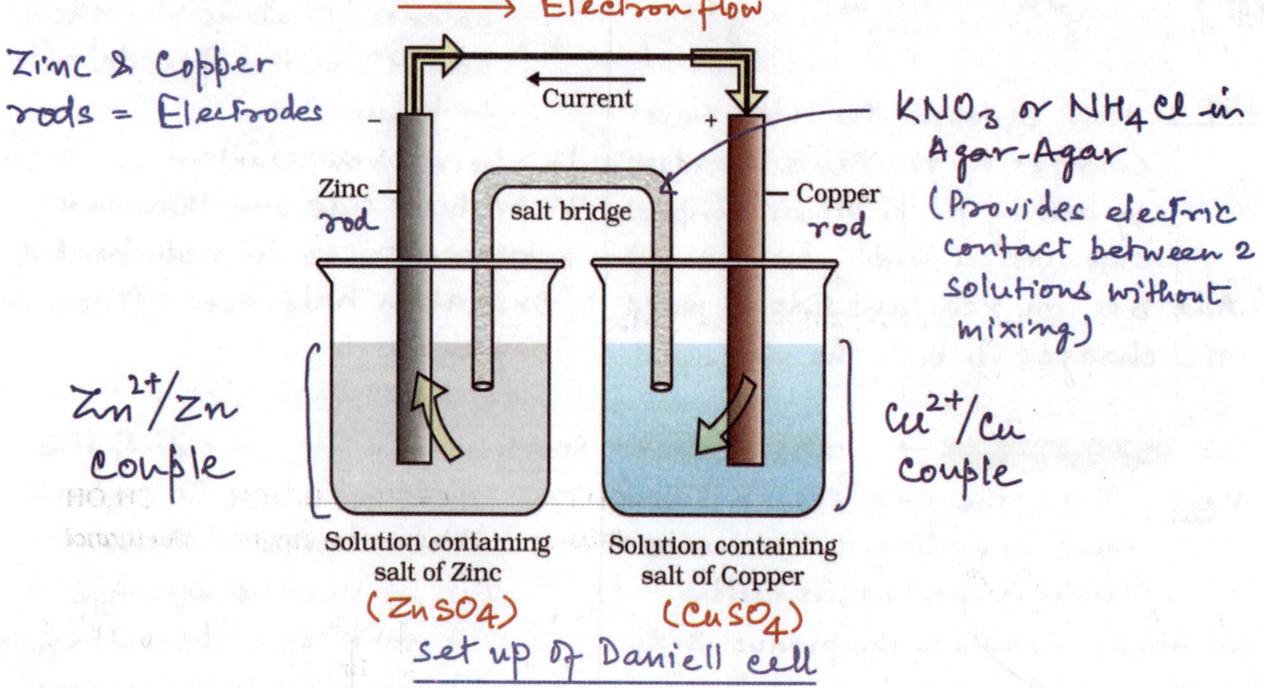

Set up of Daniell cell

- Potential associated with electrodes → Electrode Potential
  When electrode potential is measured at unit concentration and 298 K then electrode potential is called standard electrode potential (SEP)
- By convention SEP of Hydrogen is taken as 0.00 V.

Elements with (−)ve SEP → loose e^- more easily than Hydrogen. → Good Reducing Agents

Elements with (+)ve SEP → loose e^- with lesser ease in comparison to Hydrogen → Good Oxidising Agents

This is the basis for the formation of Electrochemical Series.

8. Organic Chemistry - Some Basic Principles & Techniques

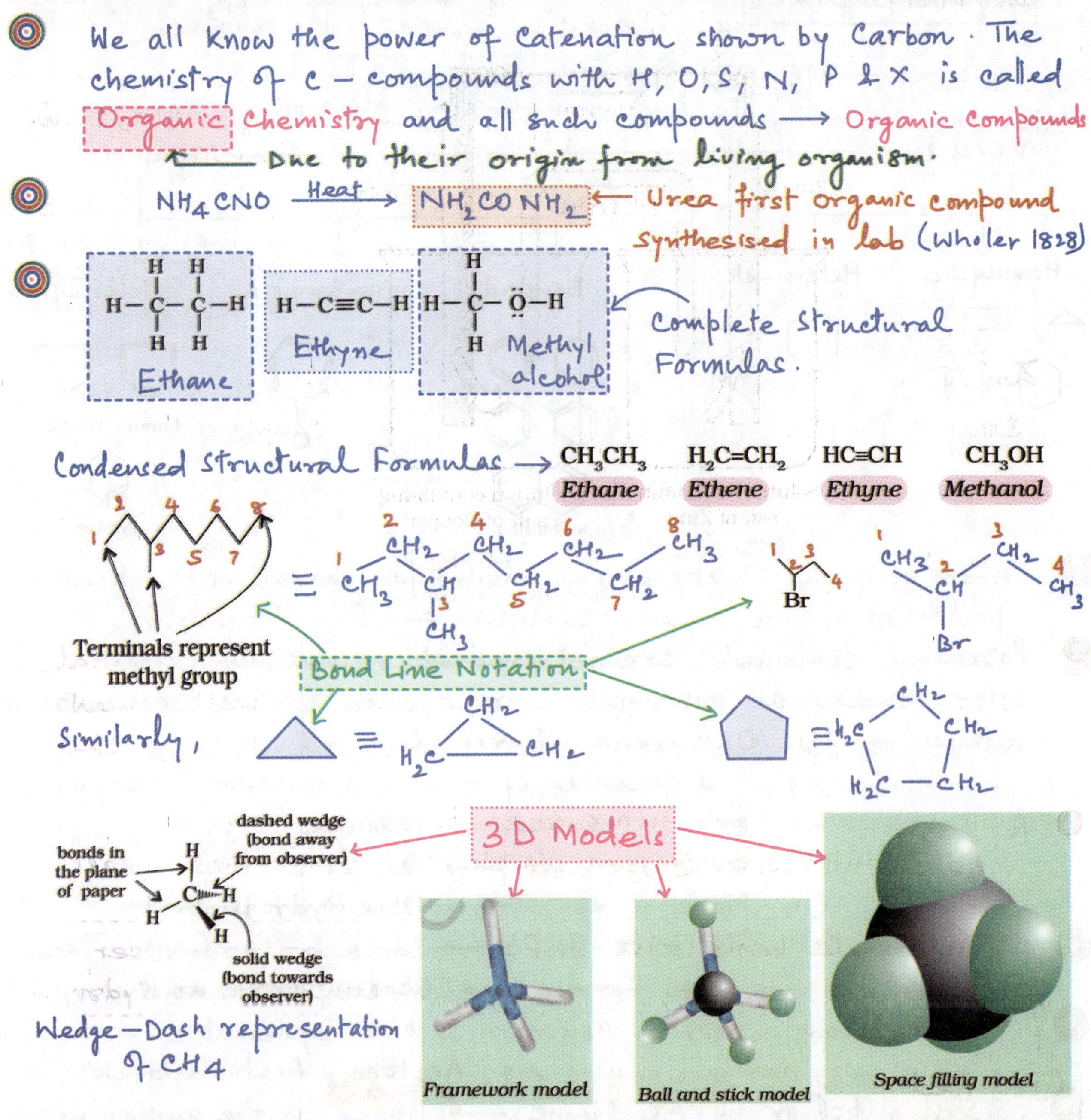

Dhyan Rakhna | Bonds are not shown in space filling model. It emphasises the relative size of each atom based on their vander Waals radius. It simply conveys the volume occupied by each atom in the molecule.

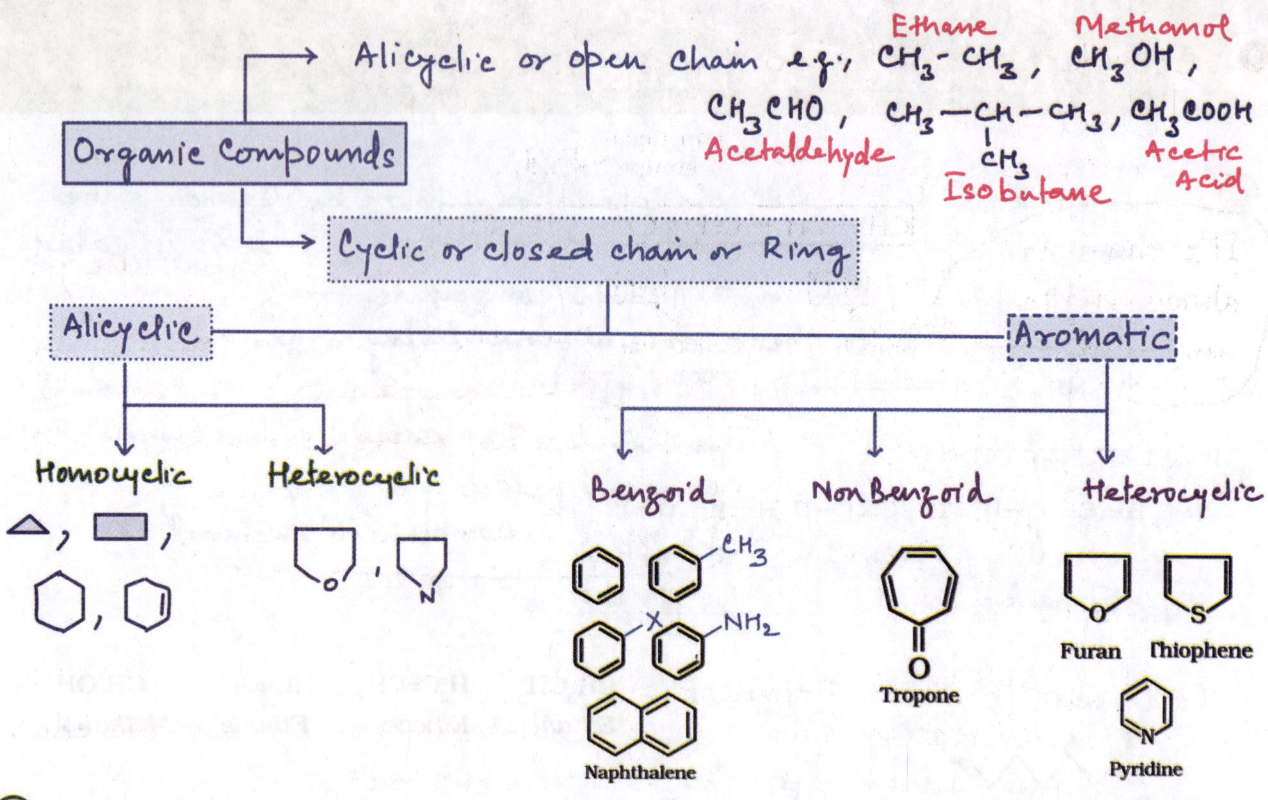

- Atom or group of atoms responsible for characteristic chemical properties of an organic compound ⟶ Functional Group.
- Organic compounds are not studied individually rather these are studied as Homologous series. Each of these series will have —
  - (i) One General formula
  - (ii) A difference of $-CH_2$ (or 14 amu) between any two successive members
  - (iii) Gradation in physical properties
  - (iv) More or less similar chemical properties.
- Traditional Names based on origin or source ⟶ Common or Trivial Names e.g., Formic acid (HCOOH), Citric acid etc.,
- Name having a portion common & other systematic ⟶ Semi trivial or derived names e.g., Acetone, Acetic acid etc.
- Systematic or IUPAC Name ⟶ Based on the guidelines provided by International union of Pure and Applied chemistry. These names have following portions

Prefixes + Root word + Suffixes

- Consider a prototype organic compound as given below –

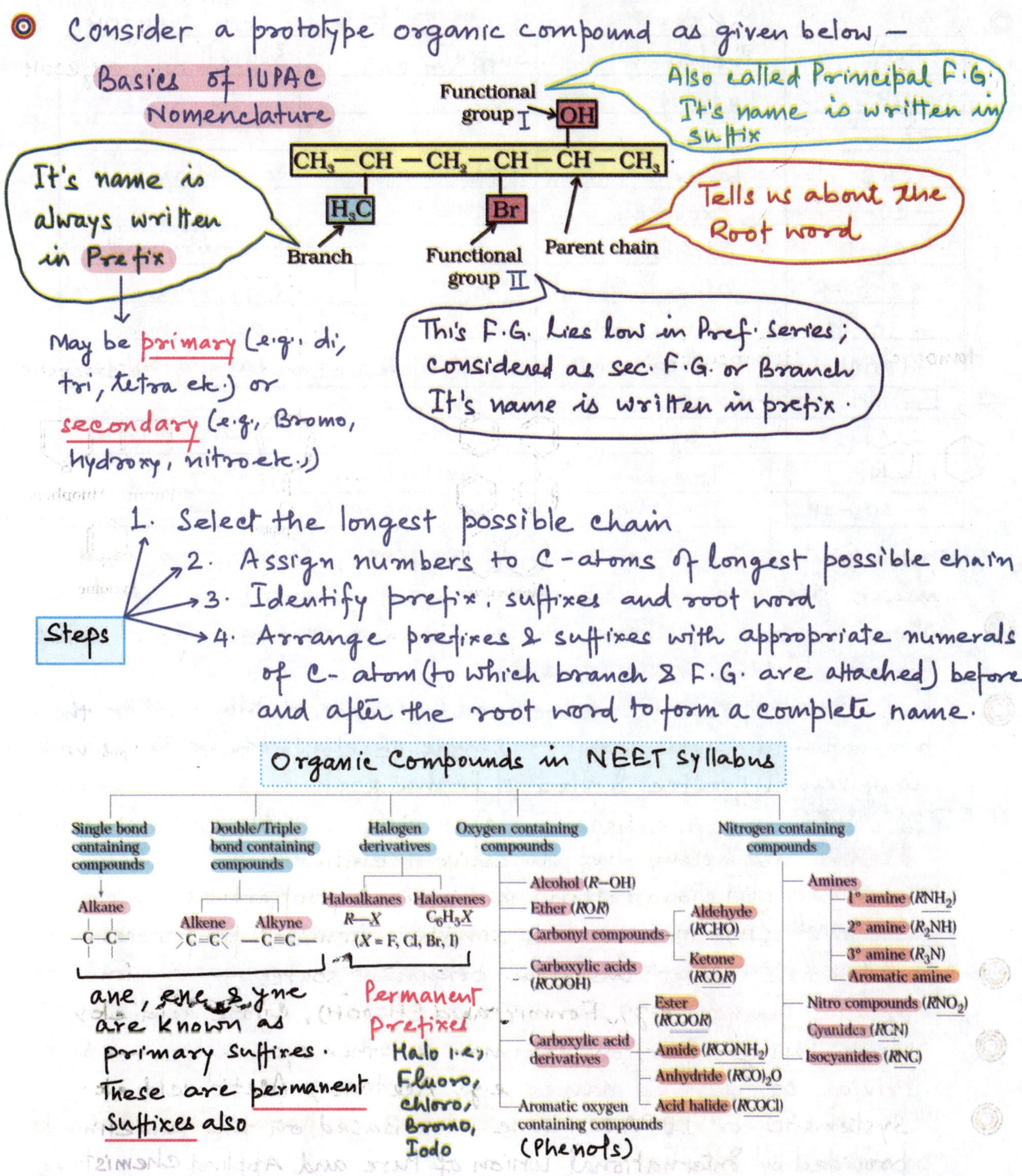

- Except first 4 i.e., Meth-, Eth-, Prop- & But- rest all the root words are based on number of C-atoms present in longest possible chain.

Prefixes & Suffixes of F.G.

F.G.	Prefix	Suffix I	Suffix II
—OH	Hydroxy	ol	—
—O—	Alkoxy	—	—
—CHO	formyl	al	Carbaldehyde
—CO—	Oxo or keto	one	—
—COOH	Carboxy	oic acid	Carboxylic acid
—COO—R	alkoxy carbonyl	oate	carboxylate
—$CONH_2$	carbamoyl	amide	carboxamide
—COCl	halocarbonyl	oyl halide	carbonyl halide
—NH_2	amino	amine	—
—CN	cyano	Nitrile	carbonitrile
—NC	isocyano	isonitrile	—
—SO_2—OH	sulpho	Sulphonic acid	—

Dhyan Rakhna 1 Among the given suffixes, suffix I is used under all normal conditions while suffix II is used when due to any reason we are unable to count the C-atom of F.G. in the main chain.

2 The prefix of any F.G. is used when more than 1 F.Gs. are present in the compound ⟶ Name of F.G. with lower preference is given in prefix & that of higher pref. is given as suffix.

NEET concentrate

Preference Series (as per 1993 recommondations)

Carboxylic Acids ⟶ Sulphonic Acids ⟶ Acid Halides ⟶ Anhydrides ⟶ Esters ⟶ Amides ⟶ Nitriles ⟶ Aldehydes ⟶ Ketones ⟶ Alcohols & Phenols ⟶ Amines ⟶ Ethers ⟶ Peroxides ⟶ Alkene ⟶ Alkyne ⟶ Halo, nitroso, nitro, alkoxy ⟶ Oxiranes (cyclic ethers)

Dhyan Rakhna | Preference Series mein jo group pehle hai uski preference high hai.

Rules to select longest Possible chain

I. Normally the continuous C-chain with max. no. of C-atoms is the longest possible chain.

II. If 2 or more chains of equal length are present, then select the chain with max. no. of side chains

III. If any double bond, triple bond or F.G. is present in the compound, then it must be included with in the longest possible chain.

IV. If more than 1 F.G. or multiple bonds are present in the compound, then only the presence of principal F.G. is necessary with in the longest possible chain.

Dhyan Rakho | Principal F.G. is chosen in accordance with the preference series given on the last page.

Rules to assign numbers to the C-atoms of longest possible chain

I. For symmetrical compounds ⟶ Numbering can be done from either of their ends.

II. If a branch is present ⟶ Numbering must be done from the end near to the branch (so that the C-atom bearing the branch will get least possible number)

III. If more than 1 branch is present —

Case 1. Of equal length ⟶ then numbering must be done in accordance with lowest sum rule

Case 2. Of unequal length ⟶ then numbering must be done in accordance with lowest set of locants rule

(A): $CH_3-\underset{\overset{|}{CH_2-CH_3}}{CH}-CH(CH_2-CH_3)-CH_2-CH_2-CH_3$; numbered 3, 4, 5, 6, 7 along the main chain, 2, 1 on the branch

(B): $CH_3-CH(CH_3)-CH(CH_3)-CH_2-CH_2-CH_3$ chain numbered 5, 4, 3, 2, 1 and 6, 7

(A) correct sum of locants =3+4=7

(B) wrong sum of locants =4+5=9

Dhyan Rakhna | whenever there is a dispute b/w these two rules then ⟶ Lowest set of locants is given preference over Lowest sum rule.

$\overset{10}{CH_3}-\overset{9}{CH_2}-\overset{8}{CH}(CH_3)-\overset{7}{CH}(CH_3)-\overset{6}{CH_2}-\overset{5}{CH_2}-\overset{4}{CH_2}-\overset{3}{CH_2}-\overset{2}{CH}(CH_3)-\overset{1}{CH_3}$

Set of locants :2, 7, 8 (Correct)

$\overset{1}{CH_3}-\overset{2}{CH_2}-\overset{3}{CH}(CH_3)-\overset{4}{CH}(CH_3)-\overset{5}{CH_2}-\overset{6}{CH_2}-\overset{7}{CH_2}-\overset{8}{CH_2}-\overset{9}{CH}(CH_3)-\overset{10}{CH_3}$

Set of locants :3, 4, 9 (Wrong)

Case 3. Of unequal length but present at equal distance from the ends ⟶ then the smaller branch must get the least possible number.

IV. If any multiple bond or F.G. is present → Numbering must be done from the end near to this (so that multiple bond or F.G. will get lowest possible no.)

V. If more than 1 F.G. are present in the compound → → Numbering must be done from the end near to the principal F.G. (So that this group will get lowest possible no.)

VI. If more than 1 F.G. of similar nature are present at equal distance from the ends → These are preferred alphabetically.

e.g., I and Br on C-1, F and Cl on C-2: $\overset{1}{C}=\overset{2}{C}$

All the 4 groups are halogens & B of Bromo comes first alphabetically.

VII. Special cases for multiple bonds

Case 1. If double bond & triple bonds are present at the same footings → then always give preference to double bond

Case 2. If double bond and triple bond are not present at the same footings → Prefer the bond which is near to end.

e.g., In $CH_2=CH-CH_2-C\equiv CH$ → Double bond is preferred while in $CH_3-CH=CH-C\equiv CH$ → Triple bond is preferred

Functional Groupwise Nomenclature

1. Alkene → Alkane − ane + ene → Alkene
2. Alkyne → Alkane − ane + yne → Alkyne
3. Halogen compounds → Halo (chloro, Bromo, iodo etc.) + alkane → → Halo alkanes.
4. Alcohols → Alkane − e + ol → Alkanol
5. Ether → alkyl gp. + O → Alkoxy + main chain as alkane → Alkoxy alkane → CH_3O C_2H_5

Smaller alkyl gp + Oxygen → Methoxy ethane

If both the groups are similar then any one can be taken as alkoxy.

6. Aldehyde → Alkane − e + al → Alkanal ; (cyclopropane)–CHO →

Imp → Cyclopropane Carbaldehyde (as it is not possible to include C-atom of −CHO into main chain.

7. Ketone ⟶ Alkane − e + one ⟶ Alkanone
8. Carboxylic Acid ⟶ Alkane − e + oic acid ⟶ Alkanoic acid

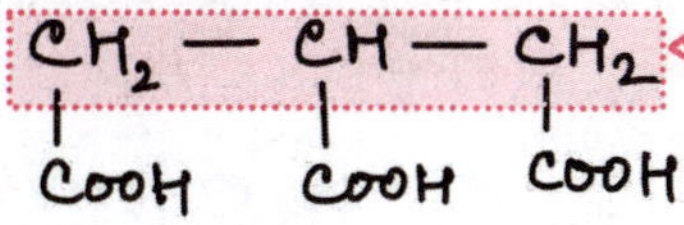

$CH_2 - CH - CH_2$ ⟵ Longest Possible chain
(each carbon bearing a COOH group: COOH, COOH, COOH)

Propane-1,2,3-tri carboxylic Acid

9. Cyanide ⟶ Alkane + nitrile ⟶ Alkane nitrile
10. Acyl halides ⟶ Alkane − e + oyl halide ⟶ Alkanoyl halide.
11. Esters ⟶ $R - \underset{\underset{O}{\|}}{C} - OR'$

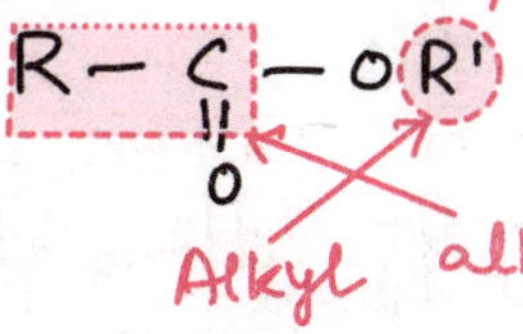

Alkyl, alkane − e + oate ⟶ Alkyl alkanoate

12. Acid Amide ⟶ Alkane − e + amide ⟶ Alkanamide
13. Acid Anhydride ⟶ Alkane − e + oic anhydride ⟶ Alkanoic anhydride.

NEET concentrate

Acid anhydrides can be pure or mixed and both of them are named differently

Ethanoic anhydride: $CH_3 - \overset{O}{\overset{\|}{C}} - O - \underset{\underset{O}{\|}}{C} - CH_3$

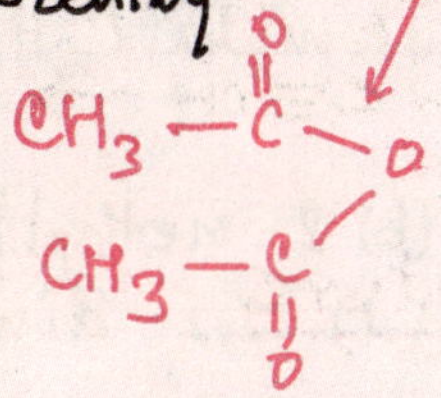

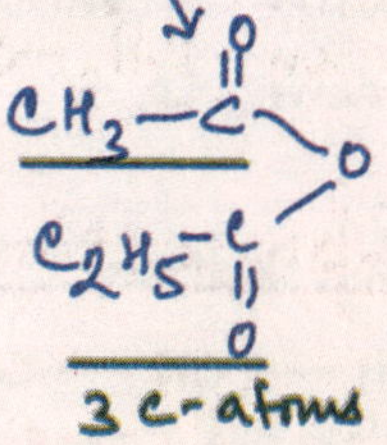

Ethanoic Propanoic anhydride: $CH_3 - \overset{O}{\overset{\|}{C}} - O - \underset{\underset{O}{\|}}{C} - C_2H_5$ (3 C-atoms)

14. Amines ⟶ Alkane − e + amine ⟶ Alkanamine

Amines can be 1°, 2° and 3° (depending upon the fact that how many alkyl groups are directly attached to Nitrogen)

$-NH_2$ (1°), $-\underset{H}{\underset{|}{N}}-$ (2°), $-\underset{|}{N}-$ (3°)

Named as alkanamine, N-alkyl alkanamine, N,N-dialkyl alkanamine

Dhyan Rakhna | Vo sabhi F.G. jinme C-atom nahi hota ⟶ longest possible chain mein kahi bhi attach ho sakte hain

N-ethyl ⟶, N-methyl ⟶ (longest possible chain) = N-ethyl-N-methyl, pentan-3-amine

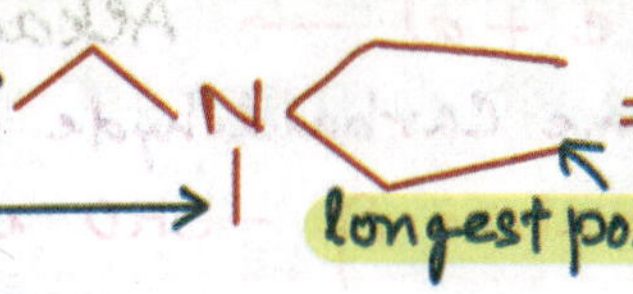

- C – atoms in a compound can be
  - 1° → Attached to 1 or no C-atom
  - 2° → Attached to 2 C- atoms
  - 3° → Attached to 3 C- atoms
  - 4° → Attached to 4 C- atoms

H–C(H)(H)–R: Primary (1°) carbon; H–C(R)(H)–R: Secondary (2°) carbon; R–C(R)(H)–R: Tertiary (3°) carbon; R–C(R)(R)–R: Quarternary (4°) carbon

Correct Numbering →

$$\overset{1}{CH_3}(1^\circ) - \overset{2}{CH}(3^\circ)(CH_3\ 1^\circ) - \overset{3}{C}(4^\circ)(CH_3\ 1^\circ)(CH_3\ 1^\circ) - \overset{4}{CH_2}(2^\circ) - \overset{5}{CH_3}(1^\circ)$$

Compound with all types of C- atoms

2,3,3-trimethyl pentane

PYQ Punch

Q.1. A compound with a molecular formula C_6H_{14} has 2 tertiary carbons Its IUPAC name is – NEET-2024

(a) n- hexane
(b) 2- methyl pentane
(c) 2,3- dimethyl butane ✓
(d) 2,2- dimethyl butane.

Sol $CH_3 - CH(CH_3) - CH(CH_3) - CH_3$ ← 3° Carbons

Q.2. The correct IUPAC name of following compound is NEET 2022

[Structure: Cl, OH substituted chain with methyl, ending in Br]

(a) 6 – bromo – 2 – chloro – 4 – methylhexan – 4 – ol
(b) 1 – bromo – 4 – methyl – 5 – chlorohexan – 3 – ol
(c) 6 – bromo – 4 – methyl – 2 – chlorohexan – 4 – ol
(d) 1 – bromo – 5 – chloro – 4 – methylhexan – 3 – ✓

Sol [Structure numbered 6, 5 (Cl), 4 (methyl), 3 (OH), 2, 1 (Br)]

–OH group is principal functional group and it is nearest to C- atom bearing Br.

NEET concentrate

- An extra a is added to the root word → If the primary suffix to be added begins with a consonant
- Always remember the carbon atom of a side chain which is attached directly to the longest possible chain must be numbered as 1st carbon atom of that side chain.

$\overset{1}{C}H_3 - \overset{2}{C}H_2 - \overset{3}{C}H - \overset{4}{C}H_2 - \overset{5}{C}H_3$, with $CH_3 - \overset{1}{C}(H) - CH_3$ attached at C-3 (← 1st C-atom of side chain)

ISOMERISM

- Compounds with same molecular formula but different properties due to the difference in their 2D & 3D structures → Isomers & this phenomenon is called Isomerism.

Dhyan Rakhna ① Technically a chemical compound show the properties of its constituent elements. So, if molecular formula of 2 compounds is same → their properties are also expected to be same

② However, Organic compounds are made up of very limited elements i.e., only C, H, O, N, S, P and X contribute in their production. So, According to technical know how, their properties must be more or less same. But the definition of isomerism indicates the importance of 2D & 3D structure as the major contributors of their properties.

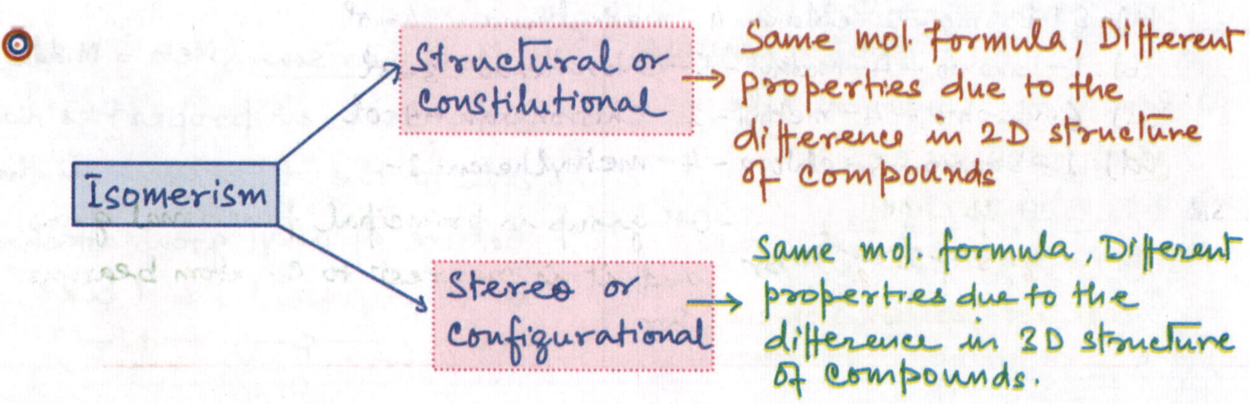

Structural Isomerism

1. Chain Isomerism

Difference in properties due to difference in carbon skeleton

① $CH_3CH_2CH_2CH_2CH_3$

② $CH_3CH(CH_3)CH_2CH_3$

③ $CH_3-C(CH_3)_2-CH_3$

Mol. formula → C_5H_{12}

2. Position Isomerism

Difference in properties due to the difference in position of monovalent F.G. attached

↑ with 1 valency free e.g., $-OH$, $-CHO$, $-Cl, Br, I, F$, $-CN$ etc.

$CH_3CH_2CH_2OH$ & $CH_3CH(OH)CH_3$

Mol. formula → C_3H_8O

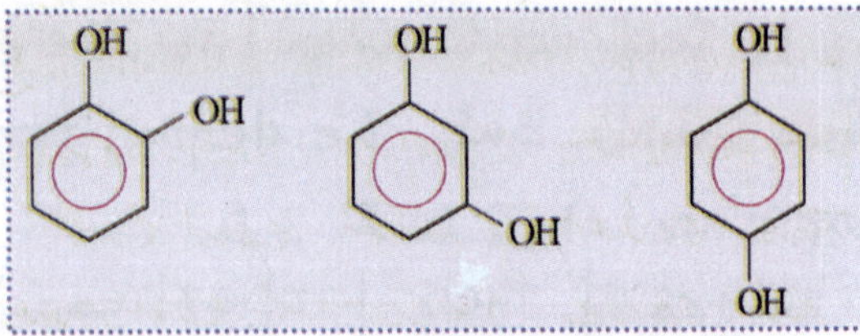

Mol. formula → $C_6H_6O_2$

NEET concentrate

- Remember | compounds like
  ① $CH_3COCH_2CH_2CH_3$ & $CH_3CH_2COCH_2CH_3$
  ② $CH_3CH_2NH_2$ & CH_3NHCH_3
  are not position isomers

3. Functional Isomers

Difference in properties due to difference in F.G. attached.

C_2H_5OH & CH_3OCH_3

mol. formula → C_2H_6O

F.G. → Alcohol & Ether

Some more other such groups –

1. Aldehyde & ketone
2. Aldehyde & Oxirane (cyclic ether)
3. Ketone & Oxirane
4. Cyanide & Isocyanide
5. Carboxylic acid & Ester.

Always remember | although functional isomers show different properties towards a reagent but their approach towards a reagent is always same i.e., their reaction centres are more or less similar.

e.g., $CH_3-CH_2-\ddot{O}-H$

$CH_3-\ddot{O}-CH_3$

Reaction centre of Both the isomers

4. Metamerism (Meta = Middle)

Difference in properties is due to the difference in the nature of alkyl group attached to a polyvalent F.G. (like $-O-$, $-C(=O)-$, $-N(-)-$)

NEET concentrate

Metamers can never be considered as chain or position isomers.

① $CH_3COCH_2CH_2CH_3$
② $CH_3CH_2COCH_2CH_3$
③ $CH_3COCH(CH_3)CH_3$

F.G. —C(=O)—

Mol. Formula → $C_5H_{10}O$

① $CH_3CH_2CH_2NH_2$
② $CH_3CH(CH_3)NH_2$
③ $CH_3CH_2NHCH_3$
④ $CH_3N(CH_3)CH_3$

F.G. —N(—)—

Mol. Formula C_3H_9N

5. Tautomerism

→ Difference in properties due to the the motion of a mobile α Hydrogen
→ Specialised Functional isomerism
→ Isomers must have
 — One highly electronegative atom
 — Multiple bond
 — Atleast 1 acidic H

$$CH_3-\underset{\underset{O}{||}}{C}-CH_3 \underset{\bar{O}H}{\overset{H^+}{\rightleftharpoons}} CH_3-\underset{\underset{OH}{|}}{C}=CH_2$$

keto form — enol form

Structural Isomerism

→ In a solution both the isomers coexist and have the tendency of interconversion.
→ Their interconversion is acid or base catalysed.
→ Due to this interconversion a dynamic equilibrium is established between both the isomers.

NEET concentrate

⊙ Keto-enol tautomerism serves as the basis of very important reactions like aldol condensation

→ Compounds like

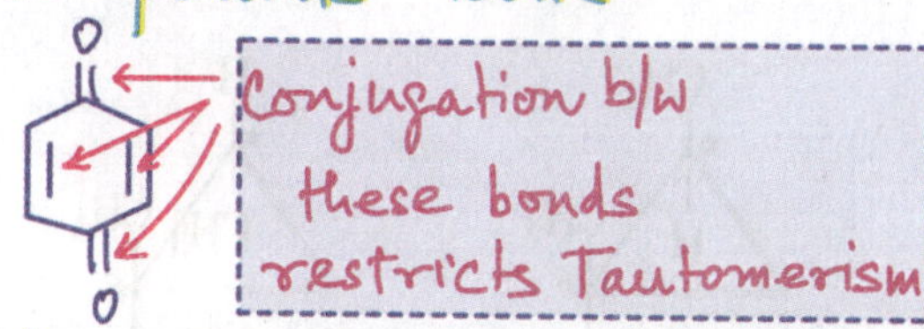

does not show keto-enol tautomerism. This compound prefers to stay in keto form.

→ The order of enol content in some important compounds is —

$CH_3CHO < CH_3COCH_3 < CH_3COCH_2CHO < CH_3COCH_2COCH_3$

6. Ring Chain Isomerism

→ Specialised functional group isomerism.
→ Open chain & cyclic structures are isomeric as both share similar degree of unsaturation

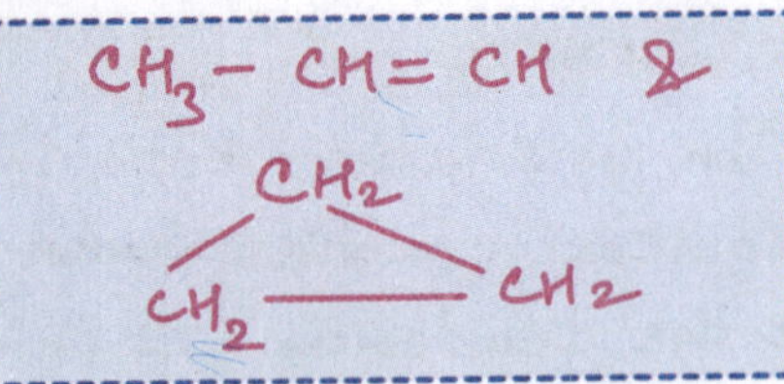

mol. formula C_3H_6

Degree of Unsaturation → No. of Hydrogen pairs absent in an unsaturated compound in comparison to its saturated counter part. e.g.. DOU of C_3H_6 = 1 (as it contains 1 pair or 2 Hydrogens less from its saturated counterpart i.e., C_3H_8.

Stereoisomerism

Geometrical — Difference in properties due to **hindered rotation** along a C–C, C–N or N–N double bond

Optical — Differential behaviour towards Polarised Light (Discussed in detail in Haloalkanes and Haloarenes)

But-2-ene

H_3C and H on C=C, H_3C and H below — cis form

H_3C and H on C=C, H and CH_3 below — trans form.

→ C-atoms of cyclic forms which show geometrical isomerism → stereocentres

cis-form; trans-form (1,2-dimethylcyclopropane); cis, trans (1,2-dimethylcyclohexane) OR cis, trans

cis form → less stable, more polar, more soluble in polar solvents, with more b.p., Less m.p.

trans form → More stable, less polar, less soluble in polar solvents, with less b.p., more m.p ← due to more symmetry in comparison to cis form.

R—C—H ‖ :N—OH syn oxime; R—C—H ‖ HO—N: anti oxime

Syn and anti forms → Seen in C—N and N—N double bonds.

→ Syn ≈ cis ; Anti ≈ trans.

NEET concentrate

Geometrical isomers for those compounds which have dissimilar groups attached to double bonded C-atoms are classified as E (Entgagen = opposite ≈ trans) and Z (Zusammen = together ≈ cis) forms

Formulae to calculate No. of Geometrical Isomers

Imp

1. compounds with dissimilar ends ⟶ 2^n
2. compounds with similar ends and even number of stereocentres ⟶ $2^{n-1} + 2^{\frac{n}{2}-1}$
3. compounds with similar ends and odd number of stereocentres ⟶ $2^{n-1} + 2^{\frac{n-1}{2}}$

Fundamental Concepts of Organic Reaction Mechanism

Organic Molecule (substrate) $\xrightarrow[\text{Reagent}]{\text{Attacking}}$ [Intermediate] ⟶ Product

[Intermediate] ⟶ By Products

Organic Molecule and Attacking Reagent ↓ Both undergo Bond Fission and New Bond formations in them results to Products.

[Intermediate] ↑ seen in the form of mainly Carbocations, carbanions and free radicals.

→ A sequential account of each step describing e^- movement, energetics during bond fission and formation, and kinetics i.e., rates of product formation from reactants ⟶ ⟶ Reaction mechanism.

Covalent Bond Fission

Homolysis ⟵ Covalent Bond Fission ⟶ Heterolysis

Homolysis

→ Equal distribution of shared electron.

$$CH_3-CH_3 \xrightarrow{\text{Light/heat}} \dot{C}H_3 + \dot{C}H_3$$

$$Cl-Cl \xrightarrow{\text{Light/heat}} \dot{Cl} + \dot{Cl}$$

→ Species formed — free radical

→ seen in non polar bonds & in the presence of Non polar solvents.

→ Presence of peroxides, high temp. UV light, pre existing free rad. favours this fission.

Heterolysis

→ Unequal distribution of shared electron.

$$A-B \xrightarrow{\text{Heterolysis}} A^+ + B^-$$

(B is more electronegative)

→ Species formed — Carbocation & carbanion

→ seen in polar bonds

→ Presence of polar solvents and low temperature favours the reaction.

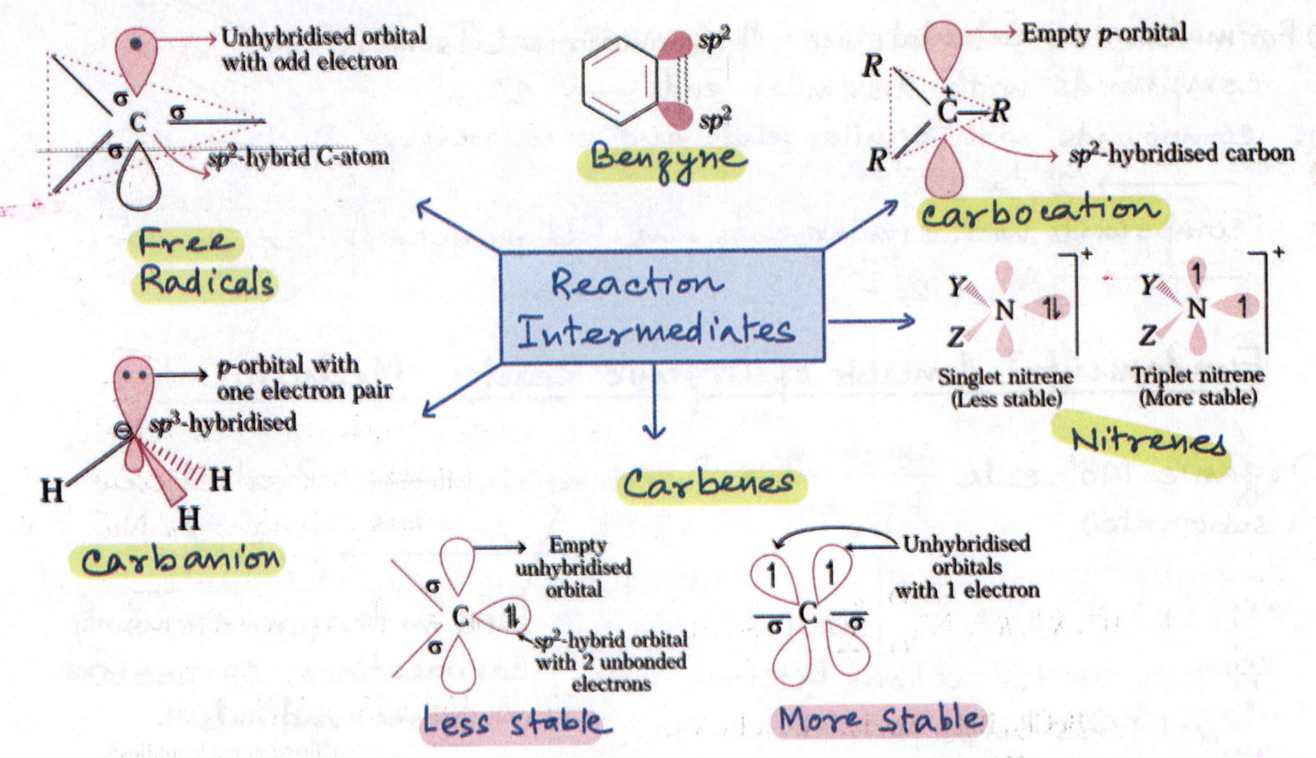

→ Free radicals are paramagnetic in nature (due to the presence of single odd e^- in them) and because of this reason only these are of very reactive nature.

→ Free radical reactions are loop based chain reactions & involve chain Initiation, Propagation & Termination steps.

→ Cyclopropyl methyl carbocations i.e.,

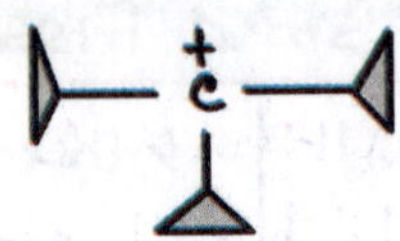

most stable carbocations (due to conjugation between the bent orbitals of cyclopropyl ring and vacant p-orbitals of the cationic carbon)

→ The stability of Nitrenes and Carbenes is based upon pairing or separation of electrons according to Hund's rule

→ Benzyne is a hypothetical species (Not seen practically ever). Its uniqueness is its 3rd bond which is by nature a π bond ⟶ Formed by the sidewise overlapping of 2 sp^2 hybrid orbitals.

- The agent responsible for a reaction i.e., initiates, propagates and terminates the reaction ⟶ Reagent.

- Reagent
  - → Homolysis ⟶ Free radicals (A•)
    Very reactive species due to the presence of odd e^- (High energy unpaired e^-)
  - → Heterolysis ⟶ Electrophile & Nucleophile
    - Electrophile: e^- deficient species which attacks on e^- rich areas; denoted as E^+
    - Nucleophile: e^- rich species which attacks on e^- deficient areas; denoted as Nu^-

	Electrophiles	Nucleophiles
Charged Examples	$H^{\oplus}$, $X^{\oplus}$, $R^{\oplus}$, $\overset{\oplus}{N}O_2$, $\overset{\oplus}{N}O{=}O$, $\overset{\oplus}{S}O_3H$	$\overset{\ominus}{H}$, $\overset{\ominus}{O}H$, $R-\overset{\ominus}{O}$, $\overset{\ominus}{C}H_3$, $\overset{\ominus}{X}$, $\overset{\ominus}{S}H$, $R-\overset{\ominus}{S}$
Neutral Examples	$BeCl_2$, BH_3, $ZnCl_2$, AlX_3, FeX_3, $\dot{C}H_3$, $\ddot{C}H_2$, $\ddot{C}X_2$. $SnCl_4$, $SiCl_4$, PCl_5, SF_6, IF_7. Cl_2, Br_2, I_2 — Lewis Acids	$\ddot{N}H_3$, $R-\ddot{N}H_2$, $R_2\ddot{N}H$, $R_3\ddot{N}$, $\ddot{N}H_2-\ddot{N}H_2$ (Nitrogen nucleophiles); $H-\ddot{O}-H$, $R-\ddot{O}-H$, $R-\ddot{O}-R$ (Oxygen nucleophiles); $H-\ddot{S}-H$, $R-\ddot{S}-H$, $R-\ddot{S}-R$ (Sulphur nucleophiles) — Lewis Bases

→ Species with 2 e^- donating centres ⟶ Ambident Nucleophile
e.g., $C{\equiv}N$ & $N{\rightleftarrows}C$

NEET concentrate

- Organic compounds in which C is bonded with EN atom (O, N, S) by a multiple bond contains both e^- rich (equivalent to Nu^-) and e^- deficient (equivalent to E^+) parts. e.g., $R-\underset{\Vert}{\overset{}{C}}-H$ (C=O), $R-\underset{\Vert}{C}-R$ (C=O), $R-\underset{\Vert}{C}-OH$ (C=O) & acid derivatives etc.

- Metal ions (like Na^+, K^+, Li^+, Mg^{2+} etc.) can never be considered as Electrophiles (because of their inability to form covalent bonds.) however H^+ can (due to its ability to form covalent bonds)

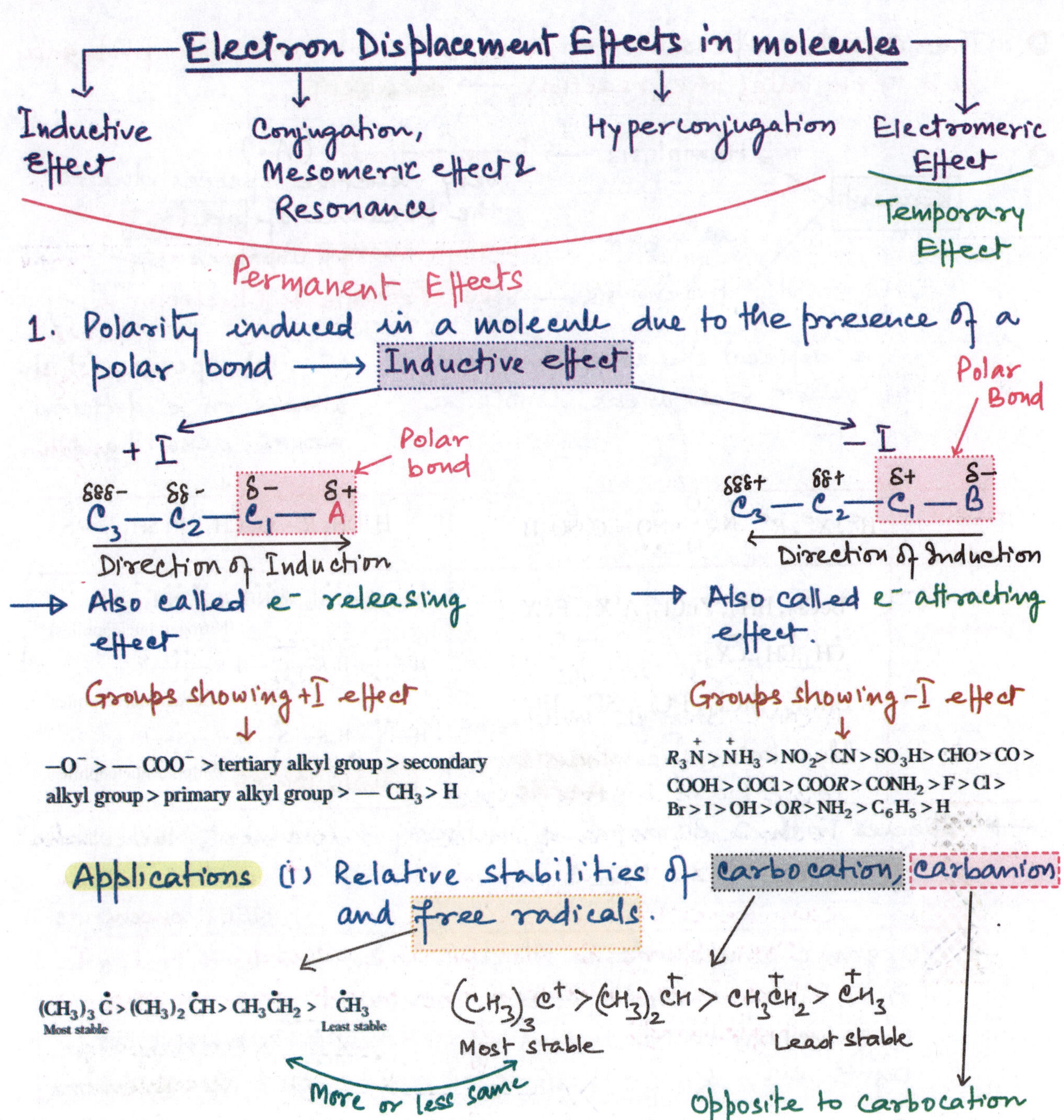

→ Simply, Groups with + I effect → stabilise carbanion but destablise free radicals and carbocations.

Groups with –I effect → stabilises carbocations and free radicals and destabilises carbanions.

(ii) Acidic and Basic Strengths

Group	Acidic Strength	Basic strength
+I	↓ Decreases	↑ Increases
−I	↑ Increases	↓ Decreases

* $CH_3OH < H_2O < C_6H_5OH$ (Acidic Strength)
* $CH_3NH_2 > NH_3 > C_6H_5NH_2$ (Basic strength)
* $CCl_3COOH > CHCl_2COOH > CH_2ClCOOH > CH_3COOH$ (Acidic strength)
* $CH_2FCOOH > CH_2ClCOOH > CH_2BrCOOH > CH_2ICOOH$ (Acidic strength)

2. Partial bonding in π bonded organic molecules → Conjugation or conjugative bonding.

→ It can be seen between
 a. 2 or more π bonds
 b. A π bond & lone pair of e⁻
 c. A π bond & (+)ve & (−)ve charges
 d. A π bond & odd e⁻ of free radical
 e. A (+)ve charge and lone pair.

→ It can be seen when above written objects are at
 a. same plane & same angle
 b. Technically at a distance of single bond from each other (as (i) 2 different orbitals of a single atom can never be in same plane & at same angle
 (ii) Overlapping is not possible according to MOT if distance between the objects is more than a single bond)

2p orbitals of c-atom
C
90°

>C — C — C — C<

Overlapping Possible

Overlapping not possible

→ Result of conjugation
 a. Partial = Improper bond length
 b. Extra stability in molecule
 c. Unpredictable results in reactions.

→ Example Buta-1,4-diene is simplest & best example.

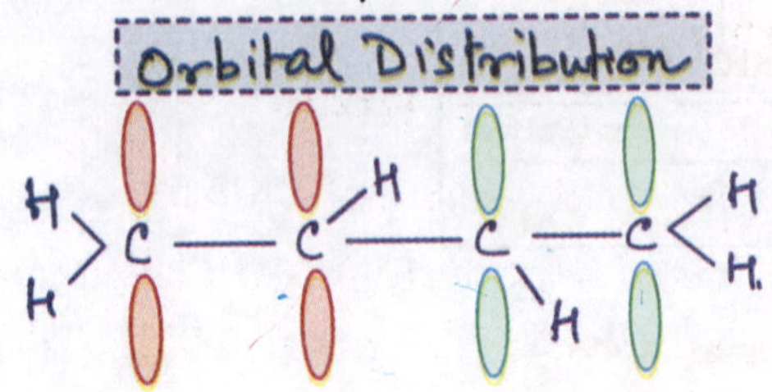

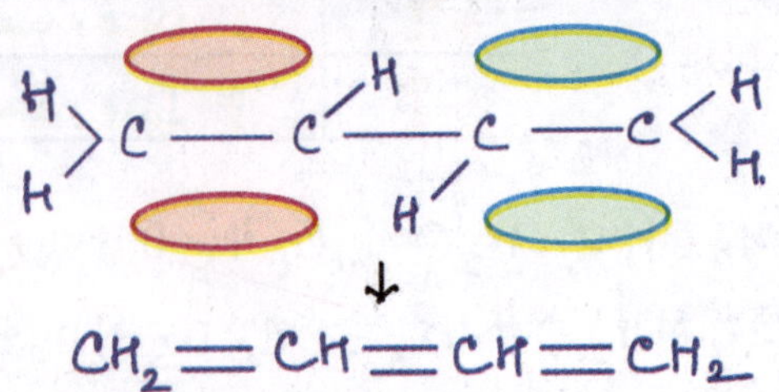

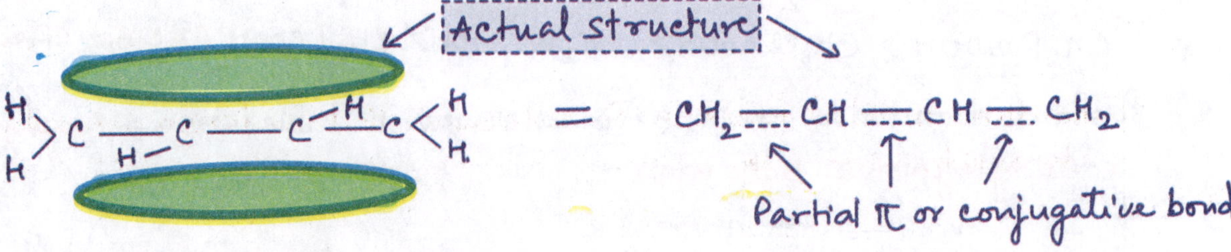

3. Polarity produced in a molecule due to the process of conjugation

→ **Mesomeric Effect**

+ M effect

→ Also called e^- donating effect

① $H_2C{=}CH{-}CH{=}CH{-}\ddot{N}H_2 \longleftrightarrow H_2\overset{\ominus}{C}{-}CH{=}CH{-}CH{=}\overset{\oplus}{N}H_2$

② $H_2C{=}CH{-}\ddot{Cl}: \longleftrightarrow H_2\overset{\ominus}{C}{-}CH{=}\overset{\oplus}{Cl}$

③ (Resonance structures of chlorobenzene: $:\ddot{Cl}:$ on benzene ⟷ $\oplus Cl$ with negative charge at ortho ⟷ $\oplus Cl$ with negative charge at para ⟷ $\oplus Cl$ with negative charge at other ortho ⟷ $:\ddot{Cl}:$ on benzene)

→ Groups showing +M effect

$O^- > NH_2 > OH > OR > NHAc >$ alkyl gps. ($CH_3 > 1° > 2° > 3°$) > phenyl

− M effect

→ Also called e^- withdrawing effect

① $H_2C{=}CH{-}\overset{O}{\overset{\|}{C}}{-}H \longleftrightarrow H_2\overset{\oplus}{C}{-}CH{=}\overset{O^{\ominus}}{\overset{|}{C}}{-}H$

② (Resonance structures of nitrobenzene: $\overset{\ominus}{O}{-}\overset{\oplus}{N}{=}O$ on benzene ⟷ positive charge at ortho ⟷ positive charge at para ⟷ positive charge at other ortho ⟷ nitrobenzene)

→ Groups showing −M effect

$NO_2 > CN > SO_3H > CHO > COOH > COCl > COOR > CONH_2$

4. When we can not draw exact electronic picture of a compound which explains all of its properties → → → →

We draw 2, 3 or more structures each of which explains some of its properties

↓

Resonating structures or Canonical forms

→ The phenomenon → Resonance (completly Hypothetical)

→ The actual structure is considered as hybrid of these forms → Resonance Hybrid.

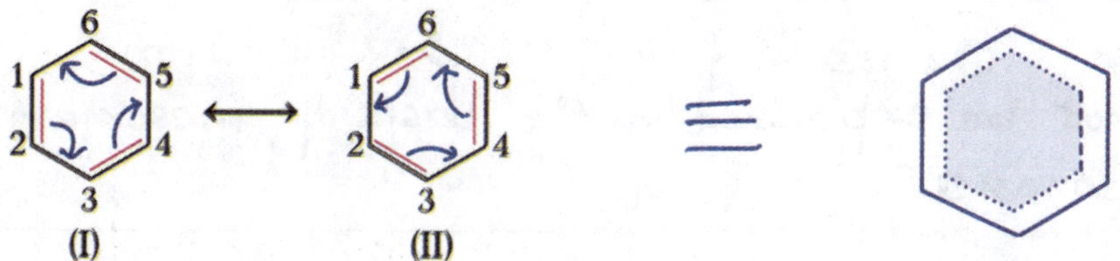

Canonical forms of Benzene   Resonance Hybrid

→ Conditions for Resonance

a. Arrangement of atoms, electonic distribution. no. of charges, and no. of unpaired e^- → More or less same in all contributing structures

b. Energy content of all canonical forms → nearly the same

→ Stability of canonical forms

a. Structure without charges → Most stable

b. Among the charged structures

(i) structure with max. no. of covalent bonds → Most stable

(ii) Structure with less charge separation → IInd in queue

(iii) Structure with conventionally correct charges → Comes at last place

→ More no. of canonical forms → More will be stability of compound.

→ The difference between the energy of most stable canonical form (Theoritical value) and energy of resonance hybrid (actual or experimental value) ⟶ Resonance Energy.

→ Exceptional properties of compounds showing resonance
a. Extra stability
b. Improper bond length & type

NEET concentrate

Resonance & Mesomeric effects are not at all same. Infact we can say " All the cases of mesomeric effect can be explained on the basis of conjugation but all the the cases of Resonance can not be explained on the basis of mesomeric effect or resonance." For Example, Structure of HCl –

$$HCl \longleftrightarrow H^+Cl^-$$

(In gaseous form) (In aqueous form)

can not be explained on the basis of mesomeric effect or resonance.

→ Application wise Mesomeric effect is equivalent to Inductive effect. Infact +M = +I and –M = –I But,
Always Remember,
+M = e^- donating while +I = e^- releasing
–M = e^- withdrawing while –I = e^- attracting
Words releasing and attracting are related to Induction only while donating and withdrawing are related with hypothetical e^- transference.

5. Conjugation of odd e^-, (+)ve charge or π bond with a C–H bond of alkyl group → Hyperconjugation

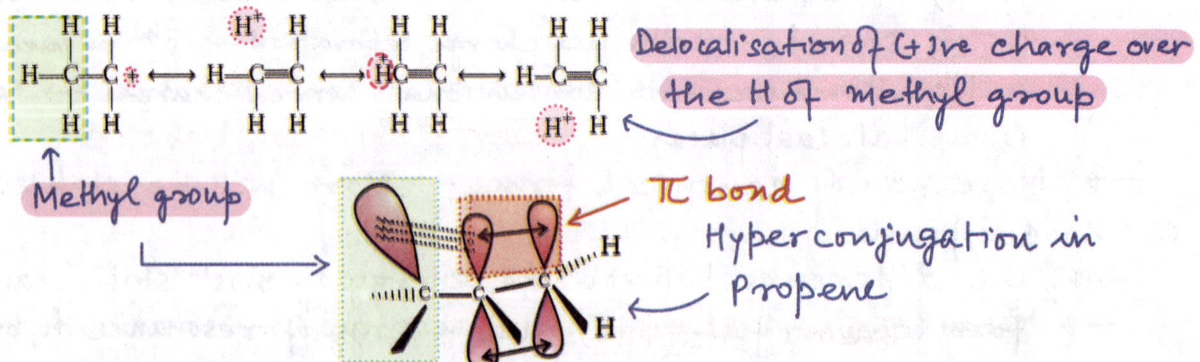

→ Applications

a. Stability of alkenes = No. of Hydrogens present at alternate position to π bond

Means no. of H-atoms present in adjacent alkyl groups.

① $CH_3-CH=CH_2 > CH_3-CH_2-CH=CH_2 > CH_3-CH(CH_3)-CH=CH_2$

3 Hyperconjugative structure (HS) | 2 HS | 1 HS

② $(CH_3)_2C=C(CH_3)_2 > (CH_3)_2C=CH(CH_3) > (CH_3)_2C=CH_2$

12 HS | 9 HS | 6 HS

③ $\overset{+}{C}H_3 < CH_3\overset{+}{C}H_2 < CH_3\overset{+}{C}HCH_3 < CH_3-\overset{+}{C}(CH_3)-CH_3$

No HS | 3HS | 6HS | 9HS

④ H–C(H)(H)–C₆H₅ ⟷ H–C(H)=C₆H₅⁻ H⊕ ⟷ H–C(H)=C₆H₅⁻ H⊕ ⟷ H–C(H)=C₆H₅⁻ H⊕

NEET concentrate

If any atom with High E_N (like halogens) is attached as $X-\underset{X}{\overset{X}{C}}-\underset{H}{C}=C\begin{smallmatrix}H\\H\end{smallmatrix}$, then hyperconjugation operates in opposite direction ⟶ Reverse Hyperconjugation

6. Polarity produced in a multiple bonded molecule due to the approach of a reagent ⟶ Electromeric Effect.

→ Seen because of the presence of π bond as attacking reagent always attacks the exposed e⁻ cloud.

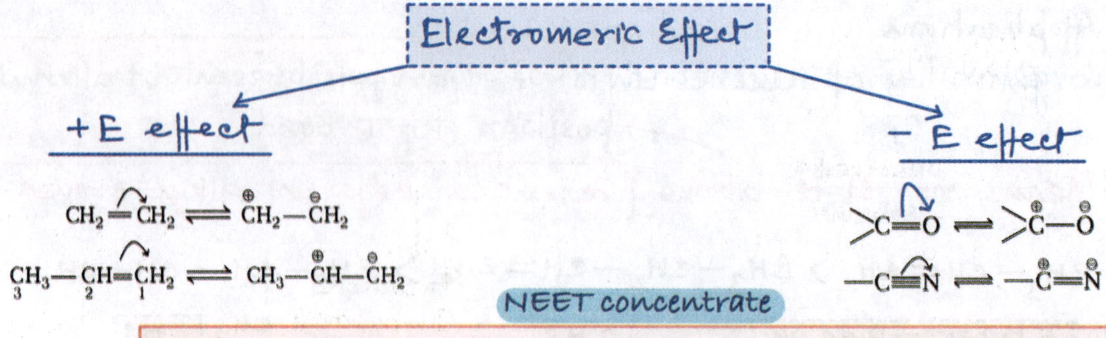

NEET concentrate

Increase in inductive effect due to the approach of any charged species towards a molecule already showing inductive effect ⟶ Inductomeric Effect

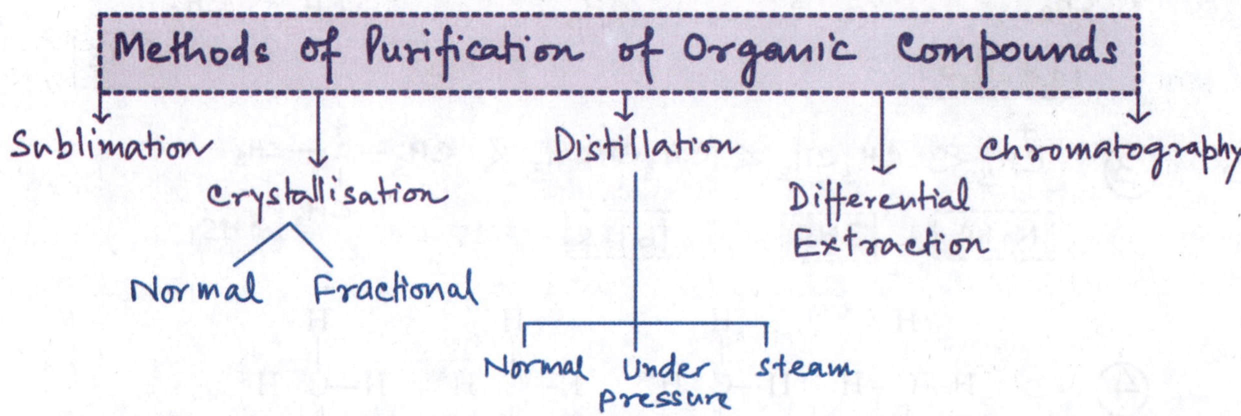

1. Process of purification used to separate sublimable volatile compounds from Non-sublimable impurities ⟶ Sublimation

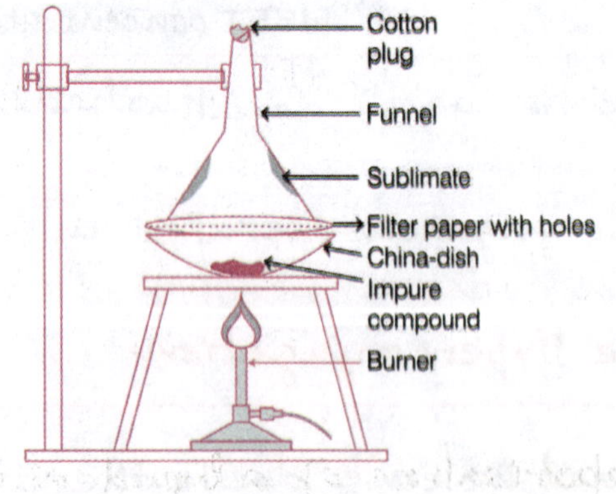

Purification of camphor, naphthalene, anthracene, benzoic acid, salicylic acid etc. from their non volatile impurities

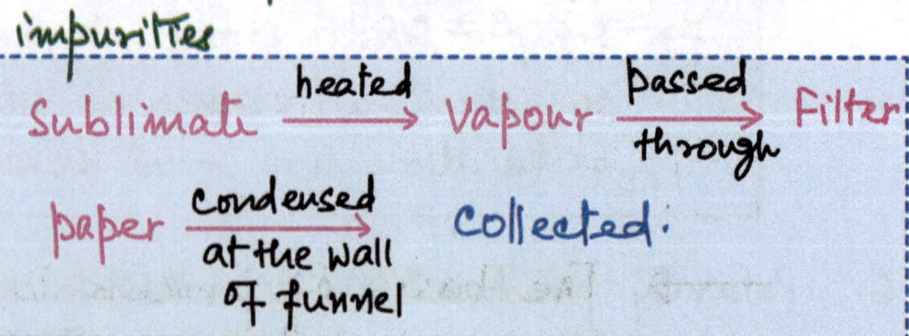

⟶ Rate of sublimation may increased if process is carried out under pressure.

2. Purification method based on the differences in solubility of organic compounds with their impurities

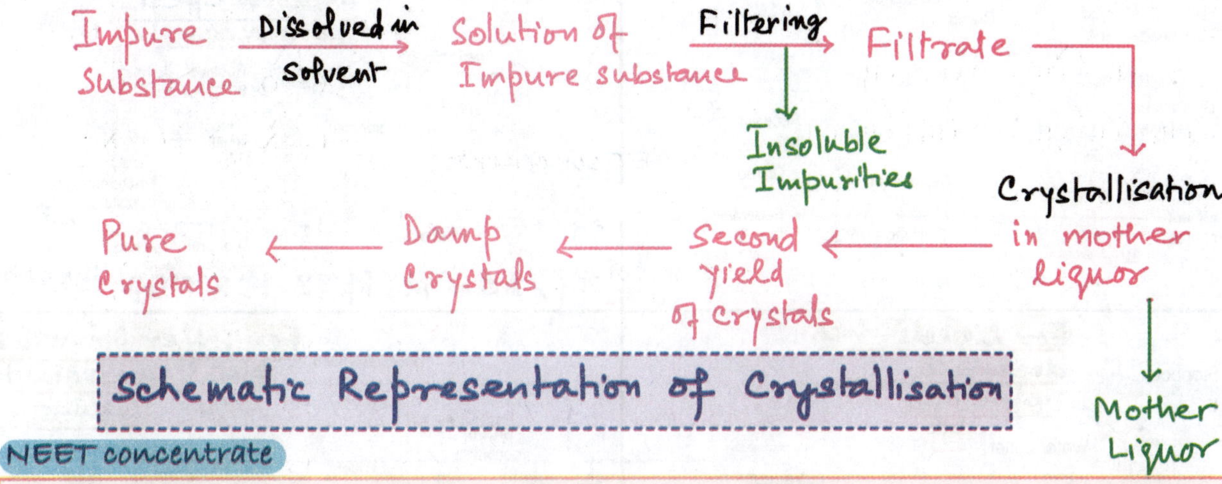

Schematic Representation of Crystallisation

NEET concentrate

- Sometimes crystallisation can be induced by adding a few crystals of the pure substance to the conc. solution → Seeding
- The role of solvent is very important in crystallisation. Usually polar solvents (like water) tend to produce better results than non-polar solvents like hydrocarbons.

3. Method of Purification which is used to purify those mixtures which have different solubilities in same solvent ⟶ ⟶ ⟶ Fractional Crystallisation.
   e.g., A mixture of $KClO_3$ & KCl

4. Method of Purification used if organic liquid is stable at its b.p. & contains a non-volatile impurity → Distillation
   ⟶ Simple Distillation is used in such cases where a sufficient difference is visible between the b.p. of two liquids e.g. Chloroform (bp 334k) & Aniline (bp 457k)
   Benzene (bp 308K) & Aniline (bp 384k)
   ⟶ The basis of process is Vaporisation of a liquid at its bp ⟶ Collection of Vapours separately ⟶ Condensation of vapours to get the liquid again.

Simple Distillation

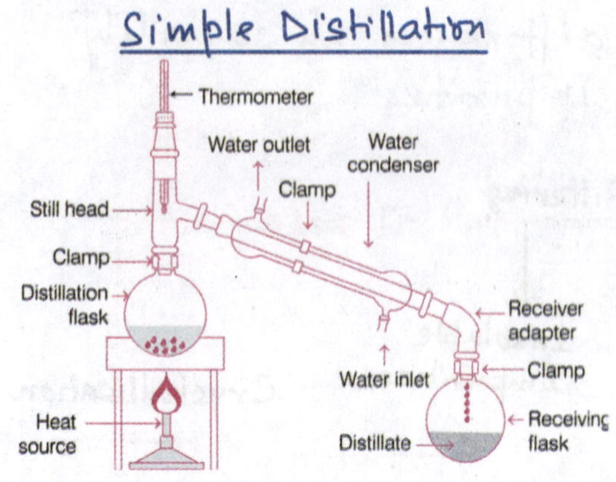

Fractional Distillation

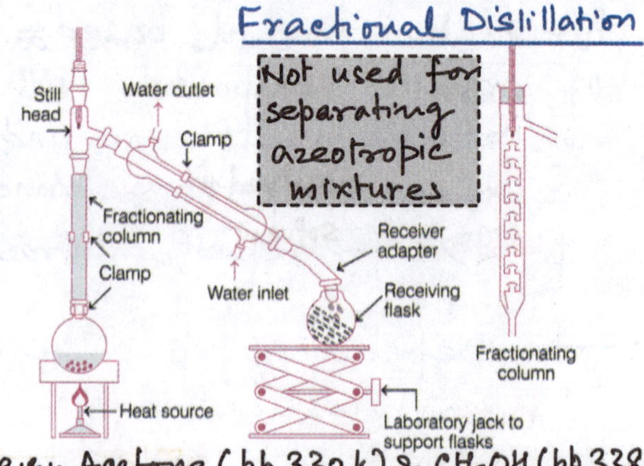

Not used for separating azeotropic mixtures

e.g., Acetone (bp 330 K) & CH_3OH (bp 338 K)

For liquids which decompose before their bp

Under Reduced Pressure

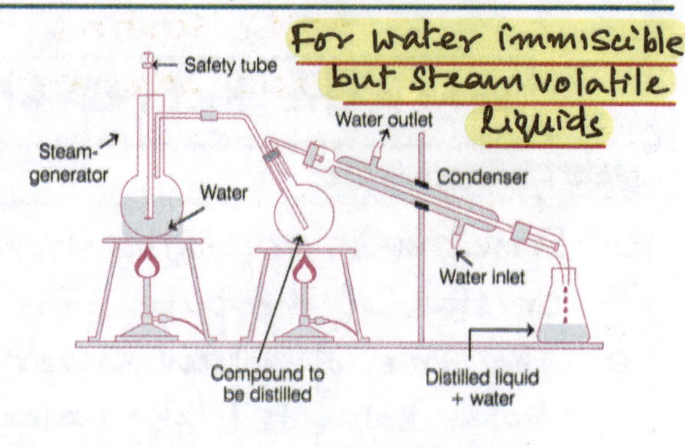

For water immiscible but steam volatile liquids

Steam Distillation

→ Recovery of glycerol from spent lye & concentration of sugar juice in sugar mills is done through Distillation under reduced pressure

→ Separation of aniline from aniline-water mixture & separation of ortho and para nitrophenols is done through steam distillation method.

5. Extraction of any organic substance from its aqueous solution into another organic liquid → Differential Extraction.

→ Based on following facts

a. Organic solvent (used for extraction) must form a distinct i.e., separable layer with water

b. Solubility of organic substance must be larger in organic solvent

c. Organic solvent must be volatile (for further purification)

d. Repeated extractions are needed
e. Process must be carried out in a separating funnel
f. K > 1 for repeated extractions

Solvent layer
Organic compound in aqueous layer
Before extraction

Organic compound in solvent layer
Aqueous layer
After extraction

→ Depending upon the aqueous phase the organic solvents used are –

Water → Chloroform
Acidic solutions → Dichloromethane
Basic solutions → Hydrocarbons.

6. Separation depending upon the differences in partition coefficients of the components of a mixture between two immiscible phases → Chromatography (Tswett, 1906)

Mobile phase ↙ ↘ Stationary phase

→ $K = \frac{C_s}{C_m}$ ← C_s: Conc. of substance in stationary phase; C_m: Conc. of substance in mobile phase

K → Partition coefficient

→ Removal of adsorbed substance from adsorbent → Elution

Classification

Gas Chromatography
Adsorbent → Solid
Eluent → Gas

Gas Chromatography
Adsorbent → Liquid
Eluent → Gas

Adsorption Chromatography
Adsorbent → Solid
Eluent → Liquid

Liquid – Liquid Partition chromatography
Adsorbent → Liquid
Eluent → Liquid.

NEET concentrate

- Chroma = Colour ; Graphy = writing
- Column chromatography → Simplest ; carried out in long glass tube or column

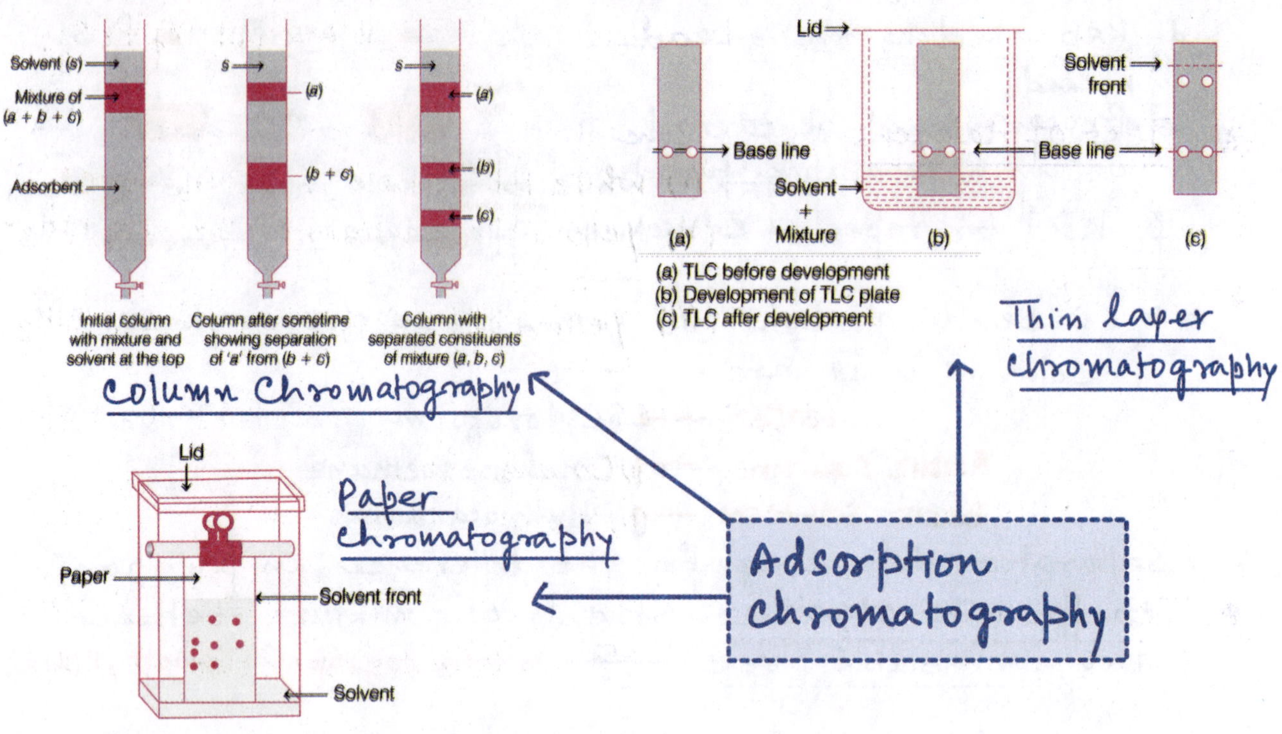

Qualitative Analysis

a. Detection of C & H ⟶ By heating compound with CuO

1. C present → CO_2 evolved (turns Lime water milky
2. H present → H_2O formed (turns anhy. $CuSO_4$ blue)
3. Other Elements (P, S, N, X) ⟶ Lassaigne's test.

→ Organic compound + Dry Na (fusion) ⟶ Boiled with H_2O after fusion and then filtered → Soda Extract (SE) is formed.

* **Test of Nitrogen** SE + Freshly prepared $FeSO_4$ + HCl $\xrightarrow[\text{cool}]{\text{boil \&}}$ Prussian Blue colour or ppt

⇒ Not given by diazo (−N=N−) compounds

* **Test of Sulphur** (1) SE + Sod. Nitroprusside ⟶ Purple (violet) colour

(ii) SE + Lead acetate ⟶ Black ppt. of PbS.

✲ **Test of Halogens** A. SE + Conc. HNO_3 + boil & cool + $AgNO_3$ ⟶

⟶ (i) white ppt. soluble in aq. NH_3 ⟶ Cl

(ii) yellow ppt. partially soluble in aq. NH_3 ⟶ Br

(iii) yellow ppt. insoluble in aq. NH_3 ⟶ I

B. SE + CS_2 or CCl_4 + Cl_2 water + $KMnO_4$ + Shake

⟶ (i) Orange colour ⟶ Br

(ii) Violet colour ⟶ I

✲ **Test of N & S together** SE + Freshly prepared $FeSO_4$ + HCl $\xrightarrow[\text{Cool}]{\text{Boil}}$ Blood Red colour ⟶ N & S

✲ **For Phosphorous** Organic Compound + Oxidising agent (Na_2O_2)

⟶ P if present oxidised to phosphate

⟶ Further boiled with HNO_3 & then Ammonium molybdate ⟶ Yellow colouration or ppt. ⟶ Phosphorous.

Quantitative Analysis

✲ **Of C and H** By Leibig's combustion method

(i) $$\% \text{ of C} = \frac{\text{Mass of } CO_2}{\text{Mass of organic compound}} \times \frac{12}{44} \times 100$$

(ii) $$\% \text{ of H} = \frac{\text{Mass of } H_2O}{\text{Mass of organic compound}} \times \frac{2}{18} \times 100$$

✲ **Of Halogens** By Carius method

(i) $$\% \text{ of Cl} = \frac{\text{Mass of AgCl formed}}{\text{Mass of organic compd.}} \times \frac{35.5}{143.5} \times 100$$

(ii) $$\% \text{ of Br} = \frac{\text{Mass of AgBr formed}}{\text{Mass of organic compd.}} \times \frac{80}{188} \times 100$$

(iii) $$\% \text{ of I} = \frac{\text{Mass of AgI formed}}{\text{Mass of organic compd.}} \times \frac{127}{235} \times 100$$

* **Of Sulphur** By Carius method

$$\% \text{ of } S = \frac{\text{Mass of } BaSO_4 \text{ formed}}{\text{Mass of Organic compd.}} \times \frac{32}{233} \times 100$$

* **Of Phosphorus** By Carius method

$$\% \text{ of } S = \frac{\text{Mass of } Mg_2P_2O_7 \text{ formed}}{\text{Mass of Organic compd.}} \times \frac{62}{222} \times 100$$

* **Of Nitrogen** a. By Duma's Method

$$C_xH_yN_z + \left(2x + \frac{y}{2}\right)CuO \longrightarrow xCO_2 + \frac{y}{2}H_2O + \frac{z}{2}N_2 + \left(2x + \frac{y}{2}\right)Cu$$

Oxides of Nitrogen + Cu ⟶ N_2 + CuO

$$\% \text{ of } N = \frac{28}{22400} \times 100 \times \frac{V}{w}$$

V ← Volume of N_2 in Nitrometer

w ← Mass of substance taken

b. By Kjeldahl's Method

N of Organic compd. + conc. $H_2SO_4 \xrightarrow{\Delta} (NH_4)_2SO_4$

$(NH_4)_2SO_4 \xrightarrow{2NaOH} Na_2SO_4 + 2H_2O + 2NH_3$

$$\% \text{ of } N = \frac{1.4 \times N_1 \times V_1}{w}$$

N_1 ← Normality of H_2SO_4

V_1 ← Volume of H_2SO_4

⟹ This method is not applicable to compounds having Nitrogen in ring or containing Nitro and —N=N— (azo) groups (as their N is not fully converted to $(NH_4)_2SO_4$.

9. Hydrocarbons

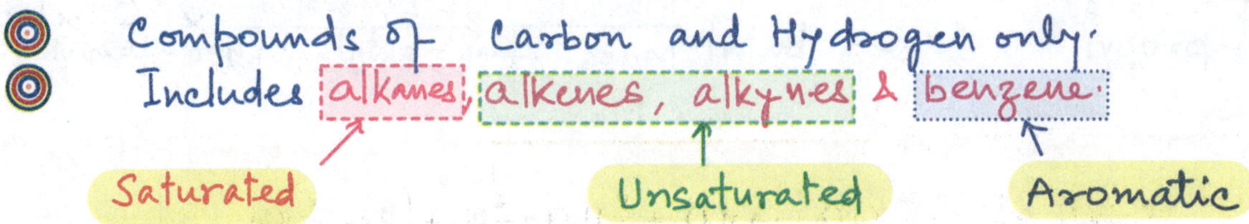

Alkanes (C_nH_{2n+2})

- Contain C — C single bonds only and rest of the valencies are satisfied by Hydrogens.
- Primary source ⟶ Mineral oil & Petroleum
- Simplest member ⟶ Methane (Commonly ⟶ Marsh gas as found in Marsh areas)
- Inert compounds (due to their saturated nature), donot react with acids, bases or other reagents ⟶ Paraffins (Latin parum = little ; affinis = affinity)
- 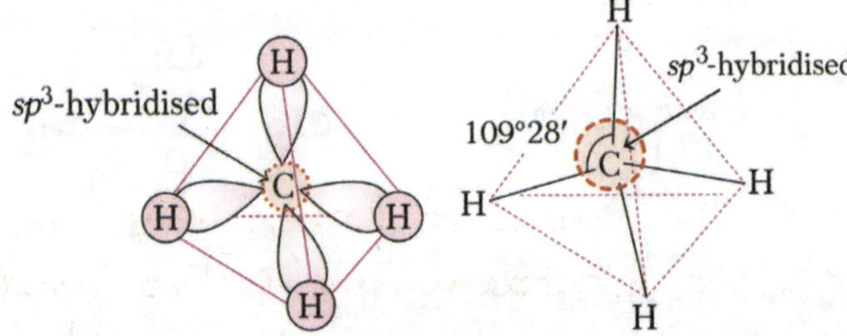

Structure of simplest alkane (CH_4)
Hybridisation of all C-atoms ⟶ sp^3

- IUPAC Names ⟶ CH_4 (Methane), C_2H_6 (Ethane), C_3H_8 (Propane), C_4H_{10} (Butane), C_5H_{12} (Pentane) and afterwards follow the same pattern of numbers i.e., Hex for 6, Hept for 7 and so on.
- Alkane — ane + yl ⟶ Alkyl groups (when saturated Hydrocarbon chain is considered as the side chain) e.g., Methyl ($-CH_3$) ; Ethyl ($-C_2H_5$) etc.
- Alkyl groups can also be seen differently on the basis of their attachment with the main chain —

$CH_3-\underset{CH_3}{\overset{H}{C}}-$ iso-propyl

$CH_3-CH_2-\underset{CH_3}{\overset{H}{C}}-$ sec. butyl

$CH_3-\underset{CH_3}{\overset{CH_3}{C}}-$ tert-butyl

$CH_3-\underset{CH_3}{\overset{CH_3}{C}}-CH_2-$ neo-pentyl

— (Free valency through which these groups will be attached to the main chain)

NEET concentrate

Technically, IUPAC donot recognise words like sec, iso, tert, neo etc. According to IUPAC nomenclature these groups are named as

$CH_3-\underset{CH_3}{\overset{H}{C}}-$ (1-methyl) ethyl

$CH_3-CH_2-\underset{CH_3}{\overset{H}{C}}-$ (1-methyl) propyl

$CH_3-\underset{CH_3}{\overset{CH_3}{C}}-$ (1,1-dimethyl)ethyl

$CH_3-\underset{CH_3}{\overset{CH_3}{C}}-CH_2-$ (2,2-dimethyl) propyl

- Alkane show chain isomerism (being devoid of any F.G.)

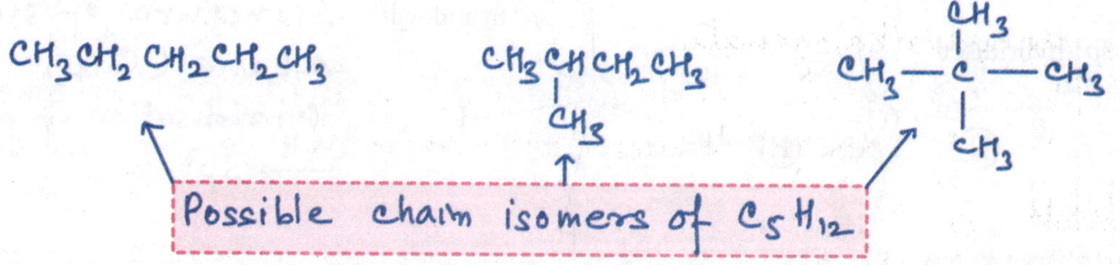

Methods of Preparation

From Unsaturated Hydrocarbons

$$CH_2=CH_2+H_2 \xrightarrow[523-573\,K]{Ni/Pt/Pd} CH_3-CH_3$$

$$CH_3-C\equiv CH+2H_2 \xrightarrow[523-573\,K]{Ni/Pt/Pd} CH_3CH_2CH_3$$

The reaction is simply called Hydrogenation.

- If only Ni is used at a temperature 200 – 300°C ⟶ Sabatiers & Senderen's Reaction.

NEET concentrate

- Methane cannot be prepared from this method
- Cycloalkanes ⟶ Unsaturated Hydrocarbons, hence can easily undergo hydrogenation. Their reactivity order is

△ > ▭ > ⬠ > ⬡

Due to angle strain ⟶ Greater the angle strain less stable or more reactive is the cyclo compound.

From Alkyl Halides

$$C_nH_{2n+1}X + H_2 \xrightarrow{Zn/H^+} C_nH_{2n+2} + HX$$

$$C_2H_5Cl + H_2 \xrightarrow{Zn/H^+} C_2H_6 + HCl$$

Reduction with Metal/Acid

The correct order of reactivity of different halides ⟶
Iodides > Bromides > Chlorides

- Reduction can also be carried out by using complex hydrides like $LiAlH_4$ (LAH), $NaBH_4$, $NaAlH_4$, Ph_3SnH (TPH)

NEET concentrate

- $LiAlH_4$ usually does not reduces 3° alkyl halide, it basically dehydrohalogenate 3° alkyl halide to give alkene.
- For 3° alkyl halide reduction, $NaBH_4$ or TPH is used.
  - $NaBH_4$: Does not reduces 1°, only works on 2° & 3°
  - TPH: Reduces all 1°, 2° & 3°

- Reduction of alkyl halides can also be carried out as

$$RI \xrightarrow{HI \text{ in Red P at } 420k}$$

Here, Red P is used to remove I as volatile PI_3 else reaction will become reversible and never reach to completion.

$$2RX + 2Na \xrightarrow[Ether]{Dry} R-R + 2NaX$$

$$2CH_3X + 2Na \xrightarrow[Ether]{Dry} CH_3-CH_3 + 2NaX$$

Wurtz Reaction

Both free radical and ionic mechanisms are suggested but ionic one is preferred as Formation of Na free radical is suspicious.

NEET concentrate

- The reaction is preferred for the formation of symmetrical alkanes (those with even no. of C-atoms)
- CH_4 can not be prepared by this reaction.
- If we use 2 different alkyl halides then a mixture of alkanes is produced i.e.,

$$CH_3X + C_2H_5X + 2\,Na \xrightarrow{\text{Dry Ether}} CH_3-CH_3 + CH_3-C_2H_5 + C_2H_5-C_2H_5 + NaX$$

Mixture of alkanes

Formed due to disproportionation (intermolecular hydrogenation of free radical)

By reduction of Acid & Carbonyl compounds

$$>C=O + 4[H] \xrightarrow{Zn-Hg/HCl} >CH_2 + H_2O$$

$$R(H)C=O + 4[H] \xrightarrow{Zn-Hg/HCl} R-CH_3 + H_2O$$

$$R_2C=O + 4[H] \xrightarrow{Zn-Hg/HCl} R-CH_2-R + H_2O$$

Clemmensen Reduction

Zn-Hg is the e^- provider while HCl is H^+ provider for the reaction & 4[H] is generated as —

$$2\,Zn \longrightarrow 2\,Zn^{2+} + 4e^-$$

$$4[H] \longleftarrow 4H^+ \text{ (taken up by } 4e^-)$$

$$>C=O \xrightarrow[-H_2O]{NH_2-NH_2} >C=N-NH_2 \text{ (Hydrazone)} \xrightarrow[450\,K]{C_2H_5O^-Na^+} >CH_2 + N_2 + H_2O$$

$$R-CHO \xrightarrow[-H_2O]{NH_2-NH_2} R-CH=N-NH_2 \xrightarrow[450\,K]{C_2H_5O^-Na^+} R-CH_3 + N_2 + H_2O$$

Wolf Kishner Reduction

Dhyan Rakhna ① Wolf kinerner reduction is the specific reaction for the reduction of $>C=O$ group to directly $>CH_2$ group ② It does not proceed through alcohol formation. ③ Hence, It is the most suitable reagent for

(ring with –OH and >C=O) ⟶ (ring with –OH) conversion.

Same reduction can also be carried out as

$RCHO \xrightarrow[\Delta]{Red\ P + HI} RCH_3$; $RCOCH_3 \xrightarrow[\Delta]{Red\ P + HI} RCH_2CH_3$

From Grignard Reagent

$RMgX + H_2O \xrightarrow[Ether]{Dry} RH + Mg(OH)X$

$RMgX + D_2O \xrightarrow[Ether]{Dry} RD + Mg(OD)X$

$RMgX + R'OH \xrightarrow[Ether]{Dry} RH + Mg(OR')X$

The reaction is an example of Protonolysis and seen in all such cases where any acid reacts with Grignard's reagent

NEET concentrate

➡ The alkyl group of alkane comes from Grignard's reagent and H from the acid taking part in the reaction

From Carboxylic Acid

$RCOO^-Na^+ + NaOH/CaO \xrightarrow{\Delta} Na_2CO_3 + RH$

$CH_3COONa + NaOH/CaO \xrightarrow{\Delta} CH_4 + Na_2CO_3$

Duma's Decarboxylation

NaOH/CaO → Sodalime in which

NaOH → Main functional partner

3:1

CaO → keep reaction medium dry.

→ This method is most effective for $CH_3COO^-Na^+$ while for higher carboxylic acids → Mixture of products are formed.

→ Directly Acid can also be taken in the reaction in which case → Sodalime first converts in to sodium salt and then decarboxylation takes place.

$2CH_3COO^-K^+(aq) \xrightarrow[current]{Electric} \underbrace{CH_3-CH_3 + 2CO_2}_{Anode} + \underbrace{2KOH + H_2}_{cathode}$

Kolbe's Electrolysis

If Pot. salts of different acids are used then mixture of Hydrocarbons are used which are difficult to separate.

NEET concentrate

- CH_4 cannot be synthesised by this method.
- Esters, lower alkanes & alkenes are obtained as by products.
- The reaction is used to create a new C–C bond as

$$\begin{matrix} CH_3COO^-K^+ \\ CH_3COO^-K^+ \end{matrix} \rightleftharpoons \begin{matrix} CH_3COO^- \\ CH_3COO^- \end{matrix} + 2K^+$$

at Cathode

$$\begin{matrix} CH_3COO^- \\ CH_3COO^- \end{matrix} \xrightarrow{-2e^-} \begin{matrix} CH_3COO \\ CH_3COO \end{matrix} \xrightarrow{-2CO_2} \begin{matrix} CH_3 \\ | \\ CH_3 \end{matrix}$$

New bond formation

Hydroboration

$$3R-CH=CH_2 + BH_3 \xrightarrow[DIGLYME]{THF} (R-CH_2-CH_2)_3B$$

$$(R-CH_2-CH_2)_3B \xrightarrow{H^+} 3RCH_2CH_3$$

$$(R-CH_2-CH_2)_3B \xrightarrow[NaOH]{AgNO_3} \begin{matrix} R-CH_2-CH_2 \\ | \\ R-CH_2-CH_2 \end{matrix}$$

THF → Tetrahydrofuran
DIGLYME → Diethylene glycol methyl ether.

Imp: The reaction is a Markovnikov's addition strictly but the products obtained appears to be Anti Markovnikov's because H is present in the reaction as H^- instead of H^+

By the Hydrolysis of Metal Carbides

$$Al_4C_3 + 12H_2O \xrightarrow{\Delta} 4Al(OH)_3 + 3CH_4$$

$$Be_2C + 4H_2O \xrightarrow{\Delta} 2Be(OH)_2 + CH_4$$

Physical Properties

- With low bp (as alkanes are non polar and have only weak van der Waal's forces between them)
- bp increases with increase in no. of C-atoms and bp decreases with increase in branching.

- The alkanes with even no. of C-atom have higher m.p. as compared to their odd no. successors. (as alkanes with even no. of C-atoms packed closely)
- Almost insoluble in water but easily soluble in organic solvents like ethanol & ether
- Alkanes are lighter than water.

Chemical Properties

Substitution Reactions

$CH_4 + Cl_2 \xrightarrow[\text{high temp.}]{h\nu \text{ or}} CH_3Cl + HCl$

$CH_3Cl \xrightarrow[-HCl]{Cl_2} CH_2Cl_2 \xrightarrow[-HCl]{Cl_2} CHCl_3 \xrightarrow[-HCl]{Cl_2} CCl_4$

Halogenation

Reactivity order of halogens

$F_2 > Cl_2 > Br_2 > I_2$

Reactivity order of Hydrogen

$3^\circ > 2^\circ > 1^\circ$

Mechanism (Free radical chain reaction)

- Initiation step (Single) $Cl_2 \xrightarrow[\text{or high temp.}]{h\nu} 2 \cdot Cl$
- Propagation steps (Multiple) $CH_4 + \cdot Cl \rightarrow \cdot CH_3 + HCl$
  $\cdot CH_3 + Cl_2 \rightarrow CH_3Cl + \cdot Cl$
- Termination steps (Multiple) $\cdot Cl + \cdot Cl \rightarrow Cl_2$
  $\cdot CH_3 + \cdot CH_3 \rightarrow C_2H_6$
  $\cdot CH_3 + \cdot Cl \rightarrow CH_3Cl$

NEET concentrate

- Propagation step proceeds in loop and continued until one of the substrate (CH_4 or Cl_2) is finished.
- The identification of all the 3 steps can be done as ⟶
  - (i) Initiation — Free radical present after the arrow
  - (ii) Propagation — Free radical present both the side of arrow
  - (iii) Termination — Free radical present before the arrow
- Iodination is very slow and reversible so it is carried out in the presence of oxidising agent like HIO_3 or HNO_3.

$$CH_3CH_2CH_3 \xrightarrow[425-750K]{HNO_3} CH_3CH_2CH_2NO_2 + CH_3\underset{NO_2}{\underset{|}{C}}HCH_3$$

Vapour Phase Nitration

In vapour phase cleavage occurs at all C–C and C–H bonds resulting to other products as well like nitromethane, nitroethane

---

$$RH + \underset{\text{(oleum)}}{H_2SO_4/SO_3} \longrightarrow RSO_3H + H_2SO_4$$

Sulphonation

Ease of Replacement of H
$3° > 2° > 1°$
Not shown by alkanes lower than hexane.

Oxidation Reactions

$$C_nH_{2n+2} + \left(\frac{3n+1}{2}\right)O_2 \xrightarrow{\Delta} nCO_2 + (n+1)H_2O + \text{Heat}$$

Generalised Equation for Combustion

$$C_nH_{2n+2} + O_2 \longrightarrow \underset{\text{Carbon Black}}{C} + H_2O + CO\uparrow$$

$$6CH_4 + 2O_2 \xrightarrow{1773K} 2CH\equiv CH + 2CO_2 + 10H_2$$

Incomplete combustion Reactions.

Controlled Oxidation

$$H-\underset{H}{\overset{H}{C}}-H \xrightarrow{[O]} H-\underset{H}{\overset{H}{C}}-OH \xrightarrow{[O]} H-\underset{OH}{\overset{H}{C}}-OH \xrightarrow[-H_2O]{[O]} H-\overset{H}{C}=O \xrightarrow{[O]} H-C(=O)-OH$$

NEET concentrate

$$CH_4 + O_2 \xrightarrow[\Delta]{Mo_2O_3} HCHO + H_2O$$

Synthesis Gas

$$CH_4 + \underset{\text{(steam)}}{H_2O} \xrightarrow[\text{Ni on alumina}]{1273K} CO + 3H_2$$

$$RCH_3 + \frac{3}{2}O_2 \xrightarrow{Ag_2O} RCOOH + H_2O$$

$$CH_3-CH_3 + 3O_2 \xrightarrow[\Delta]{(CH_3COO)_2Mn} 2CH_3COOH + 2H_2O$$

Any alkane with 3° H.

Imp. $(CH_3)_3CH + [O] \xrightarrow{KMnO_4} (CH_3)_3COH$

Thermal Catalytic Reactions

$$CH_3-CH_2-CH_2-CH_3 \xrightarrow[573\,K,\ 30-35\,atm]{anh.\ AlCl_3/HCl} CH_3-\underset{H}{\overset{CH_3}{C}}-CH_3$$

Isomerisation (involves 1,2 hydride or methyl shift)

$$n\text{-hexane} \xrightarrow[773\,K,\ 10-12\,atm]{Cr_2O_3/V_2O_5/Mo_2O_3} \text{(benzene)} + 4H_2$$

$$n\text{-heptane} \xrightarrow[773\,K,\ 10-12\,atm]{Cr_2O_3/V_2O_5/Mo_2O_3} \text{(toluene, } C_6H_5CH_3) + 4H_2$$

Aromatisation
Not shown by alkanes having less than 6 C

- All alkanes undergo pyrolysis (pyro → thermal; lysis → breakage) to give lower alkanes, alkenes and Hydrogen

$$\text{Alkane } (C_nH_{2n+2}) \xrightarrow{\text{Pyrolysis}}$$ Lower alkanes (all from n-1 to CH_4), Alkene (All possible forms from $CH_2=CH_2$ to n C atoms) H_2

$$C_3H_8 \xrightarrow{\text{Pyrolsis}} \underbrace{CH_3-CH=CH_2 + CH_2=CH_2}_{\text{Alkenes}} + \underbrace{C_2H_6 + CH_4}_{\text{Alkanes}} + H_2$$

Conformations

Infinite number of different spatial arrangements possible due to restricted rotation along C–C single bond

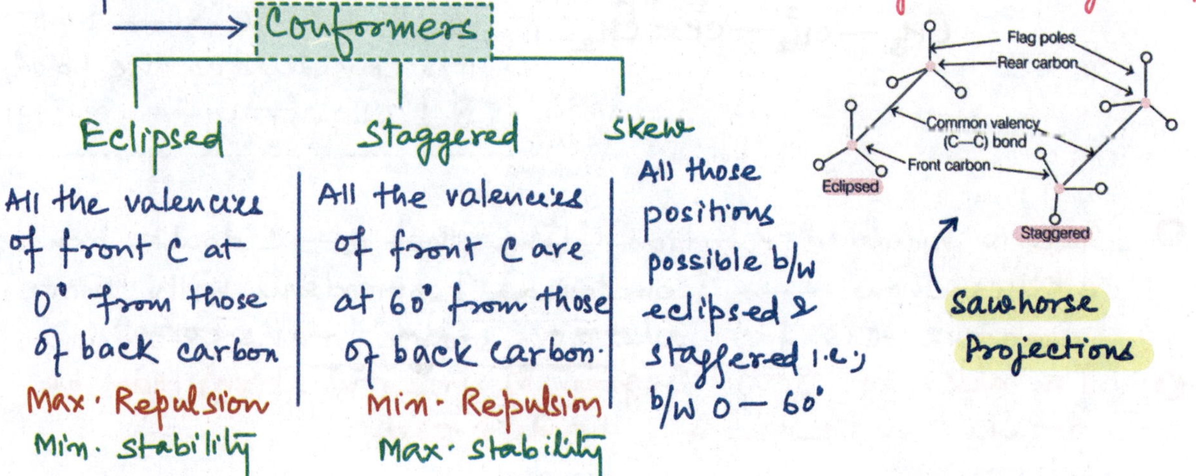

→ **Conformers**

- **Eclipsed**: All the valencies of front C at 0° from those of back carbon. Max. Repulsion, Min. stability
- **Staggered**: All the valencies of front C are at 60° from those of back carbon. Min. Repulsion, Max. stability
- **Skew**: All those positions possible b/w eclipsed & staggered i.e., b/w 0 – 60°

Sawhorse Projections

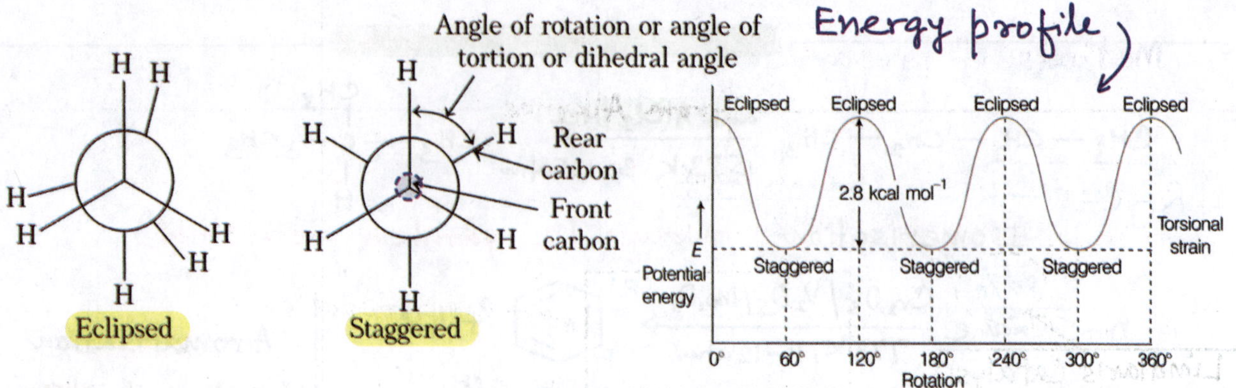

Alkene (C_nH_{2n})

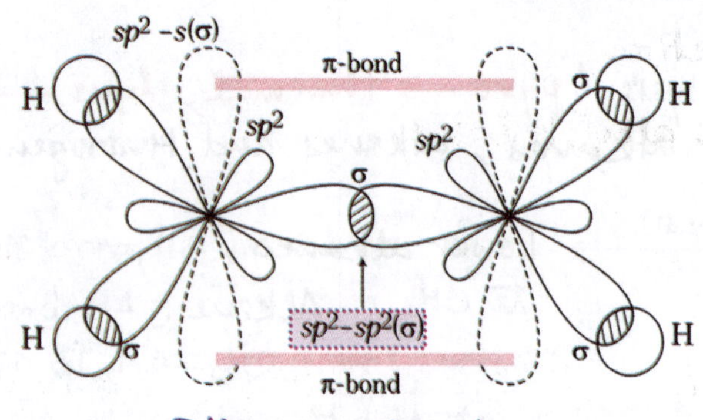

Ethene molecule

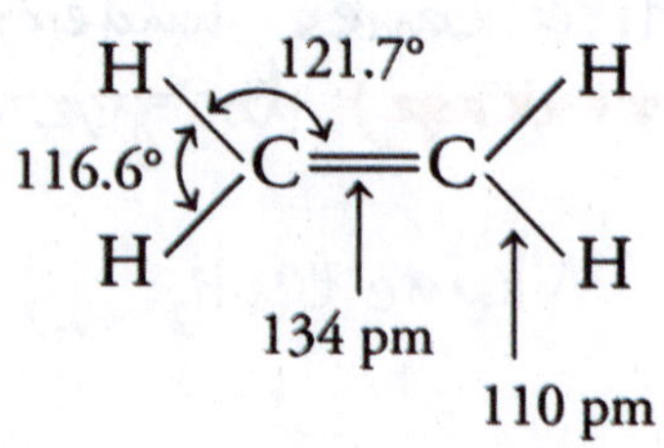

Bond Angle and Bond lengths

- Nomenclature ⟶ Alkane − ane + ene ⟶ Alkene

  Position of double bond ⟶ Always remember, double bond is considered of that C-atom which is having lower no.

  e.g.,

  $\overset{4}{C}H_3 - \overset{3}{C}H_2 - \overset{2}{C}H = \overset{1}{C}H_2$

  Although π bond is present b/w 1st & 2nd C-atom but it is considered as the bond of 1st C-atom.

- Due to hindered rotation along the C — C double bond alkenes show ⟶ Geometrical Isomerism with more reactive cis form and more stable trans form.
- In alkenes DOU (Degree of Unsaturation) can be counted by the no. of π bonds present.

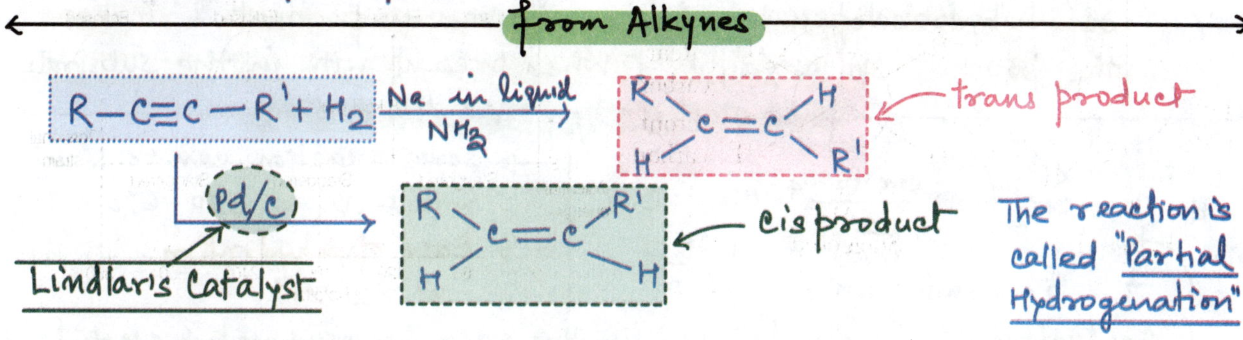

- Partial hydrogenation in the presence of Na in liquid NH_3 is called Birch Reduction.

from alkyl halides

$CH_3CH_2CH_2Cl \xrightarrow[\Delta]{alc \cdot KOH} CH_3CH=CH_2 + KCl + H_2O$

or

$CH_3\underset{|}{C}HCH_3$ (with Cl on the middle carbon)

$\overset{\beta}{CH_3}—\overset{\alpha}{CH}(X)—\overset{\beta}{CH_3}$

- Alc. KOH → Dehydrohalogenating agent i.e., removes H and X from alkyl halide
- Also called β-elimination (as H is removed from β-carbon with respect to Halogen)

→ Order of reactivity → $3° > 2° > 1°$

$RI > RBr > RCl$

NEET concentrate

For asymmetric Alkyl halides Saytzeff or Zaitsev rule is applicable → when alternatives are available then H will be removed from the C-atom with lesser no. of Hydrogens i.e., poor becomes poorer.

$\overset{}{CH_3}—\overset{\beta}{CH_2}—\overset{\alpha}{CH}(Br)—\overset{\beta}{CH_3} \xrightarrow[\Delta]{Alc \cdot KOH} CH_3—CH=CH—CH_3$ Major (80%)

$+ CH_3—CH_2—CH=CH_2$ Minor (20%)

C with less H (the CH_2 carbon)

This rule is not followed in the case of Quaternary amm salts/hydroxides like $CH_3—CH_2—CH(CH_3)N(CH_3)_3$

Dhyan Rakhna | Presence of conjugation ⟶ makes the process of Dehydrohalogenation faster if seen in product & makes the process slower/difficult when present with in the substrate

from alcohols by Acidic dehydration

$$H-\overset{\beta}{\underset{H}{\overset{H}{C}}}-\overset{\alpha}{CH_2}-OH \xrightarrow[\Delta\ 470K]{Conc.\ H_2SO_4} CH_2=CH_2 + H_2O$$

β – elimination

→ same reaction can be seen with Al_2O_3 at 620–670 K.

→ Ease of dehydration $3^\circ > 2^\circ > 1^\circ$

Saytzeff rule is also followed in this case for asymmetric alcohols.

By Hydroboration

$$3\ CH_3-C\equiv CH + BH_3 \xrightarrow[DIGLYME]{THF\ or} (CH_3-CH=CH)_3B$$

$$(CH_3-CH=CH)_3B \xrightarrow{H^+} CH_3-CH=CH_2$$

$$(CH_3-CH=CH)_3B \xrightarrow[NaOH]{AgNO_3} CH_3-CH=CH-CH=CH-CH_3 \text{ (coupling)}$$

THF & DIGLYME ⟶ form acid-base complex with B_2H_6 to form monomer BH_3

from vicinal dihalides

$$CH_3-\underset{Br}{CH}-\underset{Br}{CH}-CH_3 + Zn \xrightarrow[\Delta]{CH_3OH} CH_3-CH=CH-CH_3 + ZnBr_2$$

Dehalogenation.

NEET concentrate

→ If gem dihalide is taken as the substrate in the place of vic dihalide with Zn dust & Methanol ⟶ Alkynes are produced.

→ NaI with acetone can also be used in the place of Zn dust

* To increase the no. of C-atoms in alkenes, Grignard's reagents can be used i.e., ⟶ $RMgX + XCH_2-CH=CH_2 \xrightarrow{-MgX_2} R-CH_2-CH=CH_2$
* Electrolysis of pot. succinate gives ethene by kolbe's electrolysis.

Physical Properties

→ bp increases with increase in mol. mass (about 20–30 K per 14 amu)

→ cis alkenene ⟶ higher bp in comparison to trans counter part (as dipole moment of cis alkenes is higher)

→ mp of trans alkene > cis alkene (as packing in trans isomer is better for being more symmetrical)

→ Insoluble in polar solvents but fairly soluble in non polar solvents (e.g., benzene, petroleum ether)

→ Lighter than H_2O, density gradually increases with rise in molecular mass.

Chemical Properties

→ Due to more exposed π e^- clouds unsaturated and aromatic hydrocarbons are more prone to be attacked by electrophiles

1. $CH_2=CH_2 + H_2 \xrightarrow[250-350°C]{Ni/Pt/Pd} CH_3-CH_3$ (Hydrogenation)

2. $CH_2=CH_2 + X_2 \xrightarrow{CCl_4} \underset{X}{CH_2}-\underset{X}{CH_2}$ (Halogenation)

NEET concentrate

→ I_2 is not added under normal conditions

→ In both the above written reactions, reagent show heterolysis → E^+ & Nu^- generated, out of which E^+ initiates the reaction (e.g., $Cl_2 \rightarrow Cl^+$ (chloronium) and Cl^- (chloride) ion. Out of which chloronium ion attacks on the π e^- cloud first.

Thus these reactions are called Electrophilic additions.

→ Addition of Br_2 as bromine water → decolorises bromine water → Test of unsaturation.

Addition of Halogen halides

$-\overset{|}{C}=\overset{|}{C}- + HX \rightarrow -\underset{H}{\overset{|}{C}}-\underset{X}{\overset{|}{C}}-$

- If alkene is symmetrical → No issues, H & X can be attached to either of doubly bonded C-atom
- If alkene is asymmetrical → Issue is there and Markovnikov's rule is followed.

$CH_3-CH=CH_2 + HBr \longrightarrow CH_3-CH(Br)-CH_3$ (Major)

Asymmetrical alkene (Propene)

$CH_3-CH_2-CH_2Br$ (Minor)

Mechanism — Electrophilic addition

$HBr \longrightarrow H^+ (E^+) + Br^- (Nu^-)$

E^+ initiates the attack

① $CH(CH_3)$ = ② CH_2 — 2 possibilities:

$CH_3-\overset{+}{C}H-CH_3$ (when H^+ is attached to C-atom ②) 2° More stable

$CH_3-CH_2-\overset{+}{C}H_2$ (when H^+ is attached to C-atom ①) 1° less stable

We know that 2° carbonium Ion is more stable than 1° so 2° carbonium ion forms major product

$CH_3-\overset{+}{C}H-CH_3 \xrightarrow{Br^-} CH_3-CH(Br)-CH_3$ (Major product)

$CH_3-CH_2-\overset{+}{C}H_2 \xrightarrow{Br^-} CH_3-CH_2-CH_2Br$ (Minor product)

The rule — when an asymmetrical reagent is added to an asymmetrical alkene (Problem statement) then (+)ve part of addendum goes to that C-atom containing more no. of Hydrogen (solution statement)

→ However, in the presence of peroxide this rule is not followed (Kharasch effect or peroxide effect) → This is so because free radical mechanism is followed in this case.

Mechanism

$R-O-O-R \longrightarrow 2RO\cdot$

$H-Br \longrightarrow H\cdot + \cdot Br$

$CH_3-CH=CH_2 + \cdot Br \longrightarrow$

$CH_3-CH(Br)-\dot{C}H_2$ 1° less stable $\longrightarrow CH_3-CH(Br)-CH_3$ Minor product

$CH_3-\dot{C}H-CH_2Br$ 2° More stable $\xrightarrow{HBr} CH_3CH_2CH_2Br + \cdot Br$ Major Product

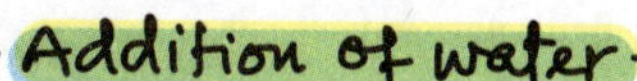

Addition of water

$CH_3-CH=CH_2 + H_2O \xrightarrow{H^+} CH_3-\underset{OH}{\underset{|}{CH}}-CH_3$

* Reaction proceeds in the presence of few drops of conc. H_2SO_4

→ Alkenes also form alkyl hydrogen sulphates on reaction with conc. H_2SO_4 at room temperature.

Ozonolysis

$>C=C< \xrightarrow{O_3}$ Ozonide $\xrightarrow[\text{Normal Hydrolysis}]{Zn}$ $2\ >C=O$ (Carbonyl compounds) $+ H_2O \longrightarrow H_2O_2$

Ozonide → Oxidative Hydrolysis → Oxidation Products of carbonyl compounds

Ozonide $\xrightarrow[\text{Reductive Hydrolysis}]{LiAlH_4}$ Reduction products of carbonyl compounds

* Ozonide formation followed by lysis.
* H_2O_2 is the byproduct of this reaction
* Oxidative hydrolysis occurs in the absence of any reagent & in it H_2O_2 → auto oxidation

NEET concentrate

→ In normal hydrolysis mild reducing agent (like Zn) is used which nullifies the oxidative activity of H_2O_2.

→ In reductive Hydrolysis strong reducing agent (like $LiAlH_4$) is used which not only nullifies the oxidative activity of H_2O_2 but also reduces the products formed i.e., carbonyl compounds.

→ The reaction is highly useful in detecting the position of π bond in alkenes & other unsaturated compounds.

Oxidation by $KMnO_4$

$>C=C< \xrightarrow[KMnO_4]{\text{cold or alkaline}} >\underset{>C-OH}{\underset{|}{C-OH}}$

* $KMnO_4$ decolorises.
* Cold or Dil. $KMnO_4$ is also called Baeyer's Reagent

It is basically mild oxidation where only π bond is oxidised to $-C-OH$ bond.

→ It is also the test of unsaturation

→ $>C=C<$ $\xrightarrow[\text{KMnO}_4]{\text{Hot or acidic}}$ $2 >C=O$ means both σ and π bonds are oxidised, even C–H bonds are also oxidised to produce either acids or acids + Ketones. It is infact vigorous oxidation.

Polymerisation

$n(CH_2=CH_2) \xrightarrow[\text{Pressure}]{O_2,\ \text{Heat}} -\!\!(CH_2-CH_2)\!\!-_n$

Polyethylene

$n(CH_2=CH-CH=CH_2) \xrightarrow[\text{Pressure}]{O_2,\ \text{Heat}} [CH_2-CH=CH-CH_2]_n$

Polybutadiene

$n(CH_2=\underset{|}{\overset{CH_3}{C}}-CH=CH_2) \xrightarrow[\text{Pressure}]{O_2,\ \text{Heat}} [CH_2-\underset{CH_3}{\underset{|}{C}}=CH-CH_2]_n$

Polyisoprene (Natural Rubber)

Alkynes (C_nH_{2n-2})

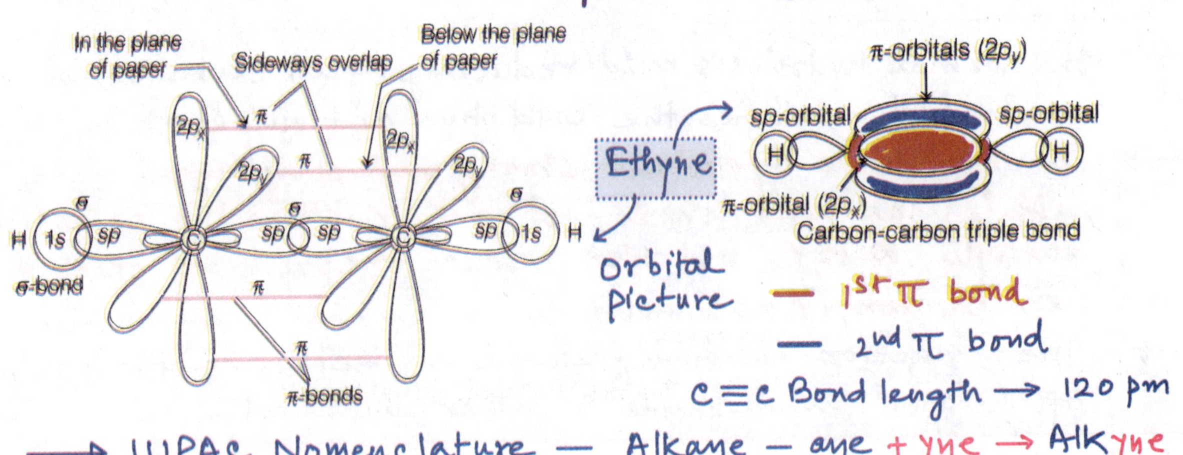

→ IUPAC Nomenclature — Alkane – ane + yne → Alkyne

Dhyan Rakhna | Just like alkyl group, the branch of alkene (i.e., Alkene – H) ⟶ Alkenyl eg. Ethenyl, Propenyl

Similarly Alkyne – H ⟶ Alkynyl eg. Ethynyl, Propynyl

so whenever you found a double bond/ triple bond in branch then don't get confused & simply use these prefixes

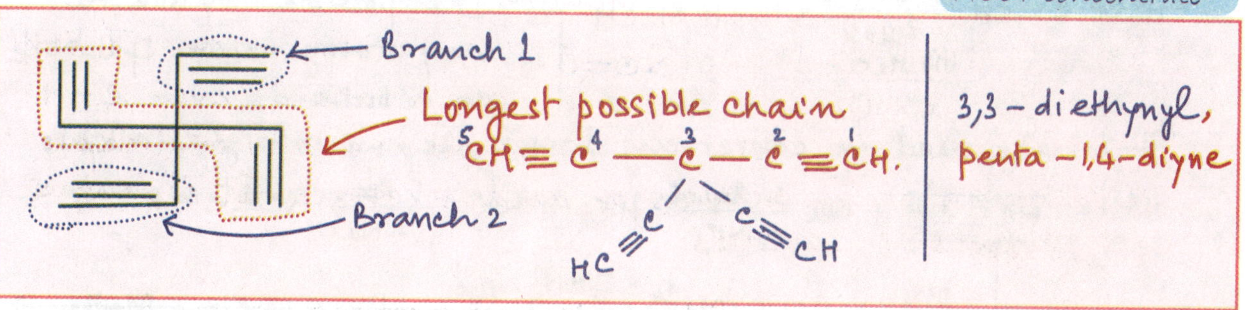

→ Alkynes only show chain, position & Ring chain isomerism while these donot show any geometrical & stereoisomerism

Methods of Preparation

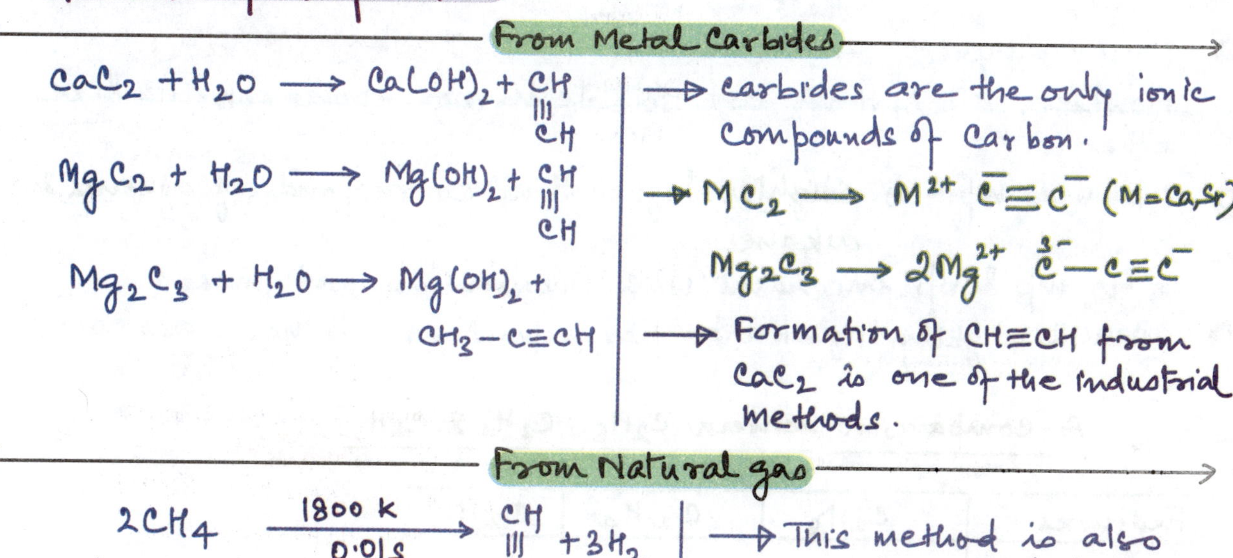

from vicinal dihalides

$$R-\underset{H}{\overset{Br}{C}}-\underset{Br}{\overset{H}{C}}-H \xrightarrow[-HBr]{Alc.\ KOH} R-\underset{H}{C}=\underset{Br}{C}-H \xrightarrow[-HBr]{alc.\ KOH} R-C\equiv C-R$$

Fast (first step); slow (second step)

$NaNH_2$ or KNH_2 single step.

$NaNH_2$ or KNH_2 is usually used with liquid NH_3

Isomerisation also results in both the cases

$CH_3CH_2C\equiv CH \xrightarrow[\text{(ii) } H_2O]{\text{(i) } NaNH_2,\ 420\,K} CH_3CH_2C\equiv CH$ → It is possible only due to very strong nature of $NaNH_2$ as a base.

It is also used in converting lower alkynes to higher alkynes

i.e., $HC\equiv CH + Na \xrightarrow{\text{In liquid } NH_3} HC\equiv C^-Na^+ \xrightarrow[-NaX]{RX} HC\equiv C-R$

$HC\equiv CH \xrightarrow{RMgX} RH + Mg\begin{smallmatrix} C\equiv CH \\ X \end{smallmatrix} \xrightarrow{RX} R-C\equiv CH + MgX_2$

Physical Properties

- First 3 alkynes → Gases; next 8 → Liquids; Rest → solids
- Lower alkynes → lighter than water & insoluble in it. However, all of them are soluble in non-polar solvents like ether.
- bp and mp → slightly higher than corresponding alkenes & alkanes.
  → mp & bp increases with increase in mol. mass.
- Density slightly higher than corresponding alkenes & alkanes.

A comparison between C_2H_6, C_2H_4 & C_2H_2

Features	C_2H_6	C_2H_4	C_2H_2
Degree of unsat. (DU)	0	1	2
C–C Bond length	153 pm	134 pm	120 pm
C–H Bond length	111 pm	110 pm	110 pm
C–C Bond Energy	368 kJ/mol	611 kJ/mol	820 kJ/mol
C–H Bond Energy	410 kJ/mol	452 kJ/mol	536 kJ/mol
Hybridisation	sp^3	sp^2	sp

820 kJ/mol ← Most difficult to break (all the 3 bonds)

Chemical Properties

Alkynes
- Terminal alkynes → Acidic Nature
- Interstial alkynes → Non acidic

- $R-C\equiv CH + Na \xrightarrow{\text{Liquid } NH_3} R-C\equiv C^-Na^+ + H_2\uparrow$
  - $\xrightarrow{\text{Tollen's Reagent}} R-C\equiv C^-Ag^+$ silver acetylide — White ppt.
  - $\xrightarrow{\text{Fehling's solution}} R-C\equiv C^-Cu^+$ copper acetylide — Red ppt.

→ Reactions of terminal alkynes
→ These are helpful in identifying the position of triple bond.

	Relative acidity		Relative basicity
Strongest acid ↑	H_2O	↑ (max)	$OH^{\ominus}$
	ROH		$RO^{\ominus}$
	$RC\equiv CH$		$RC\equiv C^{\ominus}$
	NH_3		$NH_2^{\ominus}$
	$CH_2=CH_2$		$CH_2=CH^{\ominus}$
Weakest acid	CH_3CH_3	↓	$CH_3CH_2^{\ominus}$ (max)

← Relative acidic strengths
Weaker acids have stronger conjugate bases & vice versa

Addition Reactions

1. $-C\equiv C- + H_2 \xrightarrow[250-350^\circ]{Pd/Ni/Pt} -CH=CH- \xrightarrow{H_2} -CH_2-CH_2-$

   Addition of Hydrogen → Reaction can be stopped at alkene If we use Lindlar's catalyst

2. $-C\equiv C- + X_2 \xrightarrow{CCl_4} -CX=CX- \xrightarrow{H_2} -CX_2-CX_2-$

   Addition of Halogens

   → If Br_2 water is used in the reaction ⇝ Test of Unsaturation.

3. $-C\equiv C- + HX \longrightarrow -CH=CX- \xrightarrow{HX} -CH_2-CX_2-$

   Addition of HX

   According to Markovnikov's rule

NEET concentrate

Hydrogenation in the presence of Lindlar's catalyst
Hydrogenation in the presence of P-2 catalyst } → Syn addition
Ni_2B (Nickel boride) → (P-2 catalyst)

Hydrogenation with Li or Na in the presence of Liquid NH_3 ⟶ anti addition

4. $—C\equiv C— + H_2O \xrightarrow[42\%\ H_2SO_4]{1\%\ HgSO_4} —\underset{H}{\overset{|}{C}}=\underset{OH}{\overset{|}{C}}—$

Addition of water

⇅ Tautomerise

$—\underset{H}{\overset{H}{\overset{|}{C}}}—\underset{O}{\overset{||}{C}}—$

NEET concentrate

Alkynes are less reactive than alkenes towards electrophilic additions as

Cyclic Intermediates

$>C—C<$ with $\overset{\oplus}{E}$ bridging: From alkene (Less strained more stable)

$—C=C—$ with $\overset{+}{E}$ bridging: From alkyne (More strained less stable)

Dhyan Rakho! Stability of Intermediate ∝ Reactivity of a compound

Polymerisation

$CH\equiv CH \xrightarrow[NH_4Cl]{Cu_2Cl_2} CH_2=CH—C\equiv CH \xrightarrow[Cu_2Cl_2/NH_4Cl]{HC\equiv CH} CH_2=CH—C\equiv C—CH=CH_2$

Linear Polymerisation

Cyclic Polymerisation

$3HC\equiv CH \xrightarrow[500°C]{\text{Red hot Cu or Fe tube}}$ Benzene

Ethyne

$3CH_3—C\equiv CH \xrightarrow[500°C]{\text{Red hot Cu or Fe tube}}$ Mesitylene (1,3,5-trimethylbenzene, CH_3, CH_3, CH_3)

Propyne

$4HC\equiv CH \xrightarrow[Ni(CN)_2]{\text{THF (Solvent), High Pressure}}$ Cyclooctatetraene

Isomerisation

$CH_3—CH_2—C\equiv CH \xrightarrow[THF/Heat]{alc.\ KOH} CH_3—C\equiv C—CH_3 \xrightarrow[-NH_3]{NaNH_2} CH_3CH_2—C\equiv C^-Na^+$

$CH_3CH_2—C\equiv C^-Na^+ \xrightarrow{Hydrolysis} CH_3—CH_2—C\equiv CH$

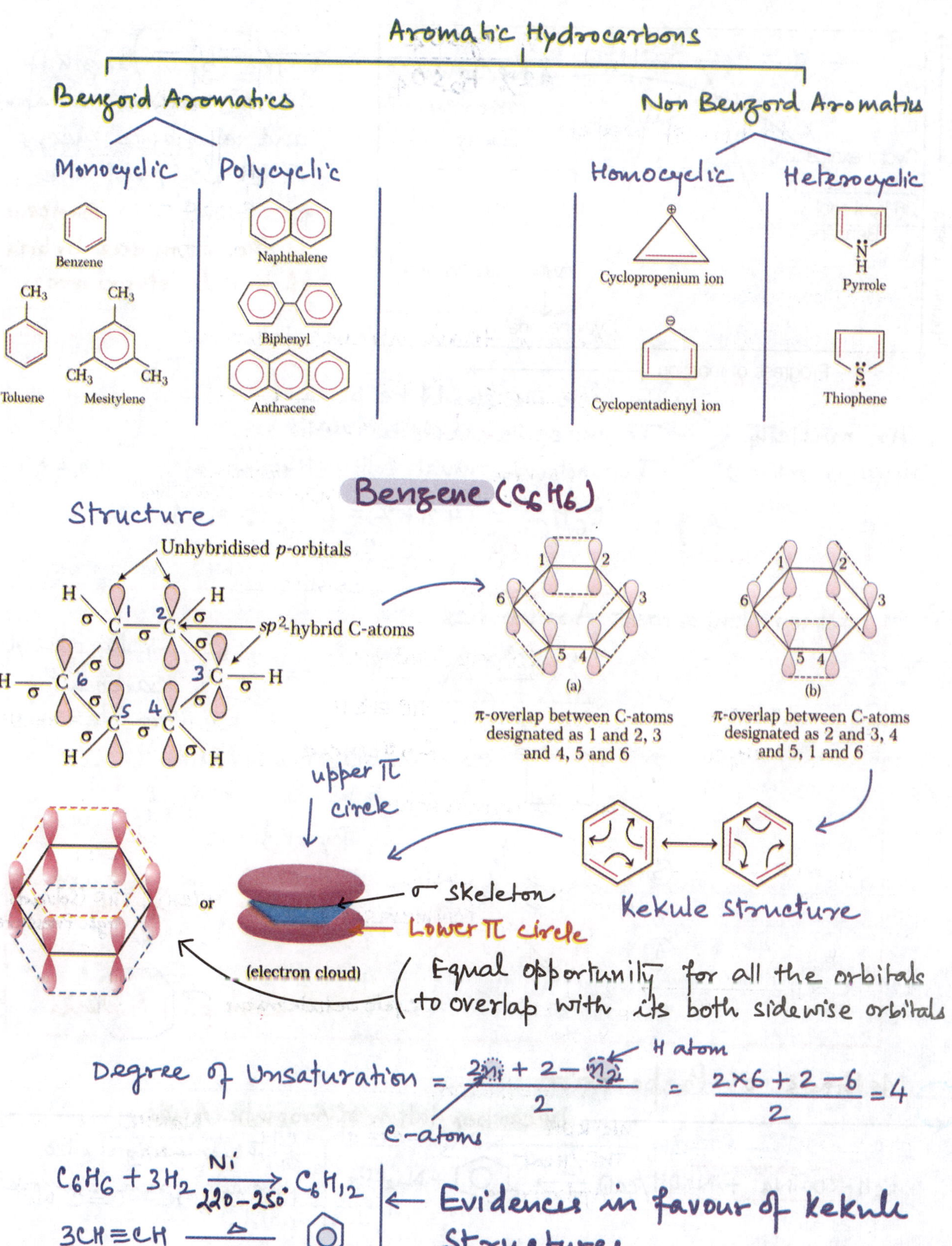
Aromatic Hydrocarbons
Benzoid Aromatics
Non Benzoid Aromatics
Monocyclic
Polycyclic
Homocyclic
Heterocyclic
Benzene
Toluene
Mesitylene
CH3
Naphthalene
Biphenyl
Anthracene
Cyclopropenium ion
Cyclopentadienyl ion
Pyrrole
Thiophene
Benzene (C6H6)
Structure
Unhybridised p-orbitals
sp2-hybrid C-atoms
(a)
π-overlap between C-atoms designated as 1 and 2, 3 and 4, 5 and 6
(b)
π-overlap between C-atoms designated as 2 and 3, 4 and 5, 1 and 6
Kekule Structure
upper π circle
σ skeleton
Lower π circle
or
(electron cloud)
Equal opportunity for all the orbitals to overlap with its both sidewise orbitals
Degree of Unsaturation = (2n1 + 2 − n2)/2 = (2×6 + 2 − 6)/2 = 4
H atom
C-atoms
C6H6 + 3H2 —Ni, 220–250°→ C6H12
3CH≡CH —Δ→
Evidences in favour of Kekule Structures.

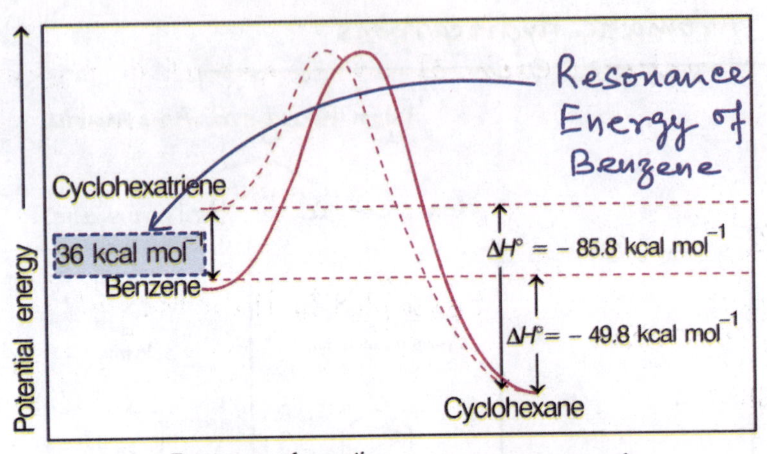

→ The bond length of 1.39 A° between C-atoms and resonance energy of 36 kcal/mol are the proves ⟶ Benzene is the resonance hybrid of Kekule structures.

Aromaticity (Necessary conditions)
- The molecule should be planar.
- The molecule should be cyclic.
- The molecule must follow Huckel Rule → $4n+2 = \pi e^-$

e.g., $C_6H_6 = 4n+2 = 6 \Rightarrow n = 1$

NEET concentrate

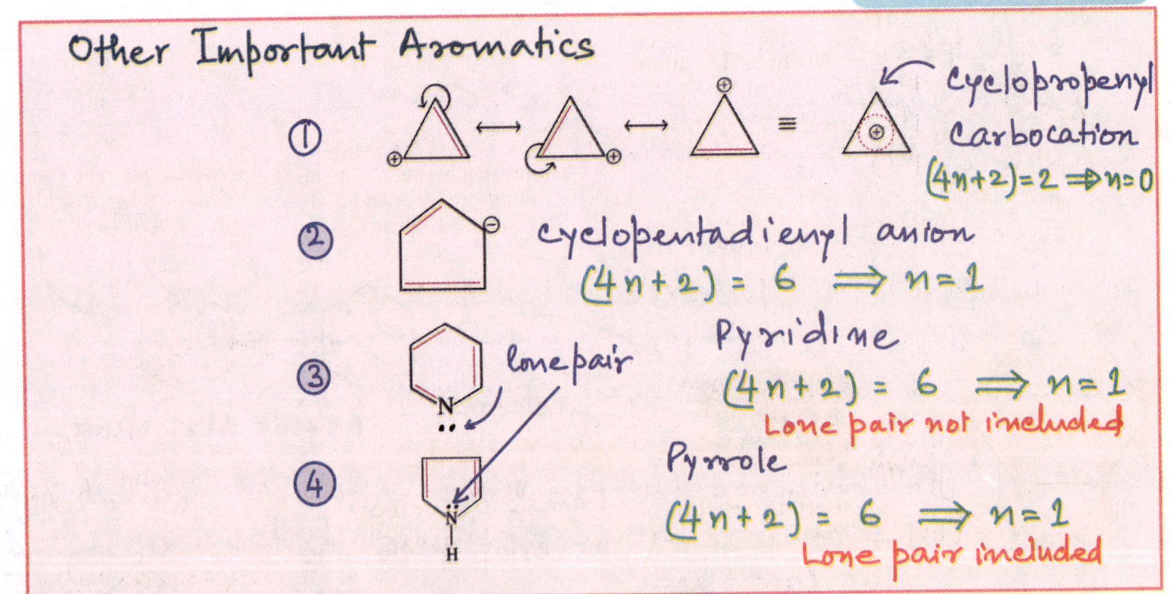

Methods of Preparation

Decarboxylation of Aromatic Acids

$C_6H_5COO^-Na^+ + NaOH/CaO \xrightarrow{\Delta}$ (benzene) $+ Na_2CO_3$

→ The reaction also proceeds from Benzoic acid.

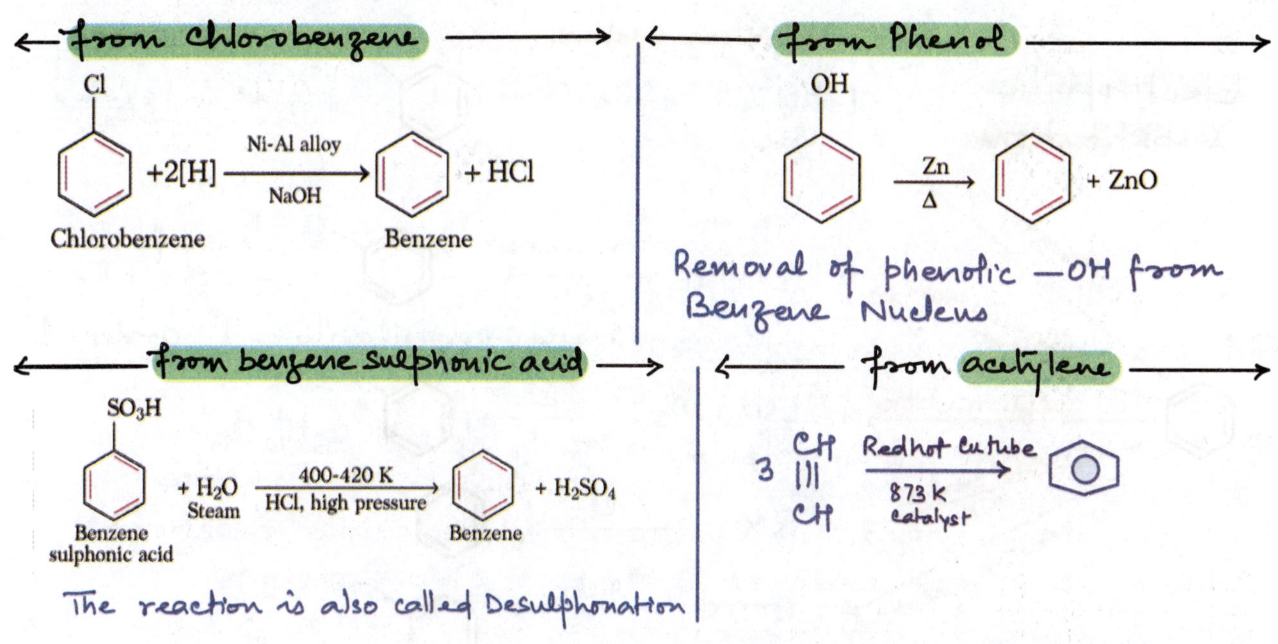

NEET concentrate

Benzene can also be prepared from $C_6H_5\overset{+}{N_2}Cl^-$ as

$$C_6H_5\overset{+}{N_2}Cl^- \xrightarrow[\text{warm}]{CH_3CH_2OH} C_6H_6 + CH_3CHO + N_2 + HCl$$

$$C_6H_5\overset{+}{N_2}Cl^- \xrightarrow[SnCl_2]{2[H] + NaOH} C_6H_6 + HCl + N_2$$

$$C_6H_5\overset{+}{N_2}Cl^- \xrightarrow{H_3PO_2 + H_2O} C_6H_6 + H_3PO_3 + N_2 + HCl.$$

Physical Properties

- Colourless, volalite liquid, insoluble in water but soluble in organic solvents.
- Inflammable & burns with sooty flame
- mp and bp of aromatic hydrocarbons increases with increase in molar mass.
- Aromatic hydrocarbons are toxic and carcinogenic in nature.

Chemical Properties

Benzene and its homologues show electrophilic substitutions.

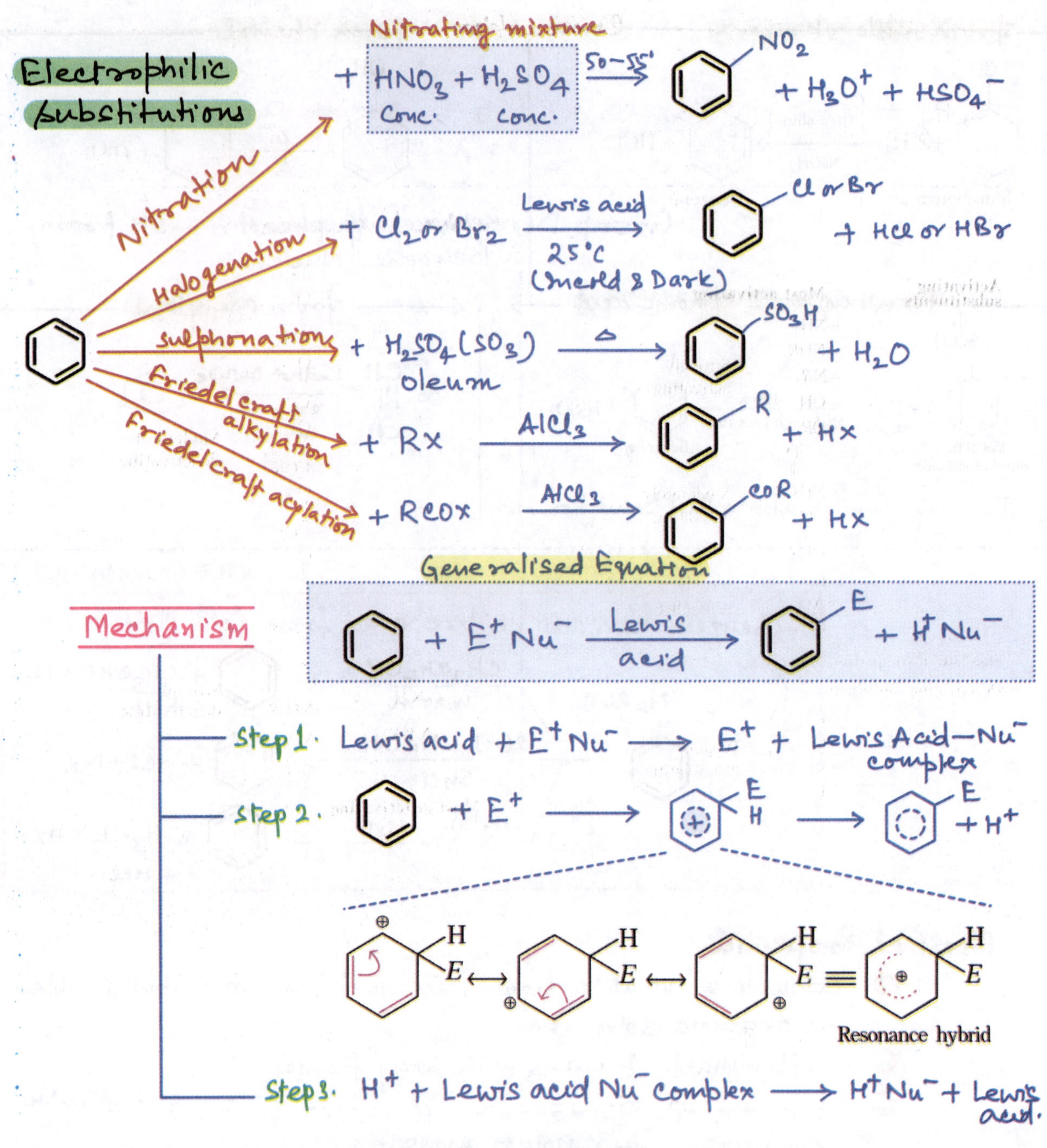

Addition Reactions

1. $C_6H_6 + 3H_2 \xrightarrow[\Delta]{Ni}$ C_6H_{12}

Hydrogenation

2. $C_6H_6 + 3Cl_2 \xrightarrow[500K]{UV}$ $C_6H_6Cl_6$

Benzene Hexa Chloride or 666 or BHC

$$C_xH_y + \left[x + \frac{y}{4}\right] O_2 \longrightarrow xCO_2 + \frac{y}{2} H_2O \quad ; \quad C_6H_6 + \frac{15}{2} O_2 \longrightarrow 6CO_2 + 2H_2O$$

Group Directive Influence

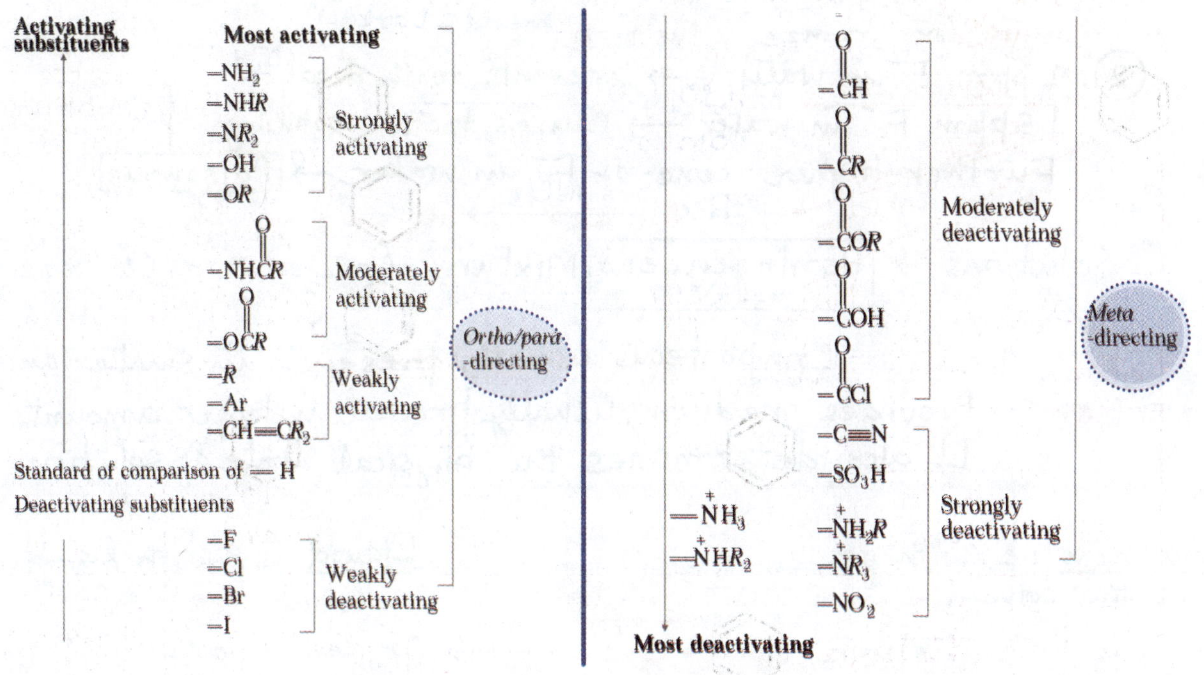

10. Solutions

- Pure substances are rare; Most of the substances around us are Mixtures. Utility of mixtures in life depends upon their composition e.g.,
  1. Brass (Cu+Zn) is quite different from German silver (Cu+Zn+Ni) or Bronze (Cu+Sn)
  2. 1 ppm F^- in water ⟶ prevents tooth decay
     1.5 ppm F^- in water ⟶ Causes tooth mottling
     Further Higher conc. of F^- in water ⟶ Poisonous → Na^+F^- Rat Poison

- Solutions — Homogeneous (All components in same phase) Mixture of 2 or more components
  - Solute – Component usually present in smaller amount.
  - Solvent – Provides medium, usually present in larger amount. It also determines the physical state of solution.

BINARY SOLUTIONS — Solutions with 2 components only i.e., Solute + Solvent

Gaseous i.e., with gas as the solvent e.g.,	Solute	Liquid i.e., with liquid solvent e.g.,
1. $N_2 + O_2$ Mixture	Gas	1. Oxygen + water mixture
2. $CHCl_3 + N_2$ Mixture	Liquid	2. Ethanol + water mixture
3. Camphor + N_2 Mixture	Solid.	3. Glucose + water mixture

Solid i.e., with solid solvent e.g.,

Solid solvent	Solute
1. H_2 + Pd mixture	Gas
2. Hg + Na Amalgam	Liquid
3. Copper + Gold Alloy (Cu dissolved in gold)	Solid

NEET concentrate

- H_2 + Pd mixture is formed by the adherence of H_2 molecules over Pd.
- Technically, the process is called OCCLUSION.
- In this solution the quantity of solute is much more than solvent
- Pd → can occlude 17 times more H_2 than its own volume.

Concentration Terms

- **Mass percentage (w/w)** – $\frac{\text{Component mass in solution}}{\text{Total mass of solution}} \times 100$

  e.g., 10% Glucose in water → 10g Glucose + 90g water

  3.62% NaOCl in water → 3.62 g NaOCl + 96.38g water

  Use – In Industrial chemical applications.

- **Volume percentage (V/V)** – $\frac{\text{Component volume in solution}}{\text{Total volume of solution}} \times 100$

  e.g., 10% C_2H_5OH in water → 10 mL C_2H_5OH + 90 mL water

  35% (V/V) Ethylene glycol solution ⟶ ANTIFREEZE → Lowers Freezing point of water to 255.4 K (−17.6°C)

  Use – In expressing concentration of liquid solutions.

→ Mass by volume (W/V) i.e., mass of solute in grams dissolved in 100 mL of solution ⟶ Used in Medicine and Pharmacy

- **Parts per Million (ppm)** – $\frac{\text{Number of component parts}}{\text{Total parts of all components}} \times 10^6$

  Used when solute present in traces.

  e.g., 1030 g H_2O (1 L sea water) with 6×10^{-3} g O_2 = 5.8 ppm.

  Use – Concentration of pollutants in water or air

- **Mole fraction (x)** – $\frac{\text{Number of moles of component}}{\text{Total moles of all components}}$

  $X_A = \frac{n_A}{n_A + n_B}$

  $X_B = \frac{n_B}{n_A + n_B}$

→ The sum of all the mole fractions of a given solution is always 1 ($X_A + X_B = 1$)

- **Molarity (M)** –

  $\frac{\text{Moles of Solute}}{\text{Volume of Solution in litre}}$

  0.25 M NaOH = 0.25 mol of NaOH in 1 Litre = 9.99925 g NaOH in 1 L solution = 0.25 mol L^{-1}

  M is temperature dependent (as volume is temp. dependent)

- **Molality (m)** –

  $\frac{\text{Moles of Solute}}{\text{mass of solvent in kg}}$

  1.00 m = 1 mol of KCl in 1 kg of water = 74.5g KCl in 1 kg solvent = 74.5g KCl in 1 kg water

  m is temperature independent (as mass is temp. independent)

NEET concentrate

Molarity, Formality and Normality are equivalent terms with slight differences –
(a) Molarity → Molecular Mass dependent
(b) Formality → Formula Mass dependent
(c) Normality → Equivalent mass dependent.

Always Remember,
Molecular Mass = formula Mass = n factor × Equivalent Mass

Solubility Maximum amount of solute that can be dissolved in specified amount of solvent at a particular temperature.

Depends upon → Nature of solute + solvent + temperature + pressure

1. **Solubility of solid in a liquid** – "LIKE DISSOLVES LIKE"
   a. Polar solutes like NaCl, Sugar easily dissolve in H_2O but Naphthalene, Anthracene donot
   b. Naphthalene, Anthracene dissolve in Benzene but NaCl, Sugar donot.

Saturated Solution – When Dissolution & Crystallisation in a solution are in Dynamic Equilibrium.

➡ Thus concentration of solute will remain constant under given conditions of temperature and pressure.

◎ It contains maximum amount of solute dissolved in given amount of solvent.

Solubility decrease in Exothermic reactions ← Temperature increase → Solubility increase in Endothermic reactions

➡ No effect of change in pressure on solubility of solids in liquids (as both solids and liquids are highly incompressible)

2. **Solubility of Gases in a liquid** – O_2 → less soluble in water
   HCl gas → Highly soluble in water.

◎ Greatly affected by temperature and pressure.

Statement of Henry's Law supported by – Dalton Independently.

Solubility of a gas in a liquid is directly proportional to the partial pressure of the gas present above the surface of liquid or solution

◎ Thus, solubility of gases increases with increase in partial pressure.

◎ If measure of solubility = Mole fraction then we can say

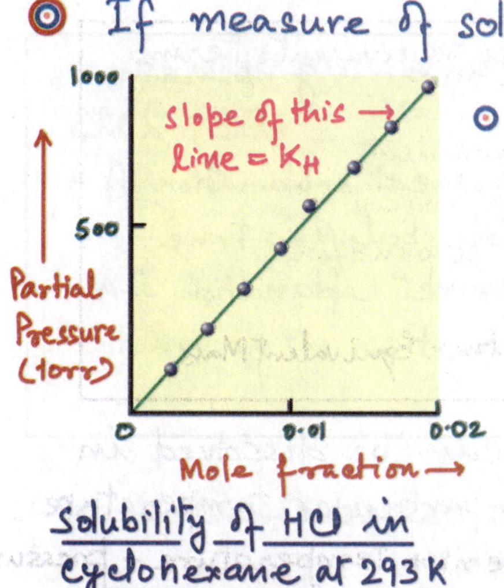

Solubility of HCl in cyclohexane at 293 K

- Mole fraction of a gas in the solution is directly proportional to the partial pressure of the gas. Or we can say
  The partial pressure of the gas in vapour phase (p) is directly proportional to the mole fraction (χ) of the gas i.e.,
  $p \propto \chi$ or $p = K_H \chi$ — Henry's law constant

At a given pressure

$$\text{solubility} \propto \frac{1}{K_H}$$

- Different gases have different K_H values at same temperature means
  $K_H \rightarrow$ Function of Nature of gas.

- Indicates solubility of these gases in water decrease with increase in temperature → (N_2, O_2 rows)

Gas	Temperature/K	K_H /kbar	Gas	Temperature/K	K_H/kbar
He	293	144.97	Argon	298	40.3
H_2	293	69.16	CO_2	298	1.67
N_2	293	76.48	Formaldehyde	298	1.83×10^{-5}
N_2	303	88.84	Methane	298	0.413
O_2	293	34.86	Vinyl chloride	298	0.611
O_2	303	46.82			

That's why aquatic organisms are more comfortable in cold waters rather than in warm waters.

PYQ Punch

The Henry's law constant (K_H) values of 3 gases (A, B, C) in water are 145, 2×10^{-5} and 35 kbar respectively. The solubility of these gases in water follows the order **NEET 2024**

(a) B > A > C ✓(b) B > C > A (c) A > C > B (d) A > B > C

Sol. Solubility $\propto \frac{1}{K_H}$ hence the gas with minimum K_H value (2×10^{-5} k bar) will have maximum solubility.

Applications of Henry's law

- Under high pressure solubility of CO_2 is increased in soft drinks
- Painful and dangerous Bends in scuba divers due to pressure variations inside sea. Air diluted with He (11·7% He, 56·2% N_2 and 32·1% O_2) is used in their tanks to avoid bends.

PYQ Punch

Assertion Helium is used to dilute Oxygen in diving apparatus
Reason Helium has high solubility in O_2 NEET 2023

(a) Both A & R are true but R is not the correct explanation of A
(b) A is true but R is false (c) A is false but R is true
(d) Both A & R are true and R is the correct explanation of A.

Sol. At normal temperature and pressure Helium is practically insoluble in Oxygen.

- Low concentrations of O_2 in the blood and tissues of people living at high altitude due to less partial pressure of O_2 in atmosphere

⇒ **Anoxia** – condition of practically no available oxygen. Anoxia in climbers results to weak body & inability to think clearly

Effect of Temperature

As Dissolution is Exothermic and involves dynamic equilibrium. ⇒ $\text{SOLUBILITY} \propto \frac{1}{\text{Temperature}}$

NEET concentrate

The gaseous phase of a liquid which is always present above its liquid phase is called vapour of that liquid

Vapour Pressure of Liquid – Liquid Solutions

Dhyan Rakho!

The pressure exerted by the vapour of a liquid over the uppermost layer of it is called VAPOUR PRESSURE.

Statement of Roult's Law ⇒ For a solution of volatile liquids the partial pressure of each component of solution is directly proportional to its mole fraction in the solution.

For any binary solution

p_1 & p_2 = partial pressures
χ_1 & χ_2 = mole fractions of components 1 & 2

$$p_{total} = \chi_1 p_1^0 + \chi_2 p_2^0 = (1-\chi_2)p_1^0 + \chi_2 p_2^0$$
$$= p_1^0 + (p_2^0 - p_1^0)\chi_2$$

Conclusions drawn from final outcome is

- Total Vapour pressure varies linearly with χ_2 (as it is related to any one component only)
- This total vapour pressure increases or decreases with the increase of x_1 (as it depends on V.P. of pure components)

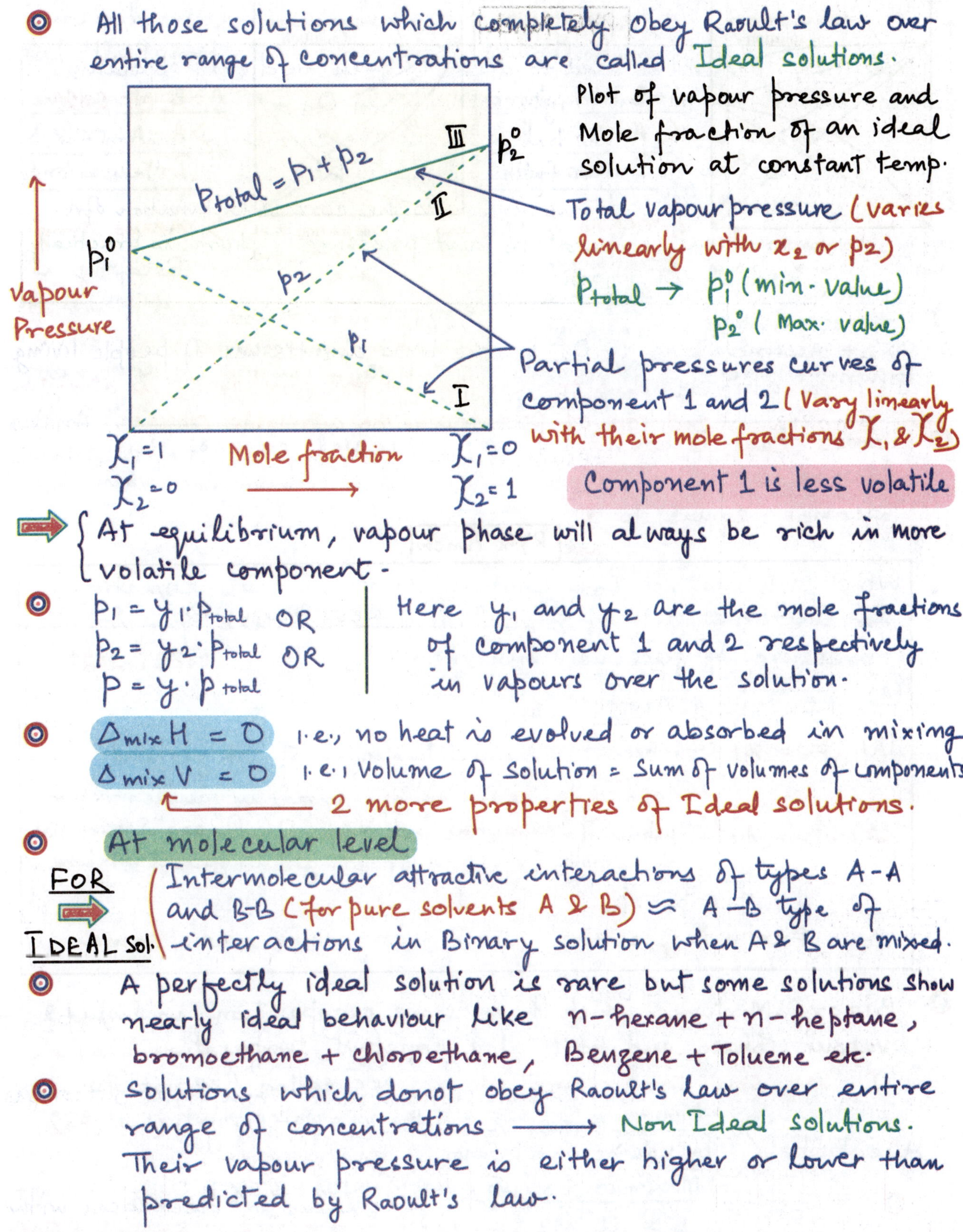

- All those solutions which completely obey Raoult's law over entire range of concentrations are called **Ideal solutions**.

Plot of vapour pressure and Mole fraction of an ideal solution at constant temp.

Total vapour pressure (varies linearly with x_2 or p_2)

$p_{total} \rightarrow p_1^0$ (min. value)

p_2^0 (Max. value)

Partial pressures curves of component 1 and 2 (Vary linearly with their mole fractions X_1 & X_2)

Component 1 is less volatile

➡ At equilibrium, vapour phase will always be rich in more volatile component.

- $p_1 = y_1 \cdot p_{total}$ OR
  $p_2 = y_2 \cdot p_{total}$ OR
  $p = y \cdot p_{total}$

  Here y_1 and y_2 are the mole fractions of component 1 and 2 respectively in vapours over the solution.

- $\Delta_{mix} H = 0$ i.e., no heat is evolved or absorbed in mixing
  $\Delta_{mix} V = 0$ i.e., Volume of solution = sum of volumes of components

  ← 2 more properties of Ideal solutions.

- **At molecular level**

  FOR ➡ IDEAL Sol. Intermolecular attractive interactions of types A–A and B–B (for pure solvents A & B) ≈ A–B type of interactions in Binary solution when A & B are mixed.

- A perfectly ideal solution is rare but some solutions show nearly ideal behaviour like n-hexane + n-heptane, bromoethane + chloroethane, Benzene + Toluene etc.

- Solutions which donot obey Raoult's law over entire range of concentrations ⟶ Non Ideal solutions. Their vapour pressure is either higher or lower than predicted by Raoult's law.

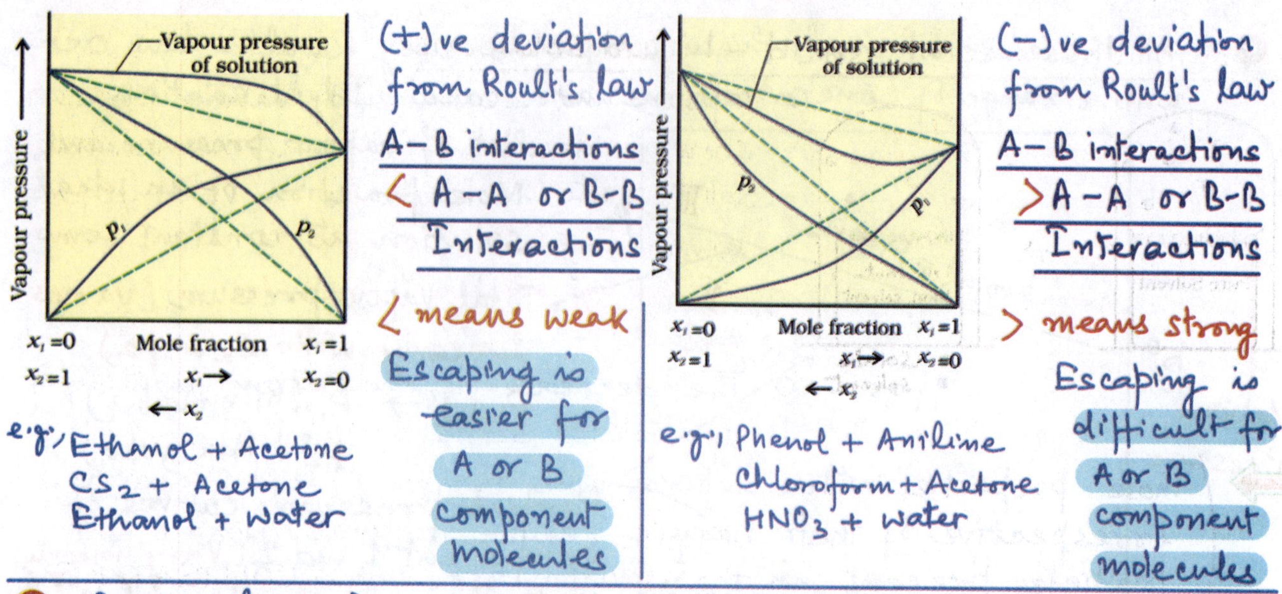

- Raoult's law is considered as a special case of Henry's law as $p_i = x_i \cdot p_i^0$ and $p = K_H x$ are comparable when K_H becomes equal to p_i^0.

PYQ Punch

Which one is not the correct mathematical equation for Dalton's Law of partial pressure? Here, p = total pressure of gaseous mixture. **NEET 2022**

(a) $p = n_1 \frac{RT}{V} + n_2 \frac{RT}{V} + n_3 \frac{RT}{V}$

(b) $p_i = x_i p$ where p_i = partial pressure of ith gas and x_i = mole fraction of ith gas in gaseous mixture

(c) ✓ $p_i = x_i p_i^0$ where p_i^0 = partial pressure of ith gas in pure state, x_i = mole fraction of ith gas in gaseous mixture

(d) $p = p_1 + p_2 + p_3$

Sol. Factual question a, b & d are more or less same

- Binary Mixtures which have same composition in liquid & vapour phase and boil at a constant temperature (better to say small temperature range) are called Azeotropes.

Azeotropes
- **Minimum Boiling** – Ethanol + water mixture at 95% by volume of ethanol (large (+)ve deviation showing mixture)
- **Maximum Boiling** – 68% HNO_3 + 32% H_2O by mass with b.p. at 393.5 K (large (–)ve deviation showing mixture)

Vapour Pressure of solid – Liquid solutions

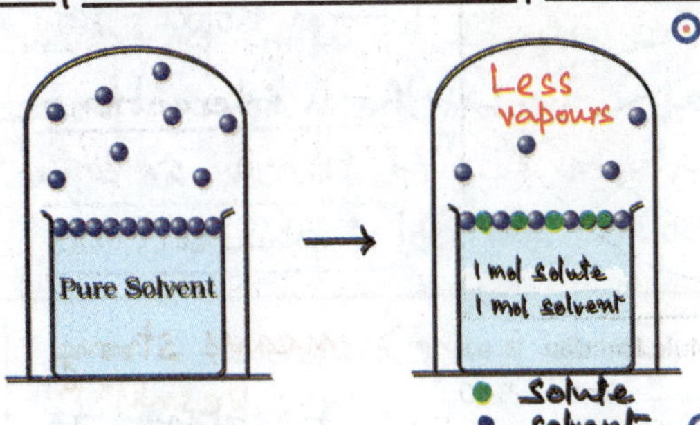

- Vapours and consequently vapour pressure show a decrease when a non volatile solid solute is added to a volatile pure solvent (as the fraction of the surface covered by solvent molecules is significantly reduced)
- The decrease depends upon quantity of non volatile solute present.

Those properties which depends upon number of solute particles irrespective of their nature relative to total number of particles present in the solution are called COLLIGATIVE PROPERTIES (Colligative Latin co = together ligare = to bind)

Colligative Properties

1. Relative lowering of Vapour pressure

$$\frac{p_1^\circ - p_1}{p_1^\circ} = \frac{n_2}{n_1} = \frac{w_2 \times M_1}{M_2 \times w_1}$$

where

w_1 = Mass of solvent
w_2 = Mass of solute
M_1 = Molar mass of solvent
M_2 = Molar Mass of solute

2. Elevation in Boiling Point or Ebullioscopy

$$\Delta T_b = K_b m$$

$$= \frac{K_b \times 1000 \times w_2}{M_2 \times w_1}$$

where

K_b = Ebullioscopic constant or Molal elevation constant or B.P. elevation constant

3. Depression in Freezing point or Cryoscopy

$$\Delta T_f = K_f m$$

$$= \frac{K_f \times 1000 \times w_2}{M_2 \times w_1}$$

where

K_f = Cryoscopic constant or Molal Depression constant or F. P. Depression constant.

4. Osmotic Pressure

$$\Pi = CRT = \frac{n_2}{V} RT$$

$$= \frac{w_2 RT}{M_2 V}$$

where

Π = Osmotic Pressure
R = Gas constant
V = volume, T = Temp.

- **Boiling point** – The temperature at which vapour pressure of a liquid becomes equal to atm. pressure
- **Freezing point** – The temperature at which the vapour pressure of a substance in its liquid phase is equal to its vapour pressure in solid phase.

NEET concentrate

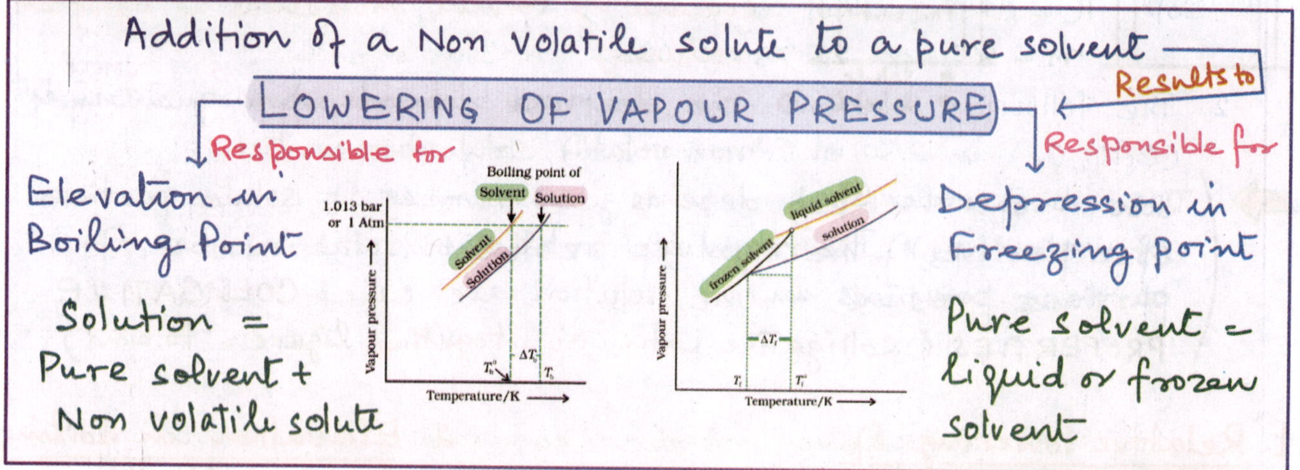

- **Osmosis** → Movement of solvent particles from their region of higher concentration to their region of lower concentration through a semi permeable membrane (SPM)

Rise in level of solution

Solvent

Solution

Semipermeable membrane

Dhyan Rakhna!

Solvent ka higher concentration = DILUTE SOLUTION

Solvent ka lower concentration = CONCENTRATED SOLUTION

Means solvent in osmosis moves from Dilute solution to concentrated solution when both are separated by SPM.

- External pressure applied to stop the flow of solvent is called Osmotic pressure (O.P.).
- Solution can be – (a) ISOTONIC – with same conc., hence same O.P. No osmosis takes place between them when connected through a SPM.

  (b) HYPERTONIC – with higher concentration. Always show endosmosis when connected to any solution by SPM.

  (c) HYPOTONIC – with lower concentration. Always show exosmosis when connected to any solution by SPM.

PYQ Punch

1. The plot of O.P. (π) vs Concentration ($mol\,L^{-1}$) for a solution gives a straight line with slope $25.73\,L\,bar\,mol^{-1}$. The temperature at which the O.P. measurment is done is NEET 2024

(a) $37°C$ ✓ (b) $310°C$ (c) $25.73°C$ (d) $12.05°C$

Sol. $\pi = CRT$, Plot is π vs C; On comparing with $y = mx + C$
$m = RT$ or $25.73 = 0.083 \times T = 310K$ or $37°C$

2. The following solutions were prepared by dissolving 10 g of Glucose ($C_6H_{12}O_6$) in 250 mL of water (p_1), 10 g of Urea (CH_4N_2O) in 250 mL of water (p_2) and 10 g of Sucrose ($C_{12}H_{22}O_{11}$) in 250 mL of water (p_3). The right option for the decreasing order of O.P. of these solutions is NEET 2021

(a) $p_2 > p_1 > p_3$ ✓ (b) $p_1 > p_2 > p_3$
(c) $p_2 > p_3 > p_1$ (d) $p_3 > p_1 > p_2$

Sol. OP = colligative property = Dependent on no. of solute particles $\longrightarrow$ dependent on no. of moles present i.e., w/M. Now for given question $w = 10g$ (same for all three solutions) so the compound with least Molar mass will have max. moles and max. OP (UREA) and vice versa.

Reverse Osmosis ⊙ Used in desalination of sea water.

⊙ Cellulose acetate – permeable to water but impermeable to impurities and ions.

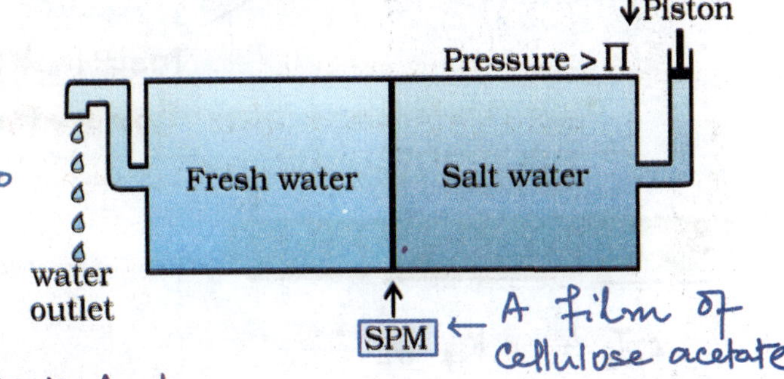

Abnormal Molar mass & van't Hoff factor

⊙ A molar mass that has either lower or higher value than the expected or normal value $\longrightarrow$ Abnormal Molar Mass (AMM)

⊙ Abnormal Molar mass of a non volatile solute is seen due to either association or dissociation of its molecules.

(a) Dissociation – $NaCl \rightleftharpoons Na^+ + Cl^-$ – Higher value than expected

(b) Association – $2CH_3COOH \rightleftharpoons (CH_3COOH)_2$ – Lower value than expected

⊙ van't Hoff Factor – Describes the extent of association or dissociation and denoted by i

- $i = \dfrac{\text{Normal Molar Mass}}{\text{Abnormal Molar Mass}} = \dfrac{\text{Observed Colligative property}}{\text{Calculated colligative property}}$

  $= \dfrac{\text{Total moles of particles after association/dissociation}}{\text{Total moles of particles before association/dissociation}}$

- $i = 1$ for Non electrolytes i.e., for solutes without any association or dissociation.

  $i < 1$ for association

  $i > 1$ for dissociation.

Values of van't Hoff factor, i, at Various Concentrations for NaCl, KCl, $MgSO_4$ and K_2SO_4.

Salt	*Values of i			van't Hoff Factor i for complete dissociation of solute
	0.1 m	0.01 m	0.001 m	
NaCl	1.87	1.94	1.97	2.00
KCl	1.85	1.94	1.98	2.00
$MgSO_4$	1.21	1.53	1.82	2.00
K_2SO_4	2.32	2.70	2.84	3.00

* represent i values for incomplete dissociation.

NaCl → $Na^+ + Cl^-$; KCl → $K^+ + Cl^-$; $MgSO_4$ → $Mg^{2+} + SO_4^{--}$: All give 2 ions on dissociation hence i_{max} for them is 2

K_2SO_4 → $(2K^+ + SO_4^{--}$: Gives 3 ions on dissociation hence i_{max} is 3

Modified Colligative properties due to i

1. Relative Lowering of V.P.

$$\frac{p_1^0 - p_1}{p_1^0} = i\frac{n_2}{n_1} = i\frac{w_2 \times M_1}{M_2 \times w_1}$$

2. Elevation of B.P.

$$\Delta T_b = i K_b m = i\frac{K_b \times 1000 \times w_2}{M_2 \times w_1}$$

3. Depression of F.P.

$$\Delta T_f = i K_f m = i\frac{K_f \times 1000 \times w_2}{M_2 \times w_1}$$

4. Osmotic pressure

$$\pi = CRT = i\frac{n_2}{V}RT = i\frac{w_2 RT}{M_2 V}$$

PYQ Punch

The van't Hoff factor (i) for a dilute aq. solution of the strong electrolyte barium hydroxide is (NEET 2016)

(a) 0 (b) 1 (c) 2 (d) 3

Sol. $Ba(OH)_2 \rightleftharpoons Ba^{2+} + 2\bar{O}H$ (Total 3 ions after dissociation)

Hence, $i = 1 + 2 = 3$

11. Electrochemistry

- It is the study of –
  (a) production of electricity from energy released during spontaneous chemical reactions (Electrochemical Methods)
  (b) use of electricity to bring about non-spontaneous chemical transformations. (Electrolytic Methods)

Electrochemical cells

- Converts chemical energy of any chemical reaction to electrical energy.
- Arrangement for Redox Reaction
  $Zn(s) + Cu^{2+}(aq) \rightarrow Zn^{2+}(aq) + Cu(s)$
  called Galvanic or Voltaic cell.

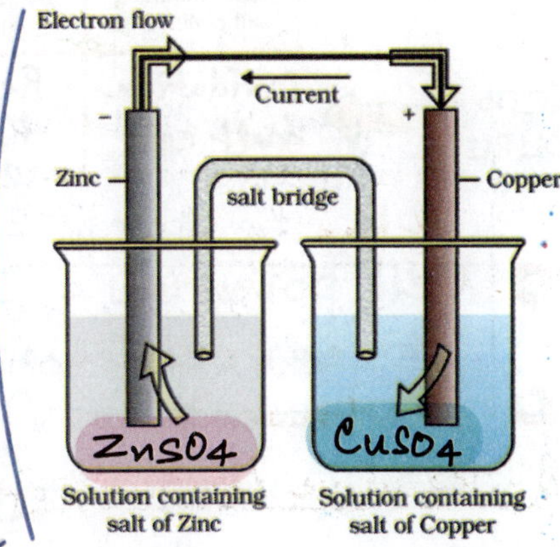

- It produces an electrical potential of 1.1 V when concentration of Zn^{2+} and Cu^{2+} ions is unity (1 mol dm^{-3}).
- Once the circuit is complete following changes are visible –
  (a) When $E_{ext} < 1.1$ V: e^- flow Zn rod $\longrightarrow$ Cu rod
  so, current flow Cu rod $\longrightarrow$ Zn rod
  Visible conclusion: Zn rod dissolution & Cu rod becomes thick due to Cu deposition.
  (b) When $E_{ext} = 1.1$ V: No e^- or current flow in any direction
  Visible conclusion: No chemical reaction
  (c) When $E_{ext} > 1.1$ V: e^- flow Cu rod $\longrightarrow$ Zn rod
  so, current flow Zn rod $\longrightarrow$ Cu rod
  Visible conclusion: Cu rod dissolution & Zn rod becomes thick due to Zn deposition i.e., the cell start behaving as an Electrolytic cell

Galvanic Cells

- Converts Gibb's energy of spontaneous Redox Reaction in to Electrical work
- Reaction $Zn(s) + Cu^{2+}(aq) \rightarrow Zn^{2+}(aq) + Cu(s)$ has 2 halves

$Cu^{2+} + 2e^- \rightarrow Cu(s)$ Reduction Half $\quad Zn(s) \longrightarrow Zn^{2+} + 2e^-$ Oxidation half

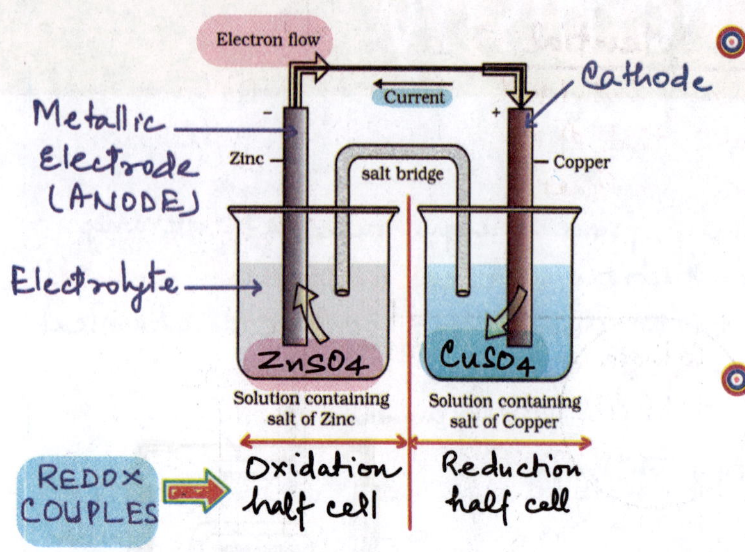

- The potential difference between electrolyte and electrode = Electrode Potential or Standard Electrode Potential (when concentration of all species involved in a half cell is unity)
- Potential difference between the electrodes = Cell Potential = Difference between the electrode (Reduction) Potential of anode and cathode.
- Cell potential = Cell electromotive force (emf) when no current is drawn through the cell.
- Representation of cell (as per IUPAC convention)

$$\underbrace{Zn(s) \mid Zn^{2+}(aq)}_{\text{ANODE}} \parallel \underbrace{Cu^{2+}(aq) \mid Cu(s)}_{\text{CATHODE}}$$

- $$E_{cell} = E_{right} - E_{left} = E_{Cu^{2+}|Cu} - E_{Zn^{2+}|Zn}$$

- $Zn^{2+}(aq, 1M) + 2e^- \longrightarrow Zn(s)$ $\quad E^\circ = -0.76V$

  $Cu^{2+}(aq, 1M) + 2e^- \longrightarrow Cu(s)$ $\quad E^\circ = +0.34V$

  So, according to $E_{cell} = E^\circ_R - E^\circ_L$

  $= 0.34V - (-0.76)V = 1.10V$

- Positive E°_{cell} value indicates that the reaction is feasible and cell will work.

PYQ Punch

Given below are half-cell reactions **NEET 2022**

$MnO_4^- + 8H^+ + 5e^- \longrightarrow Mn^{2+} + 4H_2O$ $\quad E^\circ_{Mn^{2+}/MnO_4^-} = -1.510V$

$\frac{1}{2}O_2 + 2H^+ + 2e^- \longrightarrow H_2O$ $\quad E^\circ_{O_2/H_2O} = +1.223V$

Will the MnO_4^- liberate O_2 from water in the presence of an acid

(a) No, because $E^\circ_{cell} = -0.287V$ (b) Yes, because $E^\circ_{cell} = +2.733V$

(c) No, because $E^\circ_{cell} = -2.733V$ (d) ✓ Yes, because $E^\circ_{cell} = +0.287V$

Sol. $E^\circ_{cell} = E^\circ_{MnO_4^-/Mn^{2+}} - E^\circ_{O_2/H_2O} = 1.510 - 1.223 = +0.287V$

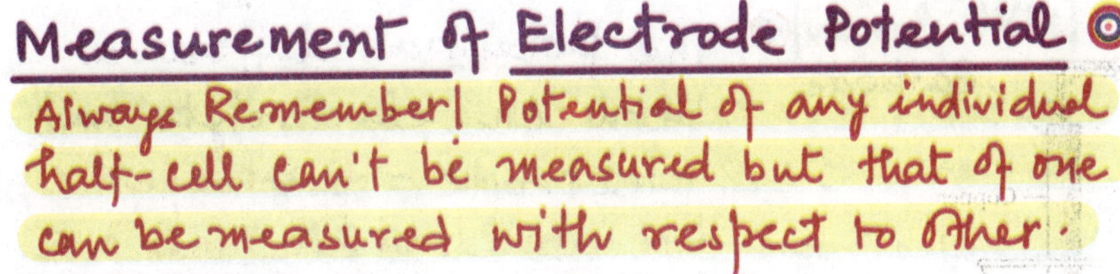

Measurement of Electrode Potential

Always Remember! Potential of any individual half-cell can't be measured but that of one can be measured with respect to other.

- It is done with the help of SHE (Standard Hydrogen electrode) represented by $Pt(s) | H_2(g) | H^+(aq)$

SHE which is Assigned Zero ✓ Potential

- $E^0 = E^0_R - E^0_L = E^0_R - 0$ (SHE = 0)

Case I –

for $Cu^{2+}[aq, 1M] + 2e^- \rightarrow Cu(s)$ standard electrode potential (SEP) is $+0.34\ V$

Case II –

for $Zn^{2+}[aq, 1M] + 2e^- \rightarrow Zn(s)$ standard electrode potential (SEP) is $-0.76\ V$.

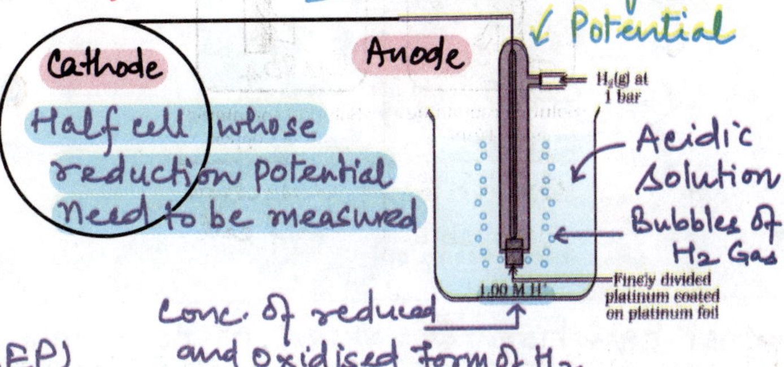

NEET concentrate

In Case I (+)ve value of SEP indicates –
- Cu^{2+} ions get reduced more easily than H^+ ions.
- Reverse of this i.e., H^+ cannot oxidise Cu.
- Cu does not dissolve in HCl
- In nitric acid it is oxidised by nitrate ions and not by H^+

In Case II (–)ve value of SEP indicates –
- H^+ ions can oxidise Zn or Zn can reduce H^+.

- Inert electrodes like those of Pt and Au does not participate in reaction rather they provide surface for Redox reaction occuring with in the cell.

Electrochemical Series

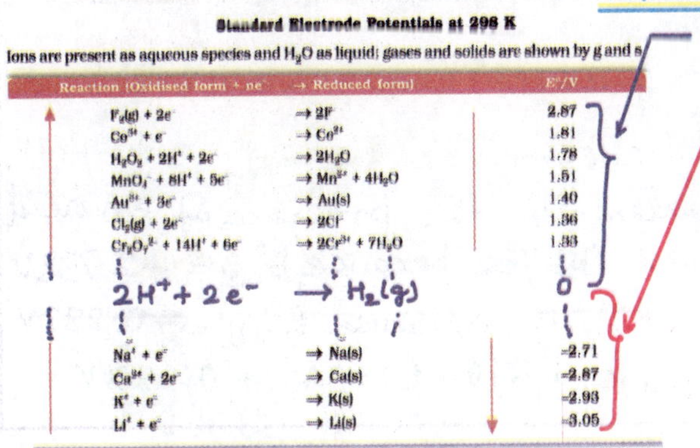

Standard Electrode Potentials at 298 K

Ions are present as aqueous species and H_2O as liquid; gases and solids are shown by g and s

Reaction (Oxidised form + ne⁻	→ Reduced form)	E°/V
$F_2(g) + 2e^-$	$\rightarrow 2F^-$	2.87
$Co^{3+} + e^-$	$\rightarrow Co^{2+}$	1.81
$H_2O_2 + 2H^+ + 2e^-$	$\rightarrow 2H_2O$	1.78
$MnO_4^- + 8H^+ + 5e^-$	$\rightarrow Mn^{2+} + 4H_2O$	1.51
$Au^{3+} + 3e^-$	$\rightarrow Au(s)$	1.40
$Cl_2(g) + 2e^-$	$\rightarrow 2Cl^-$	1.36
$Cr_2O_7^{2-} + 14H^+ + 6e^-$	$\rightarrow 2Cr^{3+} + 7H_2O$	1.33
$2H^+ + 2e^-$	$\rightarrow H_2(g)$	0
$Na^+ + e^-$	$\rightarrow Na(s)$	-2.71
$Ca^{2+} + 2e^-$	$\rightarrow Ca(s)$	-2.87
$K^+ + e^-$	$\rightarrow K(s)$	-2.93
$Li^+ + e^-$	$\rightarrow Li(s)$	-3.05

- This series provides SEPs of different elements & helps in assessment of their Redox capabilities.

- Strongest reducing agent – Li(s)
- Strongest Oxidising agent – $F_2(g)$

PYQ Punch

At 298 K, the standard electrode potentials of Cu^{2+}/Cu, Zn^{2+}/Zn, Fe^{2+}/Fe and Ag^{+}/Ag are 0.34V, −0.76V, −0.44V and 0.80V respectively. On the basis of standard electrode potential, predict which of the following reactions does not occur **NEET 2022**

(a) $CuSO_4(aq) + Fe(s) \longrightarrow FeSO_4(aq) + Cu(s)$

(b) $FeSO_4(aq) + Zn(s) \longrightarrow ZnSO_4(aq) + Fe$

✓(c) $CuSO_4(aq) + 2Ag(s) \longrightarrow Ag_2SO_4(aq) + 2Cu(s)$

(d) $CuSO_4(aq) + Zn(s) \longrightarrow ZnSO_4(aq) + Cu(s)$

Sol. As the SEP value of Ag is highest among the metals given, hence it cannot any of the metals given from their salt solutions.

Nernst Equation ◎ Used to calculate the electrode potential when conc. of electrolytes are not unity.

◎ for Reaction $M^{n+}(aq) + ne^- \longrightarrow M(s)$

Electrode Potential $E_{(M^{n+}/M)} = E^0_{(M^{n+}/M)} - \frac{RT}{nF} \ln \frac{[M]}{[M^{n+}]}$

(E^0: SEP; R: Gas constant (8.314 J/K mol); T: Temperature; n: No. of e^-; F: Faraday (96487 C/mol); $[M^{n+}]$: conc. of aq. ion)

◎ For Zn and Cu Daniell cell

$$E_{(cell)} = E^0_{(cell)} - \frac{RT}{2F} \ln \frac{[Zn^{2+}]}{[Cu^{2+}]} = E^0_{(cell)} - \frac{0.059}{2} \log \frac{[Zn^{2+}]}{[Cu^{2+}]}$$

PYQ Punch

Find the emf of the cell in which following reaction takes place at 298 K

$Ni(s) + 2Ag^+(0.001\,M) \longrightarrow Ni^{2+}(0.001\,M) + 2Ag(s)$

(Given that $E^0_{cell} = 1.05V$, $\frac{2.303RT}{F} = 0.059$ at 298 K) **NEET 2022**

(a) 1.385 V ✓(b) 0.9615 V (c) 1.05 V (d) 1.0385 V

Sol. $E_{cell} = E^0_{cell} - \frac{0.059}{n} \log \frac{[Ni^{2+}]}{[Ag^+]^2} = 1.05 - \frac{0.059}{2} \log \frac{(10^{-3})}{(10^{-3})^2}$

$= 1.05 - \frac{0.059}{2} \times 3 = 0.9615$

◎ For a generalised reaction $aA + bB \xrightarrow{ne^-} cC + dD$

Nernst equation can be $E_{cell} = E^0_{cell} - \frac{RT}{nF} \ln \frac{[C]^c[D]^d}{[A]^a[B]^b}$

Equilibrium Constant from Nernst Equation –

- For the reaction $Zn(s) + Cu^{2+}(aq) \longrightarrow Zn^{2+}(aq) + Cu(s)$ at equilibrium (when no change in the conc. of Zn^{2+} and Cu^{2+} ions is observed & Voltmeter gives zero reading)

$$E^\circ_{cell} = \frac{2.303RT}{2F} \log \frac{[Zn^{2+}]}{[Cu^{2+}]} \quad (\text{as } E_{cell} = 0)$$

$$1.1V = \frac{0.059V}{2} \log K_c \quad \left(\text{as } \frac{[Zn^{2+}]}{[Cu^{2+}]} = K_c\right)$$

or $$\log K_c = \frac{(1.1V \times 2)}{0.059V} = 37.288$$

so $$K_c = 2 \times 10^{37} \text{ at } 298\,K$$

- $$\boxed{E^\circ_{cell} = \frac{2.303RT}{nF} \log K_c}$$ ← General formula for K_c & E°_{cell} relationship

PYQ Punch

For a cell involving one electron, $E^\circ_{cell} = 0.59V$ at 298 K, the equilibrium constant for the cell reaction is [Given that $\frac{2.303RT}{F} = 0.059$ V at 298K] NEET 2019

(a) 1.0×10^2 (b) 1.0×10^5 (c) ✓ 1.0×10^{10} (d) 1.0×10^{30}

Sol. $E^\circ_{cell} = 0.59V = \frac{2.303RT}{nF} \log K = \frac{0.059}{1} \log K$

So $\log K = \frac{0.59V}{0.059V} = 10$ so $K = 10^{10}$

Electrochemical cell and Gibb's Energy for the reaction

- Change in Gibb's energy for reaction $\longrightarrow \Delta_r G = -nFE_{cell}$ (F → faraday; E_{cell} → emf of cell; n → no. of electrons)
- The reversible work done by a Galvanic cell is equal to the decrease in its Gibb's energy.
- Always Remember! $E_{cell} \longrightarrow$ Intensive Parameter while $\Delta_r G \longrightarrow$ Extensive Thermodynamic property
- Also $\boxed{\Delta_r G = -RT \ln K}$ (as $E_{cell} = E^\circ_{cell}$ at unity)

PYQ Punch

For the cell reaction $2Fe^{3+}(aq) + 2I^-(aq) \longrightarrow 2Fe^{2+}(aq) + I_2(aq)$ $E^\circ_{cell} = 0.24V$ at 298 K. The standard Gibb's energy ($\Delta_r G^\circ$) for the cell reaction is (Given that Faraday constant F = 96500 C mol^{-1}) NEET 2019

(a) $-23.16\ kJ\ mol^{-1}$
(b) $46.32\ kJ\ mol^{-1}$
(c) $23.16\ kJ\ mol^{-1}$
(d) $-46.32\ kJ\ mol^{-1}$ ✓

Sol. $\Delta_r G = -nFE^\circ_{cell} = -2 \times 96500 \times 0.24 = -46320\ J\ mol^{-1}$

Conductance of Electrolytic Solutions

- The electrical resistance of any object can be given as

$$R \propto \frac{l}{a} \quad \text{or} \quad R = \rho \frac{l}{a}$$

R → Electrical Resistance; l ← Length; a ← Area of cross section; ρ ← Resistivity or Specific Resistance (Units Ωm or Ω cm)

- As per IUPAC recommendation Resistivity prevails over the term specific Resistance. For a substance it is defined as the resistance produced by 1 m long and 1 m^2 wire of that substance.
- The inverse of resistance R is called CONDUCTANCE G, so

$$G = \frac{1}{R} = \frac{A}{\rho l} = \kappa \frac{A}{l}$$

SI unit of conductance is "Siemens" (S)

κ ← kappa, represents conductivity (specific conductance) which is opposite of Resistivity

- Magnitude of conductivity depends upon (i) Nature of material (ii) Temperature and Pressure at which measurements are made.
- Materials

Conductors
Metals, Alloys, carbon black, Graphite Polyacetylene, Polyaniline, Polypyrrole, Polythiophene

Insulators
Glass, Ceramics,

Semiconductors
Silicon, Doped silicon, Gallium Arsenide

NEET concentrate

Superconductors
Zero resistivity or Infinite conductivity
Metals & Alloys (0 to 15 K)
Ceramics & Mixed oxides (150 K)

- Conductance through metals is called electronic conductance where as conductance of electricity by ions present in a solution is called Ionic conductance.
- Ionic conductance depends on –
  (a) Nature of electrolyte, (b) size of Ions (c) Charge on ions
  (d) Solvation of ions (e) Nature & viscosity of solvent,
  (f) concentration of electrolyte (g) Temperature.
- Measurement of conductivity of ionic solutions is done through conductivity cells (as it is not possible to measure conductivity of a solution directly through Wheatstone bridge because (a) DC changes the composition of solution, (b) Direct connectivity of solution to bridge is not possible)
- Connecting wires — Area of cross section of electrodes = A
  Distance between electrodes = l
  Platinized Pt electrodes ← Coated with Pt black (Pt deposited electrochemically)
  For a cell → l/A → Cell constant $(G^*) = R\kappa$

Conductivity cell → Can be used in Wheatstone bridge as unknown resistance.

- Molar Conductivity is the conductivity of any solution having 1 Molar concentration. It is denoted by Λ_m which can be
  $\Lambda_m = \kappa/C = \kappa A/l$ (units $S\,m^2\,mol^{-1}$)
  Technically it is defined as "the conductance of volume V of solution containing 1 mole of electrolyte kept between two electrodes with area of cross section A and distance of unit length.

Variation of conductivity and molar conductivity with concentration

- Conductivity always decreases with decrease of concentration in case of weak and strong electrolytes both (as no. of ions per unit volume carrying the current decreases)
- Molar conductivity increases with decrease in concentration. (as V also increases and it more than compensates decrease in κ)
- Molar conductivity is called Limiting Molar conductivity when concentration approaches zero. It is represented by Λ°_m.

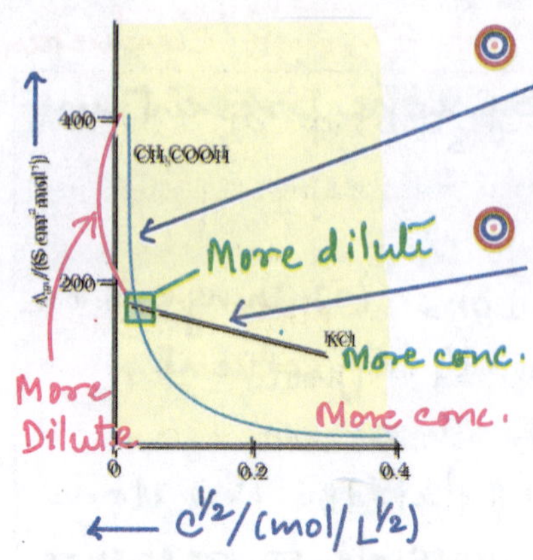

- Variation of Molar conductivity for CH_3COOH (Weak electrolyte) – Increases with dilution and max. at infinite dilution
- Variation of Molar conductivity for KCl (Strong electrolyte) – Increases slowly with dilution as

$$\lambda_m = \lambda_m^\circ - A c^{1/2}$$

(A – Constant for a given solvent)

Value of A for NaCl – 1-1, $MgCl_2$ – 2-2, $CaCl_2$ – 1-2 (Depends upon charges of cation, anion produced on dissociation of electrolyte)

- All electrolytes of a particular type have the same value of A.

PYQ Punch

The conductivity of centimolar solution of KCl is 0.0210 ohm^{-1} cm^{-1} at 25°C. The resistance of cell containing the solution at 25°C is 60 ohm. The value of cell constant is **NEET 2023**

(a) 3.28 cm^{-1} (b) 1.26 cm^{-1} (c) 3.34 cm^{-1} (d) 1.34 cm^{-1}

Sol. Cell constant $= l/a = \kappa \times R = 0.0210 \times 60 = 1.26\ cm^{-1}$

Kohlrausch law of Independent migration of Ions

Limiting molar conductivity of an electrolyte can be represented as the sum of the individual contributions of cation and anion of the electrolyte.

$$\Lambda_m^\circ = \nu_+ \lambda_+^\circ + \nu_- \lambda_-^\circ$$

(λ_+°, λ_-° – Limiting molar conductivities of ions; ν_+, ν_- – Ions produced on dissociation of electrolyte.)

- At infinite dilution (i.e., concentration c → zero) weak electrolyte dissociate completely ($\alpha = 1$) but at such low concentration the conductivity of the solution is low that it cannot be measured accurately. Hence, Kohlrausch law is used for the same.
- For weak electrolyte

$$K_a = \frac{c\alpha^2}{(1-\alpha)} = \frac{c\lambda_m^2}{\lambda_m^\circ(\lambda_m^\circ - \lambda_m)} \quad \left(\text{as } \alpha = \frac{\lambda_m}{\lambda_m^\circ}\right)$$

(K_a – Dissociation constant; c – concentration)

PYQ Punch

The molar conductance of NaCl, HCl and CH_3COONa at infinite dilution are 126.45, 426.16 and 91.0 S cm^2 mol^{-1} respectively. The molar conductance of CH_3COOH at infinite dilution is, choose the right option for your answer NEET 2021

(a) 201.28 S cm^2 mol^{-1} ✓(b) 390.71 S cm^2 mol^{-1}

(c) 698.28 S cm^2 mol^{-1} (d) 540.48 S cm^2 mol^{-1}

Sol. $\lambda^\circ_{CH_3COOH} = \lambda^\circ_{CH_3COONa} + \lambda^\circ_{HCl} - \lambda^\circ_{NaCl} = 91.0 + 426.16 - 126.45$
$= 390.71$ S cm^2 mol^{-1}

- Kohlrausch law helps in
  (a) Calculation of λ_m for any electrolyte from λ° of individual ions.
  (b) Calculation of Ka for any weak electrolyte if C, λ°_m & λ_m are given for that electrolyte.

Electrolytic cell and Electrolysis

- In electrolytic cells external source of voltage is used to bring about a chemical reaction.
- Simplest electrolytic cell is 2 copper strips dipped in the aqueous solution of $CuSO_4$. When DC voltage is applied then

  Cathode : $Cu^{2+}(aq) + 2e^- \longrightarrow Cu(s)$

  Anode : $Cu(s) \longrightarrow Cu^{2+}(s) + 2e^-$

NEET concentrate

Always Remember Anode — The electrode at which oxidation takes place. It is (+)vely charged in electrolytic cell and (−)vely charged in Galvanic cell.

Cathode — The electrode at which reduction takes place. It is (−)vely charged in electrolytic cell and (+)vely charged in Galvanic cell.

- Electrolysis of copper ⟶ Used to get high purity Cu from impure one. **Impure Cu is made anode in the process.**
- Many metals like Na, Mg, Al etc. ⟶ Produced by electrochemical reduction of their cations (as no suitable chemical reducing agents are available for the purpose) Na & Mg ⟶ By electrolysis of their fused chlorides; Al ⟶ By electrolysis of its oxide in cryolite.

- **Michael Faraday** First to describe the quantitative aspect of electrolysis. He gave 2 laws –
  - The amount of chemical reaction which occurs at any electrode (during electrolysis by a current) is proportional to the electricity passed through the electrolyte.
  - The amounts of different substances liberated by the same quantity of electricity passing through the electrolytic solution are proportional to their chemical <u>equivalent weights</u> (Atomic (Molar) Mass of Metal ÷ Number of e^- required to reduce the cation)
- Quantity of electricity → $Q = It$ ← Time in seconds; I ← current in ampere
- For $Ag^+(aq) + e^- \longrightarrow Ag(s)$ 1 mole of e^- are required to reduce 1 mole of Ag^+.
- Charge on 1 mole of e^- = 96487 C mol^{-1} ≈ 96500 C mol^{-1} (as charge on 1 e^- is 1.6021×10^{-19} C & $N_A = 6.022 \times 10^{23}$ mol^{-1})

  This is called <u>Faraday</u> quantity or simply Faraday & is represented by F.
- Similarly Mg^{2+} and Al^{3+} require 2F and 3F electrons for their reduction to Mg(s) and Al(s) respectively.

<u>Products of Electrolysis</u> – Dhyan Rakhna! Electrolysis mein Cathode (–)ve hota hai because yeh cations ko apni taraf kheenchta hai & vice versa.

- Products of electrolysis depends upon SEP of different oxidising and reducing species present in the cell.
- For Molten NaCl → Na^+ reduced at cathode, Cl^- oxidised at anode

  For aqueous NaCl → NaOH (In solution), H_2 (at cathode) and Cl_2 (at anode) are the products.

  Cathode: $Na^+(aq) + e^- \longrightarrow Na(s)$ $\quad E^\circ_{cell} = -2.71V$

  Discharged → $H^+(aq) + e^- \longrightarrow H_2(g)$ $\quad E^\circ_{cell} = 0.00V$

  Anode: $2H_2O(l) \longrightarrow O_2(g) + 4H^+ + 4e^-$ $\quad E^\circ_{cell} = 1.23V$

  Discharged → $Cl^-(aq) \longrightarrow \frac{1}{2}Cl_2(g) + e^-$ $\quad E^\circ_{cell} = 1.36V$

  Net reaction: $NaCl(aq) + H_2O(l) \longrightarrow Na^+(aq) + \bar{O}H(aq) + \frac{1}{2}H_2(g) + \frac{1}{2}Cl_2(g)$

Always Remember! Aq. NaCl solution is called BRINE SOLUTION

- Electrolysis of H_2SO_4 → Cation only H^+ so no complications at cathode

Anode: $2H_2O(l) \rightarrow O_2(g) + 4H^+(aq) + 4e^-$ (dil. H_2SO_4) $E^\circ_{cell} = 1.23$ V

$2SO_4^{--}(aq) \rightarrow S_2O_8^{--}(aq) + 2e^-$ (Conc. H_2SO_4) $E^\circ_{cell} = 1.96$V

Batteries

Primary = Non rechargeable; Secondary = Chargeable

Dry cell or Leclanche cell → Potential of cell = 1.5 V

Carbon rod (cathode)

Zinc cup (anode)

MnO_2 + carbon black + NH_4Cl paste + $ZnCl_2$

Anode: $Zn(s) \rightarrow Zn^{2+} + 2e^-$

Cathode: $\overset{+4}{Mn}O_2 + NH_4^+ + e^- \rightarrow \overset{+3}{Mn}O(OH) + NH_3$ — REDUCTION

$NH_3 \xrightarrow{Zn} [Zn(NH_3)_4]^{2+}$

Use: Transistors, clocks

$E^\circ_{cell} = 1.35$ V → Mercury cell

Use: Hearing aids, watches etc.

Zn–Hg; Anode; Anode cap; KOH + ZnO; Electrolyte; Gasket; Separator; Cathode (HgO + C); Cell can

Anode: $Zn(Hg) + 2\bar{O}H \rightarrow ZnO(s) + H_2O + 2e^-$

Cathode: $HgO + H_2O + 2e^- \rightarrow Hg(l) + 2\bar{O}H$

Overall reaction: $Zn(Hg) + HgO(s) \rightarrow ZnO(s) + Hg(l)$

Secondary Batteries:

when battery is in use:

Anode: $Pb(s) + SO_4^{--}(aq) \rightarrow PbSO_4(s) + 2e^-$

Cathode: $PbO_2(s) + SO_4^{--}(aq) + 4H^+ + 2e^- \rightarrow PbSO_4(s) + 2H_2O(l)$

Overall reaction: $Pb(s) + PbO_2(s) + 2H_2SO_4(aq) \rightarrow 2PbSO_4(s) + 2H_2O(l)$

Anode; Cathode; Negative plates: lead grids filled with spongy lead; Positive plates: lead grids filled with PbO_2; 38% sulphuric acid solution (Electrolyte)

Lead storage Battery

NEET concentrate

On charging the reaction is reversed and $PbSO_4(s)$ on anode & cathode is converted into Pb and PbO_2 respectively.

Ni – Cd cell

Jelly roll arrangement

Positive plate; Separator (Moist NaOH or KOH); Negative plate

Overall Reaction:

$Cd(s) + 2Ni(OH)_3(s) \rightarrow CdO(s) + 2Ni(OH)_2(s) + H_2O(l)$

Fuel Cell Galvanic cells that are designed to convert the energy of combustion of compounds like H_2, CH_4, CH_3OH etc., to electrical energy directly.

Cathode: $O_2(g) + H_2O(l) + 4e^- \rightarrow 4\bar{O}H(aq)$

Anode: $2H_2(g) + 4\bar{O}H(aq) \rightarrow 4H_2O(l) + 4e^-$

Overall: $2H_2(g) + O_2(g) \rightarrow 2H_2O(l)$

- The fuel cell of H_2 & O_2 to form water was used in Apollo space programme.
- The water vapours produced → Used as the drinking water for astronauts.
- H_2 and O_2 are bubbled through porous carbon electrodes in to aq. NaOH (electrolyte). Catalyst used → Finely divided Pt or Pd.

PYQ Punch

In a typical fuel cell the reactant (R) and Product (P) are — NEET 2020

(a) R = $H_2(g)$, $O_2(g)$; P = $H_2O_2(l)$

(b) R = $H_2(g)$, $O_2(g)$; P = $H_2O(l)$ ✓

(c) R = $H_2(g)$, $O_2(g)$, $Cl_2(g)$; P = $HClO_4(aq)$

(d) R = $H_2(g)$, $N_2(g)$; P = $NH_3(aq)$

Sol. Factual.

12. Chemical Kinetics

- It is the branch of chemistry that deals with the study of reaction rates and their mechanisms. (Gr. Kinesis = movement)
- Feasibility of Reaction ⟶ Thermodynamics
  Rate of a Reaction ⟶ Chemical Kinetics.

Rate of a Chemical Reaction It can be expressed in the terms of
(a) Decrease in the concentration of any of the reactants in unit time. OR
(b) Increase in the concentration of any of the products in unit time.

Dhyan Rakhna! Rate considerations sirf moderate aur slow reactions ke hote hain. Ionic exchange reactions instantaneous hoti hain. Unke Rate considerations Nahi kiye jaate.

- For any hypothetical reaction $R \longrightarrow P$

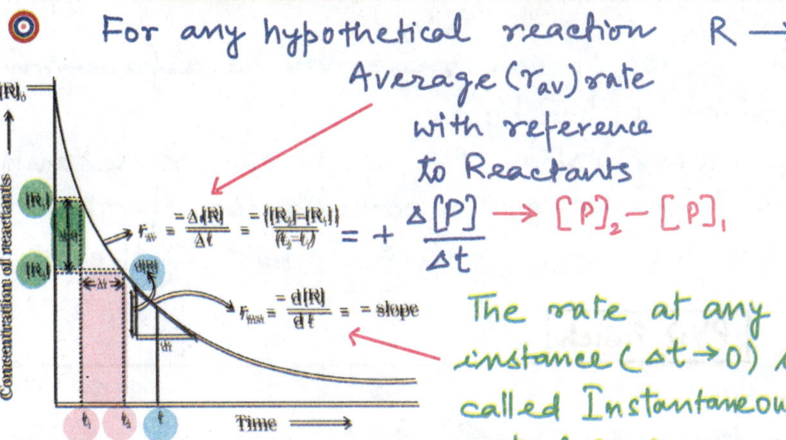

Average (r_{av}) rate with reference to Reactants $= +\frac{\Delta[P]}{\Delta t} \rightarrow [P]_2 - [P]_1$

The rate at any instance ($\Delta t \to 0$) is called Instantaneous rate (r_{inst})

Units
concentration time^{-1}
↓ $mol\,L^{-1}$ ↓ second
So, $mol\,L^{-1}s^{-1}$ or $atm\,s^{-1}$ (for gases where conc. is expressed as partial pressure

- For $2HI(g) \longrightarrow H_2(g) + I_2(g)$

$$\text{Rate} = -\frac{1}{2}\frac{\Delta[HI]}{\Delta t} = \frac{\Delta[H_2]}{\Delta t} = \frac{\Delta[I_2]}{\Delta t}$$

- Similarly for $5Br^-(aq) + BrO_3^-(aq) + 6H^+(aq) \rightarrow 3Br_2(aq) + 3H_2O(l)$

$$\text{Rate} = -\frac{1}{5}\frac{\Delta[Br^-]}{\Delta t} = -\frac{\Delta[BrO_3^-]}{\Delta t} = -\frac{1}{6}\frac{\Delta[H^+]}{\Delta t} = \frac{1}{3}\frac{\Delta[Br_2]}{\Delta t} = \frac{1}{3}\frac{\Delta[H_2O]}{\Delta t}$$

Factors influencing rate of a Reaction

1. **Concentration** More concentration fast reaction
2. **Physical state** Gases react fastest
3. **Surface area of reactant** More surface area faster reaction
4. **Temperature** More temperature faster reaction.

- Rate law is the expression in which reaction rate is given in terms of molar concentration of reactants with each term raised to some power (may or may not be the same as the Stoichiometric coefficient of reacting species in a balanced chemical equation) This expression is also called Rate expression.

- For $aA + bB \longrightarrow cC + dD$ $\quad$ Rate $= k[A]^x[B]^y$

  (Stoichiometric coefficient → x, y; Rate constant → k)

  So, $-\frac{d[R]}{dt} = k[A]^x[B]^y$ $\quad$ (as Rate $= -\frac{d[R]}{dt}$)

  ($-\frac{d[R]}{dt} = k[A]^x[B]^y$ ← differential rate equation)

NEET concentrate

> Always remember! rate law for any reaction can not be predicted by just looking at the balanced chemical equation (i.e, theoretically) rather it must be determined experimentally.

- We can measure the rate of any reaction as a function of initial concentration either by -
  - (a) Keeping the concentration of one of the reactants constant and changing the concentration of other
  - (b) By changing the concentration of both of the reactants.

PYQ Punch

For a certain reaction,

the rate $= k[A]^2[B]$, **NEET 2019**

when the initial concentration of A is Tripled keeping concentration of B constant, the initial rate would

(a) Increases by a factor of 6 $\quad$ (b) Increases by a factor of 9 ✓

(c) Increases by a factor of 3 $\quad$ (d) decreases by a factor of 9

Sol. $\frac{\text{Initial Rate}}{\text{Final Rate}} = \frac{k[A]^2[B]}{k[3A]^2[B]} = \frac{1}{9}$ or Final Rate = 9 Initial Rate

- Some Other examples $CHCl_3 + Cl_2 \longrightarrow CCl_4 + HCl$ $\quad$ Rate $= k[CHCl_3][Cl_2]^{1/2}$

  $CH_3COOC_2H_5 + H_2O \longrightarrow CH_3COOH + C_2H_5OH$ $\quad$ Rate $= k[CH_3COOC_2H_5][H_2O]^0$

- The sum of powers of the concentration of Reactants in Rate law expression is called **Order of that reaction.**
- Order can be 0, 1, 2, 3 and even in fraction.
- Zero order $[\ ]^0 \longrightarrow$ Reaction is independent of the concentration of reactants.
- Elementary Reactions $\longrightarrow$ One step Reactions
  Complex Reactions $\longrightarrow$ Multi step Reactions
- Units of rate constant for different order reactions are different.

NEET concentrate

> Infact, in competitions like NEET sometimes order of reaction is not mentioned in Question to raise the difficulty level of Questions $\longrightarrow$ In such questions the order of reaction is identified by the units of values given.

- Units of Rate Constant for
  - Zero Order Reaction = $mol\ L^{-1} s^{-1}$ $\quad 2NH_3 \xrightarrow[1130K]{Pt} N_2 + 3H_2$
  - 1st order Reaction = s^{-1} ($time^{-1}$) $\quad 2N_2O_5 \longrightarrow 4NO_2 + O_2$
  - 2nd order Reaction = $L\ mol^{-1} s^{-1}$ $\quad 2NO_2 \longrightarrow 2NO + O_2$
  - n^{th} order Reaction = $(mol\ L^{-1})^{1-n} s^{-1}$
- The number of reacting species (atoms, ions or molecules) taking part in an elementary reaction, which must collide simultaneously in order to bring about a chemical reaction is called **Molecularity of a reaction**. For Example
  - $NH_4NO_2 \longrightarrow N_2 + 2H_2O$ Unimolecular
  - $2HI \longrightarrow H_2 + I_2$ Bimolecular
  - $2NO + O_2 \longrightarrow 2NO_2$ Trimolecular or Termolecular
- The probability that more than 3 molecules can collide to form the product is very small so, reactions with molecularity above 3 are very rare and slow.
- Reactions with more than 3 molecules in stoichiometric equations must be categorised as Complex Reactions.

  e.g., $KClO_3 + 6FeSO_4 + 3H_2SO_4 \longrightarrow KCl + 3Fe_2(SO_4)_3 + 3H_2O$
  (Seems as 10th order but is actually second order reaction)

- Infact such reaction is an example of Complex i.e., multi step reaction & their order completely depends upon the order of Rate Determining step (RDS).
- Always remember in a complex reaction the slowest step is always the RDS.

Molecularity	Order
Theoritical (calculative)	Experimental
can not be fractional or zero	can be zero or fractional
Applicable only to elementary reactions.	Applicable to elementary as well as complex reactions
No meaning for complex reactions	For complex reactions given be slowest step

- For $2H_2O_2 \xrightarrow[\text{Alk. Med.}]{I^-} 2H_2O + O_2$; Rate $= -\frac{d[H_2O_2]}{dt} = k[H_2O_2][I^-]$

Because reaction proceeds through 2 steps –

1. $H_2O_2 + I^- \xrightarrow{\text{slow}} H_2O + IO^-$ ⟵ RDS
2. $H_2O_2 + IO^- \xrightarrow{\text{fast}} H_2O + I^- + O_2$

Intermediate ⟶ IO^-

- For any Zero order reaction A ⟶ Product

$\frac{d[A]}{dt} = -k$ — Differential eqn.

$k = \frac{\{[A]_0 - [A]\}}{t}$ — Integral eqn.

$\frac{[A]_0}{2k}$ — Half life

$[R]_0$ or $[A]_0$ = Initial conc. of Reactant.

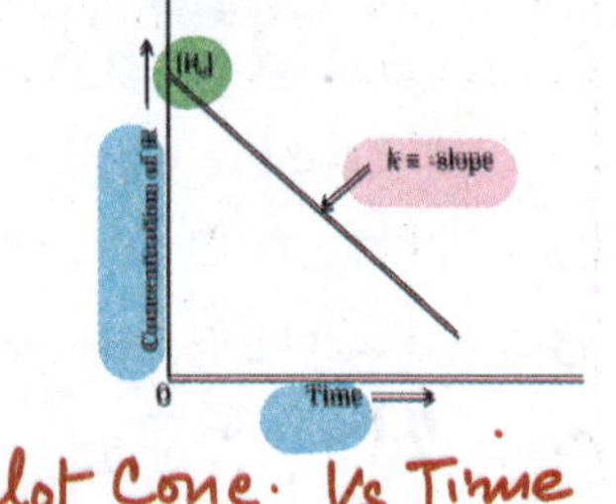

Plot Conc. Vs Time

- For any First order reaction A ⟶ Product

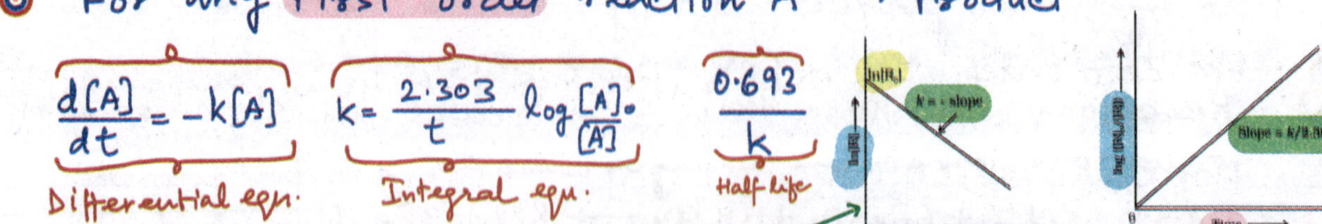

$\frac{d[A]}{dt} = -k[A]$ — Differential eqn.

$k = \frac{2.303}{t} \log \frac{[A]_0}{[A]}$ — Integral eqn.

$\frac{0.693}{k}$ — Half life

$[R]_0$ or $[A]_0$ = Initial conc.

Plot $\ln[R]$ & t

Plot $\log [R]_0/[R]$ Vs t

- **Dhyan Rakho!** All Natural and artificial radioactive decay of unstable nuclei take place by first order kinetics.

PYQ Punch

1. The given graph is a representation of kinetics of a reaction

NEET 2022

The y and x axis for zero and first order reactions, respectively are

(a) Zero order (y = Conc. & x = time) first order (y = rate constant, x = conc.)

(b) Zero order (y = rate & x = conc.) first order ($y = t_{1/2}$ & x = conc.)

(c) Zero order (y = rate & x = conc.) first order (y = rate & $x = t_{1/2}$)

(d) Zero order (y = conc. & x = time) first order ($y = t_{1/2}$ & x = conc.)

Sol.

2. For a first order reaction A ⟶ Products, initial conc. of A is 0.1 M, which becomes 0.001 M after 5 minutes. Rate constant for the reaction in min^{-1} is NEET 2022

(a) 0.9212 (b) 0.4606 (c) 0.2303 (d) 1.3818

Sol. $k = \frac{2.303}{t}\log\frac{[A]_0}{[A]} = \frac{2.303}{5}\log\frac{[0.1]}{[0.001]} = \frac{2.303 \times 2}{5} = 0.9212\ min^{-1}$

- For any first order reaction $A(g) \longrightarrow B(g) + C(g)$

$$k = \frac{2.303}{t}\log\frac{p_i}{p_A} = \frac{2.303}{t}\log\frac{p_i}{2p_i - P_t}$$

($P_t = p_A + p_B + p_C$ & $p_A = 2p_i - P_t$)

- For Zero order $t_{1/2} \propto [R]_0$; For first order $t_{1/2}$ is independent of $[R]_0$
- The order of a reaction is sometimes altered by conditions.

For example $CH_3COOC_2H_5 + H_2O \xrightarrow{H^+} CH_3COOH + C_2H_5OH$

Ester Hydrolysis with large excess of H_2O

	$CH_3COOC_2H_5$	H_2O	CH_3COOH	C_2H_5OH
t = 0	0.01 mol	10 mol	0	0
t	0 mol	9.99 mol	0.01 mol	0.01 mol

Change in conc. of H_2O is considered as negligible.

- Although the reaction given above follows Bimolecular kinetics and Rate of the reaction is affected by the conc. change of ethyl acetate and water both. But as water is taken in large excess so conc. change of water is considered as negligible hence reaction behaves as first order and called Pseudounimolecular Reaction. These reactions also follow order kinetics.
- Pseudounimolecular Reactions — Molecularity - 1, order - 1
  Although Dikhti Bimolecular Hain.
- Reaction $C_{12}H_{22}O_{11} + H_2O \xrightarrow{H^+} C_6H_{12}O_6 + C_6H_{12}O_6$
  (Cane sugar → Glucose + Fructose)
  is another example of Pseudounimolecular reactions.

Temperature dependence of the Rate of a Reaction

- For a chemical reaction with rise in temperature by 10°c, the rate constant is nearly doubled.
- Arrhenius Equation ⇒ $\{ k = A\,e^{-E_a/RT}$
  - E_a — Enegy of activation
  - R — Gas constant
  - A — Arrhenius or Frequency factor also called Pre-exponential factor.
- According to Arrhenius formation of HI through H_2 & I_2 proceeds via an intermediate formation as shown

  H–H + I–I (Collide) → H·····I / H·····I (Intermediate or Activated complex) → H—I + H—I (Product)

  Ea is required to form this Complex

Activated complex ← Intermediate
Activation energy (energy barrier)
C
A — $H_2 + I_2$ ← Reactant
B — 2HI ← Product
ΔH — Final Enthalpy of Reaction
Potential energy
Reaction coordinate ← Profile of energy change when reactants change to products

Activation Energy (Ea) — Minimum amount of energy required by reactant Molecules to form the product. It is measured in Joules per mole ($J\,mol^{-1}$)

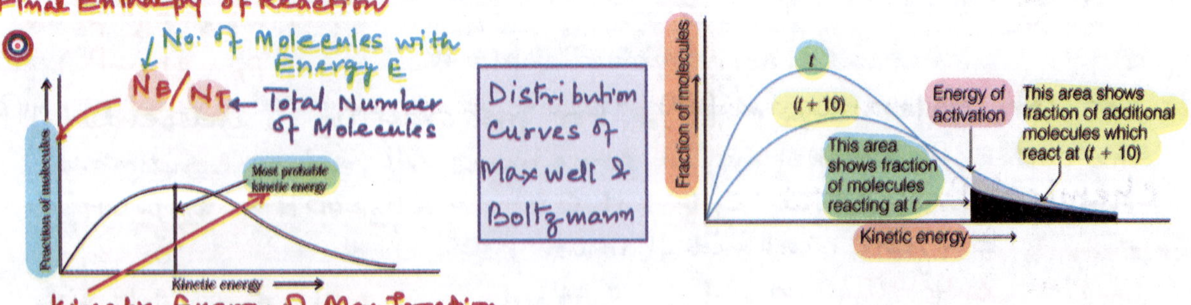

- The expressions of Arrhenius equation are
$\ln K = -\frac{E_a}{RT} + \ln A$; $\log \frac{k_2}{k_1} = \frac{E_a}{2.303R}\left[\frac{1}{T_1} - \frac{1}{T_2}\right]$

$$\log \frac{k_2}{k_1} = \frac{E_a}{2.303R}\left[\frac{T_2 - T_1}{T_1 T_2}\right]$$

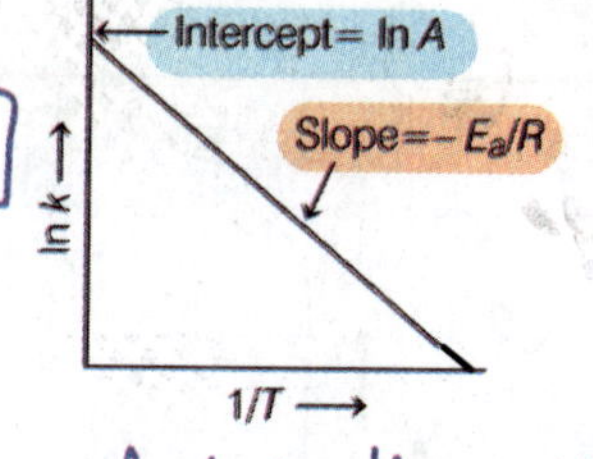

lnK Vs 1/T graph

Effect of Catalyst

- A catalyst alters the reaction rate by creating an alternate pathway of lower or higher Ea.
- A catalyst is never used up in a reaction & is always sufficient in small amounts.

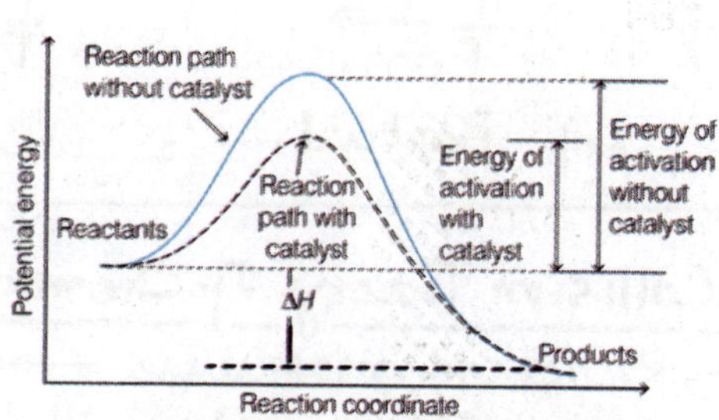

Effect of catalyst on activation energy

Dhyan Rakhna! A catalyst never alters the Gibb's Energy (ΔG) of a Reaction. It catalyses the spontaneous reactions only. It does not changes equilibrium constant, rather, it helps in attaining the equilibrium faster (as it catalyses forward and backward reactions with same extent)

PYQ Punch

1. Activation energy of any chemical reaction can be calculated if one knows the value of **NEET 2024**
(a) Rate constant at standard temperature
(b) Probability of collision
(c) Orientation of reactant molecules during collision
✓(d) rate constant at two different temperatures.

Sol. Factual (from $\log \frac{k_2}{k_1} = \frac{E_a}{2.303R}\left[\frac{1}{T_1} - \frac{1}{T_2}\right]$)

2. The rate of a reaction quadruples when temperature changes from 27°c to 57°c. Calculate the energy of activation. (Given $R = 8.314\ JK^{-1}mol^{-1}$, $\log 4 = 0.6021$ **NEET 2024**
✓(a) 38.04 kJ/mol (b) 380.4 KJ/mol (c) 3.80 kJ/mol (d) 3804 kJ/mol

Sol. Given $\frac{r_2}{r_1} = 4 = \frac{k_2}{k_1}$; so, $\log(4) = \frac{E_a \times 1000}{2.303 \times 8.314}\left[\frac{1}{300} - \frac{1}{330}\right] = 38.04\ kJ/mol$

Dhyan Rakho! Jab kisi MCQ mein options nearby digits mein given hon toh always accurate calculation karni chahiye.

PYQ Punch

3. Which plot of $\ln k$ Vs $1/T$ is consistent with Arrhenius equation? NEET 2024

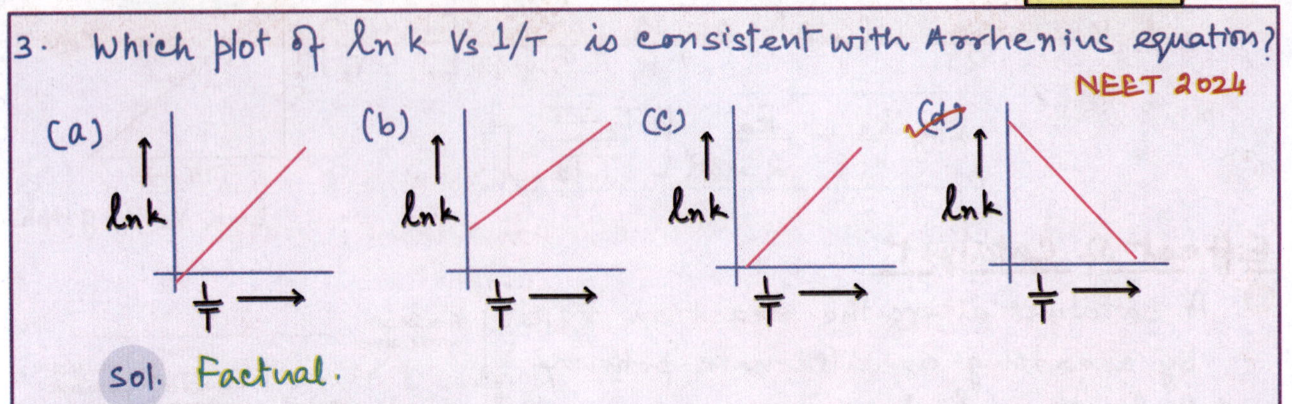

Sol. Factual.

Collision Theory of Chemical Reactions

By Max Trautz & William Lewis (1916-18)

- Reactant molecules ⟶ Hard spheres, Reaction occurs when these molecules collide with each other.
- 2 factors affect the reaction rate – (i) Collision frequency (Z) i.e., no. of collisions per second per unit volume of the reaction mixture.
  (ii) Activation Energy (E_a); So, Arrhenius equation is modified as $\text{Rate} = Z_{AB}\, e^{-E_a/RT}$ (for any reaction $A + B \rightarrow$ Product)
- But all collisions do not lead to product formation. Infact, the collisions in which molecules collide with sufficient KE (called threshold energy) and proper orientation results to product. Such collisions are called effective collisions.
- $H_3C^{\delta+}-Br^{\delta-} + \bar{O}H$
  - Improper Orientation ⟶ $H_3C^{\delta+}-Br^{\delta-}$ … $\bar{O}H$ ⟶ No Products
  - Proper Orientation ⟶ Intermediate $[\bar{O}H \cdots C^{\delta+}H_3 \cdots Br^{\delta-}]$ ⟶ $\overset{\delta-}{O}H-\overset{\delta+}{C}H_3 + Br^-$

  Proper orientation leads to product formation.
- The equation is further modified as $\text{Rate} = P\, Z_{AB}\, e^{-E_a/RT}$
  (P = Probability or Steric factor)
- Drawbacks of collision theory include –
  (i) Consideration of atoms / molecules as hard spheres
  (ii) Ignorance of structural aspect of atoms.

13. d & f Block Elements

- Elements of group 3 – 12, four series namely 3d, 4d, 5d & 6d. The elements are called transition metals.
- Elements of Group 3, two series namely 4f and 5f. The elements are called inner transition metals or rare earth metals.
- Originally word TRANSITION → chemical properties transit (midway) between s and p block elements. But according to IUPAC → Those metals which have incomplete d subshell either in atom or in their ions.

NEET concentrate

Zn, Cd and Hg have d^{10} (completely filled) configuration in their ground (atom) and oxidised (ionic) states hence, these are not regarded as Transition metals.

- 3d series (Sc – Zn), 4d series (Y to Cd), 5d series (La & Hf to Hg), 6d series (Ac and Rf to Cn)

1st Series

Z	Sc 21	Ti 22	V 23	Cr 24	Mn 25	Fe 26	Co 27	Ni 28	Cu 29	Zn 30
4s	2	2	2	1	2	2	2	2	1	2
3d	1	2	3	5	5	6	7	8	10	10

2nd Series

Z	Y 39	Zr 40	Nb 41	Mo 42	Tc 43	Ru 44	Rh 45	Pd 46	Ag 47	Cd 48
5s	2	2	1	1	1	1	1	0	1	2
4d	1	2	4	5	6	7	8	10	10	10

Sabhi Highlighted configurations ka Dhyan Rakhna! Yeh NEET point of view se Important Hain.

- d orbitals protrude more to the periphery of atom in comparison to s and p orbitals → They are more influenced by surroundings & affect more to atoms & molecules surrounding them
- There are greater similarities in the properties of transition metals of a series in contrast to their non-transition counterparts (as outermost electronic configurations of transition metals are more or less similar i.e., usually 1 or 2 electrons are present in their outermost orbits)

Physical properties of Transition metals

- Nearly all transition metals show → High tensile strength, ductility, malleability, high thermal & electrical conductivity & metallic lusture.

- All transition metals have typical metallic structures at normal temperatures (Zn, Cd, Hg and Mn are exceptions)
- Their other physical properties are –
  - Low volatility
  - High melting points (due to involvement of greater number of electrons i.e., $(n-1)d + ns$ in metallic bonding)
  - High enthalpies of atomisation with maxima at about the middle of each series (as an indication that 1 unpaired e^- per d orbital is particularly favourable for strong inter-atomic interactions)

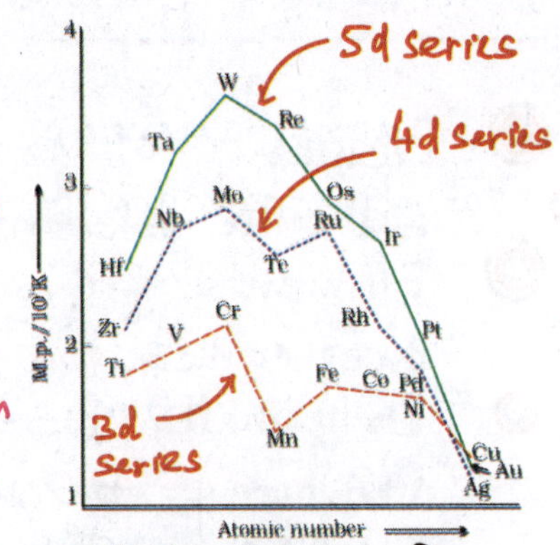

Melting Points of Transition Elements

Dhyan Rakho | Jitne zyada valence electrons utni hi strong metallic bonding.

NEET concentrate

> Enthalpy of atomisation ⟶ Important factor in determining Standard Electrode Potential So, metals with very high enthalpy of atomisation (i.e., very high B.P.) tend to be noble in their reactions. Simply, high enthalpy of atomisation ⟶ Difficulty in atomic separation ⟷ Difficulty in loss of e^- ⟷ low or almost no reactivity.

- Compounds of heavy transition metals have much more frequent metal – metal bonding (due to greater enthalpies of atomisation in contrast to those of 3d series)

Variation in atomic and ionic sizes of Transition metals

- Variation with in a series is quite small (as shielding effect of d-orbitals is not so effective so Net electrostatic attraction between Nuclear charge and outermost electron increases)
- Radii of 4d and 5d series are almost same (due to intervention of 4f orbitals which must be filled before the filling of 5d orbitals & 4f orbital filling is associated with Lanthanoid Contraction.

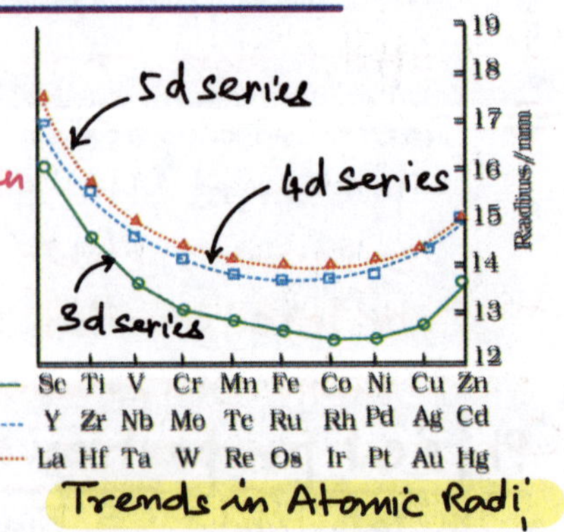

Trends in Atomic Radii

- Decrease in metallic radius + Increase in atomic mass = Increase in Density of these elements.

Ionisation Enthalpies

- In general increase in ionisation enthalpies is visible however successive I.E. donot increase as steeply as in the case of non transition elements
- Variation along a period is much less (as I.E. is typically connected directly with the atomic and ionic sizes.)
- The trend of steady increase in 2nd and 3rd I.E. break for the formation of Mn^{2+} and Fe^{3+} respectively (as in both the cases ions have stable d^5 configuration) Similar breaks visible at corresponding elements in 4d, 5d and 6d series.
- 3 terms responsible for I.E. values are–
  - (i) Attraction between outer most electrons and nucleus
  - (ii) Repulsion between electrons
  - (iii) Exchange Energy (approximately proportional to total no. of possible pairs having parallel spin in degenerate orbitals) It is calculated with the help of Hund's rule.
- Loss of exchange energy ⟶ Stability increases thus ionisation becomes more difficult.

NEET concentrate

> Mn^+ $(3d^5 4s^1)$ has lower I.E. than Cr^+ $(3d^5 4s^0)$. Similarly, I.E. of Fe^{2+} $(3d^6)$ is lower than that of Mn^{2+} $(3d^5)$. Justification of both the cases is "There is no loss of exchange energy at d^6 conf.

Oxidation States (OS)

- Lowest common oxidation state is M^{2+}. High values of 3rd I.E. of Cu, Ni and Zn indicate why it is difficult to obtain oxidation states greater than 2 for these elements.
- Variability in O.S. is due to incomplete filling of d orbitals in such a way that O.S. differ by 1.

Form most promising oxidising agents $KMnO_4$ & $K_2Cr_2O_7$

Oxidation States of the first row Transition Metal (the most common ones are in bold types)

Sc	Ti	V	Cr	Mn	Fe	Co	Ni	Cu	Zn
	+2	+2	+2	**+2**	**+2**	**+2**	**+2**	+1	**+2**
+3	+3	+3	**+3**	+3	**+3**	**+3**	+3	**+2**	
	+4	+4	+4	+4	+4	+4	+4		
		+5	+5	+5					
			+6	+6	+6				
				+7					

Always Remember! variable O.S. of p-block elements are due to Inert pair effect & always differ by 2.

- In p-block elements lower O.S. are favoured by heavier elements, the opposite is true in d-block.

- $K_2Cr_2O_7$ in acidic medium is a good oxidising agent but MoO_3 and WO_3 are not (as Mo(IV) and W(IV) are found to be more stable than Cr(IV)).
- In $Ni(CO)_4$ & $Fe(CO)_5$ the O.S. of Ni and Fe is zero (as CO group is capable enough of accepting π-character in addition to σ bonding)

Trends in M^{2+}/M Standard Electrode Potentials (SEP)

- Cu do not have the ability to liberate H_2 from acids. Only oxidising acid (HNO_3 and hot conc. H_2SO_4) react with Cu and oxidise it to Cu^{2+}. (The SEP of Cu is (+)ve as $Cu(s) \longrightarrow Cu^{2+}(aq)$ is not balanced by its hydration enthalpy) →

Thermochemical data (kJ mol^{-1}) for the first row Transition Elements and the Standard Electrode Potentials for the Reduction of M^{II} to M.

Element (M)	$\Delta_a H^\circ$ (M)	$\Delta_i H_1^\circ$	$\Delta_i H_2^\circ$	$\Delta_{hyd} H^\circ (M^{2+})$	E°/V
Ti	469	656	1309	-1866	-1.63
V	515	650	1414	-1895	-1.18
Cr	398	653	1592	-1925	-0.90
Mn	279	717	1509	-1862	-1.18
Fe	418	762	1561	-1998	-0.44
Co	427	758	1644	-2079	-0.28
Ni	431	736	1752	-2121	-0.25
Cu	339	745	1958	-2121	0.34
Zn	130	906	1734	-2059	-0.76

- SEP (E°) value of Mn, Ni & Zn are more (−)ve than expected as per trend. (as Mn^{2+} and Zn^{2+} has d^5 and d^{10} configurations respectively, whereas Ni has highest (−)ve value of Enthalpy of Hydration).

Trends in M^{3+}/M^{2+} SEP

- Among M^{3+} ions Sc^{3+} is very stable (as it has noble gas configuration) while Zn^{3+} is most unstable one (as Zn^{2+} has stable d^{10} configuration) Similarly Mn^{3+} is less stable (as Mn^{2+} has stable d^5 configuration) while Fe^{3+} (d^5) is extra stable.

Trends in stability of higher oxidation states

- Among halides TiX_4, VF_5, CrF_6 & MnO_3F show highest oxidation states of +4, +5, +6 & +7 respectively.
- All Cu^{II} halides are known except Iodides (as Cu^{2+} oxidises I^- to I_2) Further, Cu(I) compounds are unstable in aqueous solution & undergo disproportionation i.e., $Cu^+(aq) \longrightarrow Cu^{2+}(aq) + Cu$ (As Hydration energy of $Cu^{2+}(aq)$ easily compensates second ionisation enthalpy of Cu)
- Highest O.S. in oxides coincide with the group number till group 7th (Sc_2O_3 to Mn_2O_7)
- The ability of oxygen to stabilise high oxidation states exceeds F. The potential of O to form multiple bonds with metals explains its superiority

Chemical reactivity and E° values

- Many transition metals are sufficiently electropositive ⟶ easily dissolve in mineral acids with $H_2\uparrow$
- All metals of first series (except Cu) are relatively more reactive & are oxidised by 1M H^+.

- Ti and V are passive to dilute non oxidising acids at room temperature
- Mn^{3+} & Co^{3+} ⟶ Strongest oxidising agents in aqueous solutions.
  Ti^{2+}, V^{2+} & Cr^{2+} ⟶ Strong reducing agents and will liberate $H_2(g)$ from a dilute acid.
- The E° values (M^{2+}/M) of 3d series members are irregular (due to irregular first & second ionisation + sublimation enthalpies)
- Among Cr^{2+} & Fe^{2+}, Fe^{2+} is stronger reducing agent
  (As $Cr^{2+} \longrightarrow Cr^{3+}$ E° = −0.407 V → Comparatively difficult
  $Fe^{2+} \longrightarrow Fe^{3+}$ E° = −0.77 V → Easy change)
- **Magnetic Properties**
  - Diamagnetism – Repulsion to applied magnetic Field, Due to all paired e⁻
  - Paramagnetism – Attraction to applied magnetic Field, Due to unpaired e⁻
  - Ferromagnetism – Extreme case of paramagnetism, strong attraction towards applied magnetic field.
- Many transition metal ions ⟶ PARAMAGNETIC; Magnetic Moment usually calculated by 2 factors –
  1. Orbital Angular Momentum → Insignificant for 3d Transition Series
  2. spin angular momentum
- In 3d series for n unpaired e⁻ magnetic moment $\mu = \sqrt{n(n+2)}$

NEET concentrate

Calculated values of magnetic moment for 1, 2, 3, 4, 5 unpaired e⁻ are 1.73, 2.84, 3.87, 4.90 & 5.92 respectively.

- Paramagnetic substances / ions → show colouration due to the presence of unpaired electrons present in them.
- d-block elements have the tendency to form complexes like $[Cu(NH_3)_4]^{2+}$, $[Fe(CN)_6]^{3-}$, $[Fe(CN)_6]^{4-}$ & $[PtCl_4]^{2-}$. This is due to (i) Comparative smaller size of metal ions
  (ii) High charges on their ions
  (iii) Availability of vacant d-orbitals for bond formation
- Compounds of transition metals have good catalytic properties. eg:) V_2O_5 in contact process, finely divided Fe in Haber process etc.

- Reasons for their catalytic nature are -
  (i) their ability to change their oxidation state
  (ii) providing additional surface area to reactants
- Alloy → Homogeneous solid solution in which atoms of one metal are randomly distributed among the atoms of other.
  Essential condition for alloy formation → Metallic radii of atoms are with in about 15% of each other.
  Properties — Hard, Often with high melting points.
  Examples — Cr, V, W, Mo & Mn used in the production of variety of steels & stainless steel
  Brass — Cu-Zn, Bronze — Cu-Sn
- All the metals except Sc forms MO type ionic oxides. As the Oxidation number of metal increases → Ionic ch. decreases
- Mn_2O_7, CrO_3, V_2O_5 → Predominantly Acidic (V_2O_5 Amphoteric)

$K_2Cr_2O_7$

Oxidant of leather industry & helpful in the preparation of azo compounds.

- $4FeCr_2O_4 + 8Na_2CO_3 + 7O_2 \longrightarrow 8Na_2CrO_4 + 2Fe_2O_3 + 8CO_2\uparrow$
  ($FeCr_2O_4$: Chromite ore; Na_2CrO_4: Yellow solution)

  $2Na_2CrO_4 + 2H^+ \longrightarrow Na_2Cr_2O_7 + 2Na^+ + H_2O$
  $Na_2Cr_2O_7$ → crystallises as $Na_2Cr_2O_7 \cdot 2H_2O$
- $Na_2Cr_2O_7$ is more soluble than $K_2Cr_2O_7$ (Orange crystals)
  $Na_2Cr_2O_7 + 2KCl \longrightarrow K_2Cr_2O_7 + 2NaCl$
- Chromates and dichromates are interconvertible in aqueous solution depending upon the pH of the solution.
  Dhyan Rakhna | the oxidation state of Cr is same in chromates and dichromates.

  $2CrO_4^{--} + 2H^+ \rightarrow Cr_2O_7 + H_2O$; $Cr_2O_7^{--} + 2\bar{O}H \longrightarrow 2CrO_4^{--} + H_2O$

  Tetrahedral
  Chromate ion

  Different Bond Length (179 pm, 163 pm), 126°
  Dichromate ion

  2 Tetrahedra sharing 1 corner with bond angle of 126°

  Oxidising property in acidic solution can be represented as

  $Cr_2O_7^{--} + 14H^+ + 6e^- \longrightarrow 2Cr^{3+} + 7H_2O$ ($E^\circ = +1.33V$)
- $6I^- \longrightarrow 3I_2 + 6e^-$; $3Sn^{2+} \longrightarrow 3Sn^{4+} + 6e^-$; $6Fe^{2+} \longrightarrow 6Fe^{3+} + 6e^-$
  $3H_2S \longrightarrow 6H^+ + 3S + 6e^-$ (Oxidation half reactions of acidified $K_2Cr_2O_7$)

- The complete ionic equation can be obtained as
$$Cr_2O_7^{--} + 14H^+ + 6Fe^{2+} \rightarrow 2Cr^{3+} + 7H_2O + 6Fe^{3+}$$
(by adding $6Fe^{2+} \rightarrow 6Fe^{3+} + 6e^-$ with $Cr_2O_7^{--} + 14H^+ + 6e^- \rightarrow 2Cr^{3+} + 7H_2O$)

$KMnO_4$ (Dark Purple (almost black) crystals, Isostructural with $KClO_3$, solubility – 6.4g/100g water at 293K, Decomposes at 513K.)
$$2MnO_2 + 4KOH + O_2/KNO_3 \rightarrow 2K_2MnO_4 + 2H_2O$$
$$2H_2O + MnO_2 + 2KMnO_4 \leftarrow +4H^+$$

- Commercially $MnO_2 \xrightarrow[\text{Oxidised with air/}KNO_3]{\text{Fused with KOH,}} MnO_4^{2-}$ (Manganate ion)
$MnO_4^{2-} \xrightarrow[\text{in alkaline solution}]{\text{Electrolytic oxidation}} MnO_4^-$ (Permanganate ion)

- In lab. $2Mn^{2+} + 5S_2O_8^{--} + 8H_2O \rightarrow 2MnO_4^- + 10SO_4^{--} + 16H^+$
- Diamagnetic along with temperature dependent weak paramagnetic

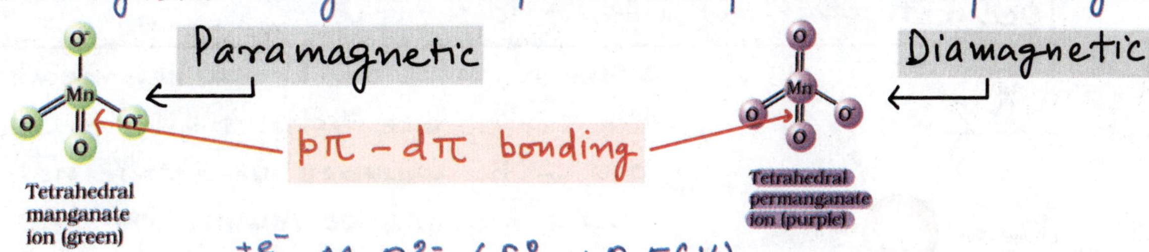

- MnO_4^-
  - $\xrightarrow{+e^-} MnO_4^{2-}$ ($E° = +0.56V$)
  - $\xrightarrow[3e^-]{4H^+} MnO_2 + H_2O$ ($E° = +1.69V$)
  - $\xrightarrow[5e^-]{8H^+} Mn^{2+} + 4H_2O$ ($E° = +1.52V$)

- **Oxidation Reactions**

In Acid solutions

- $10I^- + 2MnO_4^- + 16H^+ \rightarrow 2Mn^{2+} + 8H_2O + I_2\uparrow$
- $5Fe^{2+}$ (green) $+ MnO_4^- + 8H^+ \rightarrow Mn^{2+} + 4H_2O + 5Fe^{3+}$ (yellow)
- $5C_2O_4^{2-} + 2MnO_4^- + 16H^+ \rightarrow 2Mn^{2+} + 8H_2O + 10CO_2\uparrow$
- $5S^{--} + 2MnO_4^- + 16H^+ \rightarrow 2Mn^{2+} + 8H_2O + 5S\downarrow$
- $5SO_3^{--} + 2MnO_4^- + 6H^+ \rightarrow 2Mn^{2+} + 3H_2O + 5SO_4^{--}$
- $5NO_2^- + 2MnO_4^- + 6H^+ \rightarrow 2Mn^{2+} + 5NO_3^- + 3H_2O$

In Neutral/faintly alkaline solutions

- $2MnO_4^- + H_2O + I^- \rightarrow 2MnO_2 + 2OH^- + IO_3^-$
- $8MnO_4^- + 2S_2O_3^{--} + H_2O \rightarrow 8MnO_2 + 6SO_4^{--} + 2OH^-$
- $2MnO_4^- + 3Mn^{2+} + 2H_2O \rightarrow 5MnO_2 + 4H^+$

NEET concentrate: This reaction is catalysed by $ZnSO_4$ or ZnO

INNER TRANSITION ELEMENTS

- Lanthanoids – Members of 4f series (58 – 71); Present after Lanthanum (La); Follow Lanthanum in properties that's why called Lanthanoids.
(Gr. 3, Period 6)
$(n-2)f^{1-14}, (n-1)d^{0-1} ns^2$

- The position of all Lanthanoids is similar in periodic table but still their atomic/ionic radius decreases with increase in atomic no. This decrease is known as **Lanthanoid contraction** ⟶ Rare phenomenon seen due to zero shielding by the f electrons.

  Dhyan Rakhna | among s, p, d & f orbitals the screening or shielding effect of s & p orbitals = 65% (when outermost) d-orbitals = 15% & f orbitals = 0

- Lanthanoid contraction also affects the radii of the members of 4d and 5d transition series. (Members of both the series have almost identical radii)

NEET concentrate

> Due to almost identical radii Zr (160 pm) and Hf (159 pm) occur together and difficult to separate.

- Chemical behaviour of earlier members of the series are quite similar to Calcium but with increase in atomic no. they react more like Aluminium. (As I^st^ & IInd I.E. of Lanthanoids are comparable with those of Ca)

Ln; burns in O_2 → Ln_2O_3; with acids → H_2; with halogens → LnX_3; with H_2O → $Ln(OH)_3 + H_2$; with C, 2773 K → LnC_2, Ln_3C, Ln_2C_3; heated with N → LnN; heated with S → Ln_2S_3

Chemical reactions of the lanthanoids.

$Ln(OH)_3$ ← Definite compounds not just hydrated oxides (Basic in Nature)

- **MISCHMETALL** ⟶ Lanthanoid (≃95%) + Iron (≃5%) + S, C, Ca, Al (Trace) Used to produce bullets, shells & lighter flint.

- **Actinoids** – Members of 5f series (90 – 103); Present after Actinium (Ac); Follow Actinium in properties that's why called Actinoids.
  (Gr. 3, Period 7)
  $(n-2)f^{1-14}(n-1)d^{0-1}ns^2$

- Show Actinoid contraction just similar to lanthanoid contraction but much greater in magnitude in comparison to Lanthanoids.

Oxidation States of Actinium and Actinoids

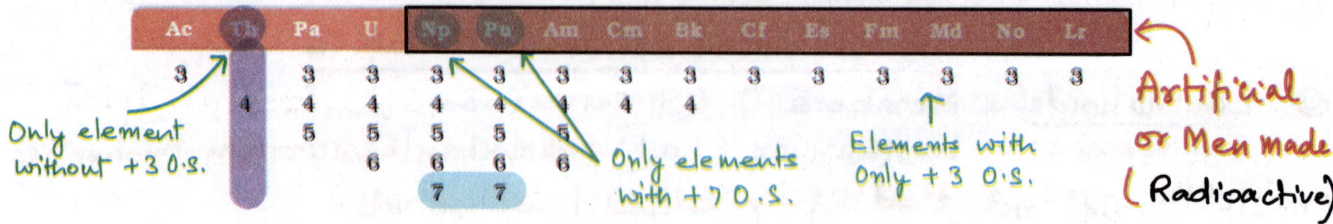

Ac	Th	Pa	U	Np	Pu	Am	Cm	Bk	Cf	Es	Fm	Md	No	Lr
3		3	3	3	3	3	3	3	3	3	3	3	3	3
	4	4	4	4	4	4	4	4						
		5	5	5	5	5								
			6	6	6	6								
				7	7									

14. Coordination Compounds

- Complex compounds in which metal atoms are bound to a number of anions or neutral molecules through coordinate linkages are called Coordination compounds.
- These are different from double salts → $KCl \cdot MgCl_2 \cdot 6H_2O$ (Carnallite) $FeSO_4 \cdot (NH_4)_2SO_4 \cdot 6H_2O$ (Mohr's salt) $KAl(SO_4)_2 \cdot 12H_2O$ (Potash alum) → Completly ionise when dissolved in solvents like water.
- Coordination compounds → do not ionise completly as they usually have Ionic (Ionisable) & Coordinate (non ionisable) linkages e.g., $K_3[Fe(CN)_6]$ have –

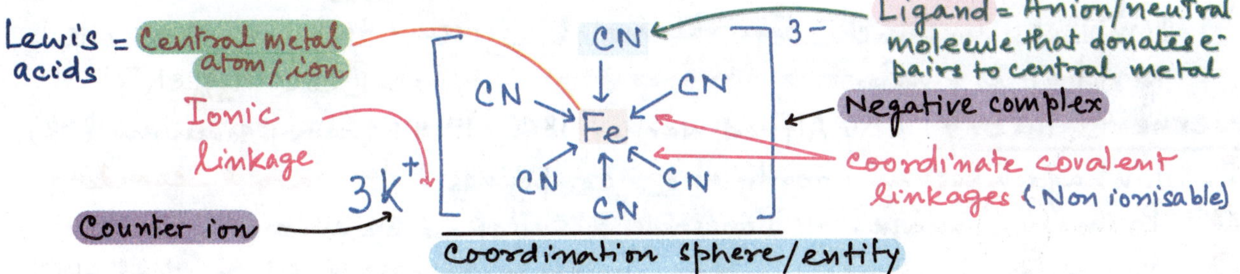

- The number of e⁻ pairs that a ligand can donate → Denticity

Ligands
- → Uni or Monodentate – with ability to donate 1 e⁻ pair (Cl^-, NH_3, H_2O)
- → Bi or Didentate – with ability to donate 2 e⁻ pairs ($C_2O_4^{--}$)
- → Polydentate – with ability to donate more than 2 e⁻ pairs. (EDTA)

$H_2\ddot{N}-CH_2-CH_2-\ddot{N}H_2$
Ethane-1,2-diamine = A di or bidentate ligand (2 e⁻-donation sites are highlighted)

COO^- | COO^-
Oxalate ion another didentate ligand.

$CH_2-N<(CH_2COO^-)(CH_2COO^-)$ | $CH_2-N<(CH_2COO^-)(CH_2COO^-)$
Ethylene diamine tetra acetate = EDTA = A Hexadentate ligand (6 e⁻ donation sights are highlighted)

Can also be called a chelate ligand as its 2 or more donor atoms binds to 1 central metal simultaneously.

- Ligands with 2 different donor atoms & either of them can donate e⁻ in the complex → Ambidentate ligands. (NO_2^-, SCN^-)

$M \leftarrow N(=O)-\bar{O}$	$M \leftarrow \bar{O}-N=O$	$M \leftarrow SNC$	$M \leftarrow NCS$
Nitrito-N	Nitrito-O	Thiocyanato-S	Thiocyanato-N

- The number of ligands surrounding the central metal is called the Coordination Number of that metal. This number is fixed for a particular metal.

- $[Pt(Cl)_6]^{2-} \rightarrow$ C.N. 6 ; $[Ni(NH_3)_4]^{2+} \rightarrow$ C.N. 4; $[Fe(C_2O_4)_3]^{3-} \rightarrow$ C.N. 6
  $[Co(en)_3]^{3+} \rightarrow$ C.N. 6 (en → ethane-1,2-diamine)

Dhyan Rakhna | Coordination Number mein central metal atom & ligands ke beech bane sirf σ bonds ko hi consider kiya jaata hai, π bonds ko nahi.

- The spatial (3D) arrangement of ligand atoms around the central metal atom ⟶ coordination Polyhedra. $[Co(NH_3)_6]^{3+}$ is octahedral; $Ni(CO)_4$ is tetrahedral; $[Pt(Cl)_4]^{2-}$ is square planar.
- The charge central metal atom carry of all ligands along with their e^- pairs are removed from coordination sphere ⟶ Oxidation state of central atom.
- Complexes in which central metal is bound to only one kind of ligand ⟶ Homoleptic complexes $[Co(NH_3)_6]^{3+}$
  Complexes in which central metal is bound to more than one kind of ligands ⟶ Heteroleptic complexes $[Co(NH_3)_4Cl_2]^+$

Werner's Theory (By Alfred Werner 1866-1919; theory given in 1898)

- Linkage types in coordination compounds – Primary & Secondary
- Primary Linkages → Ionisable & satisfied by anions.
- secondary Linkages ⟶ Non ionisable & satisfied by neutral atom or ions via coordinate bonds.
- Secondary Linkages = Coordination Number (Fixed for a metal)
- Ions / Groups attached to secondary linkages = Ligands
- Ligands have characteristic spatial arrangements corresponding to different coordination numbers = Coordination Polyhedra.

Nomenclature : Naming Mononuclear coordination compounds

- Cation is named first → for both (+)ve & (−)ve complexes.
- Ligands ⟶ named in alphabetical order & placed before the name of central metal/ion.
- Anionic Ligands name → end with – ido (as per IUPAC 2004 draft)
- Cationic Ligand name → same except aqua = H_2O; Ammine = NH_3
  Carbonyl = CO; Nitrosyl = NO.
- Number of ligands → Usually Prefix mono, di, tri etc. & bis, tris, tetrakis when ligand names include any Numerical Prefix (Concerned ligand name being enclosed in bracket)
  $[NiCl_2(PPh_3)_2]$ → dichlorido → Cl_2; bis (triphenyl phosphine) → $(PPh_3)_2$

- Metal Name → for cation & Neutral complexes - Normal element name is used. for anion complex - Metal Name ends with suffix - ate. for some metals the Latin names are used in complex anions e.g., ferrate for Fe.
- Oxidation state of Metal → As Roman Numeral in bracket after metal

$K_4[Fe(CN)_6]$ → Potassium (Cation) hexacyano ferrate (II) (Anion Complex) ← O.S.
(hexacyano: Ligand Name + No.; ferrate: Metal Name)

$[Cr(NH_3)_3(H_2O)_3]Cl_3$ (cation complex, anion) → triamminetriaqua chromium(III) chloride

$[Co(H_2NCH_2CH_2NH_2)_3]_2(SO_4)_3$ → tris(ethane-1,2-diamine)cobalt(III)sulphate

NEET concentrate

> Always Remember! Never indicate the number of cation or anions in the name of any coordination compound.

$[Ag(NH_3)_2][Ag(CN)_2]$ → diamminesilver(I) dicyanidoargentate(I)
(Cation complex, Anion Complex)

Writing Formulas of mononuclear coordination entities:

- complete formula for coordination entity is enclosed with in [ ]
- For polyatomic ligands → Formulas or ligand abbreviations are enclosed with in ( )
- Central Metal → listed first with in [ ]
- Ligands → listed in alphabetical order. Ligand placement does not depends upon its charge. For abbreviations first alphabet of abbreviation is considered.
- There should be no space between ligand and metal with in [ ].
- For Complexes charge is indicated in superscript at the right top of [ ]. In case counter ions are present so no charge is written on complete compound.
- The charge of cation is balanced by the charge on counterion.

Potassium hexacyanoferrate(III) → $3K^+[Fe(CN)_6]^{3-}$ = $K_3[Fe(CN)_6]$

tris(ethane-1,2-diamine)chromium(III) chloride → $[Cr(H_2NCH_2CH_2NH_2)_3]Cl_3$

Tetraamminediaquacobalt(III) chloride → $[Co(H_2O)_2(NH_3)_4]Cl_3$

Isomerism ◎ 2 or more compounds with same molecular formula but different properties = Isomers

◎ Difference in their properties is due to the difference in either their 2D or their 3D structures.

◎ Isomers with difference in properties due to difference in their 3D structures = stereoisomers.

◎ Isomers with difference in properties due to difference in their 2D structures = structural isomers

Stereoisomers
- Geometrical = In heteroleptic complexes, due to different geometric arrangements of ligands.
- Optical = Complexes which show different behaviour towards polarised light.

◎ **Geometrical examples** with C.N. 4 and 6

In Square planar complexes of (i) $[MX_2L_2]$ type $[Pt(NH_3)_2]Cl_2$ → Similar Groups → same side (cis) | opposite side (trans)

(ii) MABXL Type → 2 cis & 1 trans isomers

In Octahedral complexes of $[MX_2L_4]$ → 2 ligands X = Cl are oriented cis and trans to each other: $[Co(NH_3)_4Cl_2]^+$ (cis, trans)

Dhyan Rakhna! Such geometrical isomerism is not possible in tetrahedral complexes.

In octahedral complexes of formula $MX_2(L-L)_2$ → $[CoCl_2(en)_2]$ (cis, trans)

In Octahedral complexes of $[Ma_3b_3]$ type → $Co(NH_3)_3(NO_2)_3$: Facial (fac-), Meridional (mer-)

◎ **Optical**

- They can be non-superimposable mirror images of each other (Enantiomers), and are completely chiral or asymmetrical.
  - → can be either dextro (d) → Rotates polarised light to right or can be laevo (l) → Rotates polarised light to the left.
- Common in Octahedral complexes.

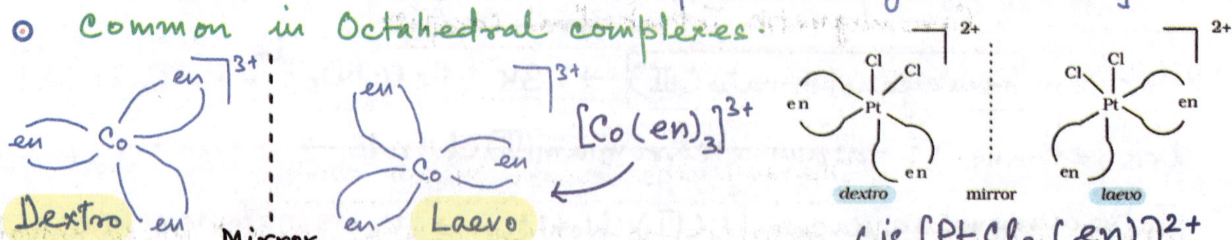

Structural Isomers

- **Linkage** → In coordination compounds with ambidentate ligands.

$[Co(NH_3)_5(NO_2)]Cl_2$
- → When NO_2 is linked through oxygen – Red
- → When NO_2 is linked through Nitrogen – Yellow

- **Coordination** → Due to interchange of ligands between cationic & anionic entities.

$[Co(NH_3)_6][Cr(CN)_6]$ & $[Cr(NH_3)_6][Co(CN)_6]$

- **Ionisation** → When counter ion is itself a potential ligand & swaps position with one of the Ligands.

$[Co(NH_3)_5SO_4]Br$ & $[Co(NH_3)_5Br]SO_4$

- **Solvate** → Also called Hydrate isomerism. Similar to ionisation with the difference that one of the ligand is solvent also. The solvent here helps in crystal lattice molecule.

Voilet → $[Cr(H_2O)_6]Cl_3$ & $[Cr(H_2O)_5Cl]Cl_2 \cdot H_2O$ ← Grey-Green.

Bonding in Coordination Compounds: Valence Bond Theory (VBT)

- Orbitals of Metal atom

→ Hybridisation → set of orbitals of equivalent energy & set geometry

→ Overlap with ligand orbitals (donating e^- for coordinate bonding)

- $[Co(NH_3)_6]^{3+}$

3d: ↑↓ ↑ ↑ ↑ ↑ | 4s: □ | 4p: □□□ ← Co^{3+} ion

↑↓ ↑↓ ↑↓ | d^2sp^3 hybrid: □□□□□□ ← e^- arrangement on approach of a ligand

↑↓ ↑↓ ↑↓ | ↑↓ ↑↓ ↑↓ ↑↓ ↑↓ ↑↓ — Six pairs of electrons from six NH_3 molecules

Inner Orbital or Low spin or spin paired complex due to (n-1) d orbital involvement

Diamagnetic Octahedral complex

- Similarly $[CoF_6]^{3-}$ → Outer Orbital or High Spin or Spin free Complex due to nd orbital involvement.

3d → ↑↓ ↑ ↑ ↑ ↑ | ↑↓ ↑↓ ↑↓ ↑↓ ↑↓ ↑↓ ← sp^3d^2

Paramagnetic Octahedral complex

- $[NiCl_4]^{2-}$ → High Spin Complex

3d → ↑↓ ↑↓ ↑↓ ↑ ↑ | ↑↓ ↑↓ ↑↓ ↑↓ ← sp^3 hybrid

Paramagnetic Tetrahedral complex

- $[Ni(CO)_4]$ → Tetrahedral Diamagnetic Complex (sp^3 hybridisation)
- $[Ni(CN)_4]^{2-}$ → 3d → ↑↓ ↑↓ ↑↓ ↑↓ | ↑↓ ↑↓ ↑↓ ↑↓ ← dsp^2

Diamagnetic Square planar complex

Dhyan Rakha | Hybridisation is a hypothetical concept which involves mathematical manipulation of wave equation for atomic orbitals.

Magnetic properties ◉ For metals up to 3 e^- in d orbitals → the magnetic behaviour of their free ions & coordination entities is similar (Ti^{3+}, V^{3+}, Cr^{3+})

◉ $[Mn(CN)_6]^{3-}$ → Magnetic Moment of 2 unpaired e^-
$[MnCl_6]^{3-}$ → Magnetic Moment of 4 unpaired e^-
$[Fe(CN)_6]^{3-}$ → Magnetic Moment of 1 unpaired e^-
$[FeF_6]^{3-}$ → Magnetic Moment of 5 unpaired e^-
$[CoF_6]^{3-}$ → Magnetic Moment of 4 unpaired e^-

} All Paramagnetic

$[Co(C_2O_4)_3]^{3-}$ → Diamagnetic with no unpaired e^-

Inner orbital complexes with d^2sp^3 hybridisation rest outer orbital complexes with sp^3d^2 hybridisation.

Limitations ◉ Many assumptions involved without quantitative interpretation of magnetic data.

◉ No light on colouration of coordination compounds.

◉ No quantitative interpretation of thermodynamic or kinetic stability of coordination compounds

◉ 4- coordination complexes whether square planar or tetrahedral → No exact prediction

◉ Unable to differentiate between weak & strong ligands.

◉ **Crystal Field Theory** ◉ Electrostatic model, considers metal-ligand bond as ionic → arising due to electrostatic interactions between metal ion and ligand.

◉ d orbitals of metal atom → Degenerate (means of exactly equal energy) → Becomes splitted when approached by a ligand.

NEET concentrate

> Remember! among the d orbitals d_{xy}, d_{yz} and d_{zx} are more or less similar as in all of these the e^- cloud lie between their respective axis (i.e., either xy, yz or zx) while in $d_{x^2-y^2}$ & d_{z^2} the e^- cloud majorly lie on their respective axis.

◉ The splitting is due to different planes of e^- clouds in these orbitals. The ligands are treated as point charges (anions) or point dipoles (neutral ligands)

◉ The pattern of splitting depends upon the nature of crystal field & results to lifting of degeneracy of d-orbitals.

Splitting in octahedral coordination entities

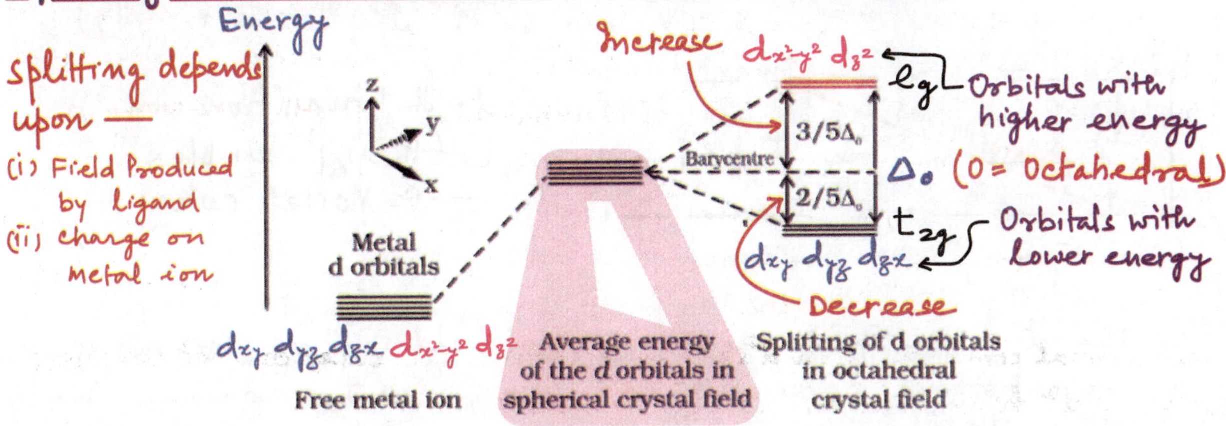

$I^- < Br^- < SCN^- < Cl^- < S^{2-} < F^- < OH^- < C_2O_4^{2-} < H_2O < NCS^- < edta^{4-} < NH_3 < en < CN^- < CO$

Spectrochemical series of increasing ligand field strength

- It is an experimentally determined series based on absorption of light by complexes with different ligands.
- Electron assignment in octahedral coordination entities –
  - (a) $d^1, d^2, d^3 \rightarrow$ lower t_{2g} in accordance with Hund's rule
  - (b) $d^4 \rightarrow$ depends upon Δ_o and P (pairing energy)
    - (i) $\Delta_o < P$ (for weak field ligands) $\rightarrow t_{2g}^3 e_g^1$
    - (ii) $\Delta_o > P$ (for strong field ligands) $\rightarrow t_{2g}^4 e_g^0$

$d^4 - d^7$ coordination entities $\longrightarrow$ more stable for strong fields than weak field.

Splitting in tetrahedral coordination entities

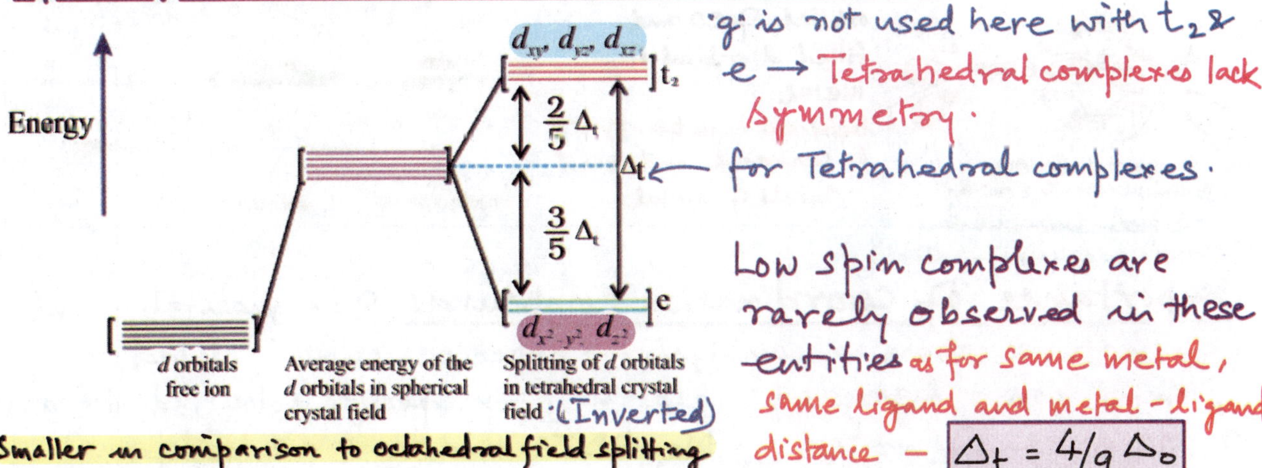

'g' is not used here with t_2 & e → Tetrahedral complexes lack symmetry.

$\Delta_t \leftarrow$ for Tetrahedral complexes.

Smaller in comparison to octahedral field splitting

Low spin complexes are rarely observed in these entities as for same metal, same ligand and metal-ligand distance – $\Delta_t = 4/9\, \Delta_o$

Colours of Coordination Compounds

- Due to d-d transition of e^- (as per crystal field theory)

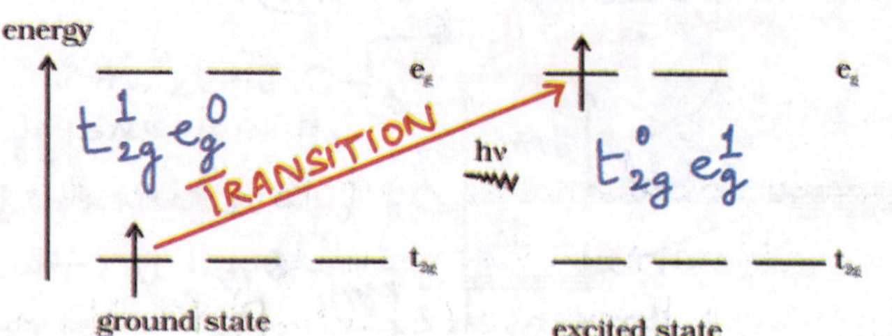

d-d transition in $[Ti(H_2O)_6]^{3+}$ complex ⟶ Voilet colour

- In the absence of ligand ⟶ crystal field splitting does not occur ⟶ substance colourless. (Anhydrous $CuSO_4$ → colourless while $CuSO_4 \cdot 5H_2O$ → Blue colour)
- $[Ni(H_2O)_6]^{2+}$ complex + en in the ratio (Ni : en) —
  - (i) 1 : 1 ⟶ Pale blue
  - (ii) 1 : 2 ⟶ Blue/ Purple.
  - (iii) 1 : 3 ⟶ Violet

  } Influence of ligand on the colour of complex

Limitations of CFT

- Unable to explain the splitting effects of anions (point charges) Vs Neutral molecules (point dipoles)
- Covalent character of bonds between Metal & ligand was not considered.

All these limitations are removed by Ligand Field Theory (LFT) and Molecular Orbital theory.

Bonding in Metal Carbonyls (Synergic bonding)

Synergic bonding

- Between vacant d orbital of CO and filled d orbital of metal
- Between lone pair of e^- of carbonyl and vacant orbitals of metal

(Complimentary bonding between 1 high energy and 1 low energy orbital)

Structure of Homoleptic carbonyls.

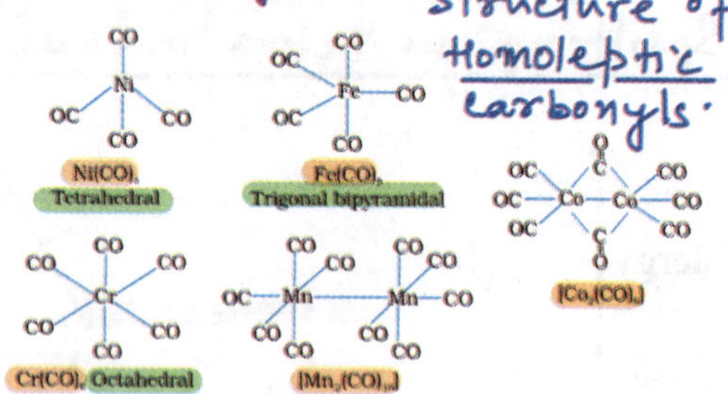

Importance of Coordination Compounds

- In qualitative and quantitative chemical analysis → Especially colour related → Metal ion + ligands (chelating) → specific colour identification.
- Hardness of water ⟶ Na_2EDTA used (as Ca^{2+} & Mg^{2+} forms stable complexes with EDTA) ⟶ selective estimation possible as

Ca^{2+} and Mg^{2+} complexes have differences in their stability constants.

- In extraction process of Metals (especially Ag & Au)
- In metal purification (By formation & subsequent decomposition of metal coordination compounds)
- Chlorophyll, Haemoglobin, Cyanocobalamine (Vit B_{12}) and many enzymes ⟶ all are coordination compounds
- As catalyst in many industrial processes ($[(Ph_3P)_3RhCl]$ is wilkinson catalyst and used in hydrogenation of alkenes)
- $[Ag(CN)_2]^-$ and $[Au(CN)_2]^-$ like complexes in electroplating.
- In Black & white photography → for film fixation and AgBr (undecomposed) removal as $[Ag(S_2O_3)_2]^{3-}$
- In Medicines; use of chelating ligands (like D-Penicillamine and desferrioxime B) for chelate therapy;

  EDTA ⟶ Lead Poisoning

  Pt coordination entities ⟶ Effectively inhibit tumour growth (cis-platin)

15. Haloalkanes & Haloarenes

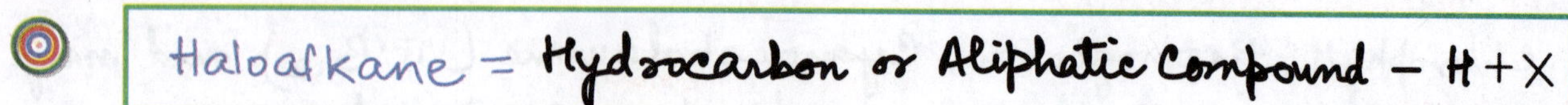

Means an alkyl halide contains one or more halogen atoms directly attached to the carbon atoms of an aliphatic system. For Example

H
H – C – X
H

sp^3 hybridised C – atom of aliphatic system

Halogen atom

Haloarenes = Benzene or Aromatic Compound – H + X

Means a haloarene contains one or more halogen atoms directly attached to the carbon atoms of an aromatic system. For Example

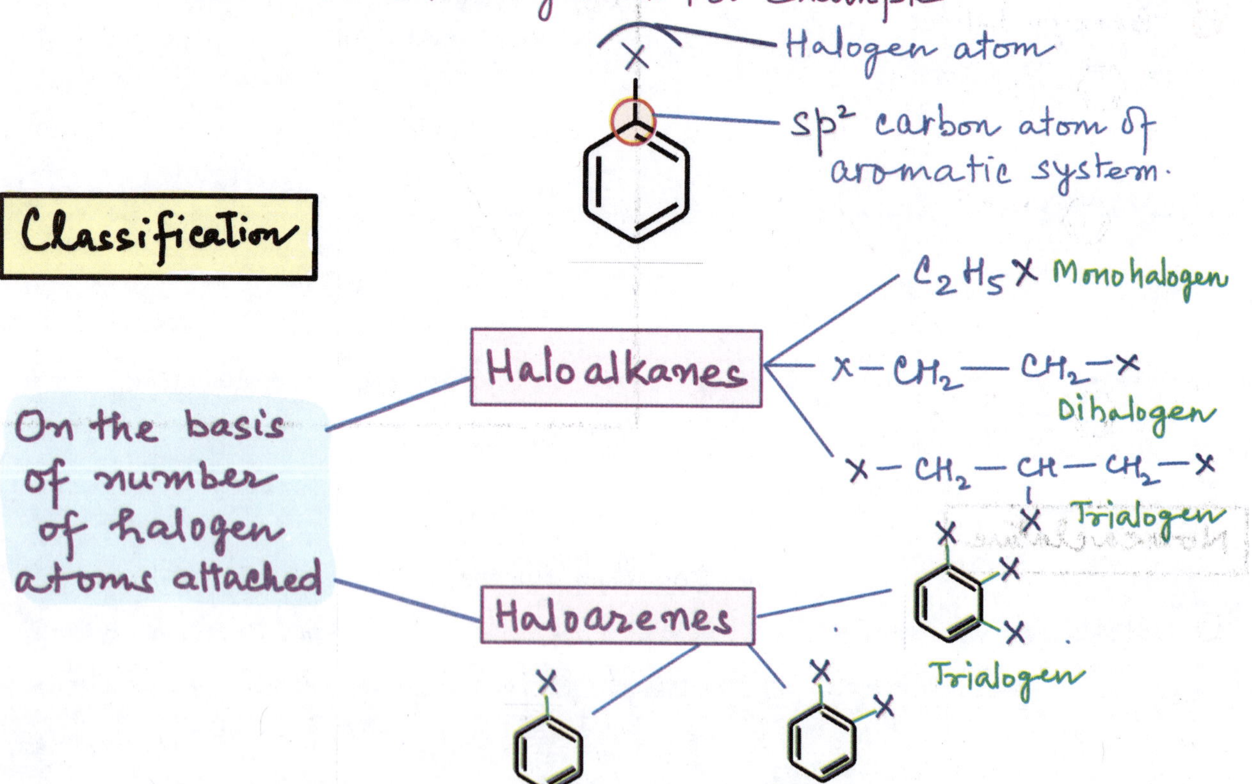

MONO HALOGEN compounds

With sp^3 C–X bond

◉ **Alkyl Halides or Halo alkanes**

$-CH_2-X$ 1°

$>CH-X$ 2°

$\geq C-X$ 3°

sp^3 Hybrid C-atom

◉ **Allylic Halides**

1° $CH_2=CH-CH_2-X$ & (cyclohexene ring with X)

2° $CH_2=CH-\underset{\substack{|\\ -C-\\ |}}{\overset{\substack{H\\ |}}{C}}-X$

3° $CH_2=CH-\underset{\substack{|\\ -C-\\ |}}{\overset{\substack{|\\ -C-\\ |}}{C}}-X$

sp^3 Hybrid Allylic C-atom

◉ **Benzylic Halides**

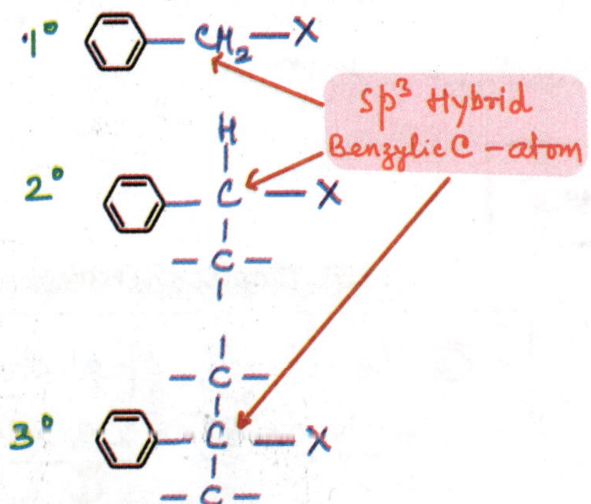

Always Remember!! Behaviour of Allyl and Benzyl group is same. Similarly behaviour of Vinyl and Aryl groups is same.

With sp^2 C–X bond

◉ **Vinylic Halide**

$CH_2=CH-X$

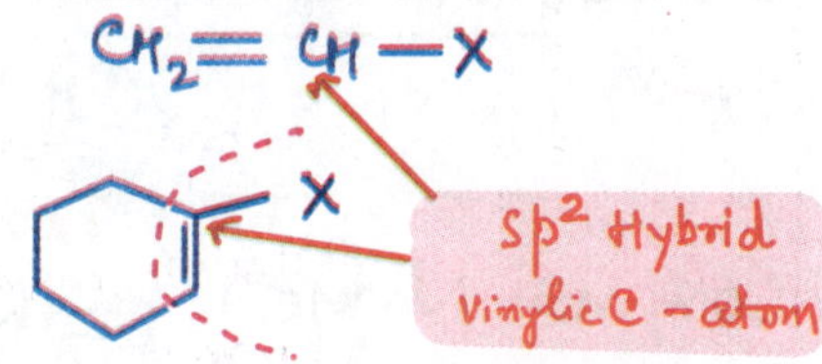

◉ **Aryl Halide**

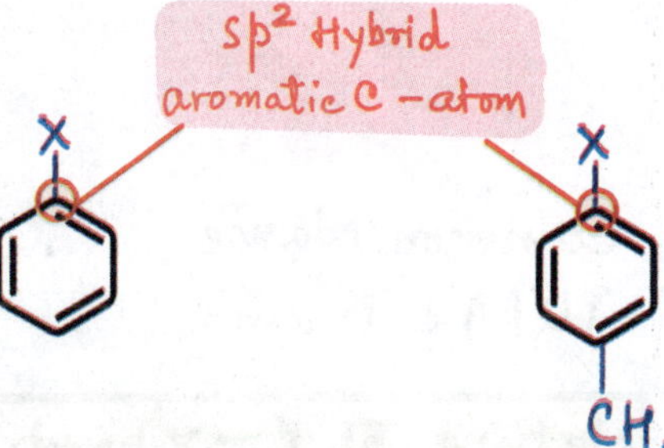

NEET concentrate

◉ Compounds with $C_{sp}-X$ bond also exist. These include –

$HC\equiv C-X$

sp Carbon

This H can be replaced by any alkyl group also.

Nomenclature

	Common Name	IUPAC Name
◉ Halogen compounds →	Alkyl Halide	Halo-alkanes
CH_3CH_2Cl →	Ethyl chloride	Chloroethane
$\overset{1}{C}H_3-\underset{\substack{|\\ Cl}}{\overset{2}{C}H}-\overset{3}{C}H_3$ →	Isopropyl chloride	2-chloropropane

◉ Aryl Halides ⟶ Common and IUPAC Name same for Monohalogen derivatives e.g., C_6H_5Br ⟶ Bromobenzene

Dihalogen derivatives

	CH_3CH (X)(X)	CH_2-CH_2 (X)(X)
Common Name	{Geminal dihalide} {Ethylidene halide}	{Vicinal-dihalide} {Ethylene dihalide}
IUPAC Name	1,1- dihaloethane	1,2-dihalo ethane

	(benzene, X at 1,2)	(benzene, X at 1,3)	(benzene, X at 1,4)
Common Name	Ortho-dihalo	meta-dihalo	para-dihalo
IUPAC Name	1,2-dihalo	1,3-dihalo	1,4-dihalo

Nature of C–X bond

Bond Nature ⟶ Polar

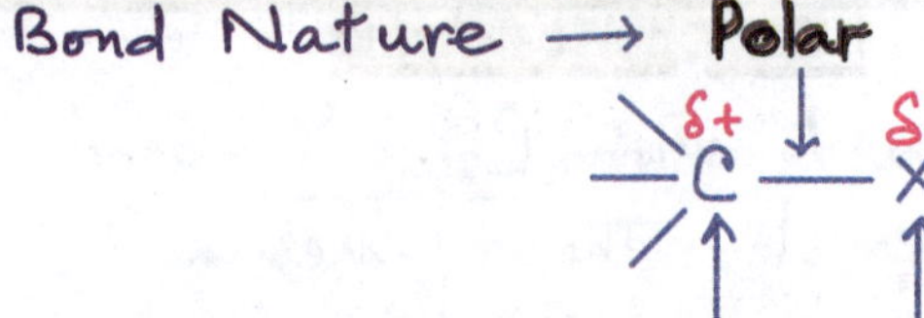

Electronegativity ⟶ Less   More

Bond	Bond length/pm	C-X Bond enthalpies/ kJmol⁻¹	Dipole moment/Debye
CH_3–F	139	452	1.847
CH_3– Cl	178	351	1.860
CH_3–Br	193	293	1.830
CH_3–I	214	234	1.636
	Increase ↓	Decrease ↓	

Haloalkanes

Methods of Preparation

1. From Alcohols

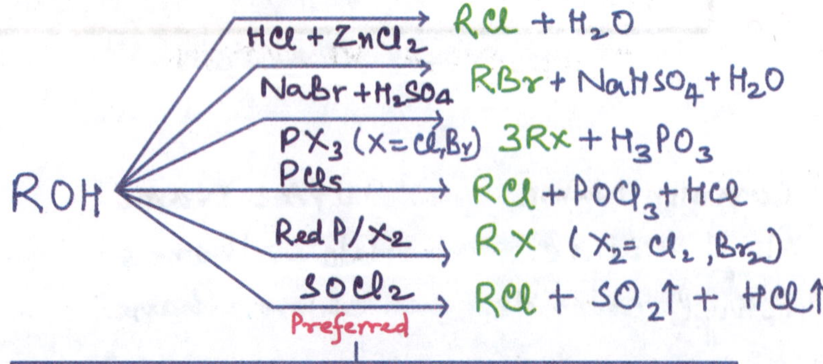

As SO_2 and HCl being gaseous escaped easily leaving pure RCl behind.

NEET concentrate

◉ Reactivity of alcohols

HCl only at room temp. ⟵ 3° > 2° > 1°

(2° > 1°) ↓ Dry HCl + Anhy. $ZnCl_2$ — LUCAS REAGENT

◉ For RBr – Constant boil with HBr (48%)

◉ For RI – NaI or KI + H_3PO_4

◉ PBr_3 and PI_3 prepared in situ i.e., with in the rxn.

- Alkyl Chloride → Dry HCl gas is passed through Alcohol solution OR Heating a mixture of alcohol and conc. HCl(aq)
- Not suitable to prepare aryl halides (as Phenols has partial double bond character in C — O bond)

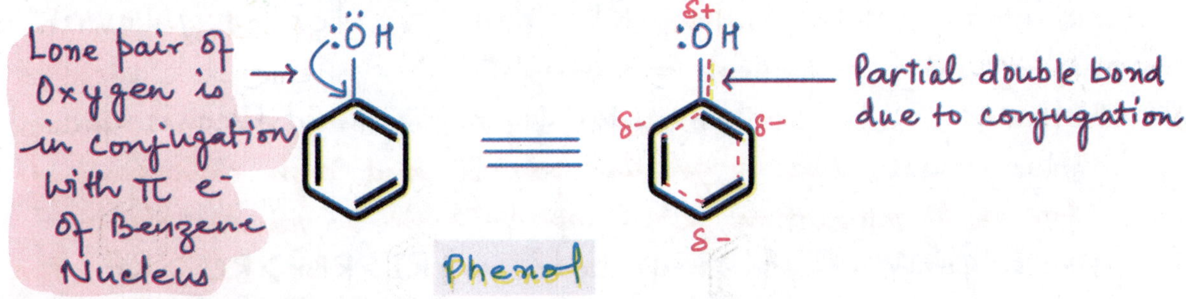

2. From Hydrocarbons

(a) From Alkanes by free radical halogenation

$$C_4H_{10} \xrightarrow[\text{or heat}]{Cl_2/\text{UV light}} CH_3CH_2CH_2CH_2Cl + CH_3CH_2CHClCH_3$$

- Complex mixture of mono and polyhaloalkanes is obtained; difficult to separate.

(b) From alkenes

$$>C=C< + HX \longrightarrow >C(H)-C(X)<$$

- Markownikoff rule is followed for alkenes & reagents with asymmetry
- Reaction proceeds through carbocation formation.

$$CH_2=CH_2 + Br_2 \xrightarrow{CCl_4} CH_2(Br)-CH_2(Br)$$

Br_2: Reddish Brown; product: vic - Dibromide, colourless

- Test of Unsaturation

3. Halogen Exchange

NEET concentrate

- Reversible, Dry Acetone facilitates forward rxn
- Hg_2F_2, CoF_2 or SbF_3 can also be used in the place of AgF

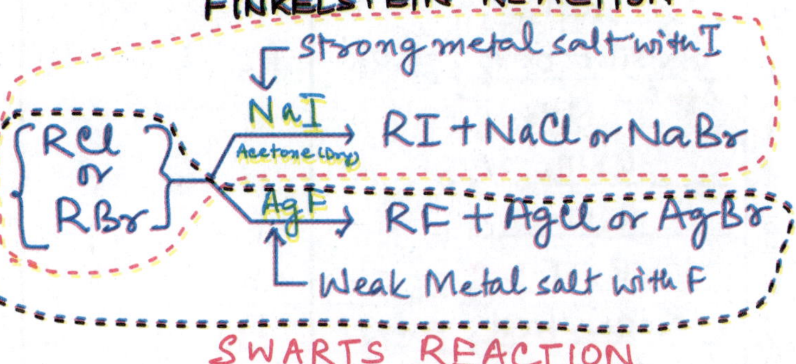

Physical Properties

- CH_3F, CH_3Cl, CH_3Br and C_2H_5Cl ⟶ Gases at room temperature
  Rest up to C_{18} ⟶ Colourless Liquids
  Beyond C_{18} ⟶ Colourless solids.
- Colourless when pure; RBr and RI develop yellowish brown colour when exposed to sunlight.
- Boiling points are considerably higher than alkanes of comparable molar mass (due to greater polarity and high intermolecular forces of attraction e.g., Dipole-Dipole & vander Waals)
- For a given alkyl group order is RI > RBr > RCl > RF (due to more van der Waals forces with increased size & mass of X atom)
- For a given halogen atom b.p. increases with increase in the size of alkyl group and decreases with more branching.
- Heavier than water, density increases with increase in carbon atom, halogen atom and atomic mass of X atom.
- Soluble in Organic solvents, Insoluble in polar solvents, less soluble in water.

Chemical Properties

→ Nucleophilic Substitution Reactions
→ Elimination Reactions
→ Reactions with Metals

1 Nucleophilic Substitution Reactions

$$\bar{Nu} + -\overset{|}{\underset{|}{C}}^{\delta+}-X^{\delta-} \longrightarrow \rangle C-Nu + \bar{X}$$

Leaving group: $\bar{X}$

Nu⁻: e^- rich species which attacks on e^- deficient areas.

- Replacement of X atom by Nu^-

	Reagent	Product	Nu^-
a.	aq. NaOH/KOH	ROH	$\bar{O}H$
b.	Moist silver oxide AgOH	ROH	$\bar{O}H$
c.	$R\bar{O}\overset{+}{Na}$	ROR	RO^-
d.	Dry silver oxide Ag_2O	ROR	RO^-
e.	NH_3	RNH_2	$\ddot{N}$
f.	RNH_2	R_2NH	$\ddot{N}$
g.	R_2NH	R_3N	$\ddot{N}$
h.	R_3N	$R_4\overset{+}{N}X^-$	$\ddot{N}$
i.	NaCN/KCN	RCN	$\bar{C}N$
j.	AgCN	$RN \overset{\rightarrow}{\equiv} C$	$C\bar{N}$

NEET concentrate

AMBIDENT NUCLEOPHILES

Groups with 2 Nucleophilic centres e.g., CN being hybrid of 2 resonating structures i.e.,

$$\bar{C}\equiv N \longleftrightarrow :C=\ddot{N}^-$$

similarly, nitrite ion

$$\bar{O}-\ddot{N}=O$$

(Linking centre show by Red)

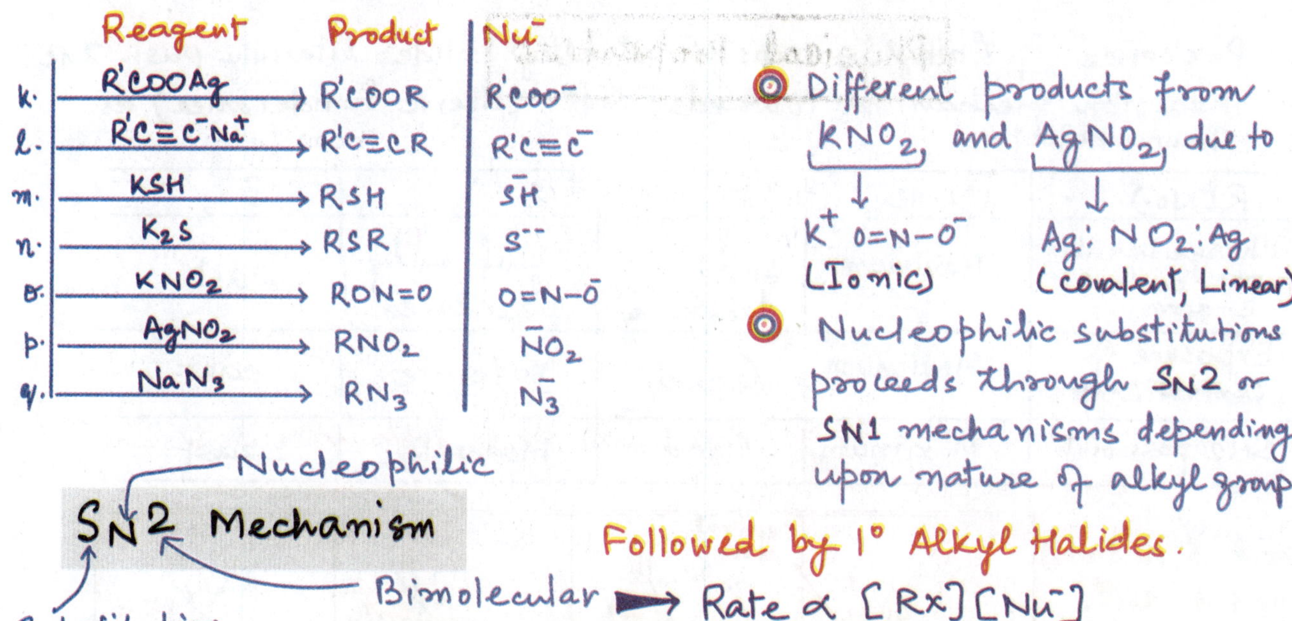

	Reagent	Product	Nu^-
k.	$R'COOAg$	$R'COOR$	$R'COO^-$
l.	$R'C\equiv C^-Na^+$	$R'C\equiv CR$	$R'C\equiv C^-$
m.	KSH	RSH	$\bar{S}H$
n.	K_2S	RSR	S^{--}
o.	KNO_2	RON=O	$O=N-\bar{O}$
p.	$AgNO_2$	RNO_2	$\bar{N}O_2$
q.	NaN_3	RN_3	N_3^-

- Different products from KNO_2 and $AgNO_2$ due to
  - KNO_2 → $K^+\ O=N-O^-$ (Ionic)
  - $AgNO_2$ → $Ag:NO_2:Ag$ (covalent, Linear)
- Nucleophilic substitutions proceeds through S_N2 or S_N1 mechanisms depending upon nature of alkyl group.

S_N2 Mechanism

S – Substitution; N – Nucleophilic; 2 – Bimolecular ⟶ Rate ∝ [RX][Nu^-]

Followed by 1° Alkyl Halides.

- Proposed by E.D. Hughes and Sir C. Ingold in 1937.

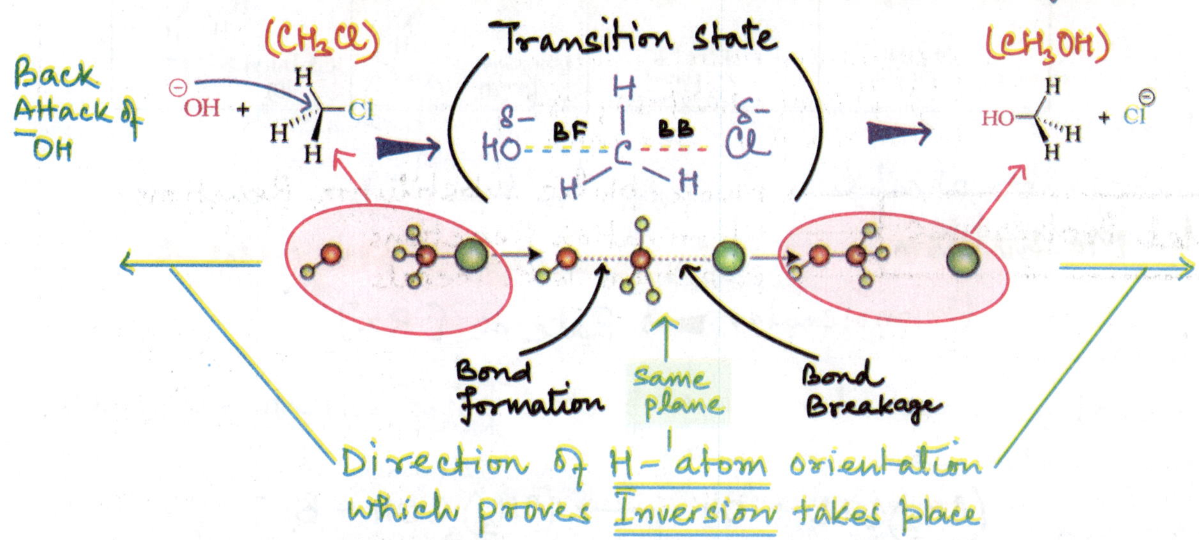

Direction of H-atom orientation which proves Inversion takes place

- Special (3D) arrangement of functional groups around C-atom is called Configuration. In S_N2 mechanism Inversion of configuration takes place
- Formation of Transition state is the slowest and Rate Determining step (RDS) of this reaction. So

$$\text{Rate} \propto [CH_3Cl][\bar{O}H]$$

(As both of them participate equally in Transition state formation)

- Order of Reactivity – 1° > 2° > 3° (as presence of bulky groups on or near the C-atom have a drastic inhibiting effect)

- Presence of 3° alkyl groups in 3° alkyl halides literally push the Reaction mechanism towards SN1 (Steric hinderance) as shown below –

R(No.)	None	1	2	3
Charge Density on central C-atom	Maximum	Slightly decreased	Significantly Decreased	Least
Exposure of central C-atom	Maximum	Good	Moderate	Least
SN2 possibility	Maximum	Good	Moderate	Least

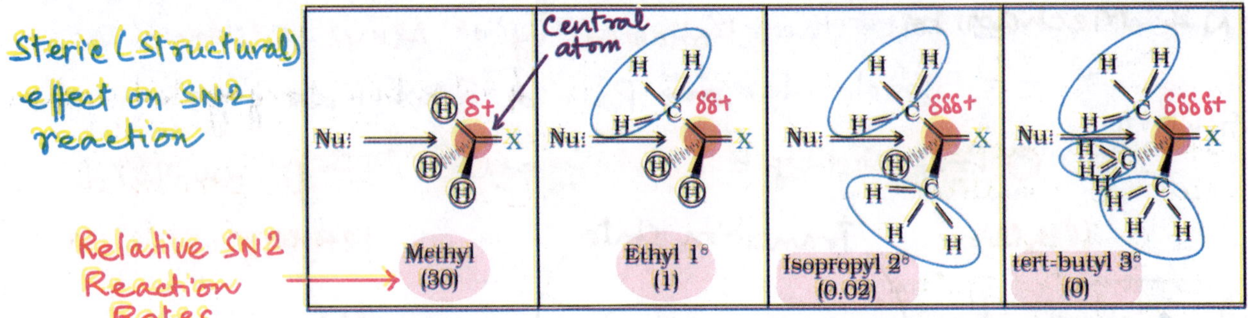

S_N1 Mechanism

S – Substitution; N – Nucleophilic; 1 – Unimolecular ⟶ Rate ∝ [Rx]

Followed by 3° Alkyl Halides.

- Generally carried out in protic polar solvents i.e., Acids, water, alcohol etc.

$$(CH_3)CCl + \bar{O}H \longrightarrow (CH_3)_3COH + Br^-$$

Mechanism

- Step 1 slowest, reversible and under the influence of $\bar{O}H$ ion.
- Rate ∝ $[(CH_3)_3CCl]$ (as $\bar{O}H$ do not participate directly in to the reaction)

Step 1:

$$(CH_3)_3CCl \underset{slow}{\overset{\bar{O}H}{\rightleftharpoons}} (CH_3)_3C^+ + Cl^-$$

Step 2:

$$(CH_3)_3C^+ \xrightarrow[fast]{\bar{O}H} (CH_3)_3COH$$

- Order of Reactivity – 3° > 2° > 1° (as 3° carbocation is most stable)

- $CH_2=CH-CH_2Cl$ and $C_6H_5CH_2Cl$ → Highly reactive via S_N1
  (as their carbocations are stabilised through resonance)

Allyl carbocation $CH_2=CH-\overset{+}{C}H_2 \longleftrightarrow \overset{+}{C}H_2-CH=CH_2$

Benzyl carbocation

NEET concentrate

Functional similarity between allyl and benzyl halides is connected with their functional similarity as shown below

4-Carbon conjugated system

Benzylic Chloride can be visualised as a 4 carbon conjugated system attached to allyl chloride

Allylic portion in Benzyl chloride

Benzylic chloride ($C_6H_5CH_2Cl$)

- Reactivity order $RI > R-Br > R-Cl \gg R-F$ (For both the mechanisms when alkyl group is same.)

Stereochemical Aspects of SN Reactions

Basic Stereochemical Principles and Notations

Asymmetric C-atom
The C- atom having 4 different groups attached to its 4 valencies

Laevorotation
Left hand side Rotation.

Polarised Light
The light beam with particulate vibrations in one plane only

Chirality
Synonym of asymmetry and basically used for asymmetry in molecules.

Optical activity
Ability of a compound to rotate the plane of polarised light.

Specific Rotation
Optical Rotation i.e., Rotation of plane of Polarised light under specific conditions

Dextrorotation
Right hand side Rotation

Optical Isomers
Isomers which differ in their behaviour towards polarised light.

- Asymmetric C-atom is also called stereocentre.
- Mirror images of asymmetrical or chiral objects are always non superimposable while symmetrical objects always has superimposable mirror images as shown below -

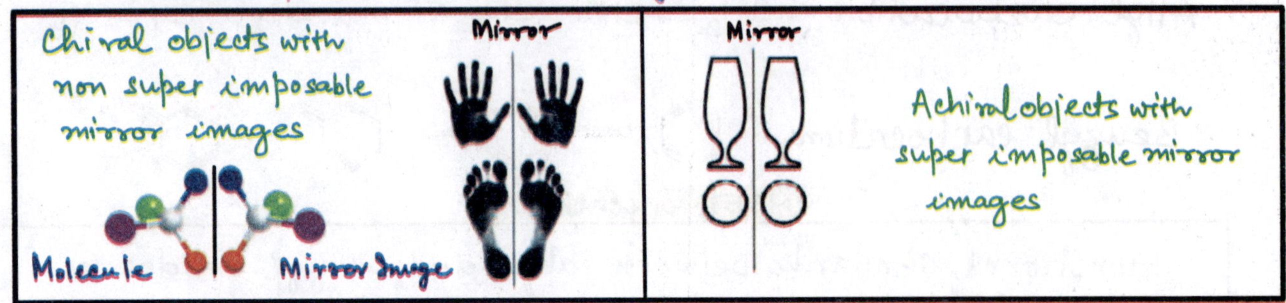

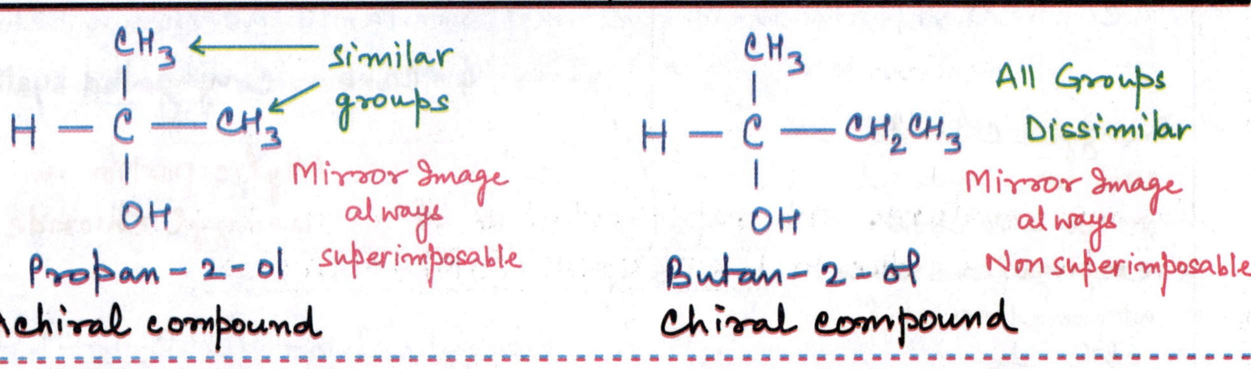

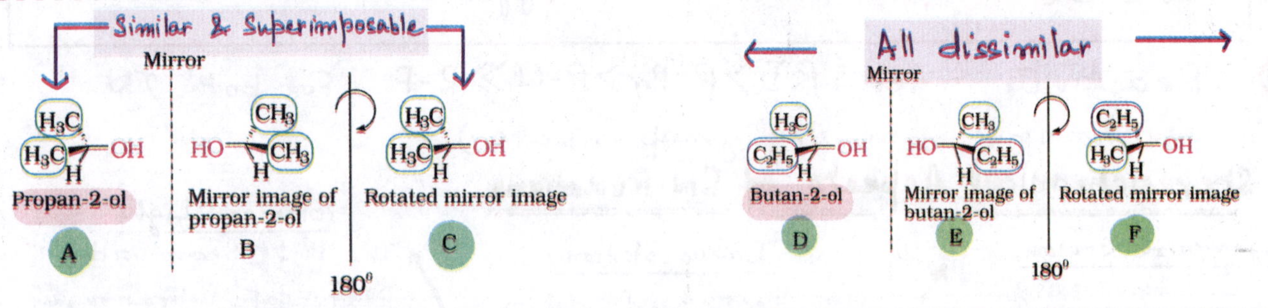

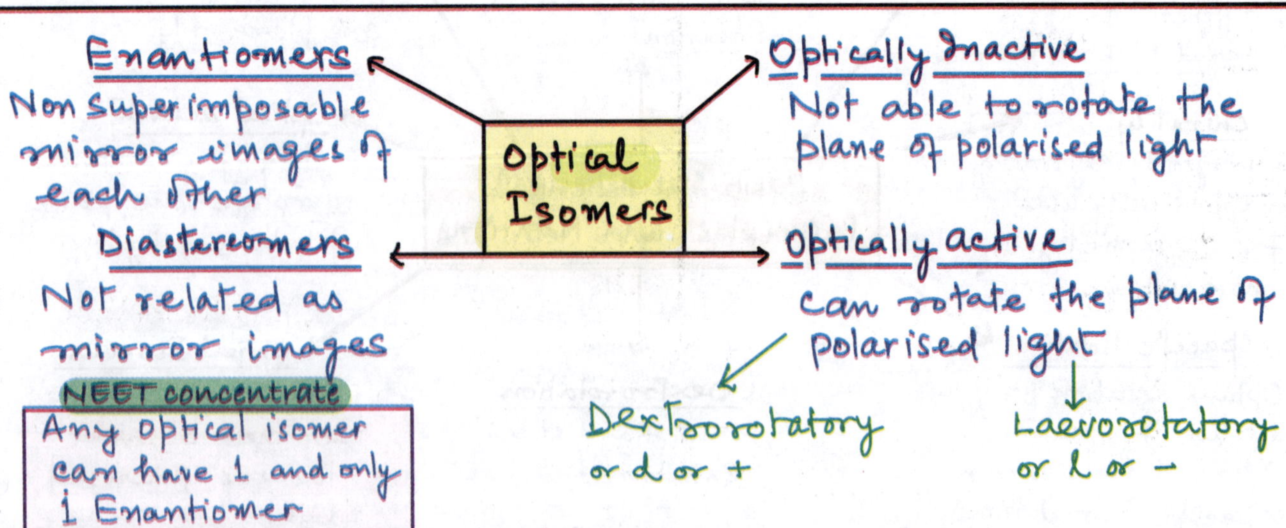

- Optical activity can be seen either in meso compounds or in Racemic mixtures (equimolar mixture of + and − forms)

Tartaric acid

Enantiomers		Meso form
COOH / H—C—OH / OH—C—H / COOH	COOH / OH—C—H / H—C—OH / COOH	COOH / H—C—OH / H—C—OH / COOH (Similar half; Line of symmetry)

Enantiomers
Have identical Physical properties like m.p., b.p., refractive index. One may be dextrorotatory while other may be laevorotatory.

Meso form
Optical rotation produced by one half is cancelled by other. It is called optical inactivation by INTERNAL COMPENSATION

- Racemic mixtures are represented as dl or ±. Their optical inactivity is due to EXTERNAL COMPENSATION (optical rotation produced by dextrorotatory form (50%) is completely cancelled by laevorotatory form)

NEET concentrate

> Always remember the dextrorotation or laevorotation is the inherent property of a compound and it has no connectivity with the absolute (actual) configuration of the molecule.

- The process of Racemic Mixture formation is called RACEMISATION while the process of separation of dextrorotatory and laevorotatory isomers from a racemic mixture is called RESOLUTION.
- Any achiral compound may have following 3 possibilities on Nu^- substitution –

X,Y = Nucleophile

Original compound (X, C_2H_5, H, CH_3) —Y→ A (Y, C_2H_5, H, CH_3): Retention of configuration

Original compound —Y→ B (H, C_2H_5, Y, CH_3): Inversion of configuration

Original compound —Y→ A+B ← Racemic mixture

- Now consider the following reaction

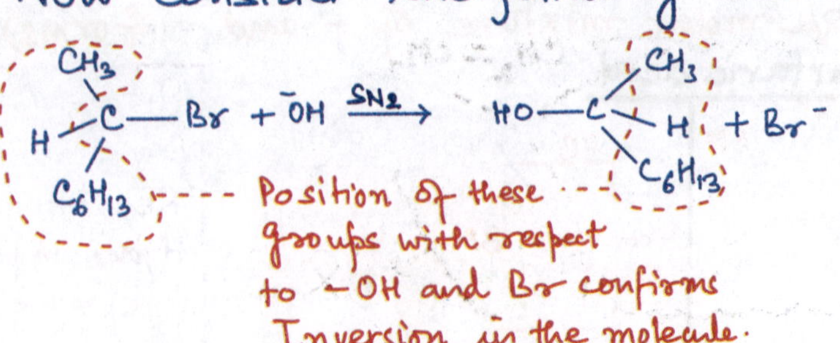

Thus we can conclude that optically active halides are accompanied by configurational Inversion in SN2 Mechanisms.

- On the other hand analyse the carbocation produced in SN1 reaction

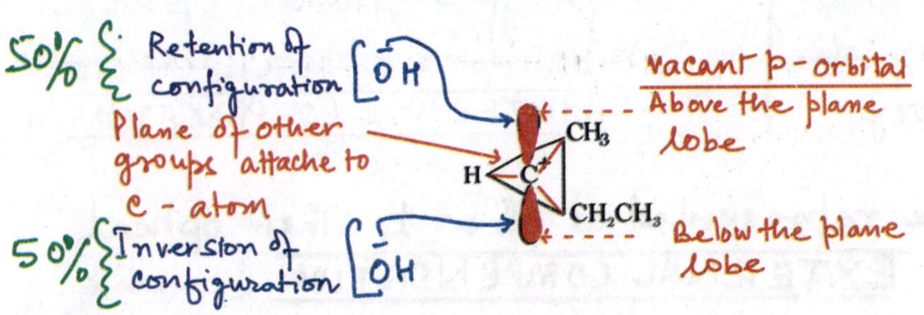

Thus we can conclude that optically active halides are accompanied by Retention & Inversion both in SN1 mechanisms Hence, Racemic mixtures are produced.

(2) Elimination Reactions

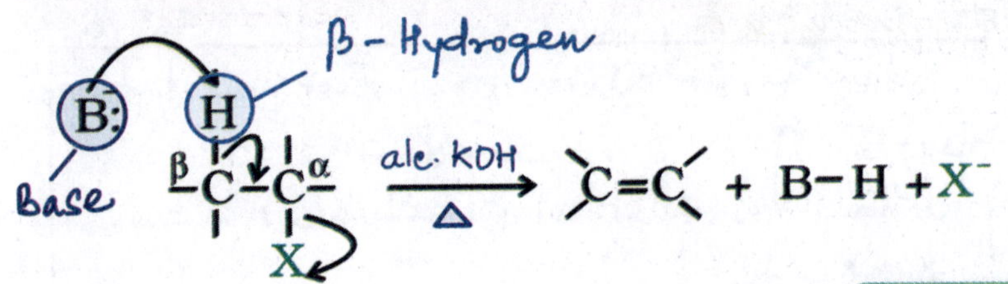

- The reaction is called Dehydrohalogenation (i.e.) Simultaneous removal of Hydrogen and Halogen)

NEET concentrate

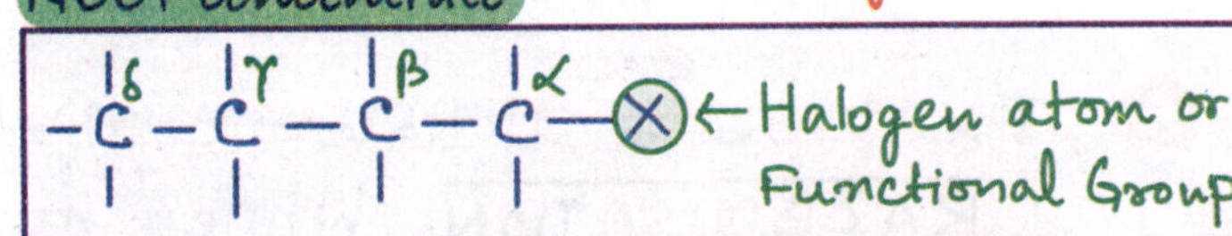

- The reaction is also called β- elimination (a Hydrogen is removed from β- carbon)

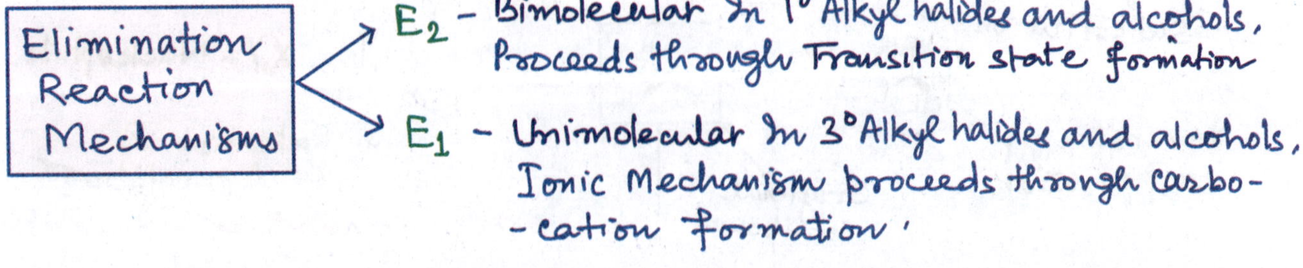

- The transition state of β-elimination in CH_3CH_2X is shown below

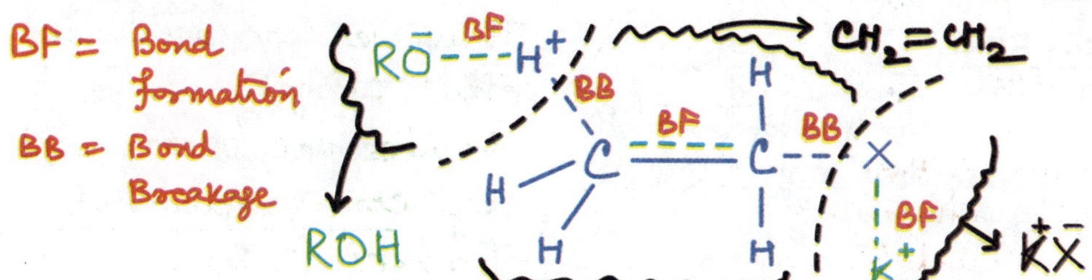

NEET concentrate

Always Remember β-elimination Reactions are Hyperconjugation based properties

- Saytzeff or Zaitsev rule will be followed in eliminations with possibility of more than 1 alkene formation i.e.,

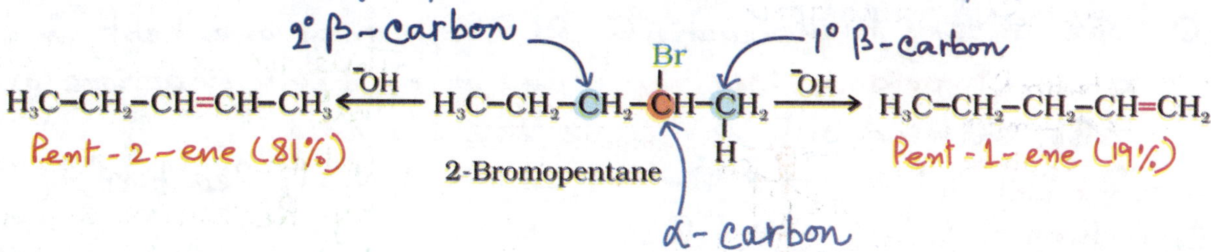

3 Interpretations of Saytzeff rule –

Saytzeff or Zaitsev rule (1875) — In β-eliminations when altnernatives are available –

1. More substituted alkene will be preferred.
2. More symmetrical alkene will be preferred.
3. Hydrogen will be removed from that C-atom which already contains lesser number of hydrogens. (Poor becomes Poorer)

H\ C = C /H ; CH_3CH_2/ \ CH_3

Pent-2-ene

1. More substituted
2. More symmetrical
3. Formed after H-removal from 2° β-carbon having less H than 1° β-carbon

- The first step of SN1 and E1 mechanisms is exactly same i.e., formation of carbocation. RO^- (of Alc. KOH) afterwords pushes the reaction towards elimination due to steric reasons.

Elimination Vs Substitution

- Elimination is favoured in 3° Alkyl halides or alcohols especially in the presence of Bulkier Nu^-/Base and slightly elevated temperatures.
- Substitution is favoured in 1° Alkylhalides and Alcohols in the presence of smaller bases, Non polar medium and comparatively lower temperatures.

3 Reaction with Metals

- Reactivity order with Mg – RI > RBr > RCl

A. $CH_3CH_2Br + Mg \xrightarrow{\text{Dry Ether}} CH_3CH_2MgBr$ (Grignard Reagent)

$\overset{\delta-}{R} - \overset{2+}{Mg} \overset{-}{X}$ — Ionic bond (Mg–X); Synergic bond (R–Mg) (Covalent but highly polar)

- Due to the presence of Mg, RMgX are very reactive and are of great synthetic importance.

Dhyan Rakhna! RMgX ki different reagents se reaction karwakar aap koi bhi ALIPHATIC COMPOUND bana sakte ho

- Due to very high reactivity of RMgX they are kept in dry ether (provides inertness) and all of their reactions are also carried out in same inert media.

B. $2RX + 2Na \longrightarrow R{-}R + 2NaX$ (Wurtz Reaction)

C. $RX + 2Li \longrightarrow RLi + LiX$

D. $2RX + Zn \longrightarrow R{-}R + ZnX_2$ (Frankland Reaction)

NEET concentrate

1. Dry Ether is the best medium for all reactions between RX and Metals shown above.
2. $C_6H_5X + 2Na + RX \xrightarrow{\text{Dry Ether}} C_6H_5{-}R + 2NaX$ (Wurtz-Fittig)
3. $2C_6H_5X + 2Na \xrightarrow{\text{Dry Ether}} C_6H_5 - C_6H_5 + 2NaX$ (Fittig reaction)
4. $4C_2H_5Cl + 4Na/Pb \longrightarrow (C_2H_5)_4Pb + 4NaCl + 3Pb$. Tetraethyl Lead (antiknock compound)

Haloarenes

Methods of Preparation

1. From hydrocarbons by Electrophilic substitution

Benzene $+ X_2 \xrightarrow[\text{Dark}]{Fe}$ C_6H_5X ; X = Cl or Br

Toluene ($C_6H_5CH_3$) $+ X_2 \xrightarrow[\text{dark}]{Fe}$ *o*-Halotoluene + *p*-Halotoluene

(Fe – Lewis's acid; Faster as –CH_3 is ring activator)

- O and p-halotoluenes are easily separable due to their different M.Ps.
- Fluoro compounds not prepared due to high reactivity of Fluorine.
- Reactions with I_2 are reversible and require HNO_3 or HIO_4 to oxidise HI formed.

2. From Amine by Sandmeyer's Reaction

HNO$_2$ can be taken directly in the place of NaNO$_2$+HX

$$C_6H_5NH_2 \xrightarrow[273-278K]{NaNO_2 + HX} C_6H_5N_2^+X^-$$

Amine → Diazonium salt (DIAZOTISATION)

$$C_6H_5N_2^+X^- \xrightarrow{Cu_2X_2} C_6H_5X + N_2$$

Aryl halide X = Cl, Br

$$C_6H_5N_2^+X^- \xrightarrow[\text{Shaking}]{KI} C_6H_5I + N_2$$

Iodobenzene

NEET concentrate

$$C_6H_5N_2^+X^- \xrightarrow[\Delta]{HBF_4} C_6H_5F + N_2 + BF_3 + HX$$

Different Reagents are required due to the differential reactivity of F, Cl, Br and I.

Physical Properties

- Aryl halides are heavier than water.
- Although polar but these are insoluble in water.
- B.P. of isomeric dihalobenzenes are more or less same.
- M.P. of para-isomers are greater than their ortho and meta counterparts

	o-isomer	m-isomer	p-isomer
b.p/K	453	446	448
m.p/K	256	249	323

More or less same range (b.p.)

Maximum (as p-isomer fits better in crystal)

Chemical Properties

→ Nucleophilic Substitution Reactions
→ Electrophilic Substitution Reactions
→ Reactions with Metals

1 Nucleophilic Substitution Reactions

- Much less reactive due to-

A. Resonance Effect

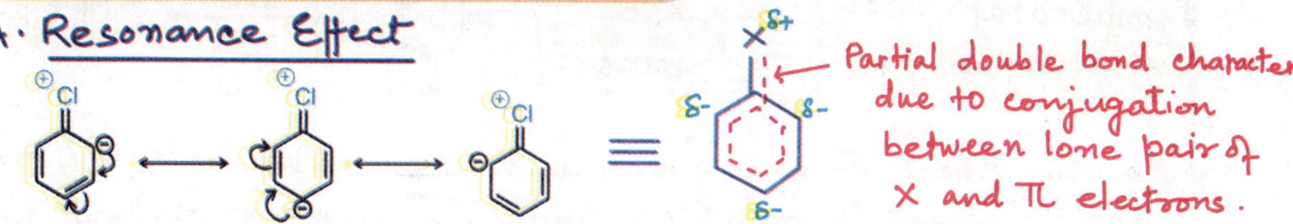

⊙ Conclusion ⟶ Difficulty in C–X bond cleavage

B. Difference in Hybridisation of C atom involved in C–X bond

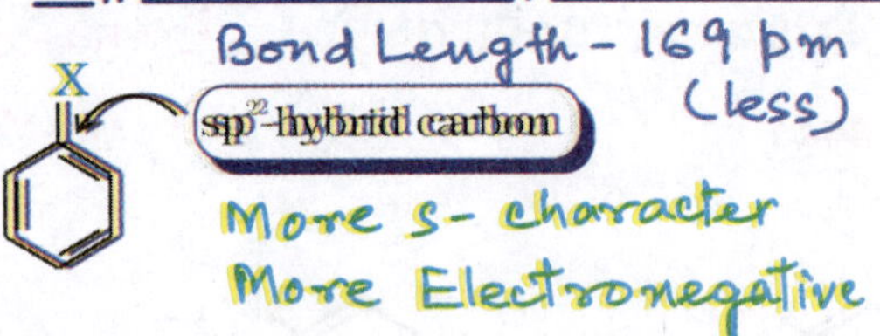

Bond Length – 169 pm (less)

More s-character
More Electronegative

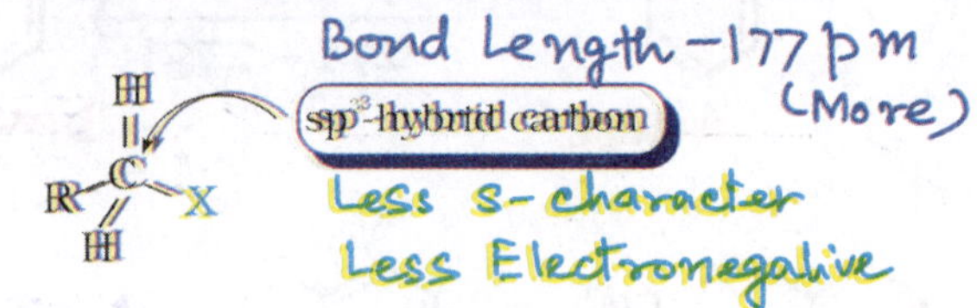

Bond Length – 177 pm (More)

Less s-character
Less Electronegative

⊙ Conclusion ⟶ Difficulty in C–X Bond cleavage (as shorter bond difficult to break than the longer bond)

C. Instability of Phenyl cation:

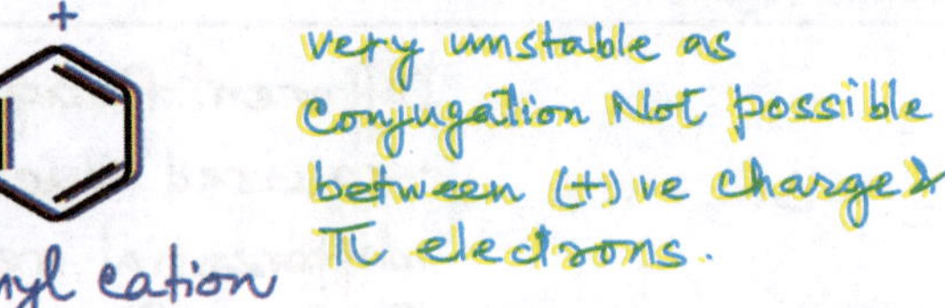

Phenyl cation

very unstable as Conjugation Not possible between (+)ve charge & π electrons.

⊙ Conclusion – No conjugation means No Resonance hence ion is highly unstable.

D. Due to possible repulsion between halogens and Nucleophiles the chances of Reactions to occur become lesser.

Overall Conclusion: Nucleophilic substitutions in aryl halides require drastic conditions of high temperature and high pressure to occur.

Chlorobenzene (:Cl:) $\xrightarrow[\text{(ii) } H^+]{\text{(i) NaOH, 623K, 300 Atm}}$ Phenol (OH)

1-Chloro-2,4-dinitrobenzene (:Cl:, NO_2, NO_2) $\xrightarrow[\text{(ii) } H^{\oplus}]{\text{(i) NaOH, 368K}}$ 2,4-Dinitrophenol (OH, NO_2, NO_2)

1-Chloro-4-nitrobenzene (:Cl:, NO_2) $\xrightarrow[\text{(ii) } H^{\oplus}]{\text{(i) NaOH, 443K}}$ 4-Nitrophenol (OH, NO_2)

Presence of an electron withdrawing group like $-NO_2$ increases the reactivity of haloarenes.

2,4,6-Trinitrochlorobenzene (:Cl:, O_2N, NO_2, NO_2) $\xrightarrow[H_2O]{\text{warm}}$ 2,4,6-Trinitrophenol (OH, O_2N, NO_2, NO_2)

Note the decrease in reaction temperature with increase in Number of $-NO_2$ groups.

As the effect of any group is always visible at 2,4,6 position with respect to group's position in Benzene nucleus hence presence of $-NO_2$ at meta position does not show this effect.

② Electrophilic Substitution Reactions

X → O & p directing and slightly deactivating.

(Resonance structures of chlorobenzene ≡ hybrid with δ+ on X and δ− at ortho and para positions)

Ortho position, para position — Enhanced e^- density

- Reason for Ring deactivation → High Electronegativity of X which results to −I effect on Benzene nucleus.

Chlorobenzene reactions:

- Conc. H_2SO_4, Δ → 2-Chlorobenzenesulfonic acid (Minor) + 4-Chlorobenzenesulfonic acid (Major)
- Cl_2, anhy. $FeCl_3$ → 1, 4-Dichlorobenzene (Major) + 1, 2-Dichlorobenzene (Minor)
- CH_3Cl, Anhy. $AlCl_3$ → 1-Chloro-2-methylbenzene (Minor) + 1-Chloro-4-methylbenzene (Major) — Friedel craft Alkylation
- HNO_3, Conc. H_2SO_4 → 1-Chloro-4-nitrobenzene (Major) + 1-Chloro-2-nitrobenzene (Minor)
- CH_3COCl, Anhy. $AlCl_3$ → 2-Chloroacetophenone (Minor) + 4-Chloroacetophenone (Major) — Friedel-Craft Acylation

③ Reaction with Metals

Wurtz-Fittig Reaction

$$C_6H_5X + Na + RX \xrightarrow{\text{Dry ether}} C_6H_5R + NaX$$

Fittig Reaction

$$2\,C_6H_5X + 2Na \xrightarrow{\text{Dry ether}} C_6H_5{-}C_6H_5 + 2NaX$$

Diphenyl

POLYHALOGEN COMPOUNDS

- Dichloromethane (CH_2Cl_2) or Methylene chloride – A solvent, a paint remover, a propellent in aerosols, a process solvent in drug manufacture, a metal cleaning and finishing solvent (Uses)
- Harms human CNS, lower levels cause slightly impaired hearing and vision, Higher levels cause dizziness, nausea, tingling and numb-ness in fingers and toes.
- Direct skin contact causes intense burning and redness, Direct eye contact can burn the cornea. (Harmful effects)

- Trichloromethane or Chloroform ($CHCl_3$) – A solvent for fats, alkaloids and iodine but majorly used to produce R-22 i.e freon refrigerant.
- Once used as anaesthetic in surgery but now replaced by less harmful compounds like ether & N_2O.
- Causes dizziness, fatigue and headache, chronic exposurses results in liver & kidney damage.
- $2CHCl_3 + O_2 \xrightarrow[\text{air}]{\text{Light \&}} 2COCl_2 + 2HCl$ (Phosgene) | **Phosgene or Carbonyl chloride is extremely poisonous.**
- $CHCl_3$ and $COCl_2$ both largely affect the CNS of humans.

NEET concentrate

> Phosgene formation can be avoided by –
> (i) Keeping $CHCl_3$ in air tight dark coloured bottles
> (ii) Adding a small amount of 1% C_2H_5OH (which converts $COCl_2$ to less harmful ethyl carbonate)

- Triiodomethane or Iodoform (CHI_3) – Very good antiseptic but antiseptic properties are due to the liberation of free I_2.
- Tetrachloromethane or Carbon tetrachloride (CCl_4) — In manufacture of refrigerants and propellants for aerosol cans.
- General solvent, Chlorofluorocarbons and pharmaceutical manufacturing are other uses.
- Can be a spot remover, cleaning fluid, degreasing agent and fire extenguisher. (all uses)
- Can also cause dizziness, nausea, vomiting, Light headedness Liver cancer and permanent damage to nerves.
- Severe exposures → Stupor, coma, unconsciousness or death
- Release in air → depletes ozone layer
- Freons or Chlorofluoro carbons of CH_4 and C_2H_6 – extremely stable, unreactive, non-toxic, non-corrosive and easily liquefiable gases.
- Most common Freon 12 (CCl_2F_2) manf. from Swarts reaction. One of the extreme causes of ozone layer depletion.
- DDT or p,p'-Dichlorodiphenyl-trichloroethane – first chlorinated organic insecticide, Originally prepared in 1837, effectiveness as insecticide ⟶ Paul Muller in 1939 (awarded Noble Prize in 1948)

- Use was increased after World war II due to its effectiveness against Mosquitoes (causing Malaria) & Lice that carry typhus.

DDT (structure: $Cl_3C-CH(C_6H_4Cl)_2$)

→ After 1940s many insects developed DDT resistant varieties

→ significantly stable, not metabolised very rapidly by animals rather usually stored in fatty tissue (due to its fat soluble nature)

Banned in USA in the year 1973 although still used in developing countries as a cheaper insecticide.

16. Alcohols, Phenols & Ethers

Alcohols = Hydrocarbon or Aliphatic Compound − H + OH

Means an alcohol contains one or more hydroxyl (OH) groups directly attached to carbon atoms of an aliphatic system. For example

$$H-\underset{H}{\overset{H}{\underset{|}{\overset{|}{C}}}}-OH$$

C – atom of aliphatic system

Hydroxyl group

Phenols = Benzene or Aromatic Compound − H + OH

Means a phenol contains hydroxyl groups directly attached to the carbon atom(s) of an aromatic system. For example,

OH — Hydroxyl group

C atom of aromatic system

Ethers = Hydrocarbon or aliphatic system − H + R–O/Ar–O

Means an ether contains an alkoxy (R–O–) or Aryloxy (Ar–O–) group directly attached to carbon atoms of an aliphatic system. For example,

$$H-\underset{H}{\overset{H}{\underset{|}{\overset{|}{C}}}}-OR$$

C atom of aliphatic system

Alkoxy group

Classification

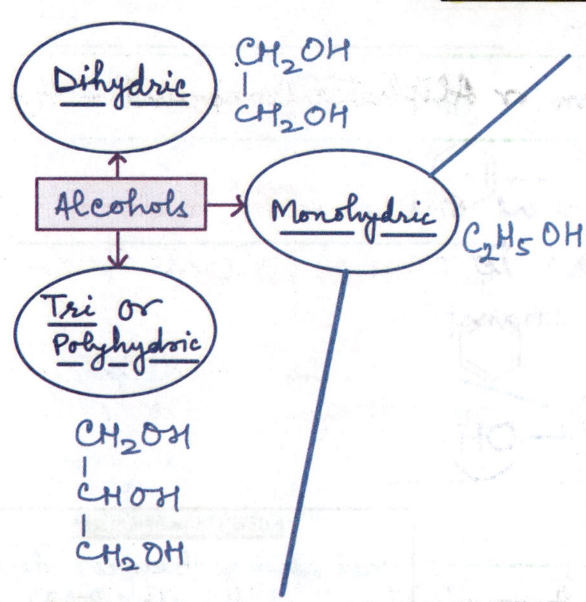

Compounds with C_{sp^3}—OH bond

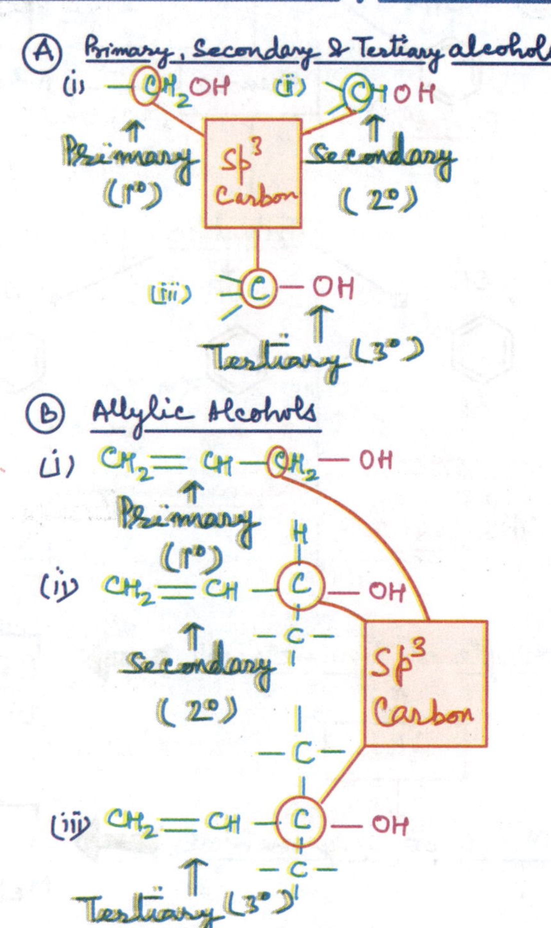

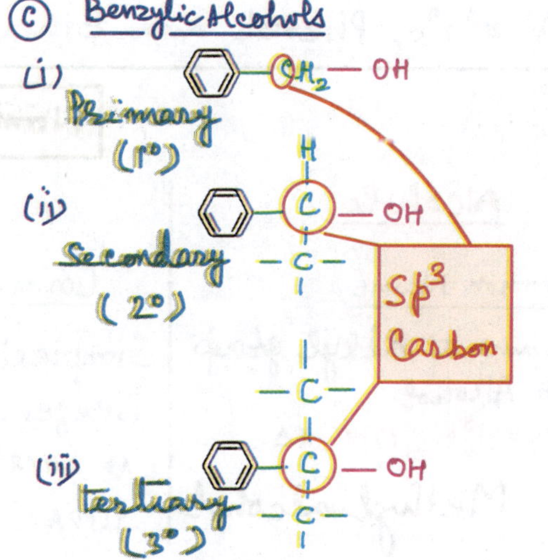

Compounds with C_{sp^2}—OH bond

(A) Vinylic Alcohol

$CH_2=CH-OH$

sp^2 Carbon

(B) Aryl Alcohol

OH (on benzene ring)

NEET concentrate

- Compounds with C_{sp}—OH bond also exist. These include –

  $HC\equiv C-OH$ (sp Carbon)

  This H can be replaced by any alkyl group also.

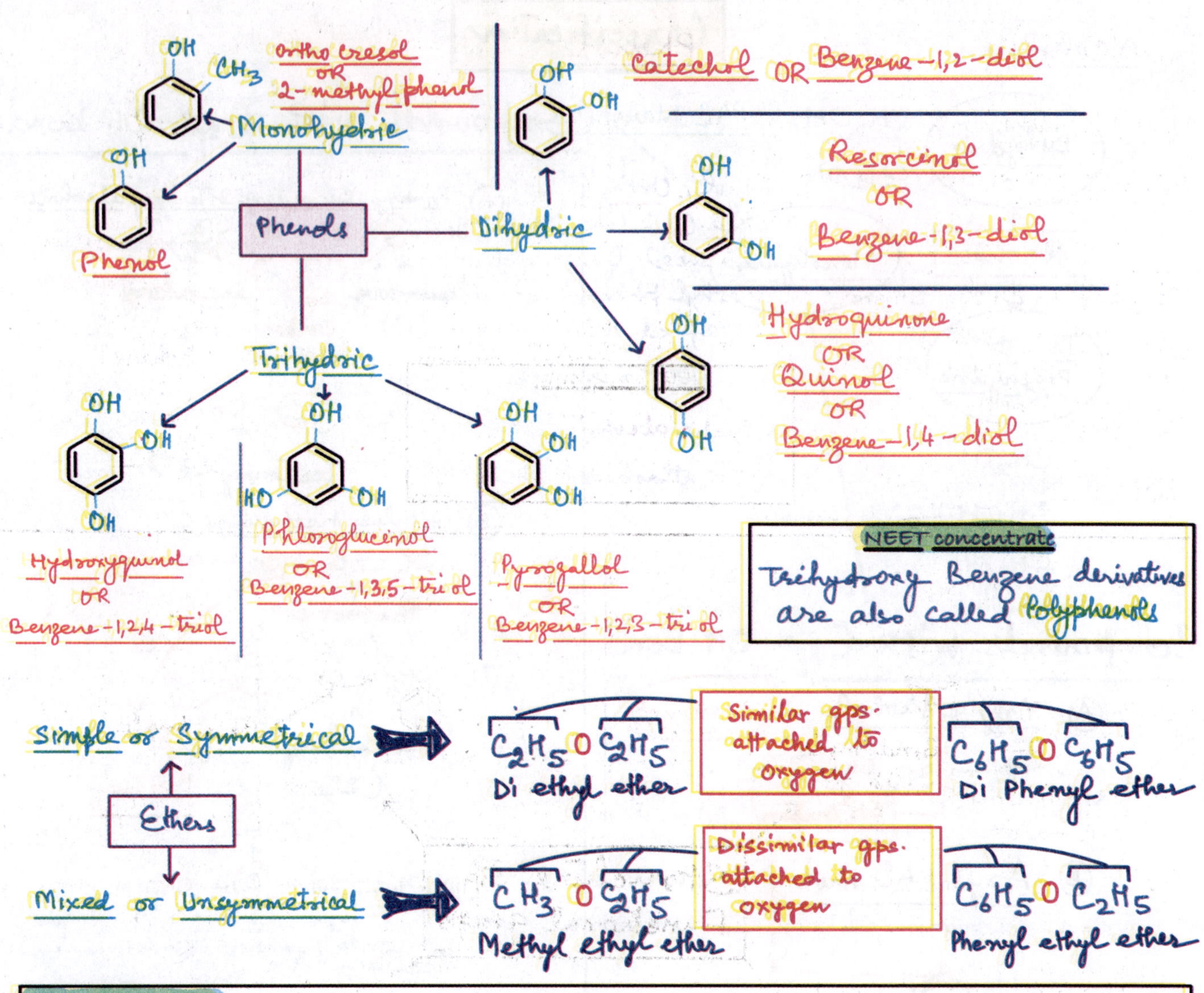

NEET concentrate

Alcohols, Phenols and Ethers all have Oxygen as their reaction centre.

Nomenclature

Alcohols

Common Name

Name of alkyl group + Alcohol

eg: CH_3OH is Methyl alcohol

Phenols

Common Name

Simplest hydroxy derivative of Benzene is Phenol, which is is accepted as common as well as IUPAC name.

Ethers

Common Name

Name of alkyl group + Ether

eg: CH_3OCH_3 is Di Methyl Ether

Alcohols	Phenols	Ethers
IUPAC Name	**IUPAC Name**	**IUPAC Name**
Alkane – e + ol = Alkanol e.g., C_2H_5OH Ethane – e + ol = Ethanol [As main chain contains 2 C atom, thus parent hydrocarbon is Ethane]	Phenol, Ortho (1,2-subs.), para (1,4 subs.) and meta (1,3 subs.) Benzene diol, Methyl phenols etc. all are accepted IUPAC Names. **NEET concentrate** Cyclic alcohols: Prefix cyclo, –OH attached to C_1 always	Alkoxy alkanes Smaller alkyl group with oxygen e.g., $CH_3OC_2H_5$ is named as Methoxy Ethane [Smaller group with Oxygen] [Main chain with 2 C atoms]

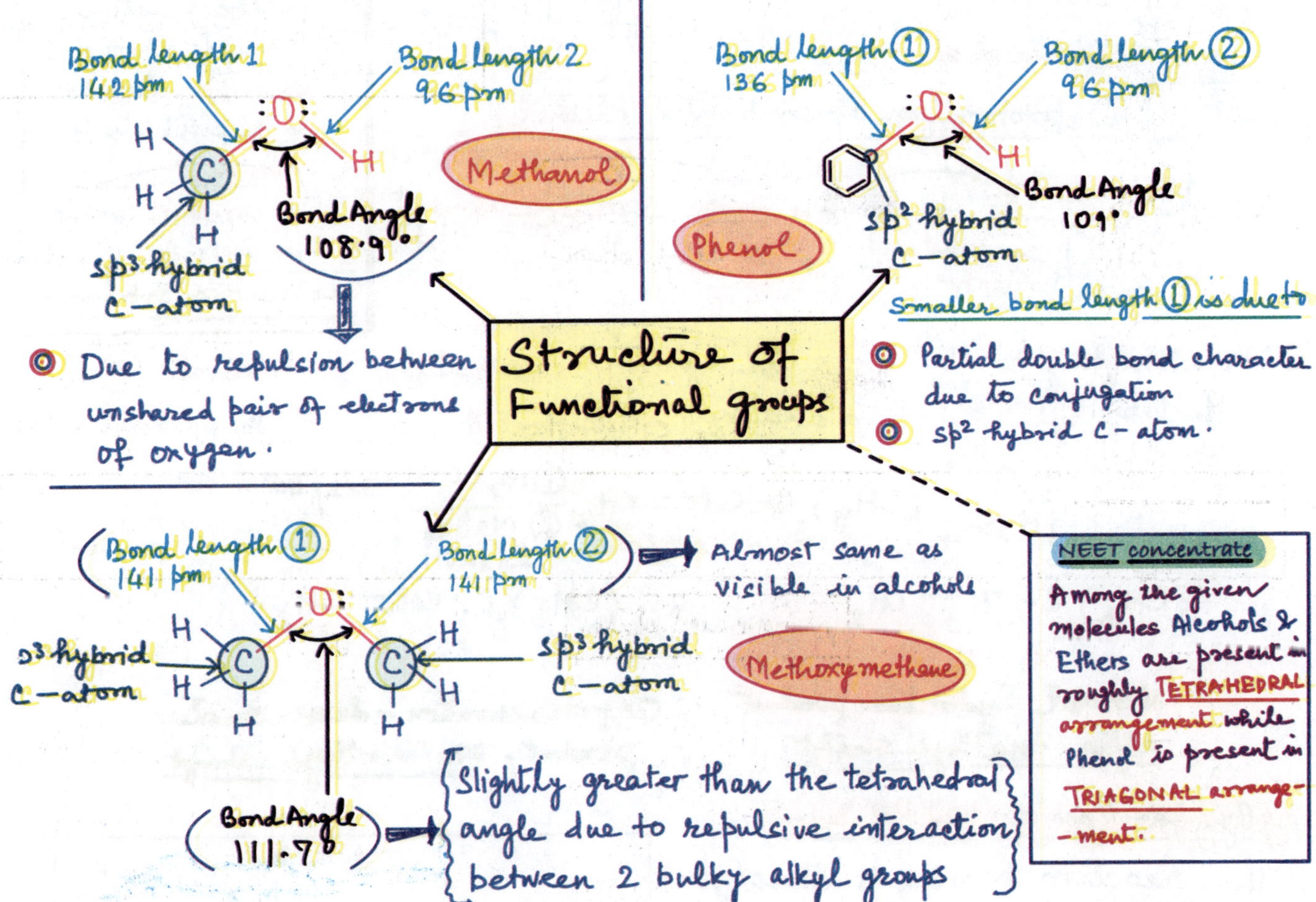

◎ Above structures also confirm the presence of Oxygen as the reaction centre in Alcohols, Phenols and Ethers.

Alcohols

Methods of Preparation

1. By acid catalysed Hydration of Alkenes

$$>C=C< + H_2O \rightleftharpoons >C(H)-C(OH)<$$

MECHANISM

Step 1 Protonation of alkene:

$$>C=C< + H-\overset{+}{O}(H)-H \rightleftharpoons -C(H)-\overset{+}{C}< + H_2O$$

Electrophile (H); carbocation

Step 2 Nucleophilic attack of water:

$$-C(H)-\overset{+}{C}< + :\ddot{O}(H)-H \rightleftharpoons -C(H)-C-\overset{+}{O}(H)-H$$

carbocation; Protonated Alcohol

Step 3 Deprotonation of protonated alcohol:

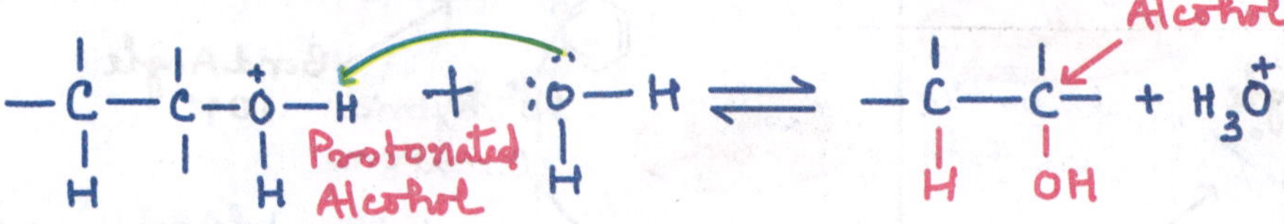

$$-C(H)-C-\overset{+}{O}(H)-H + :\ddot{O}(H)-H \rightleftharpoons -C(H)-C(OH)- + H_3O^+$$

> **NEET concentrate**
> - H_2SO_4 most suited acid for the reaction
> - step 1 is the Rate Determining step (RDS)
> - As the reaction proceeds through carbocation formation so the possibility of Hydride, Methyl or Phenyl shift can also be there for carbocation stabilisation

- This shifting can be prevented by Oxymercuration – Demercuration i.e.) attack by $Hg(OCOCH_3)_2$ followed by $NaBH_4/NaOH$.

$$(CH_3)_3C-CH=CH_2$$

With H_2O / H_2SO_4: $(CH_3)_2C(OH)-CH(CH_3)-CH_2(H)$

Normal hydration product after methyl shift

With ① $Hg(OCOCH_3)_2$/THF ② $NaBH_4$ & NaOH: $(CH_3)_3C-CH(OH)-CH_2(H)$

Oxymercuration – demercuration product, No methyl shift

2. By hydrolysis of Alkyl Halides –

The reaction proceeds through S_N1 & S_N2 mechanisms and the reagents can be aq. KOH, aq. NaOH and wet silver oxide (AgOH)

$$R-CH_2X \xrightarrow{AgOH \ / \ aq.\ KOH \ / \ aq.\ NaOH} R-CH_2-OH + AgX \text{ or } KX \text{ or } NaX$$

3. By Hydroboration – Oxidation of alkene

- For asymmetrical alkenes the reaction proceeds through Markownikov addition with Boron as (+)ve part of addendum (B^{3+}) and H as (–)ve part (H^-).

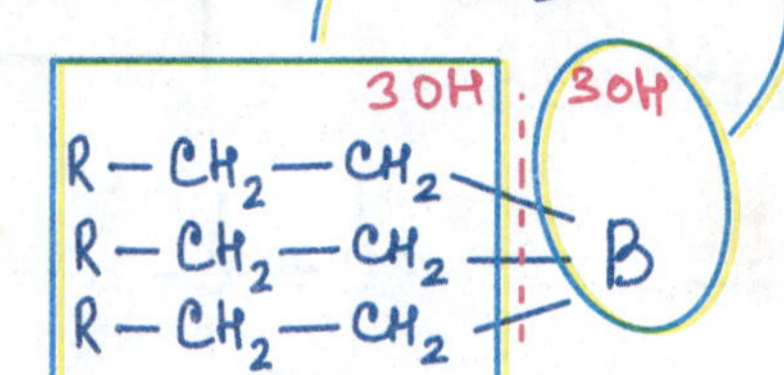

NEET concentrate: The final product looks like if it has been formed by addition of water to any asymmetrical alkene in a way opposite to Markovnikov's rule.

Attack of H_2O_2 on trialkyl borane can be visualised as

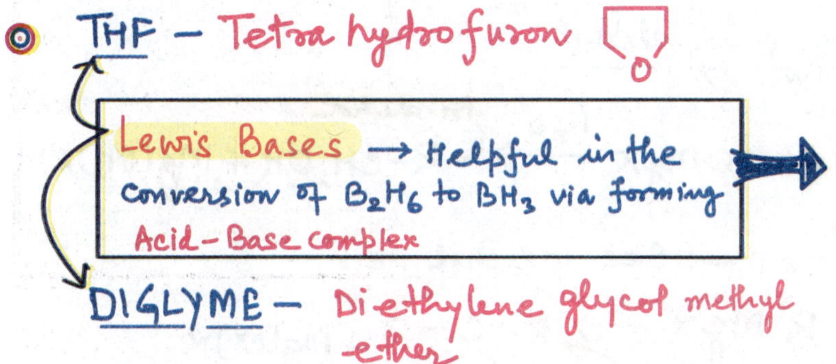

- THF – Tetra hydro furan

Lewis Bases → Helpful in the conversion of B_2H_6 to BH_3 via forming Acid–Base complex

DIGLYME – Diethylene glycol methyl ether

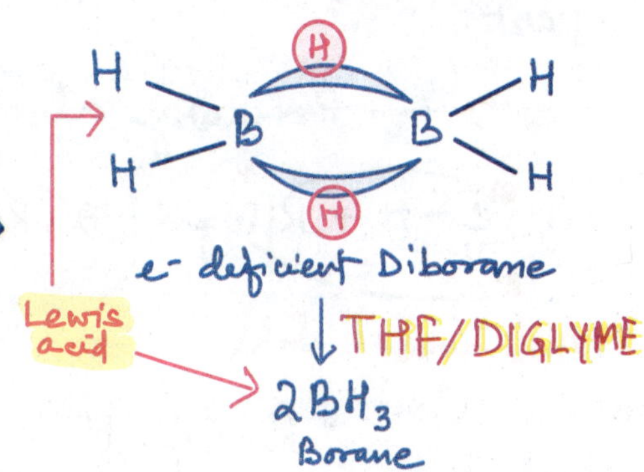

4. By the reduction of Aldehydes & ketones

- Single step reduction, requires moderate reducing agents like $NaBH_4$
- Aldehydes give Primary while Ketones give secondary alcohols.
- Hydrogenation in the presence of metals like Pd, Pt or finely Divided Ni also gives same result.

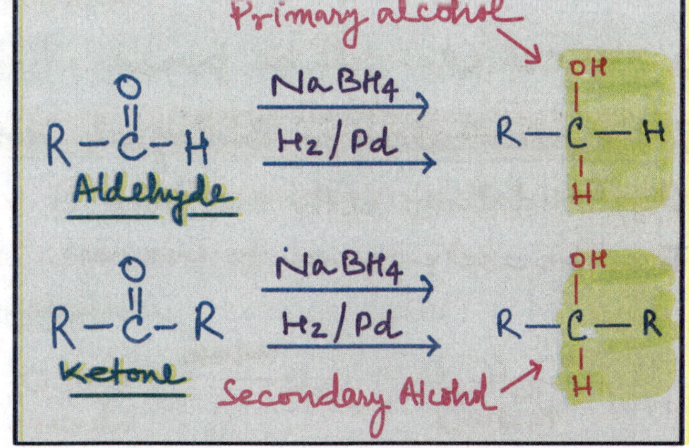

5. By the reduction of Acids and their derivatives

- Two step reduction, requires strong reducing agents like $LiAlH_4$
- $LiAlH_4$ being expensive used for special occasions only.
  Alternatively, ester formation followed by Hydrogenation is used.
- Hydrogenation in the presence of metals like Pd, Pt or Ni also gives same result.

$$R-\overset{O}{\overset{\|}{C}}-OH \xrightarrow[\text{(ii) } H_2O]{\text{(i) } LiAlH_4} R-CH_2-OH \text{ (Primary Alcohol)}$$

$$\downarrow H^+ \;/\; R'OH$$

$$R-\underset{O}{\underset{\|}{C}}-OR' \xrightarrow[\text{Catalyst}]{H_2} RCH_2OH + R'OH$$

6. From Grignard Reagent

- The alkyl group of Grignard reagent works as the Nucleophilic (Nu^-) part.
- HCHO ⟶ Primary alcohol i.e.,

$$H-\overset{\delta+}{\underset{\overset{\|}{O^{\delta-}}}{C}}-H + \overset{-}{R}\overset{+}{Mg}X \longrightarrow R-CH_2OMgX \xrightarrow{H_2O} R-CH_2OH + Mg(OH)X \text{ (Pri. alcohol)}$$

Aldehydes other than HCHO ⟶ Sec. alcohol i.e.,

$$R-\underset{O}{\underset{\|}{C}}-H + R'MgX \longrightarrow R-\underset{H\;\;OH}{C}-R' + Mg(OH)X \text{ (sec. alcohol)}$$

ketones ⟶ Tert. alcohol

$$R-\underset{O}{\underset{\|}{C}}-R' + R''MgX \longrightarrow R-\underset{R''\;\;OH}{C}-R' + Mg(OH)X \text{ (Tert. alcohol)}$$

- CH_3OH can not be prepared from this reaction

7. Fermentation or Biological Oxidation

- Oxidation with the help of enzymes or Biological catalysts.
- Precisely used to prepare C_2H_5OH

$$\underset{\text{Maltose}}{C_{12}H_{22}O_{11}} + H_2O \xrightarrow{\text{Maltase}} \underset{\text{Glucose}}{2C_6H_{12}O_6} \xrightarrow{\text{Zymase}} \underset{\text{Ethyl alcohol}}{2C_2H_5OH} + 2CO_2$$

(Enzyme: Maltase, Zymase)

Physical Properties

- Colourless toxic liquids, boiling point increases regularly with increase in number of C-atoms.
- Boiling points more than corresponding alkanes (due to inter-molecular H-bonding present in them)

C_2H_5OH – Ethanol (Mol. mass – 46, B.P. – 351K)

$CH_3CH_2CH_3$ – Propane (Mol. mass – 44, B.P. – 231K)

- Boiling points of lower members less than water (due to less H-bonding than water)
- Lower members miscible with water (due to intermolecular H-bonding between alcohol and water molecule)

→ Solubility falls rapidly as we move down the homologous series.

Chemical Properties

Alcohols as Nucleophiles

$R-\ddot{O}-H + C^+ \longrightarrow R-\overset{+}{O}(H)-C \xrightarrow{-H^+} R-\ddot{O}-C$

The bond between O and H is broken

Protonated alcohols as Electrophiles

$R-CH_2-\ddot{O}-H \xrightarrow{H^+} R-\overset{\delta+}{C}H_2-\overset{+}{O}H_2 \xrightarrow[Br^-]{-H_2O} Br-CH_2-R$

The bond between C and O is broken

Reactions with cleavage of O-H Bond

① Acidity

- Due to polar nature of O–H bond
- $1° > 2° > 3°$ (As larger alkyl group increases e^- density on Oxygen thus decreasing polarity)
- With active metals like Na, K and Al they evolve H_2 as

$2ROH + 2Na \longrightarrow 2RO^-Na^+ + H_2\uparrow$ BRONSTED ACID behaviour

- Weaker acids than water ($H_2O > ROH$)

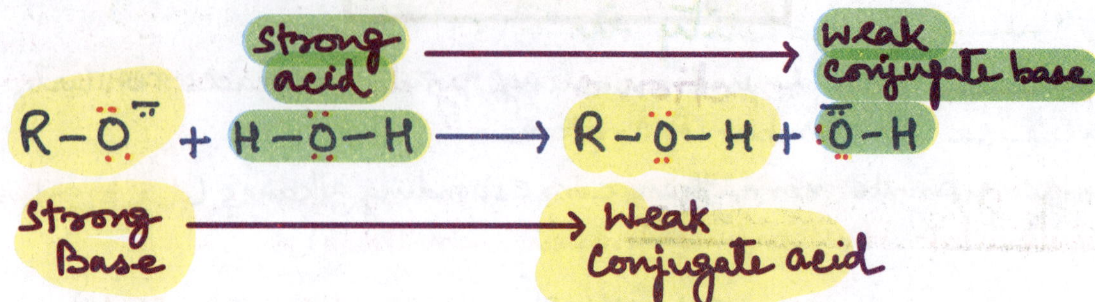

- Alcohols are Bronsted bases as well (Due to the presence of lone e⁻ pair on O)

$$C_2H_5\bar{O}Na^+ > Na^+\bar{O}H \text{ (Basicity)}$$

2 Esterification

- $$ROH + R'COOH \xrightleftharpoons{H^+} R'COOR + HOH$$
  $$ROH + (R'CO)_2O \xrightleftharpoons{H^+} R'COOR + R'COOH$$
  $$ROH + R'COCl \xrightarrow{Pyridine} R'COOR + HCl$$

- First two reactions are reversible hence one of the products need continuous removal for their completion.
- In 3rd reaction base (pyridine) reacts and neutralises HCl continuously, thus making the reaction Unidirectional.

Reactions with cleavage of C–O Bond

1 Reaction with HX

- RX are produced
- 1°, 2° and 3° react differently and can be distinguished with Lucas Reagent (conc. HCl + anhy. $ZnCl_2$) as Lucas Test

- $3^\circ \longrightarrow$ Immediate Reaction (turbidity)
- $2^\circ \longrightarrow$ Turbidity in 5 minutes (approx.)
- $1^\circ \longrightarrow$ No reaction or very delayed reaction

② With PX_3, PX_5 & $SOCl_2$

- Alkyl Halides are produced along with the formation of
  - ⓐ $H_3PO_3 \longrightarrow$ In case of PX_3
  - ⓑ $HX, POX_3 \longrightarrow$ In case of PX_5
  - ⓒ $SO_2, HCl \longrightarrow$ In case of $SOCl_2$
- Reactions follow $S_N i$ mechanism. (S_N ← Nucleophilic Substitution; i ← Ionic)

③ Dehydration

- With protic solvents or catalysts like alumina, anhy. $ZnCl_2$
- Alkenes are produced
- Relative ease of Dehydration – $3^\circ > 2^\circ > 1^\circ$

$$(CH_3)_3COH \xrightarrow[358\,K\ -H_2O]{20\%\ H_3PO_4} CH_3-\underset{}{\overset{CH_2}{\overset{\|}{C}}}-CH_3$$

$$(CH_3)_2\overset{H}{\overset{|}{C}}OH \xrightarrow[440K\ -H_2O]{80\%\ H_3PO_4} CH_3-\overset{H}{\overset{|}{C}}=CH_2$$

$$CH_3CH_2OH \xrightarrow[443K\ -H_2O]{H_2SO_4} CH_2=CH_2$$

> **NEET concentrate**
>
> Protic Solvents means any H^+ donor solvent or SIMPLY ANY ACID like H_2SO_4, H_3PO_3 etc.

Explanation

3° Carbocations are most stable therefore they give alkenes most easily (at lowest temperature)

Mechanism:

Step ① Protonated alcohol formation

$$CH_3CH_2\ddot{O}H \xrightarrow{H^+} CH_3CH_2\overset{+}{\ddot{O}}H - H$$

Protonated alcohol

Step ② Carbocation formation

$$CH_3CH_2-\overset{+}{O}H-H \xrightarrow{-H_2O} CH_3\overset{+}{C}H_2$$

Dhyan Dena Reaction Mein Carbocation form To hota hai but uska actual reason Neeche Box mein given hai

NEET concentrate

- In reality this reaction proceeds through E_2 mechanism which involves following Transition state

BF = Bond formation

BB = Bond Breakage

HSO_4^- --(BF)-- H^+ --(BB)-- CH_2 ==(BF)== CH_2 --(BB)-- $O-H$ with O --(BF)-- H^+; products: H_2SO_4, $CH_2=CH_2$, H_2O

- The yield of alkene formed is less than expected due to the establishment of following equilibrium

$$CH_2=CH_2 \underset{}{\overset{H^+}{\rightleftharpoons}} CH_3\overset{+}{C}H_2$$

Step ③ Alkene formation with H^+ Elimination

$$H-\underset{H}{\overset{H}{C}}-\underset{H}{\overset{H}{C^+}} \longrightarrow \begin{matrix}H\\H\end{matrix}>C=C<\begin{matrix}H\\H\end{matrix} + H^+$$

> **NEET concentrate**
>
> This step is the real application of the process HYPERCONJUGATION

④ Oxidation

- C—H bond oxidises to C—OH bond.

$$>C<\begin{matrix}OH\\H\end{matrix} \longrightarrow >C<\begin{matrix}OH\\OH\end{matrix} \xrightarrow[\text{Can't be attached to same C - atom}]{H_2O \text{ Removal as 2 OH groups}} >C=O$$

Final product

- Primary alcohols $\xrightarrow{[O]}$ Aldehydes $\xrightarrow{[O]}$ Carboxylic acids

  Secondary alcohols $\xrightarrow{[O]}$ Ketones $\xrightarrow{[O]}$ ✗

  Tertiary alcohols ⟶ { No oxidation under normal conditions; Carboxylic acid mixture with lesser carbon atoms under drastic conditions ($KMnO_4$ + elevated temp.)

- Oxidising agents

  Acidified $KMnO_4$ ⟶ Carboxylic acid (being strongest)

  PCC (Pyridinium ChloroChromate) ⟶ CrO_3 + Pyridine + HCl

  Anhydrous CrO_3

  (PCC and Anhydrous CrO_3) ⟶ Aldehydes (being moderate)

  Anhydrous CrO_3 ⟶ Also gives ⟶ Ketones with Secondary alcohols

- These reactions are also called DEHYDROGENATIONS (Removal of Hydrogen) or Catalytic dehydrogenations

  Primary alcohols ⟶ Aldehydes

  Secondary alcohols ⟶ Ketones

  Tertiary alcohols ⟶ Alkenes (Dehydration)

  Under Similar conditions i.e.) Cu/Ag 543K

Some Commercially Important alcohols

Methyl Alcohol

- CH_3OH or Methanol

- Also called "WOOD SPIRIT" as produced by destructive distillation of wood. Today commercially produced by

$$CO + 2H_2 \xrightarrow[\substack{200-300\,Atm \\ 573-673\,K}]{ZnO-Cr_2O_3} CH_3OH$$

- Colourless liquid, b.p. 337 K, Highly poisonous

  Ingestion in small quantities ⟶ Blindness

  Ingestion in larger quantities ⟶ Death

- Uses (a) as solvent in paints + varnishes

  (b) for making HCHO

Ethyl Alcohol

- C_2H_5OH or ethanol

- Commercially obtained by FERMENTATION as

from Molasses or Sugarcane or fruits (grapes) ⟹

$$\underset{\text{Sugar}}{C_{12}H_{22}O_{11}} + H_2O \xrightarrow{\text{Invertase}} \underset{\text{Glucose}}{C_6H_{12}O_6} + \underset{\text{Fructose}}{C_6H_{12}O_6}$$

Conditions ANAEROBIC

$$C_6H_{12}O_6 \xrightarrow{\text{Zymase}} \underset{\text{Ethyl alcohol}}{C_2H_5OH} + CO_2\uparrow$$

- In Wine making Grapes ⟶ Sugars (Juice) + yeast (Outer skin)

NEET concentrate

If percentage of C_2H_5OH exceeds 14% ⟶ Zymase action decreases

If air gets in ⟶ Taste of alcoholic drink destroyed as

$$C_2H_5OH \xrightarrow{O_2 \text{ of air}} CH_3COOH$$

- Nowadays $CH_2{=}CH_2 + H_2O \longrightarrow$ Large Quantities of C_2H_5OH

- Colourless liquid, b.p. 351 K, Highly poisonous

Ingestion in moderate quantities $\longrightarrow$ Poor Judgement

Ingestion in larger quantities $\longrightarrow$ Nausea + Loss of consciousness

↓

"Also interferes with spontaneous Respiration and can be fatal"

NEET concentrate

DENATURATION of alcohol

Done to prevent the drinking of Commercial alcohol

Commercial alcohol + Copper sulphate (Gives Blue Colour) + Pyridine (Gives foul smell)

↓

Denatured Spirit

Alcohols in Human Body

- $CH_3OH \xrightarrow{[O]} HCHO \xrightarrow{[O]}$ $\boxed{HCOOH}$ ➡ Blindness and death

(By Dehydrogenases)

Treatment → Infusions of $C_2H_5OH \xrightarrow{\text{Removes}}$ Dehydrogenases

thus Prevents → HCOOH formation

This helps in → CH₃OH removal through kidneys

- C_2H_5OH ➡ Central Nervous system directly

- Uses (a) as solvent in paints

(b) preparation of many carbon compounds

Phenols

- Also called "Carbolic Acid"
- first isolated from Coal tar in 19th century.
- Nowadays produced synthetically from Cumene method.

Methods of Preparation

1. From Haloarenes

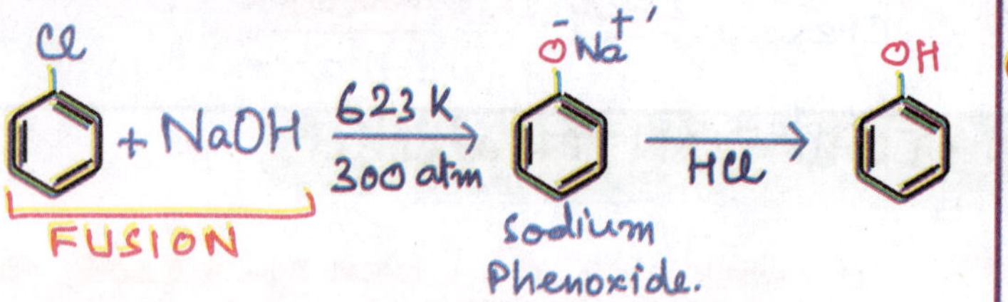

$C_6H_5Cl + NaOH \xrightarrow[300\ atm]{623\ K} C_6H_5O^-Na^+ \xrightarrow{HCl} C_6H_5OH$

FUSION — Sodium Phenoxide

NEET concentrate

- Reaction 1 is also called Dow Process.
- Some other important reactions are –
  - $C_6H_5MgBr \xrightarrow[(ii)\ H_2O/H^+]{(i)\ [O]} C_6H_5OH$
  - $C_6H_6 + O_2 \xrightarrow[315°C]{V_2O_5} C_6H_5OH$ (Latest method of Manufacture)

2. From Benzene Sulphonic acid

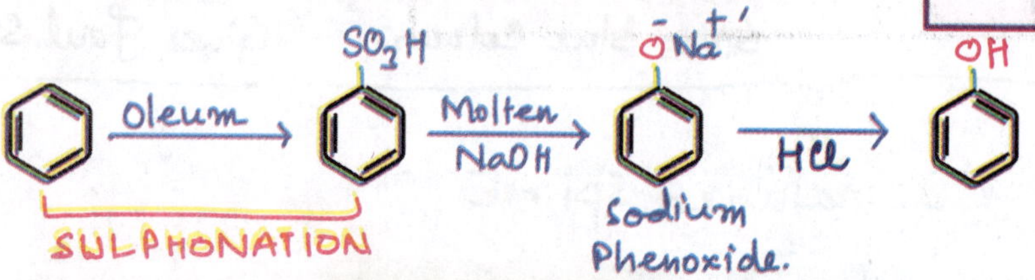

$C_6H_6 \xrightarrow{Oleum} C_6H_5SO_3H \xrightarrow[NaOH]{Molten} C_6H_5O^-Na^+ \xrightarrow{HCl} C_6H_5OH$

SULPHONATION — Sodium Phenoxide

Dhyan Rakhna! Grignard Reagent ko Dry Ether Mein Rakha jaata hai aur iski sabhi reactions bhi dry ether ki hi presence mein hoti hai

3. From Diazonium Salts

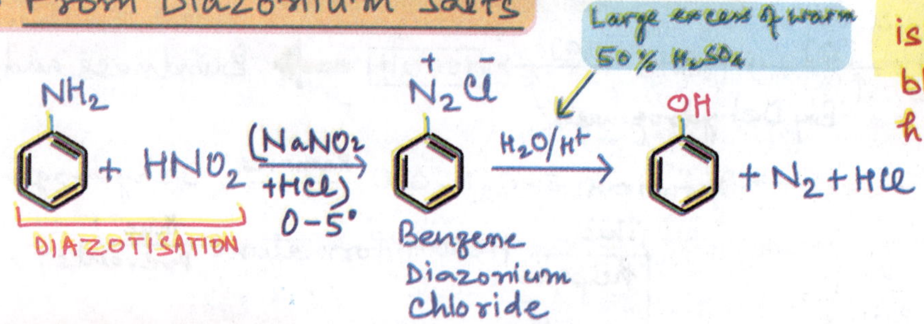

$C_6H_5NH_2 + HNO_2 \xrightarrow[0-5°]{(NaNO_2 + HCl)} C_6H_5N_2^+Cl^- \xrightarrow{H_2O/H^+} C_6H_5OH + N_2 + HCl$

DIAZOTISATION — Benzene Diazonium Chloride

Large excess of warm 50% H_2SO_4

4. From Cumene

- Also called as Auto-oxidation.
- Most of the world wide production from this method

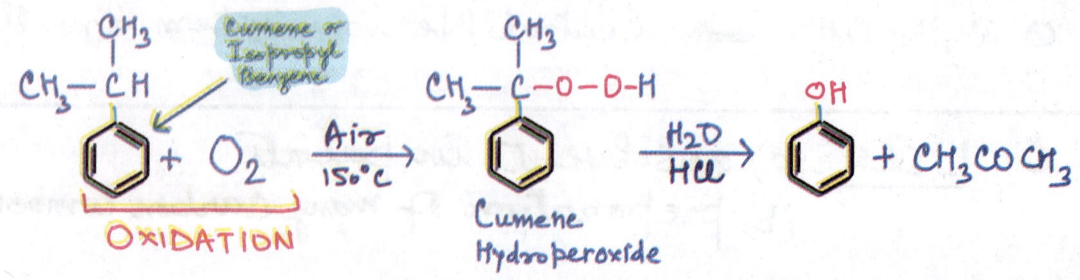

- Middle oil fraction of coaltar distillation has naphthalene and Phenolic compounds. Their isolation can be done as –

① Middle oil fraction $\xrightarrow[H_2SO_4]{\text{Washed}}$ ② Middle oil fraction – Basic Impurities (like Pyridine) $\xrightarrow[\text{cooling}]{\text{Excessive}}$ ③ Middle oil fraction – Naphthalene

③ $\xrightarrow{\text{aq. NaOH},\ CO_2,\ H_2O}$ ④ Phenols + Na_2CO_3

④ Phenols + Na_2CO_3 → Fractional Distillation →
- Phenols (180°c)
- Cresols (190–205°)
- Xylols (211–235°)

NEET concentrate

Actual Products of step ④ are phenoxides which liberate Phenols when CO_2 is blown through them

Physical Properties

- Colourless liquids or solids with red tint & Carbolic odour
- Highly Toxic, Boiling points higher than corresponding alcohols (due to stronger intermolecular H-bonding)
- Further, Boiling points are higher than hydrocarbons, ethers, haloalkanes and haloarenes of corresponding molecular masses
- More Miscible with water (due to their ability to form H-bonding with H_2O molecules) Miscibility decreases with increase in the size of aryl group (being hydrophobic in nature)
- Stronger acids than aliphatic alcohols due to –
  - ⓐ –I effect of benzene ring (sp^2 hybridised)
  - ⓑ Conjugation of lone pair of oxygen atom (Provides extra stability to phenoxide ion formed after loss of H^+)

OH (phenol) ⇌ O^- (Phenoxide ion) + H^+ → resonance structures ↔ ↔ ↔ ↔

Phenoxide ion

Stabilisation of Phenoxide ion by conjugation due to charge delocalisation

- Among substituted Phenols e^- withdrawing groups (like NO_2) increases acidic strength while e^- donating groups (like alkyl) decreases acidic strength.

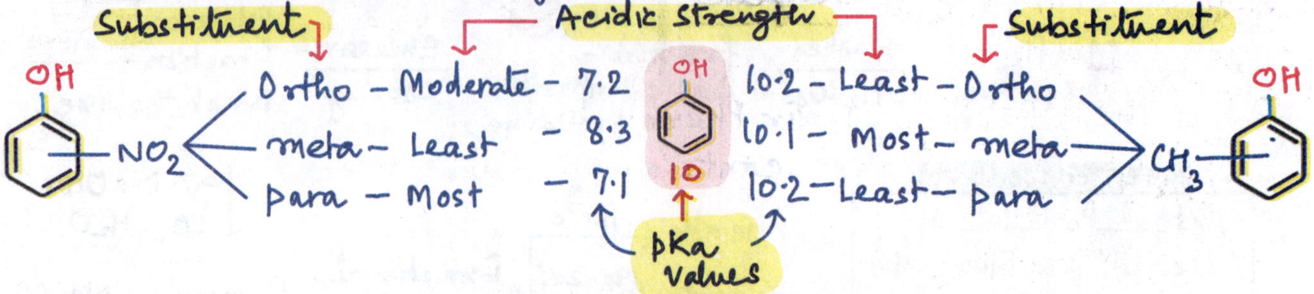

Chemical Properties

1 Kolbe's Reaction

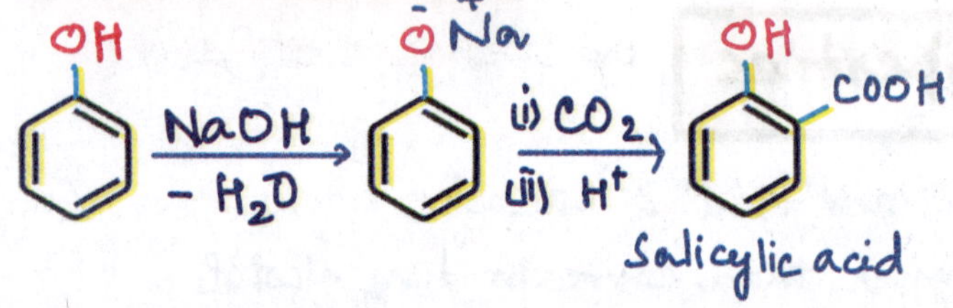

- CO_2 is a weak electrophile.
- Salicylic acid is also called ortho or 2-hydroxy benzoic acid.

2 Reimer – Tiemann Reaction

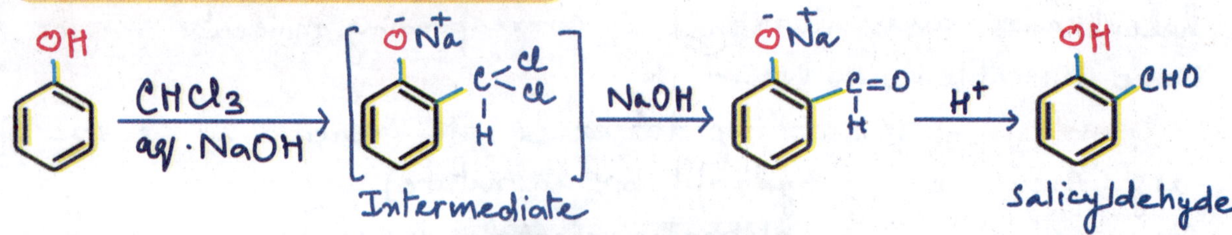

NEET concentrate

The attacking electrophile on the benzene ring is $:CCl_2$ (Dichloro carbene) which is formed as

$$\overset{\delta+}{H}-\overset{\delta+}{C}(\overset{\delta-}{Cl})_3 \xrightarrow[-H_2O]{NaOH} \bar{C}Cl_3 \xrightarrow{-Cl^-} :CCl_2$$

→ –I effect of 3 Cl

Dichlorocarbene

③ Reaction with Zn Dust

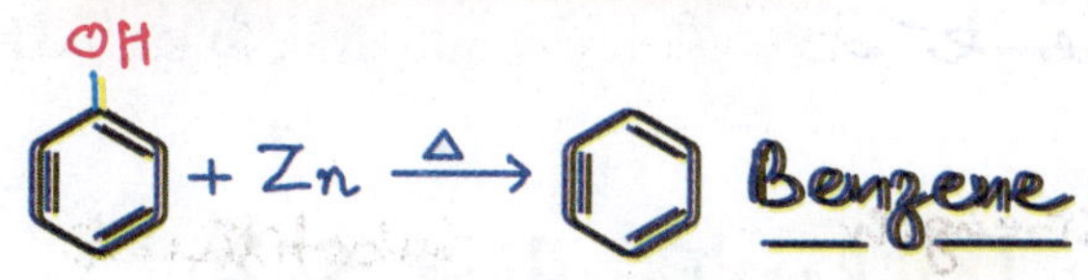

④ Oxidation

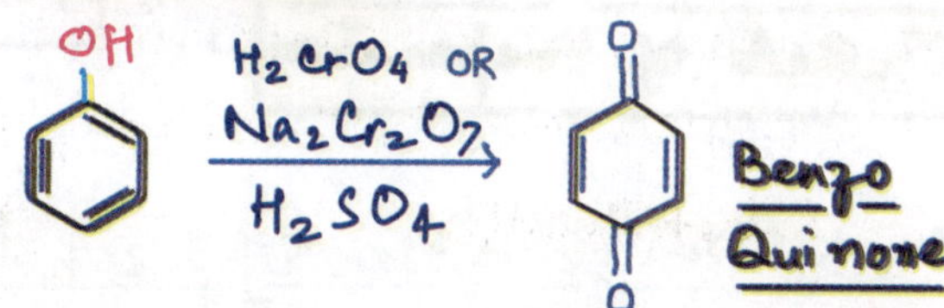

- In the presence of air Phenols are slowly oxidised to dark coloured mixtures containing Quinones.

④ Electrophilic Substitution

OH ← [Ortho, para directing and Ring activator group.]

(i) Nitration

Phenol $\xrightarrow[298\,K]{\text{Dilute } HNO_3}$ p-nitrophenol + o-nitrophenol

- Products are separated by steam-Distillation.

p-nitrophenol: Less steam volatile ← [Due to Intermolecular H-bonding.]

o-nitrophenol: More steam volatile ← [Due to Intramolecular H-bonding.]

Phenol $\xrightarrow{\text{Conc. } HNO_3}$ 2,4,6-trinitrophenol (Picric Acid) $\xleftarrow{\text{Conc. } HNO_3}$ 2,4-disulphonicacid $\xleftarrow{\text{Conc. } H_2SO_4}$ Phenol

(ii) Halogenation

(a) Phenol $\xrightarrow[273K]{Br_2 \text{ in } CS_2}$ p-bromophenol + o-bromophenol

- No Lewis acid required for Reaction due to activating nature of -OH group.

(b) Phenol + $3Br_2$ (Bromine water) ⟶ 2,4,6-tribromophenol

- In Polar solvent Phenol is in equilibrium with Phenoxide ion (actual substrate)

Ethers

Methods of Preparation

1. By Dehydration of Alcohols

C_2H_5OH (Excess) $\xrightarrow[140°C \text{ or } 413 K]{H_2SO_4}$ $C_2H_5OC_2H_5$ Diethyl ether

- Reaction type S_N2.
- H_3PO_4 can also be used as protic agent
- Suitable for ethers with Primary alkyl group only.

Mechanism:

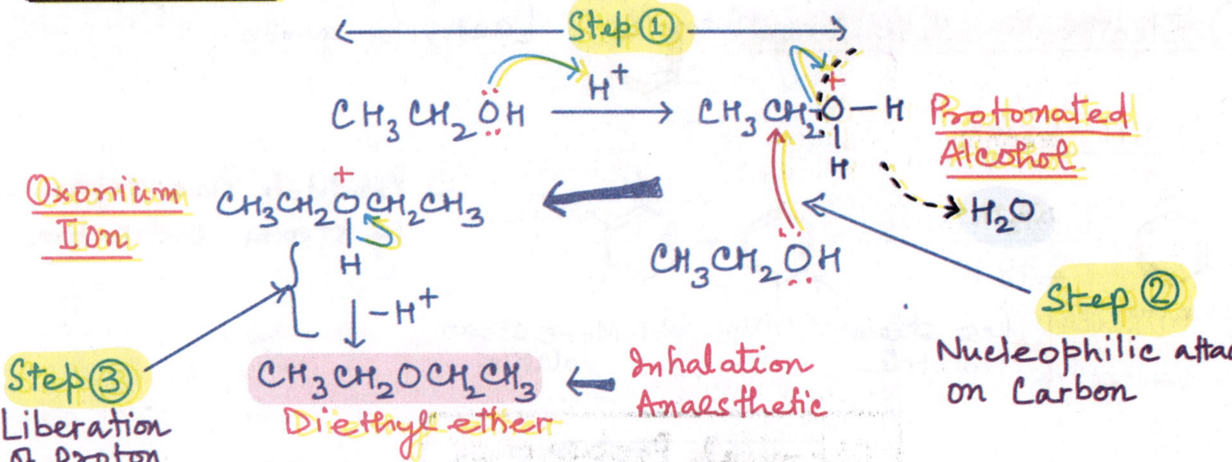

NEET concentrate

- Special conditions for reaction – ① Unhindered alkyl group ② Low temperature ③ Excess of Alcohol
- For 2° and 3° alcohols → No Ether formation (as elimination competes over substitution i.e., alkenes are formed)

2. Williamson's Ether Synthesis

$R-X + R'\bar{O}\overset{+}{Na} \longrightarrow ROR' + NaX$

$(CH_3)_3C\bar{O}\overset{+}{Na} + CH_3Br \xrightarrow{-NaBr} (CH_3)_3COCH_3$

$(CH_3)_3CBr + CH_3\bar{O}\overset{+}{Na} \xrightarrow{-NaBr} CH_3-\underset{CH_3}{\underset{|}{C}}=CH_2 + CH_3OH$

- Lab method for symmetrical & asymmetrical ethers
- SN2 with oxygen of alkoxide ion as Nucleophile
- For 2° and 3° alkyl halides elimination competes over substitution.

- 3° Alkyl halide with 1° alkoxide → No ether formation (as alkoxides are stronger bases)

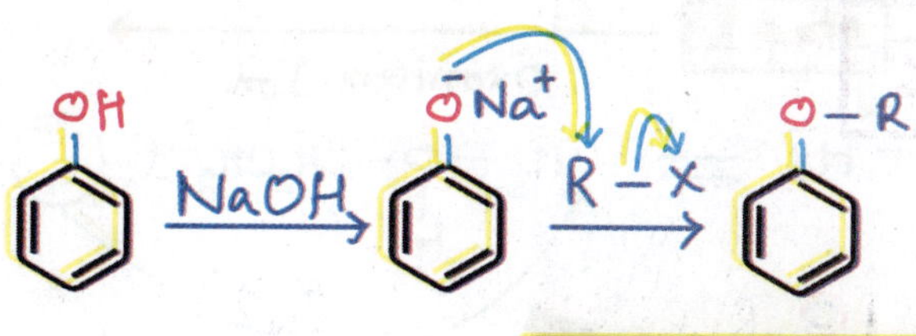

- Extension of Williamson ether synthesis.
- Remember, here Phenol is used as Phenoxide

Physical Properties

- Dimethyl ether & Ethyl Methyl ether are gases at room temp. Rest colourless liquids with characteristic ethereal smell.
- Net Dipole moments – 1.15D to 1.30D (due to polar C–O bond)
- Boiling Points lower than corresponding isomeric alcohols, but comparable with corresponding alkanes as

No H-Bonding →

Formula	$CH_3(CH_2)_3CH_3$ n-Pentane	C_2H_5-O-C_2H_5 Ethoxyethane	$CH_3(CH_2)_3$-OH Butan-1-ol
b.p./K	309.1	307.6	390

← Rigrous H-bonding

- Miscibility with water is same as that of alcohols (due to H-bonding between water molecule and oxygen of ether.

Chemical Properties

- Least reactive of the functional groups.

1 Cleavage of C–O bond

$$R_1-O-R_2 + HX \longrightarrow R_1X + R-OH$$

$$R-OH \xrightarrow{HX} H_2O + R_2X$$

← Only when HX taken in Excess

- Under drastic conditions with excess of hydrogen halides
- HI > HBr > HCl (Reactivity order)
- Usual Mechanism – SN2

- For Unsymmetrical ethers ⟶ Smaller alkyl group forms RX.
- For Alkyl aryl ethers ⟶ Phenol is formed always along with RX
- Phenols once formed do not react further under any Conditions (due to Partial double bond character between C & O)
- When one of the alkyl group is 3° ⟶ 3° alkyl halide is formed always (as reaction follows SN1 mechanism and 3° carbocation is more stable)

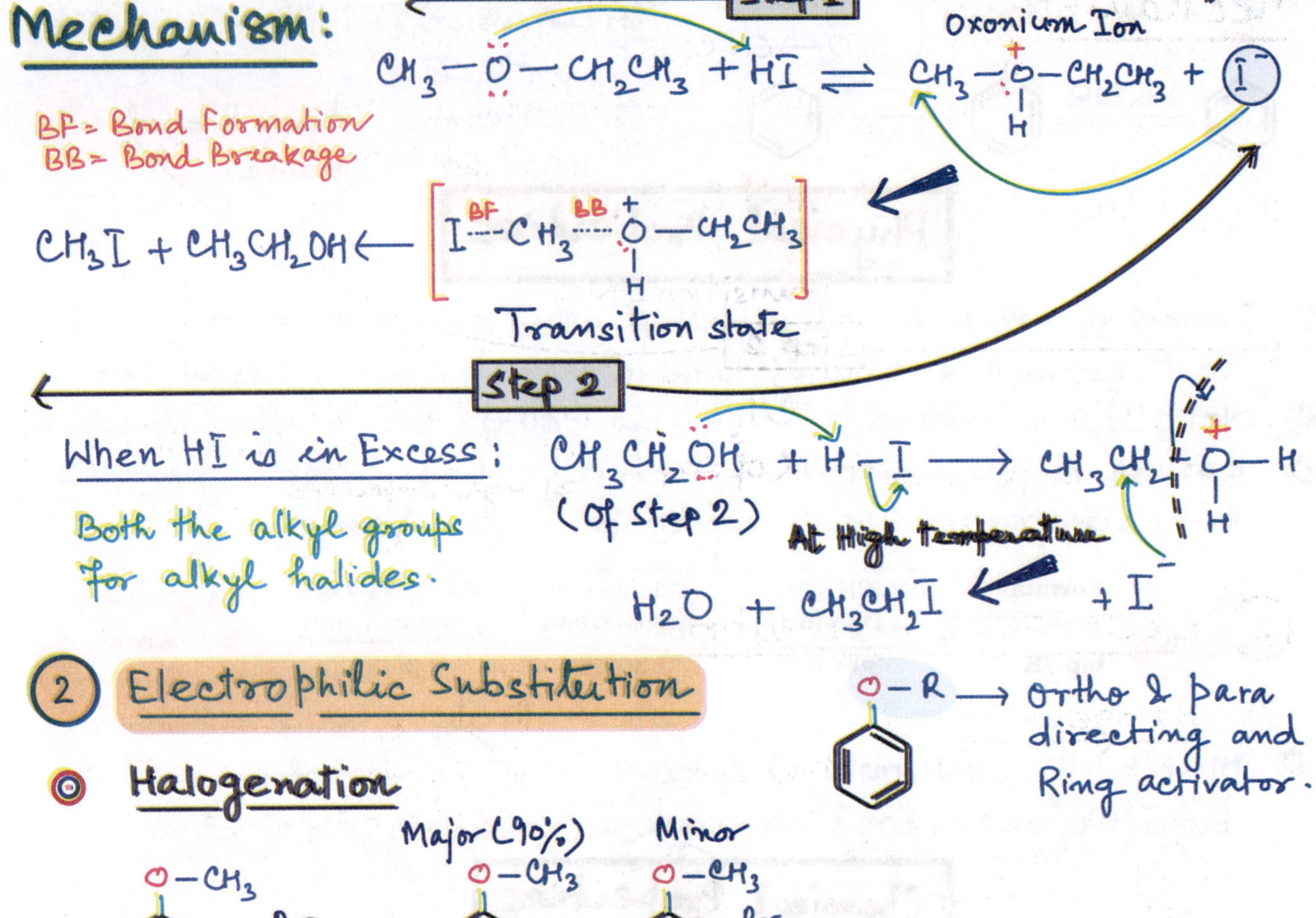

Fe(III) oxide

Br

Friedel-Crafts reaction

Anisole ($O-CH_3$) + CH_3Cl $\xrightarrow[CS_2]{\text{Anhy. } AlCl_3}$ Major: p-methylanisole ($O-CH_3$, CH_3 para) + Minor: o-methylanisole ($O-CH_3$, CH_3 ortho)

Similar case is visible with CH_3COCl

Nitration

Anisole ($O-CH_3$) $\xrightarrow[HNO_3]{H_2SO_4}$ Major (90%): p-nitroanisole ($O-CH_3$, NO_2 para) + Minor: o-nitroanisole ($O-CH_3$, NO_2 ortho)

Mechanism:

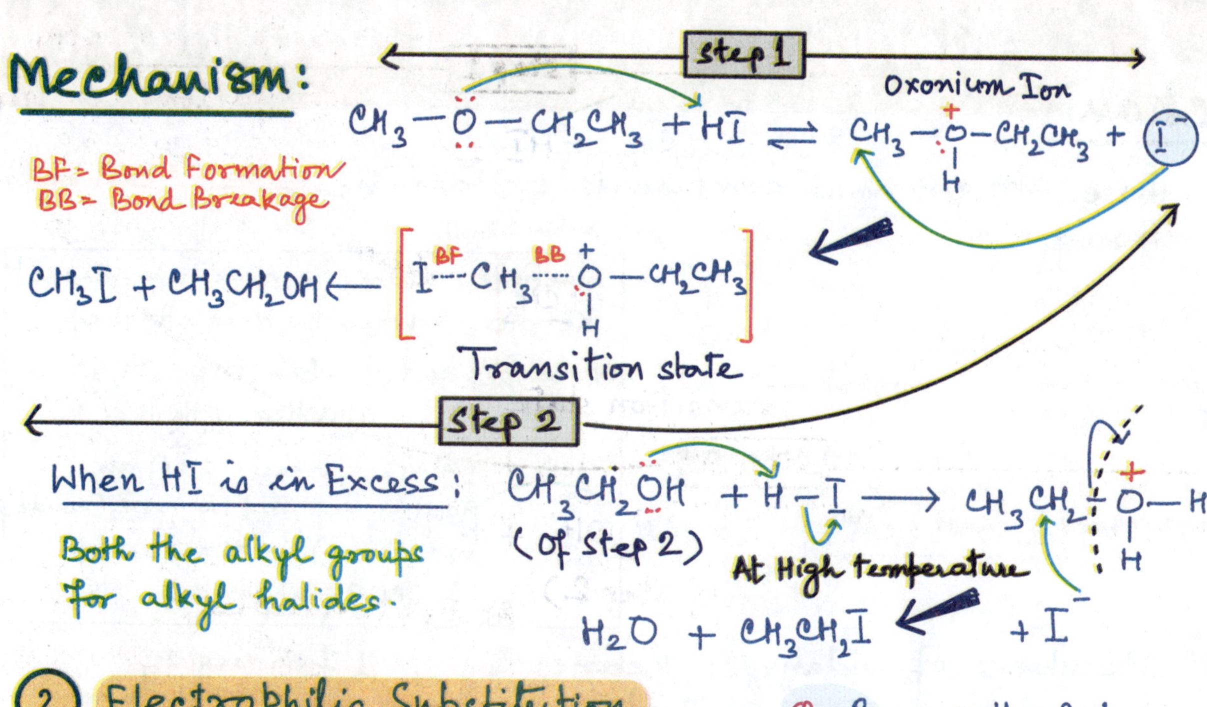

(2) Electrophilic Substitution

O — R ⟶ ortho & para directing and Ring activator.

- **Halogenation**

Anisole (C_6H_5—O—CH_3) $\xrightarrow[\text{CH}_3\text{COOH}]{\text{Br}_2 \text{ in}}$ p-bromoanisole (Major (90%)) + o-bromoanisole (Minor)

Fe(III) oxide

- **Friedel–Crafts reaction**

Anisole + CH_3Cl $\xrightarrow[\text{CS}_2]{\text{Anhy. AlCl}_3}$ p-methylanisole (Major) + o-methylanisole (Minor)

Similar case is visible with CH_3COCl

- **Nitration**

Anisole $\xrightarrow[\text{HNO}_3]{\text{H}_2\text{SO}_4}$ p-nitroanisole (Major (90%), NO_2) + o-nitroanisole (Minor, NO_2)

17. Aldehydes, Ketons & Carboxylic Acids

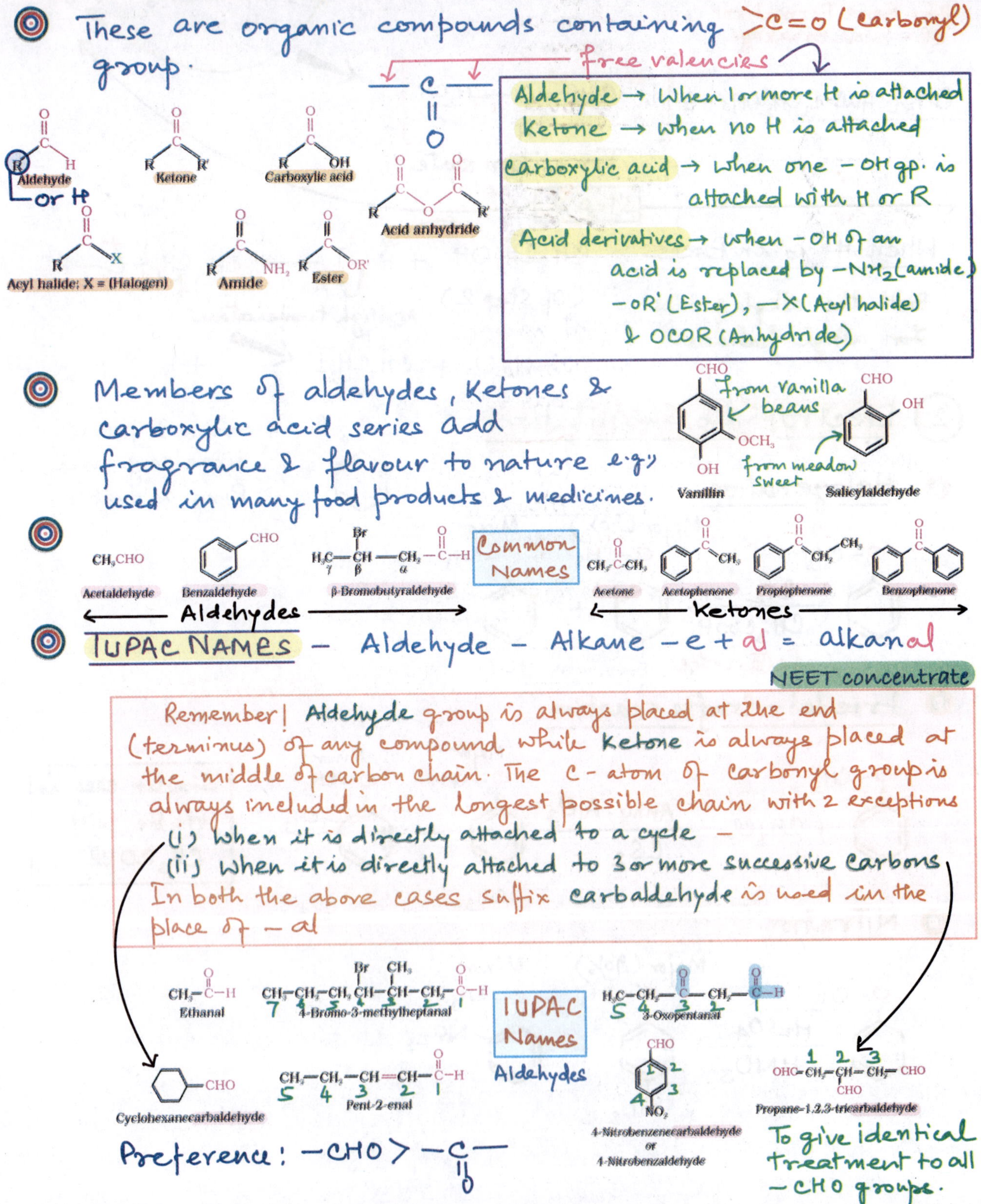

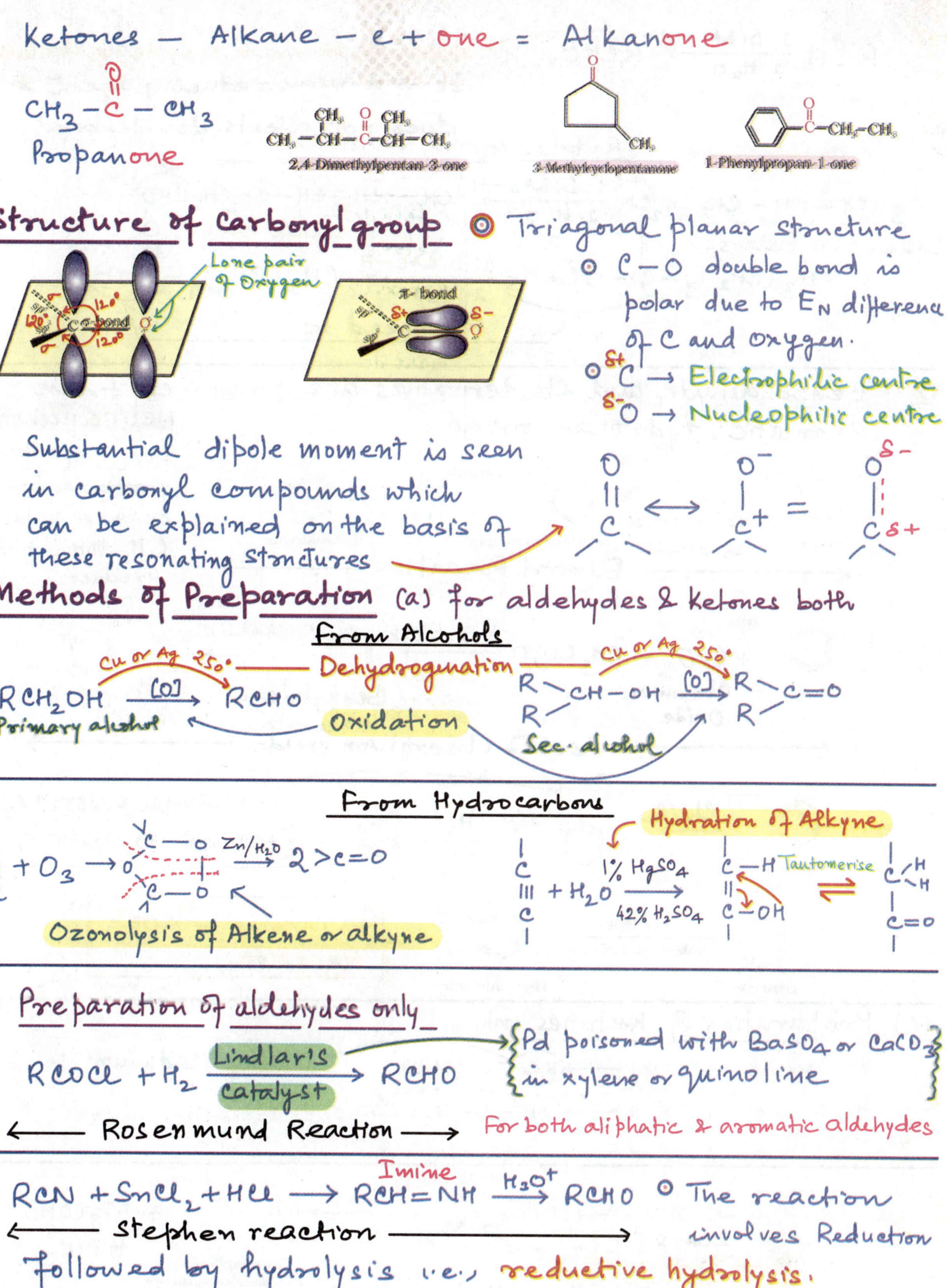

Ketones — Alkane − e + one = Alkanone
$CH_3-\overset{O}{\overset{||}{C}}-CH_3$
Propanone
2,4-Dimethylpentan-3-one
3-Methylcyclopentanone
1-Phenylpropan-1-one
Structure of carbonyl group
Triagonal planar structure
C—O double bond is polar due to E_N difference of C and oxygen.
$^{\delta+}C$ → Electrophilic centre
$^{\delta-}O$ → Nucleophilic centre
Lone pair of Oxygen
σ-bond
π-bond
120°
Substantial dipole moment is seen in carbonyl compounds which can be explained on the basis of these resonating structures
Methods of Preparation (a) for aldehydes & ketones both
From Alcohols
Cu or Ag 250° — Dehydrogenation — Cu or Ag 250°
$RCH_2OH \xrightarrow{[O]} RCHO$
Primary alcohol
Oxidation
$R_2CH-OH \xrightarrow{[O]} R_2C=O$
Sec. alcohol
From Hydrocarbons
Zn/H_2O
$2 >C=O$
Ozonolysis of Alkene or alkyne
Hydration of Alkyne
1% $HgSO_4$
42% H_2SO_4
Tautomerise
(b) Preparation of aldehydes only
$RCOCl + H_2 \xrightarrow[\text{catalyst}]{\text{Lindlar's}} RCHO$
{Pd poisoned with $BaSO_4$ or $CaCO_3$ in xylene or quinoline}
← Rosenmund Reaction →
For both aliphatic & aromatic aldehydes
$RCN + SnCl_2 + HCl \longrightarrow RCH=NH \xrightarrow{H_3O^+} RCHO$
Imine
← Stephen reaction →
The reaction involves Reduction followed by hydrolysis i.e., reductive hydrolysis.

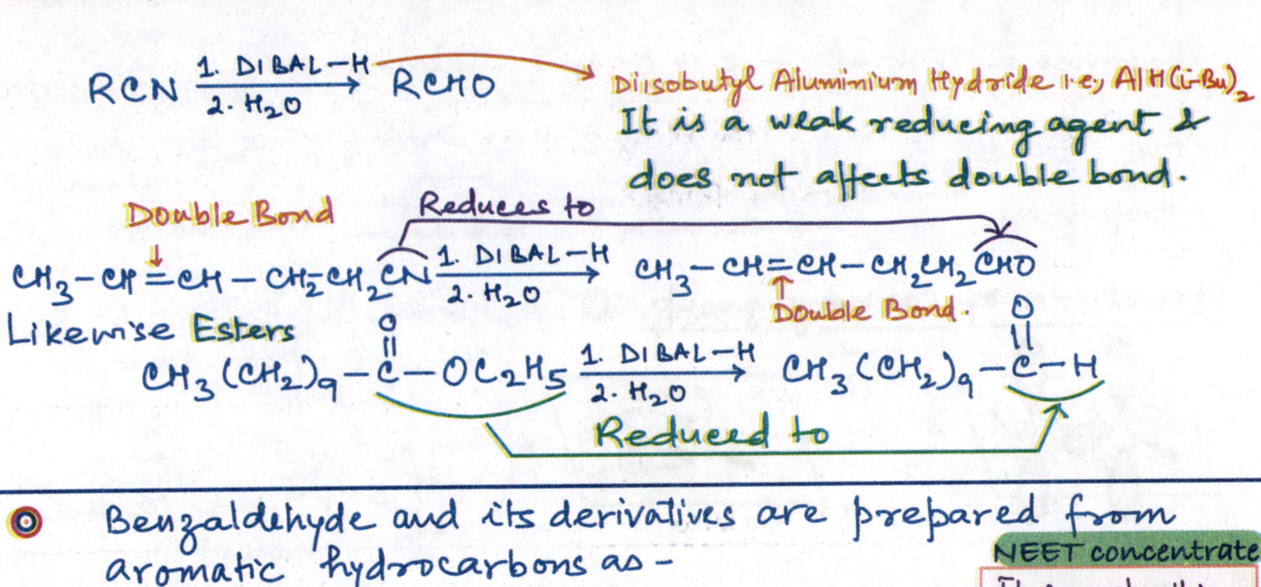

$$RCN \xrightarrow[2.\ H_2O]{1.\ DIBAL-H} RCHO$$

DIBAL-H → Diisobutyl Aluminium Hydride i.e., $AlH(i\text{-}Bu)_2$

It is a weak reducing agent & does not affects double bond.

$$CH_3-CH=CH-CH_2-CH_2CN \xrightarrow[2.\ H_2O]{1.\ DIBAL-H} CH_3-CH=CH-CH_2CH_2CHO$$

Double Bond (unchanged) — CN Reduces to CHO; Double Bond.

Likewise Esters

$$CH_3(CH_2)_9-\overset{O}{\overset{\|}{C}}-OC_2H_5 \xrightarrow[2.\ H_2O]{1.\ DIBAL-H} CH_3(CH_2)_9-\overset{O}{\overset{\|}{C}}-H$$

Reduced to

- Benzaldehyde and its derivatives are prepared from aromatic hydrocarbons as –

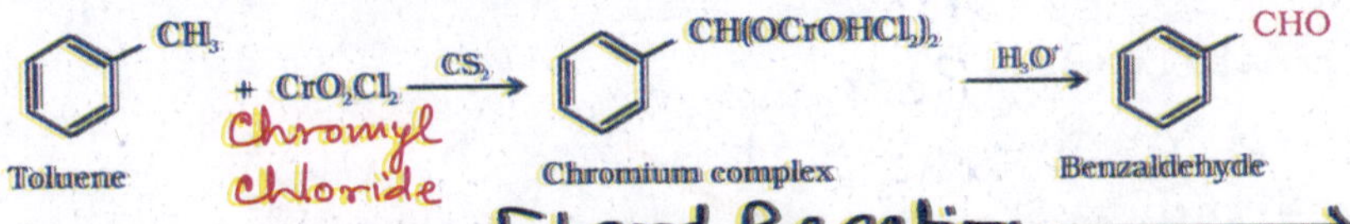

NEET concentrate: It is a specific reaction as normal oxidation yields C_6H_5COOH as final product

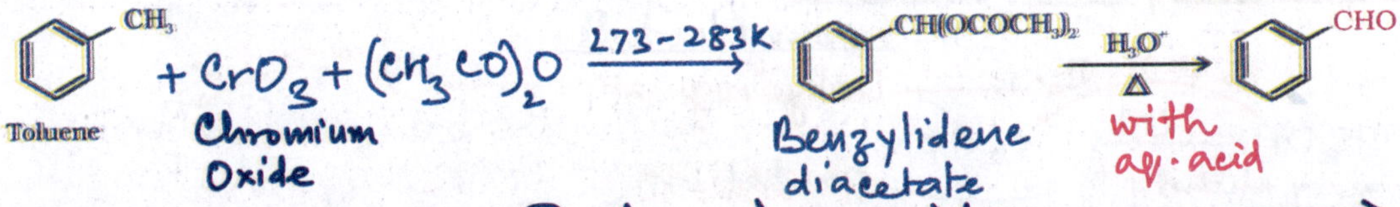

Toluene ($C_6H_5CH_3$) + CrO_2Cl_2 (Chromyl Chloride) $\xrightarrow{CS_2}$ $C_6H_5CH(OCrOHCl_2)_2$ (Chromium complex) $\xrightarrow{H_3O^+}$ C_6H_5CHO (Benzaldehyde)

← Etard Reaction →

Toluene ($C_6H_5CH_3$) + CrO_3 (Chromium Oxide) + $(CH_3CO)_2O$ $\xrightarrow{273-283K}$ $C_6H_5CH(OCOCH_3)_2$ (Benzylidene diacetate) $\xrightarrow[\Delta]{H_3O^+}$ C_6H_5CHO (with aq. acid)

← use of chromium oxide →

Toluene ($C_6H_5CH_3$) $\xrightarrow{Cl_2/h\nu}$ $C_6H_5CH_2Cl$ $\xrightarrow[373K]{H_2O}$ C_6H_5CHO

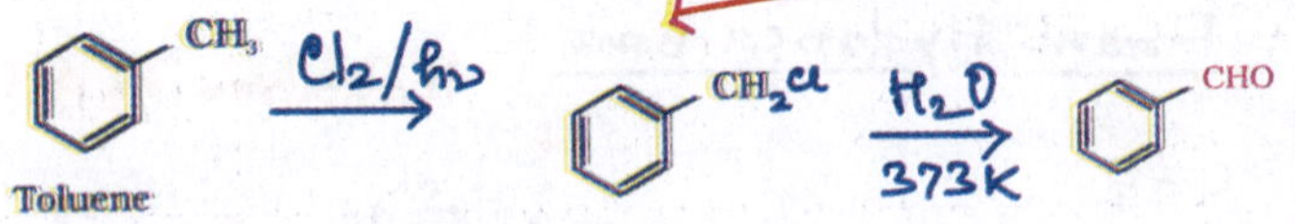

Side chain chlorination followed by hydrolysis

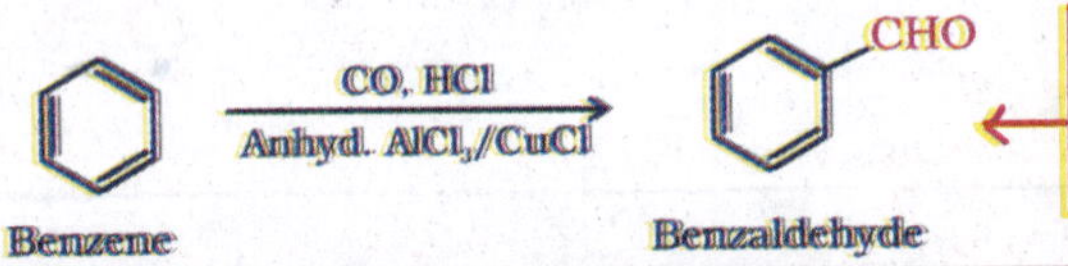

Benzene $\xrightarrow[\text{Anhyd. } AlCl_3/CuCl]{CO,\ HCl}$ Benzaldehyde ← Gatterman – Koch Reaction

---

(c) Preparation of Ketones only

$$2R-Mg-X + CdCl_2 \longrightarrow R_2Cd + 2Mg(X)Cl$$

R_2Cd → Dialkyl cadmium

$$2R'-\underset{\overset{\|}{O}}{C}-Cl + R_2Cd \longrightarrow 2R'-\underset{\overset{\|}{O}}{C}-R + CdCl_2$$

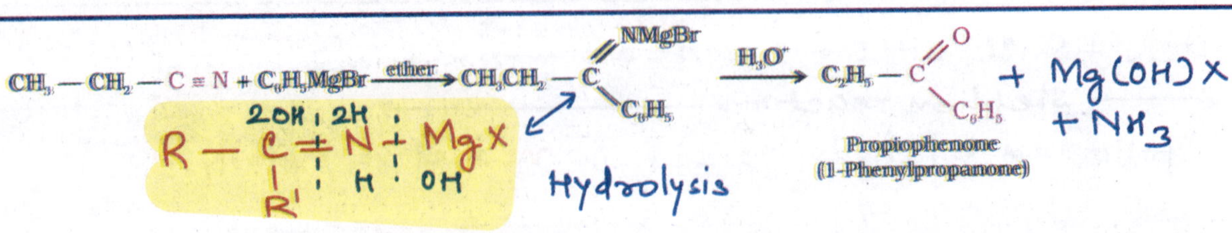

$$CH_3-CH_2-C\equiv N + C_6H_5MgBr \xrightarrow{ether} CH_3CH_2-C(=NMgBr)-C_6H_5 \xrightarrow{H_3O^+} C_2H_5-C(=O)-C_6H_5 + Mg(OH)X + NH_3$$

Propiophenone (1-Phenylpropanone)

Hydrolysis: $R-\underset{R'}{C}=N-MgX$ (2OH : 2H ; H : OH)

NEET concentrate

Reaction of HCN with RMgX gives aldehydes as –

$$H-C\equiv N + RMgX \longrightarrow H-\underset{R}{\underset{|}{C}}=NMgX \xrightarrow{H_2O} H-\underset{R}{\underset{|}{\overset{O}{\overset{||}{C}}}} + NH_3 + Mg(OH)X$$

Remember all aldehydes except HCHO can be prepared from this reaction

$$C_6H_6 + Ar/R-\overset{O}{\overset{||}{C}}-Cl \xrightarrow{\text{Anhyd. } AlCl_3} C_6H_5-\overset{O}{\overset{||}{C}}-Ar/R$$

← Friedel – crafts Acylation →

This reaction is an example of electrophilic substitution reaction.

Physical properties

- HCHO – Gas, CH_3CHO – volatile liquid. Rest either liquid or solid at room temp.
- BP higher than hydrocarbons and ethers of comporable molar mass (due to weak dipole – dipole interactions)
- BP lower than alcohols of similar molecular mass (due to the absence of intermolecular H - bonding)
- Lower members miscible with water in all proportions (due to their ability to form H – bonds with water molecules) this miscibility decreases rapidly with increase of alkyl chain.
- All of them are fairly soluble in organic solvents like benzene, ether, CH_3OH, $CHCl_3$ etc.
- Lower members with pungent smell, higher members – less pungent more fragrant.

Many naturally occurring aldehydes & ketones are used in the blending of perfumes & flavouring agents

Chemical Properties

1. Nucleophilic additions

← Mechanism outline →

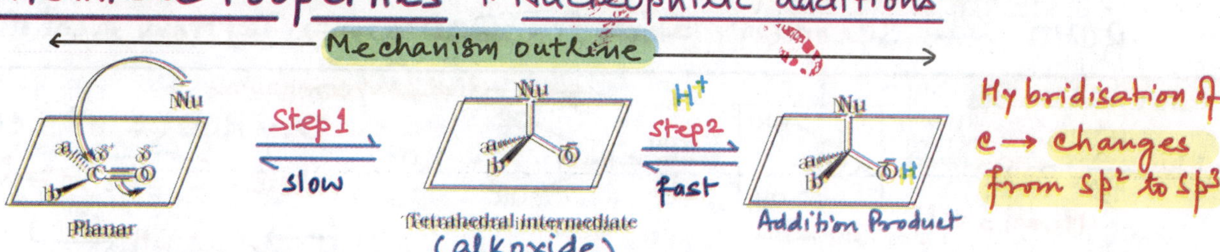

The net result → Addition of Nu^- & H^+ across the carbon oxygen double bond.

◉ Reactivity → Aldehydes > Ketones (Sterically larger and more alkyl groups attached to C - atom → more hinderance in Nucleophilic attack, Electronically +I effect of alkyl group is responsible for decrease in charge on carbonyl C-atom)

NEET concentrate

$HCHO > CH_3CHO > C_2H_5CHO > C_6H_5CHO > CH_3COCH_3$

← Increasing order of reactivity towards Nu^- addition

Among C_6H_5CHO & C_2H_5CHO the reactivity of latter is more as (+)ve charge of carbonyl carbon is delocalised due to benzene ring in C_6H_5CHO.

Examples

$HCN + OH^- \rightleftharpoons :\bar{C}N + H_2O$; $\overset{\delta+}{>C}=\overset{\delta-}{O} \rightleftharpoons$ [Tetrahedral intermediate: $>C(O^-)(CN)$] $\rightleftharpoons$ $>C(CN)(OH)$ Cyanohydrin

very slow with pure HCN; catalysed by a base

Tetrahedral intermediate

Cyanohydrin – useful synthetic intermediates

← Addition of HCN →

Due to steric reasons

$>C=O + NaHSO_3 \rightleftharpoons >C(OSO_2H)(ONa)$ $\xrightarrow{\text{proton transfer}}$ $>C(OSO_2Na)(OH)$ ← Bisulphite Addition compound

← Addition of Sodium hydrogen sulphite →

Dhyan Rakho! $NaHSO_3 \rightleftharpoons \underset{(E^+)}{H^+} + \underset{Nu^-}{SO_3^-}Na^+$ Metal ions like Na^+ can never be Electrophiles.

{For aldehydes → equilibrium lies on the right hand side

{For ketones → equilibrium lies on the left hand side

Addition Product → Water soluble → Gives back original carbonyl compound (on treatment with dilute Mineral acid/alkali) → Useful for Purification & Separation

With Grignard Reagent HCHO → Primary alcohol (except CH_3OH)

RCHO → Secondary alcohols, RCOR → Tertiary alcohols.

With Alcohols

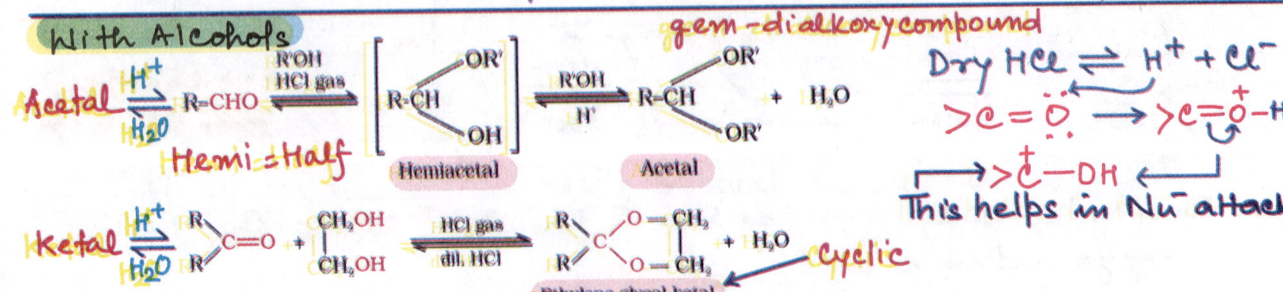

$$>C=O + H_2N\text{-}Z \rightleftharpoons \left[>C\begin{matrix}OH \\ NHZ\end{matrix}\right] \longrightarrow >C=N\text{-}Z + H_2O$$

The reaction is reversible and catalysed by acid

Technically reaction follows Nu^- – addition elimination

← **With Ammonia & its derivatives** →

$>C=O + NH_2OH \underset{H^+}{\rightleftharpoons} >C=NOH$; $>C=O + NH_2NH_2 \underset{H^+}{\rightleftharpoons} >C=NNH_2$

Hydroxyl amine → Oxime ; Hydrazine → Hydrazone

$C_6H_5NH\cdot NH_2 \longrightarrow >C=N\cdot NHC_6H_5$; $NH_2-NHCONH_2 \longrightarrow >C=N-NHCONH_2$

Phenyl Hydrazine → Phenyl Hydrazone ; semicarbazide → semicarbazone

◎ Likewise 2,4 dinitrophenyl hydrazine gives 2,4 dinitrophenyl hydrazone. These derivatives are yellow, orange or red solids and useful for characterisation of aldehydes and ketones.

NEET concentrate

With NH_3 → HCHO gives $(CH_2)_6N_4$ (Hexa methylene tetra amine or urotropine); CH_3CHO gives acetaldehyde ammonia $\left(\begin{matrix}CH_3 \\ H\end{matrix}>C<\begin{matrix}OH \\ NH_2\end{matrix}\right)$ CH_3COCH_3 gives diacetone amine $\left(\begin{matrix}CH_3 \\ CH_3\end{matrix}>C<\begin{matrix}CH_2COCH_3 \\ NH_2\end{matrix}\right)$.

The reaction of NH_3 & CH_3CHO is Nu^- addition while rest 2 are Nu^- addition elimination reactions.

Reduction ◎ Moderate reducing agents like $NaBH_4$ or Sn/HCl or 1 mole H_2/Ni — Aldehydes → Primary alcohols ; ketones → Sec. alcohols

◎ Strong reducing agents – $>C=O \longrightarrow >CH_2$ (like Zn-Hg/HCl)

$$>C=O \xrightarrow[HCl]{Zn\text{-}Hg} >CH_2 + H_2O \qquad >C=O \xrightarrow[-H_2O]{NH_2NH_2} >C=NNH_2 \xrightarrow[heat]{KOH/ethylene\ glycol} >CH_2 + N_2$$

← Clemmensen Red. → ← Wolf kishner Reduction →

Dhyan Rakho! Wolf kishner reduction mein >C=O group hi specific way mein reduce hota hai isme doosre attached groups mein koi change nahi hota hai.

Oxidation ◎ $RCHO \xrightarrow{[O]} RCOOH$ by agents like $KMnO_4$, $K_2Cr_2O_7$, HNO_3 and even Tollen's reagent & Fehling's solution. (as H of CHO group easily oxidises to –OH)

◎ $R_1-\underset{1}{CH_2}-\underset{2}{\overset{}{C}}(=O)-\underset{3}{CH_2}-R_2 \xrightarrow{[O]}$ $R_2CH_2COOH + R_1COOH$ + $R_2COOH + R_1CH_2COOH$

By Oxidation of C_1-C_2 Linkage → $R_2CH_2COOH + R_1COOH$

By Oxidation of C_2-C_3 Linkage → $R_2COOH + R_1CH_2COOH$

So as ketones do not have C—H bond for oxidation hence these generally oxidise under vigorous conditions (strong oxidising agents + elevated temperatures). C—C linkage is oxidised in them resulting to → Carboxylic acids with lesser C-atoms.

NEET concentrate

Tollen's reagent → Ammoniacal $AgNO_3$ → forms Silver mirror with aldehydes; No Reaction with ketones.

$$RCHO + 2[Ag(NH_3)_2]^+ + 3\bar{O}H \longrightarrow RCOO^- + 2Ag + 2H_2O + 4NH_3$$

Fehling's solution → Ammoniacal cuprous chloride (Formed by mixing Fehling's solution A (aq. $CuSO_4$) and Fehling's solution B (alk. sodium Potassium tartarate = Rochelle salt) → forms Red Brown PPt with aldehydes; No reaction with ketones.

$$RCHO + 2Cu^{2+} + 5\bar{O}H \longrightarrow RCOO^- + Cu_2O + 3H_2O$$

$$R-\overset{O}{\overset{\|}{C}}-CH_3 \xrightarrow{NaOX} R-\overset{O}{\overset{\|}{C}}-ONa + CHX_3 \quad (X=Cl, Br, I)$$

Intact double bond

$$(CH_3)(H)C{=}C(CH_3)-\overset{O}{\overset{\|}{C}}-CH_3 \xrightarrow{NaOCl} (CH_3)(H)C{=}C(CH_3)-\overset{O}{\overset{\|}{C}}-ONa + CHCl_3$$

← **Haloform Reaction** →

Reaction is very diversified CH_3CH_2OH (among primary Alcohols) $CH_3-\underset{OH}{CH}-$ (all sec. alcohols with OH at 2nd position, their oxidation products and their halogen substitution products all give this reaction.

- Sodium hypohalite is formed in situ by the reaction between X_2 (halogen) and alkali. All those combinations which can give X_2 and alkali can be used directly e.g., $Na_2CO_3 + I_2$
- The oxidation does not affects even a $>C=C<$ if present with in the molecule.

Aldol Condensation $2\underset{\alpha}{CH_3}CHO \underset{}{\overset{dil.\,NaOH}{\rightleftharpoons}} CH_3\underset{OH}{CH}CH_2CHO \xrightarrow[-H_2O]{\Delta} CH_3CH=CHCHO$

Aldol

Aldol = β-hydroxy aldehyde; Reaction is shown by those aldehydes or ketones which contain atleast 1 α-Hydrogen. Product of ketones is called ketols.

$$2\underset{\alpha}{CH_3}CO\underset{\alpha}{CH_3} \overset{dil.\,NaOH}{\rightleftharpoons} CH_3-\underset{OH}{\overset{CH_3}{C}}-CH_2COCH_3 \xrightarrow[-H_2O]{\Delta} CH_3-\overset{CH_3}{C}=CH-COCH_3$$

ketol α-β unsaturated ketone

NEET concentrate

Always use this tip to form aldol → $CH_3-\overset{|}{C}=O + H\cdot CH_2-\overset{O}{\overset{\|}{C}}- \longrightarrow CH_3-\underset{CH_2-\overset{}{\underset{O}{\underset{\|}{C}}}-}{\overset{}{C}}-OH$ ← aldol

Molecule 1 Molecule 2

$$CH_3CHO + CH_3CH_2CHO \xrightarrow[2.\ \Delta]{1.\ NaOH} CH_3CH{=}CHCHO + CH_3CH_2CH{=}C(CH_3)CHO + CH_3CH{=}C(CH_3)CHO + CH_3CH_2CH{=}CHCHO$$

Self aldol products (first two); Cross aldol products (last two)

Cross aldol condensation

$$C_6H_5CHO + C_6H_5COCH_3 \xrightarrow[293\,K]{\bar{O}H} C_6H_5CH{=}CH{-}\overset{O}{\overset{\|}{C}}{-}C_6H_5$$

Without α-H   with α-H   Major Product

NEET concentrate

Above reaction shows that aldehydes without α-H can also participate in aldol condensation as carbanion acceptors with other molecule having α-H.

Cannizzaro Reaction For aldehydes which do not have α-H.

$$HCHO + HCHO \xrightarrow[\Delta]{conc.\ KOH} CH_3OH + HCOO^-K^+$$

(Reduction → CH_3OH; Oxidation → $HCOO^-K^+$) Disproportionation reaction

$$C_6H_5CHO + C_6H_5CHO \xrightarrow[\Delta]{conc.\ KOH} C_6H_5CH_2OH + C_6H_5COO^-K^+$$

NEET concentrate

$$C_6H_5CHO + HCHO \xrightarrow[\Delta]{conc.\ KOH} C_6H_5CH_2OH + HCOO^-K^+$$ Crossed cannizzaro

Remember! In crossed cannizzaro if HCHO is involved then it will always form Oxidation product i.e., $HCOO^-$. Secondly, the acid formed in cannizzaro reaction always forms salt with the base (alkali) present in the reaction.

Cannizzaro reaction proceeds through intermolecular hydride or phenyl or methyl shift.

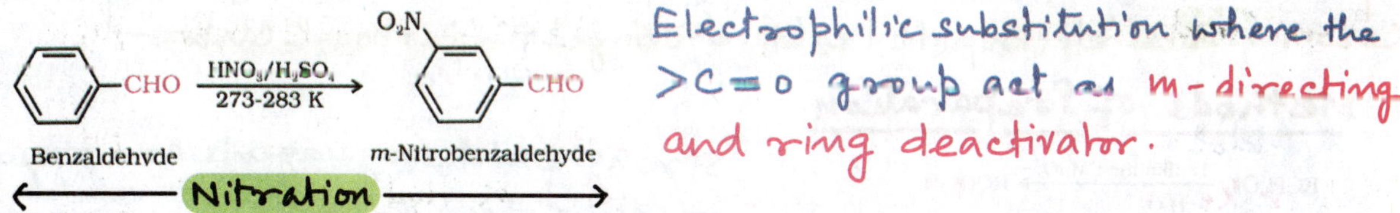

Electrophilic substitution where the >C=O group act as m-directing and ring deactivator.

Nitration

- HCHO → 40% solution is Formalin a lab preservative for specimens of Biology; Phenol + HCHO → Bakelite.

CH_3CHO → starting material to form CH_3COOH & many polymeric products

C_6H_5CHO → In Perfume & Dye industry

CH_3COCH_3 → Industrial solvents

Carboxylic Acids

- $-\underset{\underset{O}{\|}}{C}-OH$. ← Hydroxyl, ← Carbonyl } Carbo + xyl = carboxyl; can be aliphatic or aromatic

- Some higher members of aliphatic ($C_{12}-C_{18}$) carboxylic acids occur as esters of glycerol in natural fat - fatty acids

-

Formula	Common Name	IUPAC Name
HCOOH	Formic acid	Methanoic acid
CH_3COOH	Acetic acid	Ethanoic acid
CH_3CH_2COOH	Propionic acid	Propanoic acid
$CH_3CH_2CH_2COOH$	Butyric acid	Butanoic acid
$(CH_3)_2CHCOOH$	Isobutyric acid	2-Methylpropanoic acid
HOOC-COOH	Oxalic acid	Ethanedioic acid
HOOC $-CH_2-$COOH	Malonic acid	Propanedioic acid
HOOC $-(CH_2)_2-$COOH	Succinic acid	Butanedioic acid
HOOC $-(CH_2)_3-$COOH	Glutaric acid	Pentanedioic acid
HOOC $-(CH_2)_4-$COOH	Adipic acid	Hexanedioic acid
HOOC $-CH_2-CH(COOH)-CH_2-$COOH	Tricarballylic acid or carballylic acid	Propane-1, 2, 3-tricarboxylic acid
C_6H_5-COOH	Benzoic acid	Benzenecarboxylic acid (Benzoic acid)
C_6H_5-CH_2COOH	Phenylacetic acid	2-Phenylethanoic acid
C_6H_4(COOH)(COOH)	Phthalic acid	Benzene-1, 2-dicarboxylic acid

In IUPAC names suffix -oic acid is used under normal conditions and C-atom of -COOH is counted with in the chain. However, in all such situations where it is not possible to include this C-atom in the main chain carboxylic acid is used as suffix

- 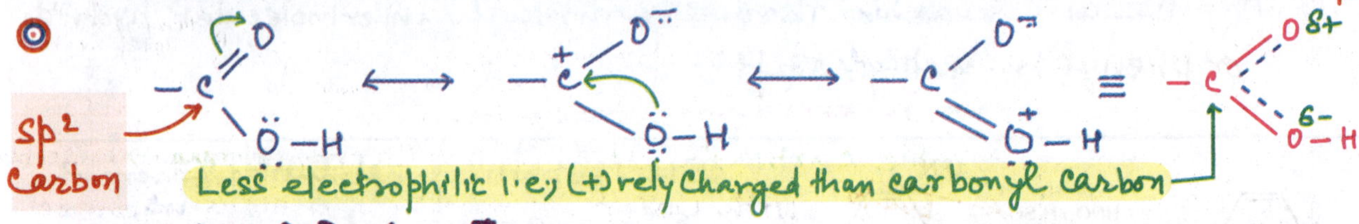

Methods of Preparation

$$RCH_2OH \xrightarrow[2.\ H_3\overset{+}{O}]{1.\ \text{alkaline } KMnO_4} RCOOH$$

$$\underset{\text{1-Decanol}}{CH_3(CH_2)_8CH_2OH} \xrightarrow[\text{Jones reagent}]{CrO_3-H_2SO_4} \underset{\text{Decanoic acid}}{CH_3(CH_2)_8COOH}$$

← Oxidation of alcohols →

Strong oxidising agents are required to show these reactions. Aldehydes show similar reactions with mild oxidising agents.

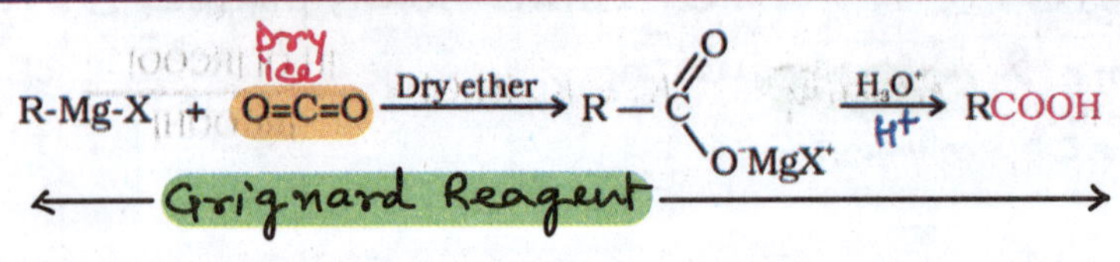

$$R\text{-}Mg\text{-}X + O{=}C{=}O \xrightarrow{\text{Dry ether}} R-\overset{O}{\overset{\|}{C}}-O^-MgX^+ \xrightarrow[H^+]{H_3O^+} RCOOH$$

← Grignard Reagent →

Method is very useful in converting alkyl halides in to corresponding carboxylic acid with 1 C more than that present

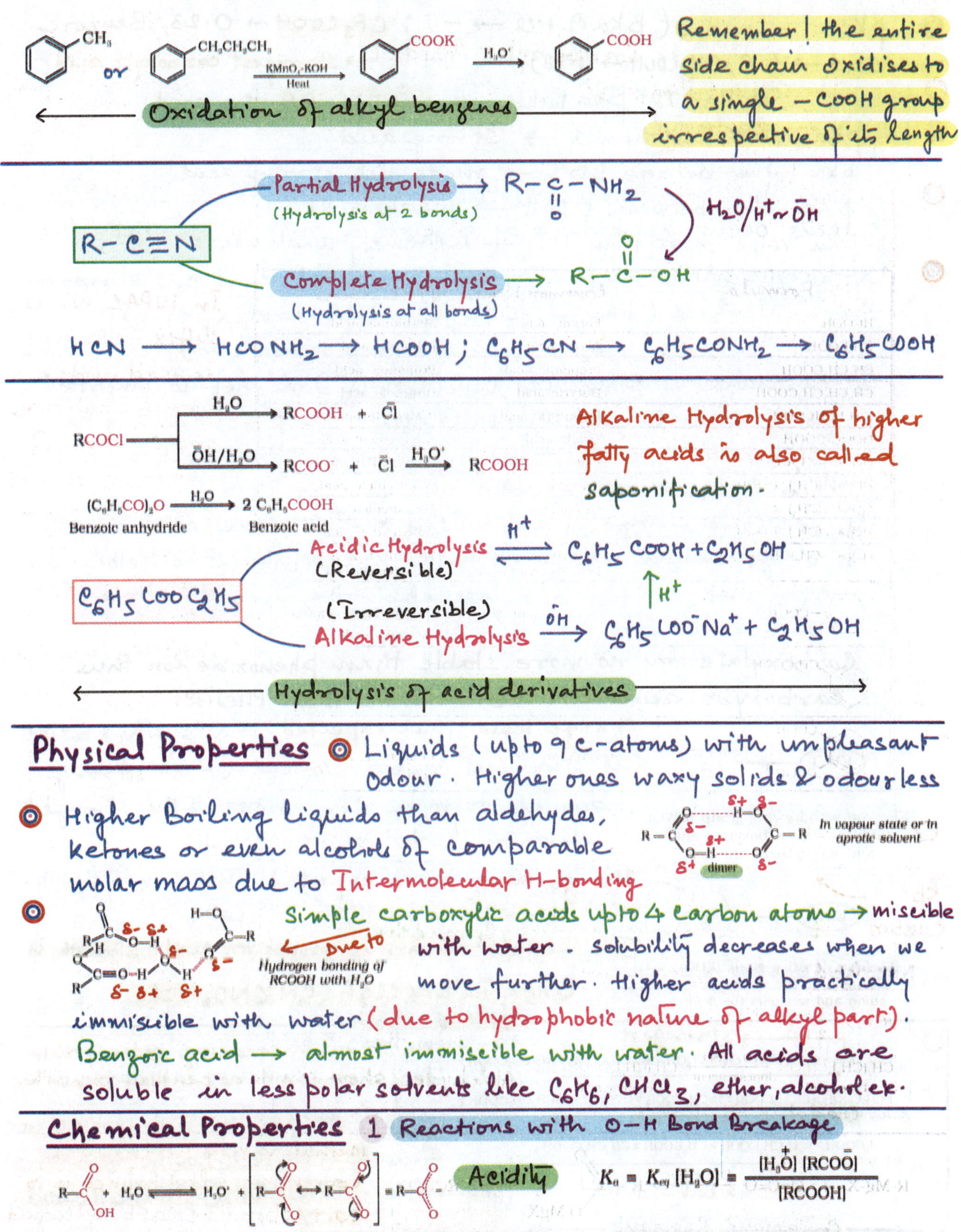
CH3
or
CH2CH2CH3
KMnO4-KOH
Heat
COOK
H3O+
COOH
Oxidation of alkyl benzenes
Remember! the entire side chain oxidises to a single –COOH group irrespective of its length
R–C≡N
Partial Hydrolysis → R–C(=O)–NH2
(Hydrolysis at 2 bonds)
H2O/H+ or OH−
Complete Hydrolysis → R–C(=O)–OH
(Hydrolysis at all bonds)
HCN → HCONH2 → HCOOH ; C6H5CN → C6H5CONH2 → C6H5COOH
RCOCl
H2O → RCOOH + Cl−
OH−/H2O → RCOO− + Cl− → H3O+ → RCOOH
(C6H5CO)2O → H2O → 2 C6H5COOH
Benzoic anhydride
Benzoic acid
Alkaline Hydrolysis of higher fatty acids is also called saponification.
C6H5COOC2H5
Acidic Hydrolysis (Reversible) H+ ⇌ C6H5COOH + C2H5OH
↑H+
(Irreversible)
Alkaline Hydrolysis OH− → C6H5COO−Na+ + C2H5OH
Hydrolysis of acid derivatives
Physical Properties
Liquids (upto 9 C-atoms) with unpleasant odour. Higher ones waxy solids & odourless
Higher Boiling liquids than aldehydes, ketones or even alcohols of comparable molar mass due to Intermolecular H-bonding
In vapour state or in aprotic solvent
dimer
Simple carboxylic acids upto 4 carbon atoms → miscible with water. solubility decreases when we move further. Higher acids practically immiscible with water (due to hydrophobic nature of alkyl part).
Due to
Hydrogen bonding of RCOOH with H2O
Benzoic acid → almost immiscible with water. All acids are soluble in less polar solvents like C6H6, CHCl3, ether, alcohol etc.
Chemical Properties
1 Reactions with O–H Bond Breakage
Acidity
Ka = Keq [H2O] = [H3O+] [RCOO−] / [RCOOH]

- $pK_a = -\log K_a$ (pK_a of HCl → −7; CF_3COOH → 0.23, Benzoic acid → 4.19, CH_3COOH → 4.76)
  (CF_3COOH → strongest carboxylic acid)

  Smaller the pK_a value → STRONGER the acid

- pK_a value less than 1 → strong acid
  pK_a value between 1 to 5 → moderately strong acid
  pK_a value between 5 to 15 → weak acids
  pK_a value more than 15 → extremely weak acids.

- Carboxylic acids → weaker than mineral acids but stronger than alcohols (pK_a $C_2H_5OH \approx 16$) and Phenol (pK_a 10)

- Phenol Vs Carboxylic acid → Due to 2 reasons i.e.,

  (A) Resonance in phenoxide ion ($C_6H_5O^-$) is not as important as it is in carboxylate ion ($RCOO^-$) [as phenoxide ion has non equivalent resonating structures while carboxylate ion has 2 equivalent resonating structures]

  (B) The (−)ve charge is delocalised over 2 more electronegative Oxygen atoms in carboxylate ion while it is delocalised over one oxygen & 3 less electronegative C-atoms in phenoxide ion.

  Carboxylate ion is more stable than phenoxide ion thus carboxylic acids are more acidic than Phenol.

- EWG ← C (O, O, −)

  Electron withdrawing group (EWG) stabilises the carboxylate anion and strengthens the acid

  Charge lesser than expected. That's why CF_3COOH is strongest carboxylic acid. (F is strong enough to make CF_3 as one of the strongest electron withdrawing group)

- EDG → C (O, O, −)

  Electron donating group (EDG) destabilises the carboxylate anion and weakens the acid

  Charge more than expected. That's why HCOOH is stronger acid than CH_3COOH.

  The effect of various groups on acidic strength is

  $C_6H_5 < I < Br < Cl < F < CN < NO_2 < CF_3$

NEET concentrate

- CF_3COOH (strongest) > CCl_3COOH > $CHCl_2COOH$ > NO_2CH_2COOH > $NC\text{-}CH_2COOH$ >
  FCH_2COOH > $ClCH_2COOH$ > $BrCH_2COOH$ > $HCOOH$ > $ClCH_2CH_2COOH$ >
  (continue)
  C_6H_5COOH > $C_6H_5CH_2COOH$ > CH_3COOH > CH_3CH_2COOH (Weakest)
  (continue)

  Acids in increasing order of their acidic strength as per their pK_a values

  C_6H_5COOH ($pK_a = 4.19$) is less acidic than ($p\text{-}OCH_3$)C_6H_4COOH (OCH_3 is EDG) but more acidic than ($p\text{-}NO_2$)C_6H_4COOH ($-NO_2$ is EWG)

- Always Remember | C_6H_5COOH & $CH_2=CH-COOH$ are more acidic than RCOOH but less acidic than HCOOH (as C-atom in $-C_6H_5$ & $CH_2=CH-$ is sp^2 hybridised i.e., more electronegative)

- $R-COOH + NaOH \longrightarrow R-CO\bar{O}Na^+ + H_2O$
  $R-COOH + NaHCO_3 \longrightarrow R-CO\bar{O}Na^+ + H_2O + CO_2$

  Acidic Reactions

  Similar reaction is seen with Metal directly also in which H_2 is liberated.

2 Reactions with –C–OH bond breakage

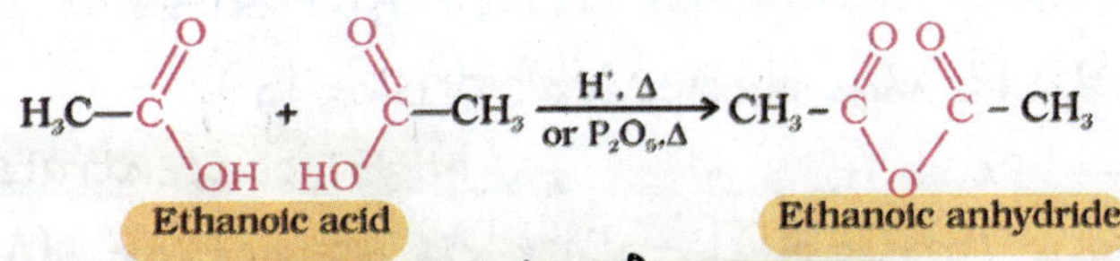

← Anhydride formation →

Its a proper dehydration reaction and of reversible nature. Anhydrides are acid derivatives.

$RCOOH + R'OH \underset{}{\overset{H^+}{\rightleftharpoons}} RCOOR' + H_2O$

← Esterification →

R–C(=O)–OH (Carboxylic acid) $\overset{H^+}{\rightleftharpoons}$ R–C⁺(OH)–OH $\overset{R'-\ddot{O}H}{\rightleftharpoons}$ R–C(OH)(:OH)–O⁺(H)–R' (Tetrahedral intermediate)

← Site creation for Nu⁻ attack →

Proton transfer ⇅ → R–C(:Ö–H)(–O–R')–O⁺H₂ $\overset{-HOH}{\rightleftharpoons}$ R–C(=O⁺H)–O-R' (Protonated ester) $\overset{-H^+}{\rightleftharpoons}$ R–C(=O)–O-R' (Ester)

Nu⁻ Addition Elimination Mechanism

- The reaction can be acid or base catalysed.
  Base catalysed esterification is irreversible while acid catalysed is reversible.

RCOOH:
- $\xrightarrow{PCl_5}$ $RCOCl + POCl_3 + HCl$
- $\xrightarrow{PCl_3}$ $RCOCl + H_3PO_3$
- $\xrightarrow{SOCl_2}$ $RCOCl + SO_2\uparrow + Cl_2\uparrow$

Reaction with $SOCl_2$ is pref. as SO_2 & Cl_2 formed are gases & escape from reaction mixture.

$R/ArCOOH + NH_3 \rightleftharpoons R/ArCOONH_4 \xrightarrow[-H_2O]{\Delta} R/ArCONH_2$
(Amm. salt) (Amide)

Phthalic acid (C₆H₄(COOH)₂) $+ NH_3 \rightleftharpoons$ C₆H₄(COO⁻NH₄⁺)₂ (Ammonium phthalate) $\xrightarrow[-2H_2O]{\Delta}$ C₆H₄(CONH₂)₂ (Phthalamide) $\xrightarrow[\Delta]{\text{Strong Heating}}$ C₆H₄(CO)₂NH (Phthalimide) $+ NH_3$

3 Reaction involving –COOH as a whole

(A) **Reduction** – Strong red. agents → Alcohols; mild/moderate reducing agents → Aldehydes. $NaBH_4$ does not reduces them

(B) **Decarboxylation** – $RCOOH/RCOONa \xrightarrow[CaO, \Delta]{NaOH} RH + Na_2CO_3$
Kolbe's electrolysis is also decarboxylation.

4 Substitution in alkyl part

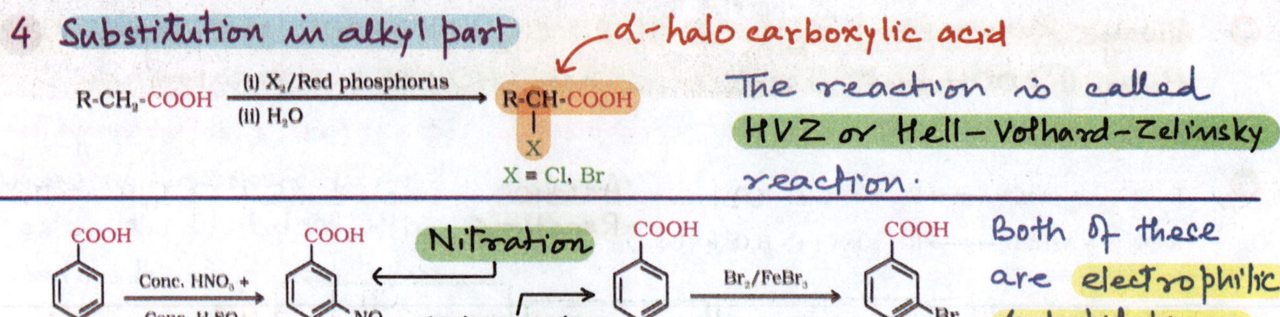

- $-COOH \longrightarrow$ M-directing & Ring deactivator

NEET concentrate

C_6H_5COOH does not show Friedel-Crafts reaction. (As $AlCl_3$ has more tendency to bound with $-COOH$ group in comparison with alkyl or acyl halide.)

- $HCOOH \longrightarrow$ used in rubber, textile, dyeing, leather & electro-plating industry.

  $CH_3COOH \longrightarrow$ Solvent & Vinegar

  Hexanedioic acid $\longrightarrow$ manufacture of Nylon 6-6.

  Esters of $C_6H_5COOH \longrightarrow$ Perfumery

  $C_6H_5COO^-Na^+ \longrightarrow$ Food preservative

  Higher fatty acids $\rightarrow$ soaps and detergents.

18. Amines

- Derivatives of NH_3; Obtained by the replacement of 1, 2 or all 3 H atoms of NH_3 by alkyl or aryl groups.

1 H Replacement: CH_3-NH_2, $C_6H_5-NH_2$ | 2 H Replacement: $CH_3-NH-CH_3$ | 3 H Replacement: $CH_3-N(CH_3)_2$

- Hybridisation ⟶ sp^3; Geometry - Pyramidal

lesser angle than typical tetrahedral one (due to bp - bp and lp - bp repulsion)

$(CH_3)_3N$ — unshared electron pair; CH_3; CH_3; CH_3; 108°

Structure — e^- density of alkyl or aryl groups also play very important role in their properties.

Classification

$R-\ddot{N}H_2$ — 1° or Primary

$R_2\ddot{N}-H$ — 2° or secondary

$R_2\ddot{N}-R$ — 3° or Tertiary

For 2° or 3°:
- Simple — with same R/Ar
- Mixed — with different R/Ar

Nomenclature

- Common system — alkyl amine e.g., methyl amine

IUPAC system — Alkane - e + amine = Alkanamine

e.g., CH_3NH_2 - Methanamine; $C_2H_5NH_2$ - Ethanamine

- IUPAC does not recognises 2° and 3° amines. According to IUPAC, 2° amines are — N-substituted 1° Amines and 3° amines are — N, N-disubstituted 1° Amines.

- e.g., $CH_3NHC_2H_5$ — N-methyl, ethanamine (Larger alkyl group will be considered as longest possible chain)

$CH_3N(C_2H_5)_2$ — N-ethyl-N-methylethanamine (for more than 2 alkyl groups attached to N as substituents alphabetical order is followed); $NH_2(CH_2)_6NH_2$ — Hexane-1,2-diamine;

$C_6H_5NH_2$ — Aniline or Benzenamine (In case of benzene or its derivatives common names are also accepted)

(skeletal structure with N) — N-ethyl-N-methyl, pentan-3-amine (Being Non carbon functional group Amine can be attached to any C-atom of the parent chain)

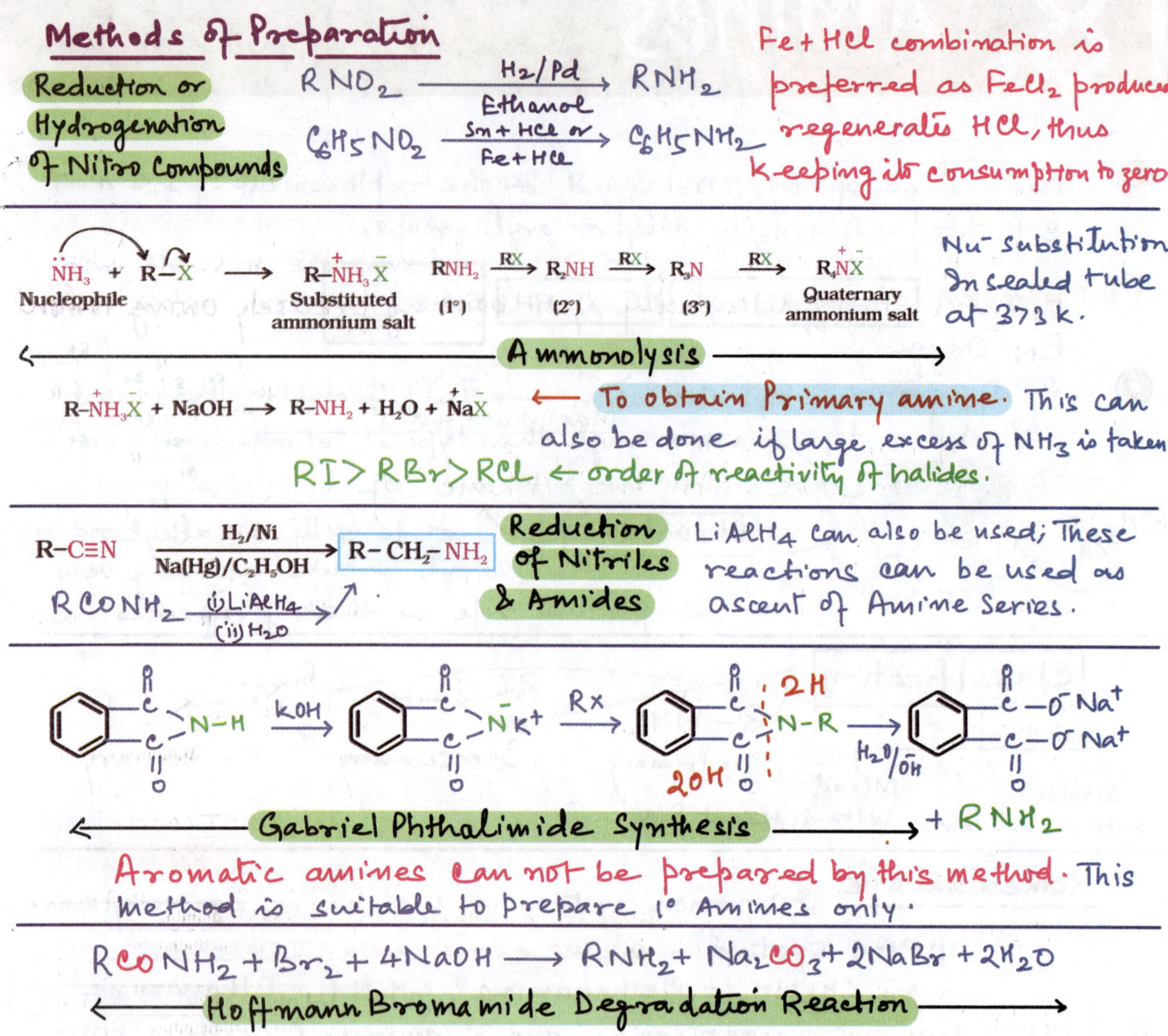

Methods of Preparation

Reduction or Hydrogenation of Nitro Compounds

$$RNO_2 \xrightarrow[\text{Ethanol}]{H_2/Pd} RNH_2$$

$$C_6H_5NO_2 \xrightarrow[\text{Fe + HCl}]{\text{Sn + HCl or}} C_6H_5NH_2$$

Fe + HCl combination is preferred as $FeCl_2$ produced regenerates HCl, thus keeping its consumption to zero.

Ammonolysis

$$\ddot{N}H_3 + R{-}X \longrightarrow R{-}\overset{+}{N}H_3\overset{-}{X}$$

Nucleophile; Substituted ammonium salt

$$\underset{(1^\circ)}{RNH_2} \xrightarrow{RX} \underset{(2^\circ)}{R_2NH} \xrightarrow{RX} \underset{(3^\circ)}{R_3N} \xrightarrow{RX} \underset{\text{Quaternary ammonium salt}}{R_4\overset{+}{N}\overset{-}{X}}$$

Nu^- substitution In sealed tube at 373 K.

$$R{-}\overset{+}{N}H_3\overset{-}{X} + NaOH \longrightarrow R{-}NH_2 + H_2O + \overset{+}{Na}\overset{-}{X}$$

← To obtain Primary amine. This can also be done if large excess of NH_3 is taken.

RI > RBr > RCl ← order of reactivity of halides.

Reduction of Nitriles & Amides

$$R{-}C{\equiv}N \xrightarrow[\text{Na(Hg)}/C_2H_5OH]{H_2/Ni} R{-}CH_2{-}NH_2$$

$$RCONH_2 \xrightarrow[\text{(ii) } H_2O]{\text{(i) } LiAlH_4} R{-}CH_2{-}NH_2$$

$LiAlH_4$ can also be used; These reactions can be used as ascent of Amine Series.

Gabriel Phthalimide Synthesis

Phthalimide $\xrightarrow{KOH}$ Potassium phthalimide ($\overset{-}{N}K^+$) $\xrightarrow{RX}$ N-alkylphthalimide (N–R) $\xrightarrow{H_2O/\overset{-}{O}H}$ Sodium phthalate ($-C-O^-Na^+$, $-C-O^-Na^+$) + RNH_2

(2H, 2OH)

Aromatic amines can not be prepared by this method. This method is suitable to prepare 1° Amines only.

Hoffmann Bromamide Degradation Reaction

$$RCONH_2 + Br_2 + 4NaOH \longrightarrow RNH_2 + Na_2CO_3 + 2NaBr + 2H_2O$$

NEET concentrate

The reaction proceeds through the formation of $R{-}N{=}C{=}O$ (alkyl isocyanate) as a stable intermediate. Hydrolysis of this isocyanate leads to decarboxylation & formation of amine as

$$RNH_2 \leftarrow \underset{2H}{R{-}N} \,\vdots\, \underset{2OH}{C{=}O} \rightarrow HO{-}\overset{O}{\overset{\|}{C}}{-}OH = H_2CO_3$$

Only 1° amines can be prepared from this method also.

$RCONH_2$ → On Reduction → RCH_2NH_2 (1° Amine)

$RCONH_2$ → Hoffmann Degradation → RNH_2 (1° Amine)

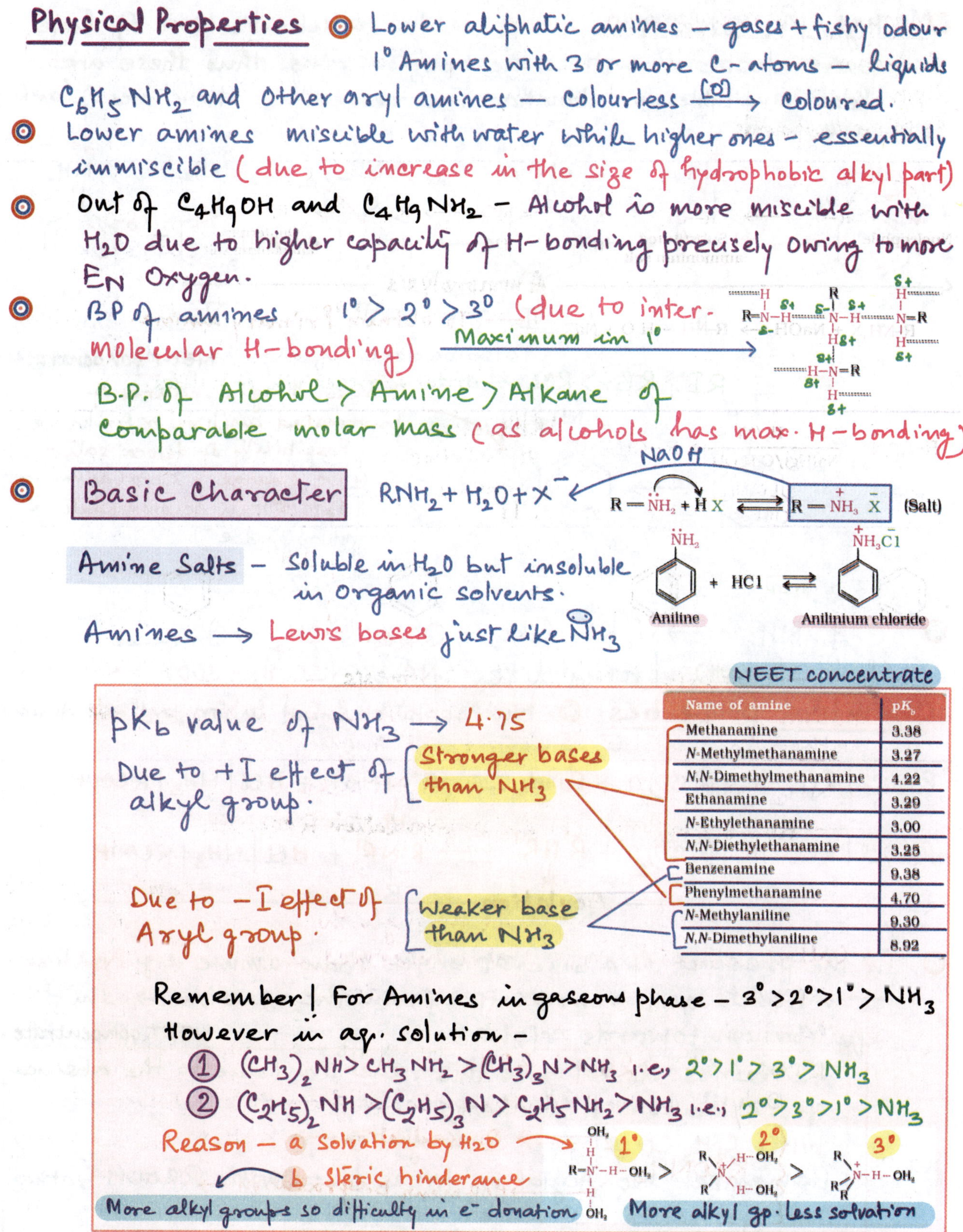

Physical Properties

- Lower aliphatic amines – gases + fishy odour
  1° Amines with 3 or more C-atoms – liquids
  $C_6H_5NH_2$ and other aryl amines — colourless $\xrightarrow{[O]}$ coloured.
- Lower amines miscible with water while higher ones – essentially immiscible (due to increase in the size of hydrophobic alkyl part)
- Out of C_4H_9OH and $C_4H_9NH_2$ – Alcohol is more miscible with H_2O due to higher capacity of H-bonding precisely owing to more EN Oxygen.
- BP of amines $1^\circ > 2^\circ > 3^\circ$ (due to inter-molecular H-bonding) Maximum in 1° →

B.P. of Alcohol > Amine > Alkane of comparable molar mass (as alcohols has max. H-bonding)

- **Basic Character**

$RNH_2 + H_2O + X^-$ ← NaOH — $R-\ddot{N}H_2 + HX \rightleftharpoons R-\overset{+}{N}H_3\ \overset{-}{X}$ (Salt)

Amine Salts – Soluble in H_2O but insoluble in organic solvents.

$C_6H_5NH_2$ + HCl $\rightleftharpoons$ $C_6H_5\overset{+}{N}H_3\overset{-}{Cl}$

Aniline → Anilinium chloride

Amines → Lewis bases just like $\ddot{N}H_3$

NEET concentrate

pK_b value of NH_3 → 4.75

Due to +I effect of alkyl group. — Stronger bases than NH_3

Due to –I effect of Aryl group. — Weaker base than NH_3

Name of amine	pK_b
Methanamine	3.38
N-Methylmethanamine	3.27
N,N-Dimethylmethanamine	4.22
Ethanamine	3.29
N-Ethylethanamine	3.00
N,N-Diethylethanamine	3.25
Benzenamine	9.38
Phenylmethanamine	4.70
N-Methylaniline	9.30
N,N-Dimethylaniline	8.92

Remember! For Amines in gaseous phase – $3^\circ > 2^\circ > 1^\circ > NH_3$
However in aq. solution –

1. $(CH_3)_2NH > CH_3NH_2 > (CH_3)_3N > NH_3$ i.e., $2^\circ > 1^\circ > 3^\circ > NH_3$
2. $(C_2H_5)_2NH > (C_2H_5)_3N > C_2H_5NH_2 > NH_3$ i.e., $2^\circ > 3^\circ > 1^\circ > NH_3$

Reason – (a) Solvation by H_2O → 1° > 2° > 3°
(b) Steric hinderance

More alkyl groups so difficulty in e^- donation

More alkyl gp. less solvation

- High pK_b value of $C_6H_5NH_2$ is due to delocalisation of lone pair electrons within the benzene ring thus these are less available for donation. The resonating structures of aniline are

$\ddot{N}H_2$ / $\overset{+}{N}H_2$ / $\overset{+}{N}H_2$ / $\overset{+}{N}H_2$ / $\ddot{N}H_2$ ≡ $\overset{\delta+}{N}H_2$ ($\delta-$, $\delta-$, $\delta-$)

I ⟷ II ⟷ III ⟷ IV ⟷ V

NEET concentrate

$\overset{+}{N}H_3$ ⟷ $\overset{+}{N}H_3$

2 resonating structures of protonated aniline or Anilinium Ion. Possibility of delocalisation of (+)ve charge = Zero (as Valence shell of N (2nd) can accommodate a maximum of 8 e^-)

- $C_6H_5NH_2$ (Basic Strength) ⟶ { ERG like $-OCH_3$, $-CH_3$ → Increase; EWG like $-NO_2$, $-SO_3H$, $-COOH$, $-X$ → Dec. }

Chemical properties

- Nucleophilic substitution by 1° & 2° Amines

$$RCOCl \mid RCONH_2 \mid (RCO)_2O + R'NH_2 \rightleftharpoons R'N(H)-\overset{O}{\overset{\|}{C}}-R + HCl \mid NH_3 \mid RCOOH$$

$$RCOCl \mid RCONH_2 \mid (RCO)_2O + R'N(H)R' \rightleftharpoons R'N(R)R' + HCl \mid NH_3 \mid RCOOH$$

⟵ Acylation ⟶

- In the presence of a base stronger than amine e.g. Pyridine ⟶ Reacts and removes HCl from the reaction → shift equilibrium towards right.

NEET concentrate

3° Amines do not give this reaction (due to the absence of replaceable H in them)

With C_6H_5COCl ⟶ Benzoylation.

Remember No Acylation takes place with RCOOH rather salt formation is visible.

$R-NH_2 + CHCl_3 + 3KOH \xrightarrow{Heat} R-NC + 3KCl + 3H_2O$

← Isocyanide Test →

The reaction is shown by 1° Amines only (Aliphatic + Aromatic)

- Isocyanides are known for their foul smell (that of bitter almonds)
- For $C_6H_5NH_2 + CHCl_3 + 3KOH \xrightarrow{\Delta} C_6H_5NC + 3KCl + 3H_2O$ term Carbylamine reaction is also used (as C_6H_5NC = Carbylamine = Phenyl isocyanide)

$RNH_2 + HONO \xrightarrow{NaNO_2 + HCl} [R-\overset{+}{N}_2Cl^-] \xrightarrow{H_2O} ROH + N_2 + HCl$

Unstable.

Used in the estimation of Proteins & Amino acids

$C_6H_5NH_2 + HONO \xrightarrow[273-278K]{NaNO_2 + HCl} C_6H_5\overset{+}{N}_2Cl^- + NaCl + H_2O$

(stable)

← Reaction with HNO_2 →

NEET concentrate

2° amines form N-nitrosoamines (yellow oily liquid $R-\underset{}{\overset{R}{N}}-N=O$) while 3° amines give tri alkyl ammonium nitrite ($R_3\overset{+}{N}HNO_2$) which is soluble in water.

$C_6H_5-\overset{O}{\underset{O}{S}}-Cl + H-\underset{H}{N}-C_2H_5$ (1°) $\longrightarrow C_6H_5-\overset{O}{\underset{O}{S}}-\underset{H}{N}-C_2H_5 + HCl$

Hinsberg reagent

Strongly e⁻ withdrawing (the SO_2 group); strongly acidic (the N–H hydrogen)

N-Ethylbenzenesulphonamide (soluble in alkali)

← Hinsberg Test →

$C_6H_5-\overset{O}{\underset{O}{S}}-Cl + H-\underset{C_2H_5}{N}-C_2H_5$ (2°) $\longrightarrow C_6H_5-\overset{O}{\underset{O}{S}}-\underset{C_2H_5}{N}-C_2H_5 + HCl$

No acidic Hydrogen

Insoluble in NaOH.

N,N-Diethylbenzenesulphonamide

3° Amines ⟶ Do not react with $C_6H_5SO_2Cl$.

- The property is used to distinguish & separate 1°, 2° & 3° Amines. $C_6H_5SO_2Cl$ is also replaced with p-toluene sulphonyl chloride i.e., $C_6H_4(CH_3)SO_2Cl$.

$C_6H_5NH_2 + 3Br_2 \xrightarrow{Br_2/H_2O}$ 2,4,6-tribromoaniline (Br at both ortho positions and para position) $+ 3HBr$

White ppt.

NH_2 ← Ortho & para directing + Ring activator

← Electrophilic substitution →

High reactivity of benzene ring in ES reactions of $C_6H_5NH_2$

creates problem. To resolve this issue $-NH_2$ group is masked with CH_3CO- group i.e., Acylation first as shown below

$$\underset{\text{Aniline}}{C_6H_5NH_2} \xrightarrow[\text{Pyridine}]{(CH_3CO)_2O} \underset{\substack{N\text{-Phenylethanamide} \\ \text{(Acetanilide)}}}{C_6H_5-NH-\overset{O}{\overset{\|}{C}}-CH_3} \xrightarrow[CH_3COOH]{Br_2} \underset{\text{(Major)}}{p\text{-}Br-C_6H_4-NH-\overset{O}{\overset{\|}{C}}-CH_3} \xrightarrow{\bar{O}H \text{ or } H^+} \underset{\text{4-Bromoaniline}}{p\text{-}Br-C_6H_4-NH_2}$$

NEET concentrate

The lone pair of N interacts with C–O bond to reduce their delocalisation on C_6H_5

$$>\ddot{N}-\overset{:O:}{\overset{\|}{C}}-CH_3 \longleftrightarrow >\overset{+}{N}=\overset{:\ddot{O}:^-}{\overset{|}{C}}-CH_3$$

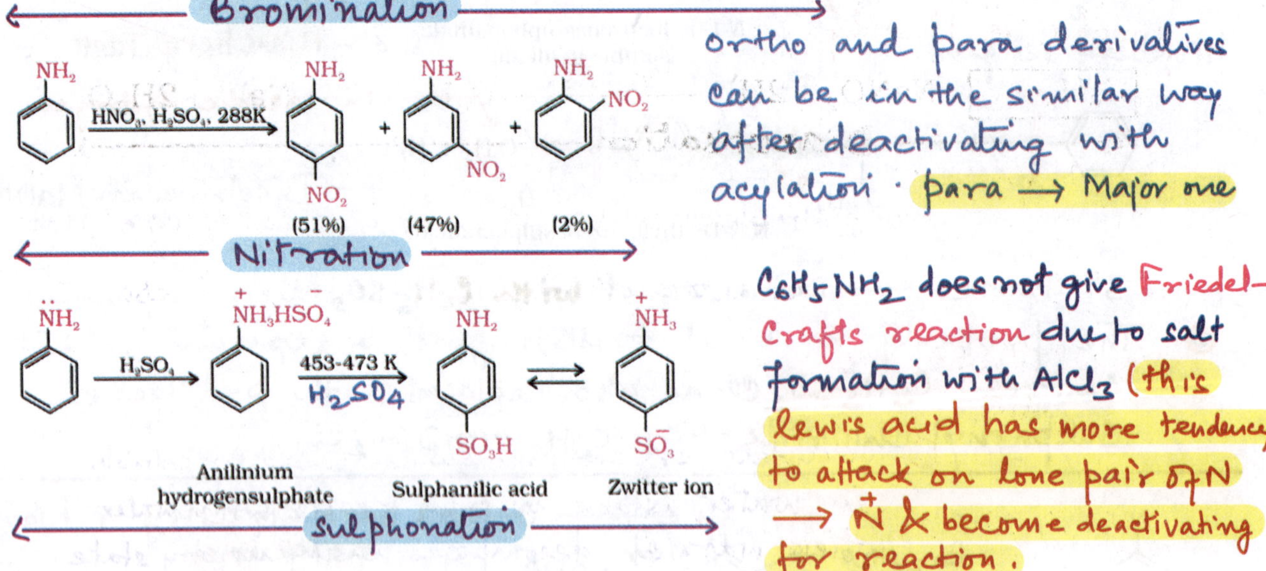

ortho and para derivatives can be in the similar way after deactivating with acylation. para → Major one

$C_6H_5NH_2$ does not give Friedel-Crafts reaction due to salt formation with $AlCl_3$ (this lewis acid has more tendency to attack on lone pair of N → $\overset{+}{N}$ & become deactivating for reaction.

Diazonium Salts

$Ar\overset{+}{N_2}X^-$ ← Cl^-, Br^-, HSO_4^-, BF^- etc.

Aryl group → Ar; ↑ Diazonium Group.

$C_6H_5\overset{+}{N_2}Cl^-$ = Benzene diazonium chloride

$C_6H_5N_2^+\ HSO_4^-$ = Benzene diazonium hydrogensulphate.

$\overset{\oplus}{N}\equiv N:$ ↔ $N=\overset{\ominus}{N}:$ ↔ $N=\overset{\ominus}{N}:$ ↔ $N=\overset{\ominus}{N}:$

Explanation of the stability of Benzene diazonium ion

Stable for a short duration between 273 – 278 K or 0 – 5°C.

should be 1° only.

$$C_6H_5NH_2 + NaNO_2 + 2HCl \xrightarrow{273-278K} C_6H_5\overset{+}{N_2}\overset{-}{Cl} + NaCl + 2H_2O$$

Diazotisation

Due to their less stable nature, Diazonium salts are not stored generally and used immediately after their preparation.

Physical Properties

- Colourless crystalline solids, readily soluble in water, stable in cold, reacts with water when warmed, decomposes easily in dry state.

- $C_6H_5\overset{+}{N_2}BF_4^-$ → water insoluble, stable at room temperature.

Chemical Reactions

With Displacement of N_2 ← Chemical Reactions → With Retention of diazo gp.

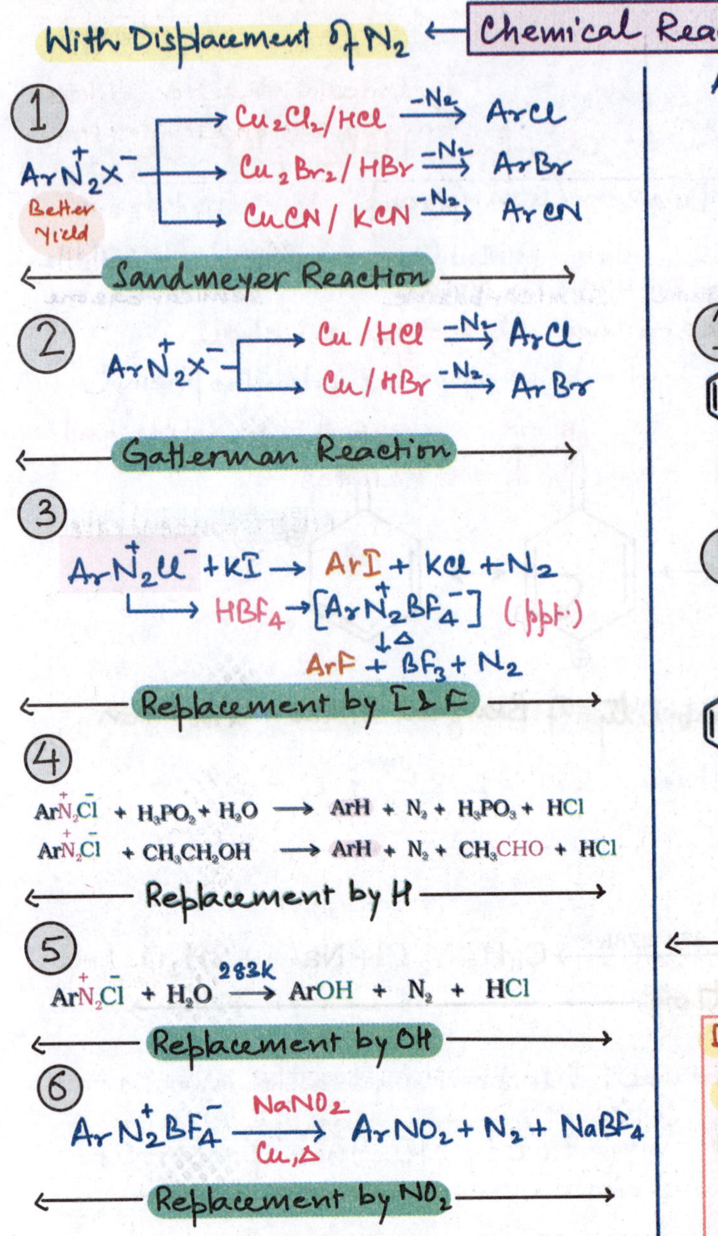

With Displacement of N_2

① $Ar\overset{+}{N}_2X^-$ →
- $Cu_2Cl_2/HCl \xrightarrow{-N_2} ArCl$
- $Cu_2Br_2/HBr \xrightarrow{-N_2} ArBr$
- $CuCN/KCN \xrightarrow{-N_2} ArCN$

Better Yield

← Sandmeyer Reaction →

② $Ar\overset{+}{N}_2X^-$ →
- $Cu/HCl \xrightarrow{-N_2} ArCl$
- $Cu/HBr \xrightarrow{-N_2} ArBr$

← Gatterman Reaction →

③ $Ar\overset{+}{N}_2Cl^- + KI \rightarrow ArI + KCl + N_2$

→ $HBF_4 \rightarrow [Ar\overset{+}{N}_2BF_4^-]$ (ppt.)

$\downarrow \Delta$

$ArF + BF_3 + N_2$

← Replacement by I & F →

④ $Ar\overset{+}{N}_2\overset{-}{Cl} + H_3PO_2 + H_2O \rightarrow ArH + N_2 + H_3PO_3 + HCl$

$Ar\overset{+}{N}_2\overset{-}{Cl} + CH_3CH_2OH \rightarrow ArH + N_2 + CH_3CHO + HCl$

← Replacement by H →

⑤ $Ar\overset{+}{N}_2\overset{-}{Cl} + H_2O \xrightarrow{283K} ArOH + N_2 + HCl$

← Replacement by OH →

⑥ $Ar\overset{+}{N}_2\overset{-}{BF_4} \xrightarrow[Cu,\Delta]{NaNO_2} ArNO_2 + N_2 + NaBF_4$

← Replacement by NO_2 →

With Retention of diazo gp.

Azo products are produced with extended conjugate system (as both the aromatic rings are joined by $-N=N-$ bond)

These products are called azo dyes.

① $C_6H_5\overset{+}{N}_2X^-$ + H–C_6H_4–OH $\xrightarrow{\overline{O}H}$ C_6H_5–N=N–C_6H_4–OH $+ Cl^- + H_2O$

p-hydroxyazobenzene (ORANGE)

② $C_6H_5\overset{+}{N}_2X^-$ + H–C_6H_4–NH_2 $\xrightarrow{H^+}$ C_6H_5–N=N–C_6H_4–NH_2 $+ Cl^- + H_2O$

p-aminoazobenzene (Yellow)

← Electrophilic Substitution →

NEET concentrate

Dhyan Rakho! Diazonium salt se Harek aromatic compound prepare kiya ja sakta hai Theek usi tarah jaise RMgX se harek aliphatic compound bana sakte hain.

19. Biomolecules

- Living system ⟶ contains Non living molecules & atoms → still has ability to grow, sustain & reproduce itself.
- Biochemistry ⟶ Study of biomolecules like carbohydrates, proteins Lipids, Nucleic acids, vitamins, hormones etc.

Interactions of these complex molecules constitute the molecular logic of life processes.

Carbohydrates Polyhydroxy aldehydes or ketones OR compounds which on hydrolysis produce such units.

↳ Also called saccharides = Greek sakcharon means Sugar

Classification
- → Monosaccharides (Mono = Single)
- → Oligosaccharides (Oligo = few)
- → Polysaccharides (Poly = many)
- → Reducing — Reduce Tollen's Reagent & Fehling's solution
- → Non reducing – Don't have ability to reduce.

All Monosaccharides (whether aldoses or ketoses) are reducing sugars.

aldoses ⟶ Polyhydroxy aldehydes; ketoses ⟶ Polyhydroxy ketones.

- Monosacharides are the simplest units (No further hydrolysis is possible). These can be

C-atoms	General Name	If aldehyde	If ketone
3	Triose	Aldotriose	Ketotriose
4	Tetrose	Aldotetrose	Ketotetrose
5	Pentose	Aldopentose	Ketopentose
6	Hexose	Aldohexose	Ketohexose
7	Heptose	Aldoheptose	Ketoheptose

Examples

Ribose, deoxyribose (Pentoses)

Glucose, Fructose, Galactose (Hexoses)

Glucose Aldohexose, present in sweet fruits, honey, ripe grapes.

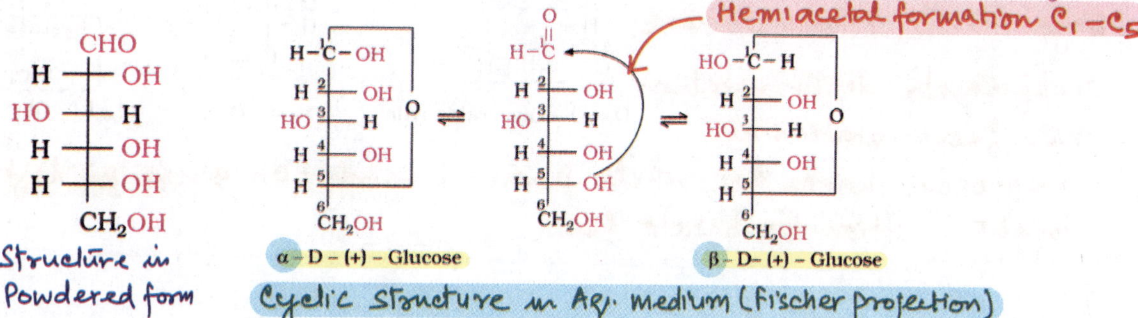

α-D-(+)-Glucopyranose β-D-(+)-Glucopyranose

Howarth Projection (see C_1 configuration)

Evidences in favour of openchain structures

1. Mol. formula – $C_6H_{12}O_6$

$C_6H_{12}O_6$

② $\xrightarrow{HI/\Delta}$ n-Hexane → All 6 C are linked in a straight chain.

③ $\xrightarrow{NH_2OH}$ $HC{=}NOH - (CHOH)_4 - CH_2OH$ (Oxime)

④ HCN → $HC(OH)(CN)-(CHOH)_4-CH_2OH$ (Cyanohydrin)

→ >C=O group is present preferably at position no. 1.

⑤ $\xrightarrow{Br_2\ water}$ $COOH-(CHOH)_4-CH_2OH$ → $-\overset{H}{C}=O$ is present at C_1

⑥ $\xrightarrow{(CH_3CO)_2O}$ $CHO-(CHOOCCH_3)_4-CH_2OOCCH_3$ → 5 –OH groups are present (C_2-C_6)

⑦ $C_6H_{12}O_6$ & $COOH-(CHOH)_4-CH_2OH$ (gluconic acid) both on oxidation with HNO_3 ⟶ $COOH-(CHOH)_4-COOH$ saccharic acid ⟶ –OH group at C_6 is primary alcoholic ($-CH_2OH$) group.

Methods of Preparation

- $C_{12}H_{22}O_{11}$ (Sucrose) $\xrightarrow[H^+]{Hydrolysis}$ $C_6H_{12}O_6$ (Glucose) + $C_6H_{12}O_6$ (Fructose)
- $(C_6H_{10}O_5)_n$ (Starch) + nH_2O $\xrightarrow[393K;\ 2-3atm]{H^+}$ $n\ C_6H_{12}O_6$

⟵ By Hydrolysis ⟶

NEET concentrate

D & L Configuration

Dhyan Rakho! yahan (+) aur (–) respectively dextrorotation aur laevorotation ko represent karta hai while D aur L sirf –OH group ki left aur right position ko batata hai

D-(+)-Glyceraldehyde: CHO; H–C–OH; CH_2OH

D-(+)-Glucose: CHO; H–C–OH; HO–C–H; H–C–OH; H–C–OH; CH_2OH

L-(–)-Glyceraldehyde: CHO; HO–C–H; CH_2OH

Evidences in favour of cyclic structure

- No Schiff's test and No reaction with $NaHSO_3$ ⟶ $-CHO$ group is less reactive.
- Penta acetate of Glucose gives no reaction with NH_2OH ⟶ free $-CHO$ group is not present.
- 2 crystalline forms of Glucose ⟶ α-(m.p. 419 K) & β-(m.p. 423 K) are obtained at 303 K and 371 K respectively ⟶ Presence of these forms can not be explained without cyclic structures.

α & β-forms of Glucose ⟶ Anomeric forms or Anomers.

Fructose

- Ketohexose, natural monosaccharide found in fruits, honey & vegetables.
- Sweetest naturally occurring sugar.

CH_2OH, $C=O$, HO–H, H–OH, H–OH, CH_2OH

D – (–) – Fructose

Open Chain

1 HOH_2C – 2 C – OH, 3 HO–H, 4 H–OH, 5 H–, O, 6 CH_2OH

α-form

2 HO – C – 1 CH_2OH, 3 HO–H, 4 H–OH, 5 H–, O, 6 CH_2OH

β-form

Closed chain (cyclic) Fischer Projection

C-atoms outside the ring

Fructose structures

6 HOH_2C, O, 1 CH_2OH, 5, 2, H, H, OH, OH, 4, 3, OH, H

α – D – (–) – Fructofuranose

C-atoms outside the Ring

6 HOH_2C, O, OH, 5, 2, H, H, OH, 1 CH_2OH, 4, 3, OH, H

β – D – (–) – Fructofuranose

Howarth projection

NEET concentrate

Dhyan Rakhna ! (a) Glucose mein ring $C_1 - C_5$ ke beech banti hai aur Fructose mein $C_2 - C_5$ ke beech.
(b) Glucose mein -CHO (aldehyde) group present hota hai while Fructose mein >C=O (ketonic) group.

- In Diasaccharides, monosaccharide units are joined through Glycosidic Linkages.
- Glycosidic bond is formed by the removal of H_2O from 2-OH gps.

C_1 is involved in Glycosidic bonding so not free to reduce

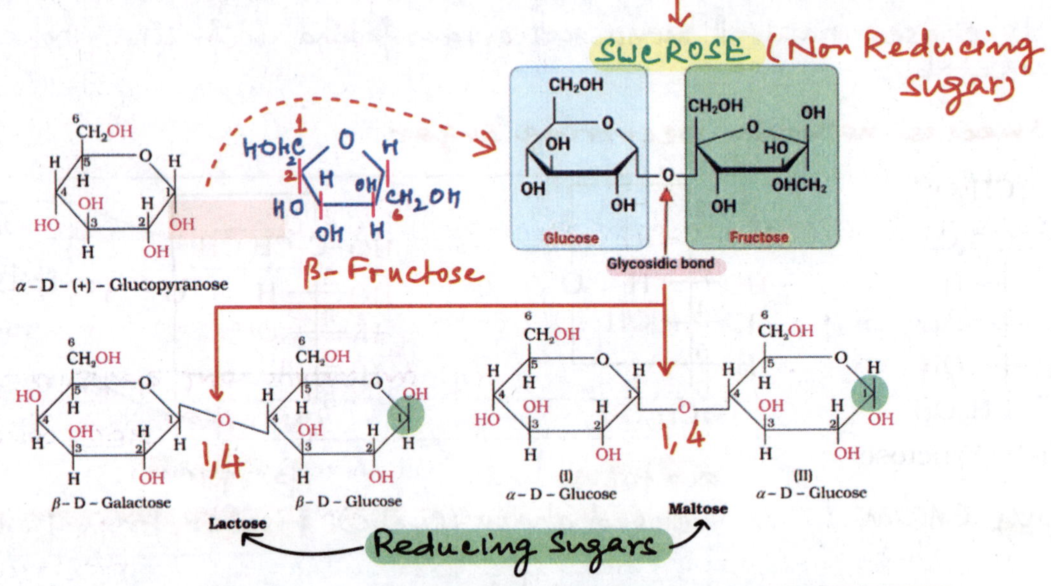

C_1 is not involved in Glycosidic bonding and free to reduce

- Sucrose (Dextrorotatory) $\xrightarrow{\text{Hydrolysis}}$ Glucose (+52.7°) (Dextrorotatory) + Fructose (−92.4°) (Laevorotatory)

  Invert Sugar ← change in rotation ← Overall mixture Laevorotatory

- Polysaccharides → most commonly encountered carbohydrates; Mainly involved in food storage or structure development

- Starch → Main storage polysaccharide of plants; polymer of α- Glucose
  - → Amylose − 15-20%, water soluble,
  - → Amylopectin − 80−85%, water insoluble

Amylose

Long unbranched chain of 200–1000 α– D Glucose units.

Amylopectin

(1,6) α-Link, Branch at C_6

Branched & more dense

- Most important dietary source for humans ⟶ found in cereals, roots, tubers + some vegetables.
- Cellulose ⟶ Exclusive to plants (especially cell walls), contains β– D Glucose joined with 1,4– linkages.
- Glycogen ⟶ Animal starch, structure similar to amylopectin and even more profusely branched. Present in mucles, liver & Brain + yeast & Fungi

Proteins

- Most abundant biomolecules; seen in milk, cheese, pulses, peanuts, fish, meat etc.
- Building Blocks of Body (as required for growth & maintanance of body)

NEET concentrate

> All Enzymes are proteins (except RNAase) so all metabolic activities of our body require proteins.

- These are heteropolymer like compounds of α-amino acids.

$R-CH(NH_2)-COOH$
α-amino acid (R = side chain)

These acids are lined with specific peptide linkages between amino group of one acid & carboxylic acid group of other.

$$H_2N-CH_2-COOH + H_2N-CH(CH_3)-COOH \xrightarrow{-H_2O} H_2N-CH_2-\boxed{CO-NH}-CH(CH_3)-COOH$$

Peptide linkage

- More than 200 Amino acids known ⟶ approx. 20 are involved in protein synthesis (Simplest – Glycine; most complex – Tryptophan)
- Sulphur containing ⟶ Methionine & Cysteine
- Essential or essentially required in diet ⟶ Valine, Leucine, Isoleucine, Arginine, Lysine, Threonine, Methionine, Phenylalanine, Tryptophan, Histidine. Rest are non-essential i.e., Not compulsorily required in diet.

- **Amino acids** → colourless, crystalline solids, water soluble, with high m.p. ; behave like salts (as Zwitter ions basically)

$$R-CH(NH_2)-COOH \rightleftharpoons R-CH(\overset{+}{N}H_3)-COO^-$$ (Zwitter ion)

← Amphoteric in nature

NEET concentrate

The pH at which any amino acid is converted into Zwitter ion is called Iso electric point.

- All naturally occurring α-Amino acids → Optically active. (Except Glycine)
- Most naturally occurring amino acids → L-configuration.
- Simplest peptide chains are known by the number of peptide bonds present in them e.g., Dipeptide, Tripeptide ..... upto poly peptides.
- Proteins
  - → Globular – spherical, coiled. polypeptide chains, water soluble. e.g., Insulin, Albumin.
  - → Fibrous – Fibre like proteins, water insoluble, e.g., Keratin (hair, wool, silk); Myosin

Structural Levels ↓

α-Helix

β-pleated sheet

Primary structure

Secondary structure

Peptide Bond only

Peptide + Hydrogen bonds

Bond support

one chain highly coiled

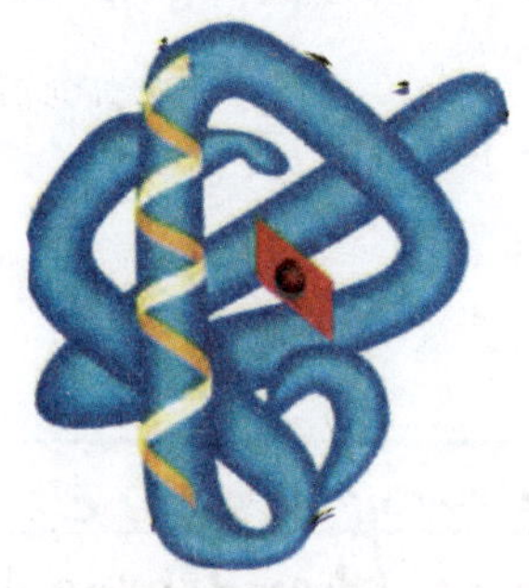

Tertiary structure

Major Contributors to Proteins Enzymes & Hormones

Many chains highly coiled

Quaternary structure

Bond Support

Peptide + Hydrogen + Ionic + Disulphide + Hydrophobic Bonds.

- Loss of Specific 3D structure of Protein = Denaturation
  It may be due to change in temperature, pH (physical change) or chemical change eg. Coagulation of egg proteins on boiling curdling of milk, Paneer formation etc.

Enzymes → Catalyst of Biological Origin; Globular Proteins, majorly involved in the catalysis of metabolic reactions of human body.

- Very specific for a particular reaction/particular substrate

→ Named after class of compounds on which they work - Maltase work on Maltose, Lactase work on Lactose etc.

NEET concentrate

> Enzymes can be categorised into 7 classes on the basis of their functional nature i.e., Isomerases, Oxidoreductases, Transferases, Hydrolases, Lyases (Breakers), Ligases (Joiners) & Translocases.

- Just like inorganic catalysts enzymes are also needed in very small quantities for a reaction and work after reducing the E_A (activation energy of the reaction)

Vitamins = Vital Amines ◉ Organic compounds required in the diet in small amounts to perform specific biological functions.

◉ Provide normal maintenance of optimal growth & health.

◉ B & C – Water Soluble ⟵ Vitamins ⟶ Fat Soluble – A, D, E & K

Source	Vitamin	Deficiency Disease
Fish liver oil, carrots Butter & Milk	A	Xerophthalmia (hardening of cornea of eye) & Night Blindness
Yeast, milk, green vegetables & cereals	B_1 (Thiamine)	Beri – Beri (loss of apetite, retarded growth)
Milk, egg white, liver kidney	B_2 (Riboflavin)	Cheliosis (fissuring at corners of mouth & lips) Digestive disorders & burning sensation of skin.
Yeast, milk, egg yolk, cereals, gram	B_6 (Pyridoxine)	Convulsions
Meat, fish, egg & curd	B_{12} (Cobalamine)	Pernicious Anaemia (RBCs deficient in haemoglobin)
Citrus fruits, Amla Green vegetables	C (Ascorbic Acid)	Scurvy (Bleeding gums)
Exposure to sun light, fish and egg yolk	D	Rickets (Bony deformity in kids) Osteoporosis and Osteomalacia (soft bones & joint pains in adults)
Vegetable oil (wheat germ oil) sun-flower oil	E Anti aging vitamin	Muscular weakness and increased fragility of RBCs
Green leafy vegetables	K Antihaemorrhagic vitamin	Increased blood clotting time

Nucleic Acids

- 2 acids → Deoxyribonucleic Acid (DNA)
  ↓
  Ribonucleic Acid (RNA)

- DNA → Present inside nucleus, forms heredity vehicle of cell.

NEET concentrate

> Chromosomes of a cell are called heredity vehicle. These are made up of DNA + Histone proteins. These are highly coiled structures and their coiling is due to attraction between (+)vely chared histones and (−)vely charged DNA.

- Nucleic acid → Pentose Sugar + Nitrogenous base
  ↓
  Nucleotide ← Nucleoside + Phosphate
  (↑ combine to form)

Sugar of RNA → β-D-ribose: HOH_2C (C5), ring O, C1 (OH, H), C4 (H), C3 (H, OH), C2 (H, OH)

Sugars

Sugar of DNA → β-D-2-deoxyribose: HOH_2C (C5), ring O, C1 (OH, H), C4 (H), C3 (H, OH), C2 (H, H)

Point of Difference (C2: OH in ribose, H in deoxyribose)

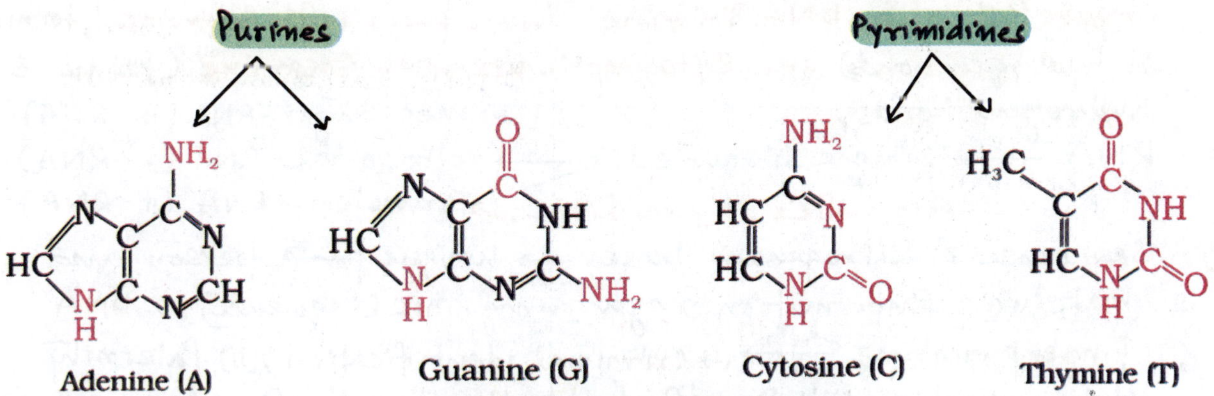

Nitrogenous bases of DNA

- Uracil is present in the place of Thymine in RNA.
- In Nucleic acids polynucleolites are linked through Phosphodiester linkages.

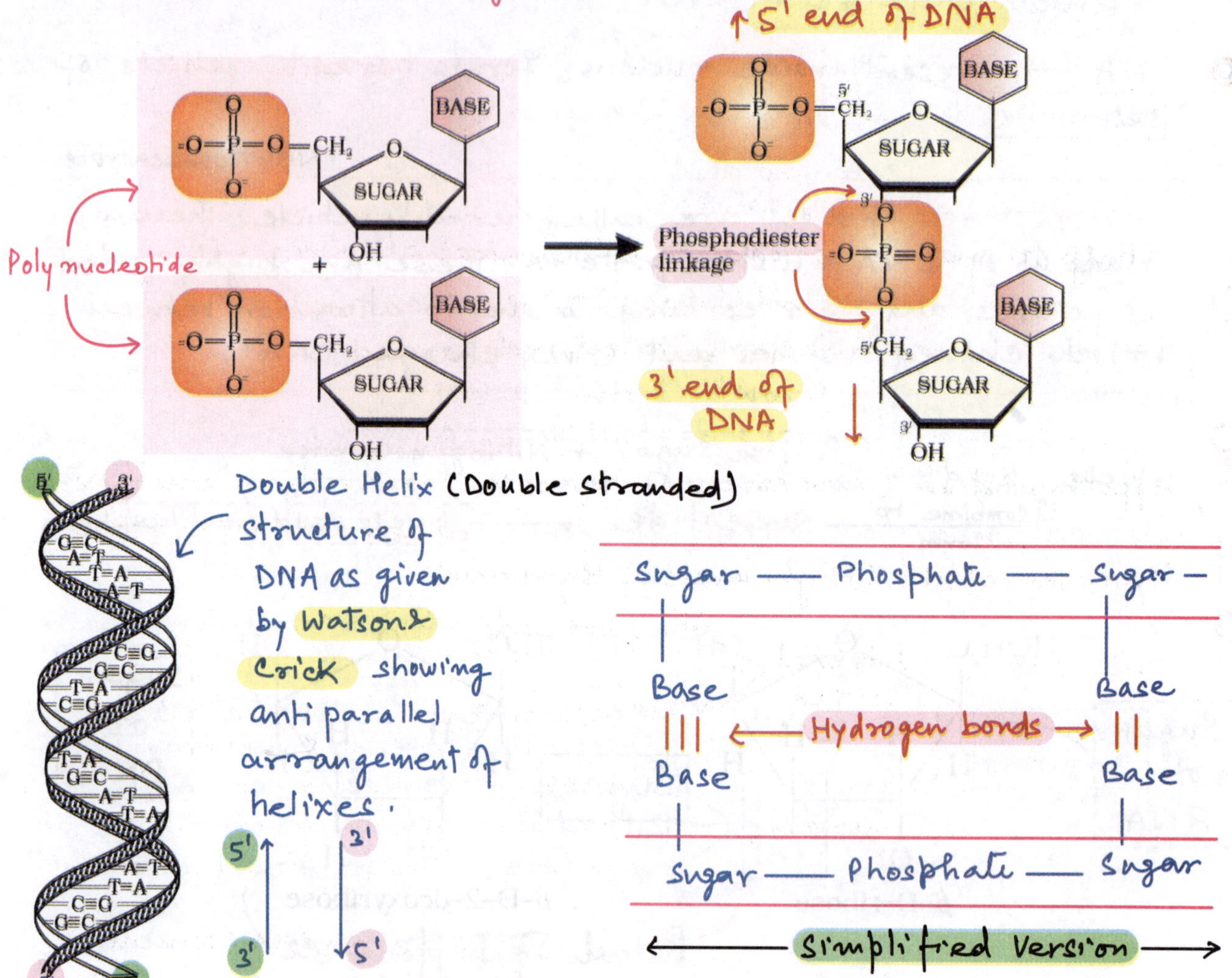

- Dhyan Rakho! In DNA Thymine always pairs with Adinine (forms 2 hydrogen bonds) and Cytosine pairs with Guanine (forms 3 hydrogen bonds)
- RNA ⟶ Single stranded ⟶ messenger-RNA (m-RNA); ribosomal-RNA (r-RNA); transfer – RNA (t-RNA) (Also called soluble-RNA)
- Sequence of Nitrogenous bases ⟶ unique for a person and matching information regarding this (sequence) ⟶ DNA fingerprinting $\xrightarrow{\text{helps in}}$ (i) Criminal identification, (ii) Paternity determination (iii) Dead Body identification (iv) Racial group identification.

- Information flow in heredity – DNA ⟶ RNA ⟶ Protein.

Hormones
- Intercellular messengers, produced by endocrine glands (those glands which pour their secretions directly into blood stream)

- Hormones
  - → Steroids – e.g., estrogens & androgens
  - → Polypeptides – e.g., insulin & endorphins
  - → Amino acid Derivatives – e.g., epinephrine & norepinephrine
  - Functions ↓ Help to maintain balance of biological activities

- ↓ Insulin ⟵ Blood Glucose level Regulation ⟶ Glucagon ↑
  - Epinephrine ⟵ Response to external stimuli ⟶ Norepinephrine
  - Growth hormone ⟵ Growth & development ⟶ Sex hormone

- Thyroxine ⟶ Iodinated derivative of Amino acid Tyrosine.
  Hypothyroidism (Low levels of thyroxine) → Obesity & Letharginess also caused by low iodine in diet. Iodised salt is the remedy
  Hyperthyroidism (High levels of thyroxine)

- Steroid Hormones
  - Adrenal cortex
    - Glucocorticoids – control carbohydrate metabolism, modulate inflammatory reactions & stress
    - Minerelocorticoids – control water & salt excretion levels by the kidney.
  - Gonads
    - Testosteron – male hormone
    - Estradiol – female hormone
    - Progesteron – female supportive hormone

NEET concentrate

- Addison's Disease ⟶ Due to improper functioning of Adrenal cortex Fatal disease; Symptoms – Hypoglycemia. weakness & increased susceptibility to stress, Treated with intake of Gluco & Mineralocorticoids.
- Deep voice, Facial hair, general physical constitution → sec. sexual characters of male.
- Besides controlling sec. sexual characters in females, Estradiol also controls menstrual cycle while Progesteron prepares uterus for implantation of fertilized eggs.

20. p-Block Elements

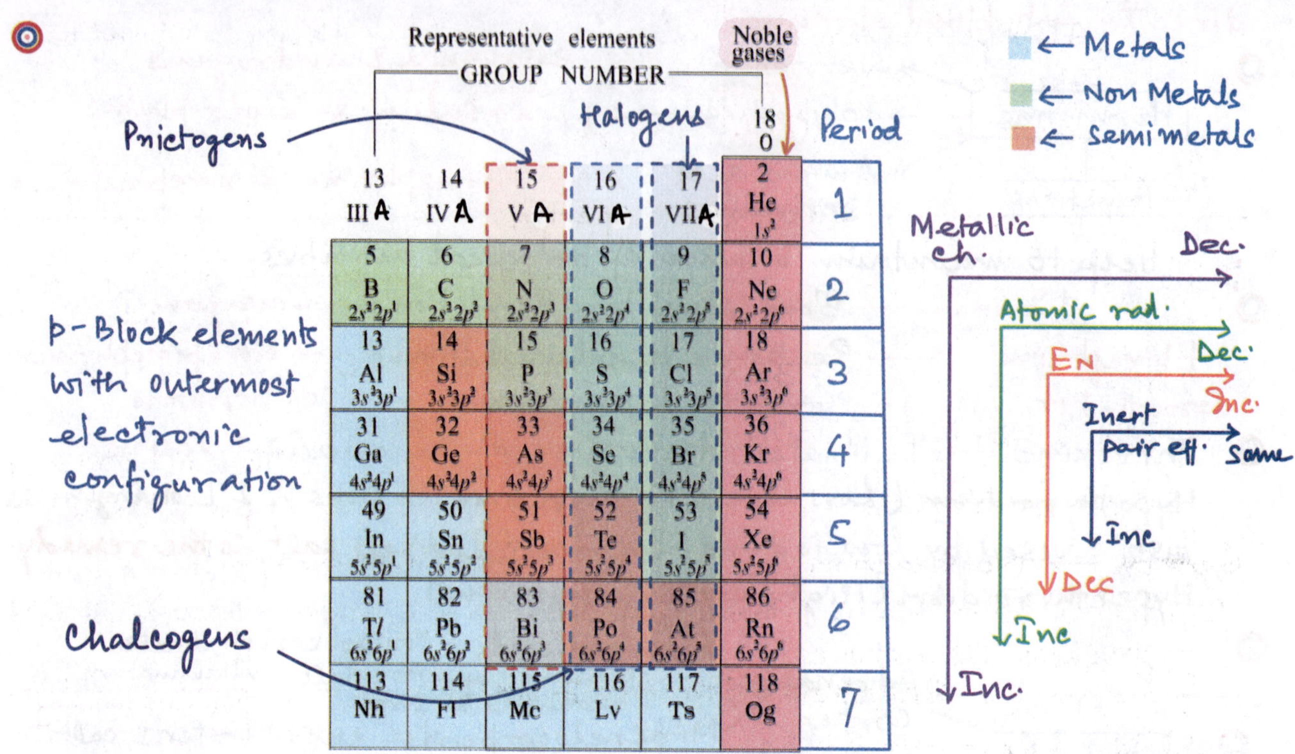

Group 13

- Most abundant – Al ; Density → Increases with Al having exceptionally low density (due to its very large molar volume),
- Oxidation state – +3 & +1 ; stability of +3 decreases while that of +1 increases down the group (due to inert pair effect i.e., tendency of s-electrons to remain together)
- B – Semimetal (more closer to non metals than to metals) It does not have capacity to form B^{3+} ion. Its compounds are largely covalent & because of which its oxides form oxoacids with water.
- Atomic Radius: B < Ga < Al < In < Tl ← Smaller radii due to poor screening of 3d e^-

  Electronegativity: Al (1.5) < Ga (1.6) < In (1.7) < Tl (1.8) < B (2)

  Melting Point: Ga < In < Tl < Al < B

  Boiling Point: Tl < In < Ga < Al < B

  Oxidation states: B & Al – +3 ; Rest – +3 & +1

  I^st I.E.: In < Al < Ga < Tl < B

NEET concentrate

Compounds of Al → covalent in anhydrous state and ionic in aq. solutions.
Always remember Nature of oxide depends upon bond type i.e., Ionic bond favours alkaline nature while covalent bond favours acidic nature.

Chemical Properties

- $4B + 3O_2 \xrightarrow{\Delta} 2B_2O_3$
  $2Al + \frac{3}{2}O_2 \longrightarrow Al_2O_3$
  $2Al + 3H_2O \longrightarrow Al_2O_3 + 3H_2\uparrow$
  $4Tl + 2H_2O + O_2 \longrightarrow 4TlOH$
  $2B + N_2 \xrightarrow{\Delta} 2BN$

Ga & In → No reaction

B → Unreactive at room temp. & reacts on heating; Totally unreactive in crystalline form.
Al → Quite reactive, reaction exothermic ($\Delta H = -1670$ kJ) → Thermite reaction

BN: structure similar to graphite hence called Inorganic Graphite

Oxides of B → Acidic; those of Al & Ga → Amphoteric; those of In & Tl → Basic in nature.

Reaction with Air & water

- $2M + 3X_2 \longrightarrow 2MX_3$

All with sp^2 hybridisation & Trigonal planar structure, Lewis acids B > Al > Ga > In

All BX_3 → covalent; Fluorides of rest group members → Ionic while other trihalides → Covalent
$AlCl_3$ (anh.) → Covalent; (Aq.) → Ionic

Reaction with Halogens

- $2B + 6HNO_3 \xrightarrow{\Delta} 2H_3BO_3 + 6NO_2$
  (Hot, conc.)
  $2M + 6HCl \longrightarrow 2MCl_3 + 3H_2\uparrow$ (M: All except B)
  $Al + 4HNO_3 \longrightarrow Al(NO_3)_3 + 2H_2O + NO$
  $O_2 + NO_2 + Al_2O_3$ ← Protective layer

Tl dissolves in Acids forming Tl^+ and becomes passive in HCl (as it forms water soluble TlCl)

Reaction with Acids

- $2M + 2NaOH + 2H_2O \longrightarrow 2NaMO_2 + 3H_2\uparrow$ (This reaction is not shown by In & Tl)
  (M: Al or Ga)
  $2Al + 2NaOH + 6H_2O \longrightarrow 2Na^+[Al(OH)_4]^- + 3H_2\uparrow$
  Sodium tetrahydroxy aluminate (III)

NEET concentrate

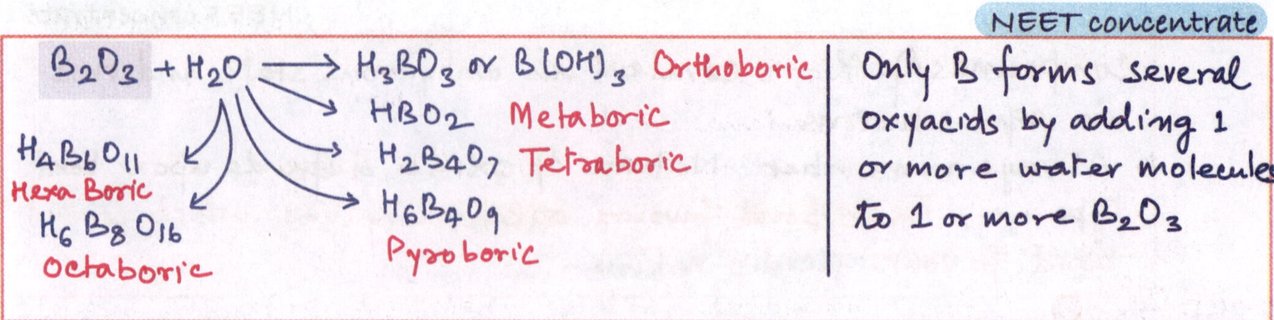

- Hydrides of Boron → Boranes (B_nH_{n+4} & B_nH_{n+6})
All of these are Lewis acids. BH_3 is the most important one which usually exist as Dimer
i.e.) B_2H_6 (Diborane) →
It restores monomeric form in the presence of Lewis bases like
THF = Tetra hydro Furan & DIGLYME = Diethylene glycol methyl ether.

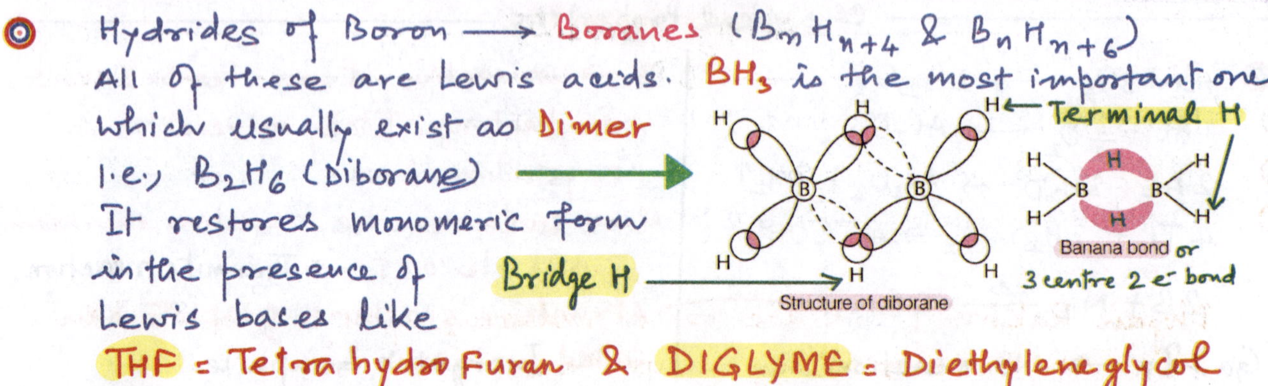

Structure of diborane

- Hydride of Al → Alane (Polymeric with Gen. formula $(AlH_3)_n$
GaH_3 → Less stable ; InH_3 & TlH_3 → extremely unstable

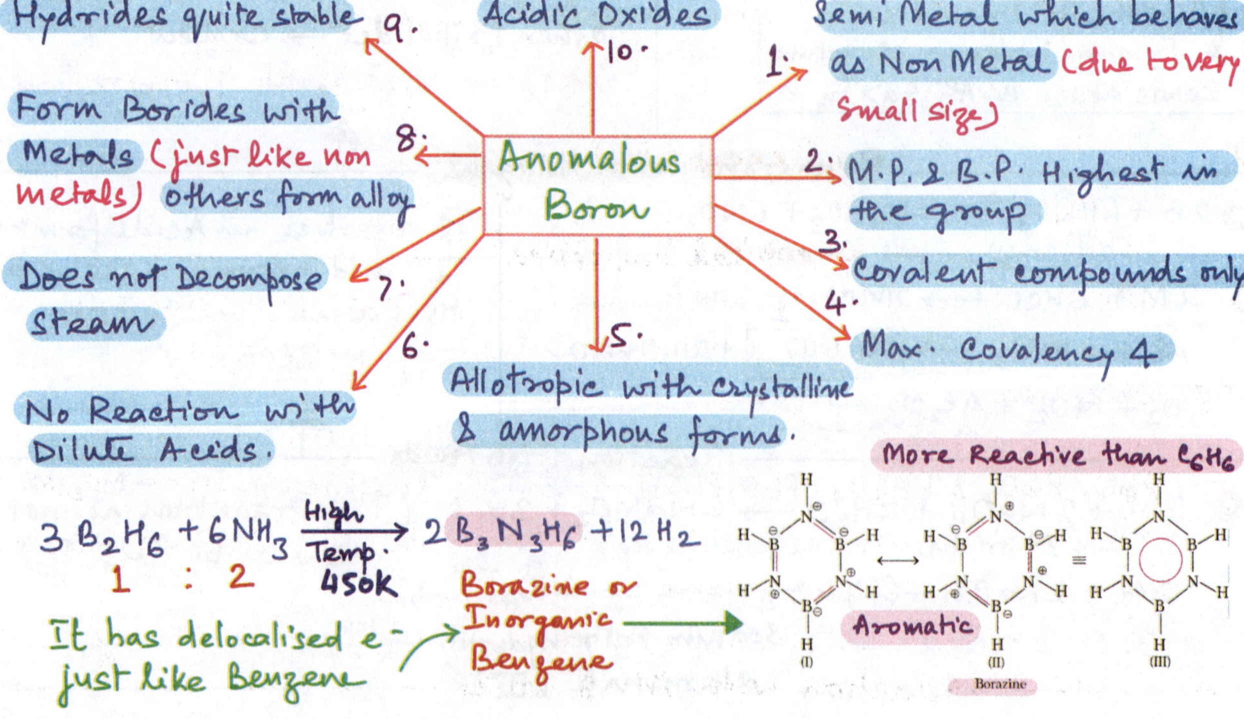

Borazine

NEET concentrate

- Al_2Cl_6 also has bridge structure but without Banana Bond (Cl–Al bridged structure: two Al atoms linked by two bridging Cl)
- Lewis acid strength of BX_3: $BF_3 < BCl_3 < BBr_3 < BI_3$ (due to strongest back bonding in BF_3)

Group 14

- C → Non metal; Si & Ge → Metalloids; Sn & Pb → Metals

At. size & Density → Inc.

B.P. → Dec.

- Density of C in Diamond > Density of Si (one exception only)
- M.P. C > Si > Ge > Pb > Sn ; Group 13 < Group 14 Similar in I.E.
- Oxidation states → +2 & +4 (stability of +2 increases down the group due to inert pair effect)

Dhyan Rakhna | Sn^{2+} are better reducing agents than Sn^{4+} & Pb^{4+} are better oxidising agents than Pb^{2+}.

- Due to its high EN C can form C_2^{2-} (acetylide) & C^{4-} (methanide) easily

Element	C	Si	Ge	Sn	Pb
Electronegativity (Pauling scale)	2.5	1.8	1.8	1.8	1.9

- Catenation C >> Si > Ge ≈ Sn (Not shown by Pb) Higher than both B & N family.

Max. hydrides due to catenation

Element	General formula of hydrides	Common name	Known number of hydride (n)
Carbon (C)	C_nH_{2n+2}	Alkane	n = 1 to 100
Silicon (Si)	Si_nH_{2n+2}	Silane	n = 1 to 8
Germanium (Ge)	Ge_nH_{2n+2}	Germane	n = 1 to 9
Tin (Sn)	Sn_2H_{2n+2}	Stannane	n = 1 or 2

Hydrides of C-family

- All show allotropy (except Pb); Tendency decreases from C to Pb.

Chemical Properties

- Oxides → MO & MO_2 ; All stable (Except SiO & GeO); CO → Neutral

$SiO_2 + Si \xrightarrow[\text{Temp.}]{\text{High}} SiO$ (formed and stable only at high temp.)

NEET concentrate

CO → Neutral; CO_2, SiO, SiO_2, GeO, GeO_2 → Acidic; SnO, SnO_2 PbO, PbO_2 & Pb_3O_4 ($PbO.PbO_2$) → Amphoteric; Acidic str. → MO_2 > MO

$MO_2 + 2NaOH \longrightarrow Na_2MO_3 + H_2O$ (Na_2MO_3: Carbonate, silicate, Germinates etc.)

$SnO_2 + 4HCl \longrightarrow SnCl_4 + 2H_2O$; $PbO_2 + 4HCl \longrightarrow PbCl_2 + Cl_2 + H_2O$

Pb_3O_4 → Red Lead or Sindoor; Pb_2O_3 → Lead sesquioxide

Reaction with Air & water

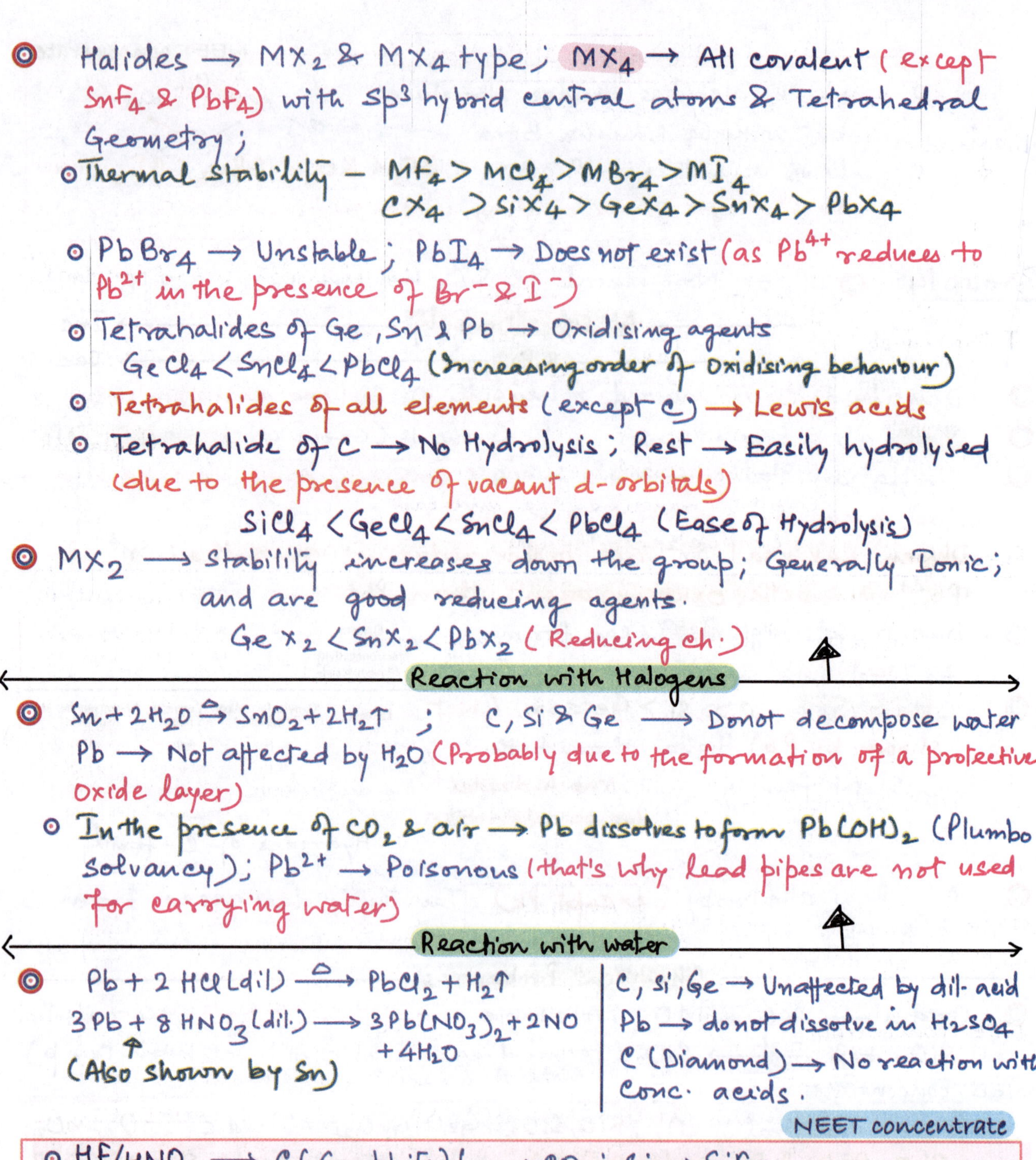

- Halides → MX_2 & MX_4 type; MX_4 → All covalent (except SnF_4 & PbF_4) with sp^3 hybrid central atoms & Tetrahedral Geometry;
  - Thermal stability – $MF_4 > MCl_4 > MBr_4 > MI_4$
    $CX_4 > SiX_4 > GeX_4 > SnX_4 > PbX_4$
  - $PbBr_4$ → Unstable; PbI_4 → Does not exist (as Pb^{4+} reduces to Pb^{2+} in the presence of Br^- & I^-)
  - Tetrahalides of Ge, Sn & Pb → Oxidising agents
    $GeCl_4 < SnCl_4 < PbCl_4$ (Increasing order of oxidising behaviour)
  - Tetrahalides of all elements (except C) → Lewis acids
  - Tetrahalide of C → No Hydrolysis; Rest → Easily hydrolysed (due to the presence of vacant d-orbitals)
    $SiCl_4 < GeCl_4 < SnCl_4 < PbCl_4$ (Ease of Hydrolysis)
- MX_2 → Stability increases down the group; Generally Ionic; and are good reducing agents.
  $GeX_2 < SnX_2 < PbX_2$ (Reducing ch.)

Reaction with Halogens

- $Sn + 2H_2O \xrightarrow{\Delta} SnO_2 + 2H_2\uparrow$; C, Si & Ge → Donot decompose water
  Pb → Not affected by H_2O (Probably due to the formation of a protective oxide layer)
  - In the presence of CO_2 & air → Pb dissolves to form $Pb(OH)_2$ (Plumbo solvancy); Pb^{2+} → Poisonous (that's why lead pipes are not used for carrying water)

Reaction with water

- $Pb + 2HCl(dil) \xrightarrow{\Delta} PbCl_2 + H_2\uparrow$
  $3Pb + 8HNO_3(dil.) \longrightarrow 3Pb(NO_3)_2 + 2NO + 4H_2O$
  (Also shown by Sn)

  C, Si, Ge → Unaffected by dil. acid
  Pb → do not dissolve in H_2SO_4
  C (Diamond) → No reaction with Conc. acids.

NEET concentrate

- HF/HNO_3 → C (Graphite) forms CO_2; Si → SiF_4
- Ge → Dissolves slowly in Hot conc. H_2SO_4 & HNO_3
  Sn → Also dissolves in conc. acids.
  Pb → does not dissolve in conc. HCl (due to $PbCl_2$ coating formation)

Reaction with Acids

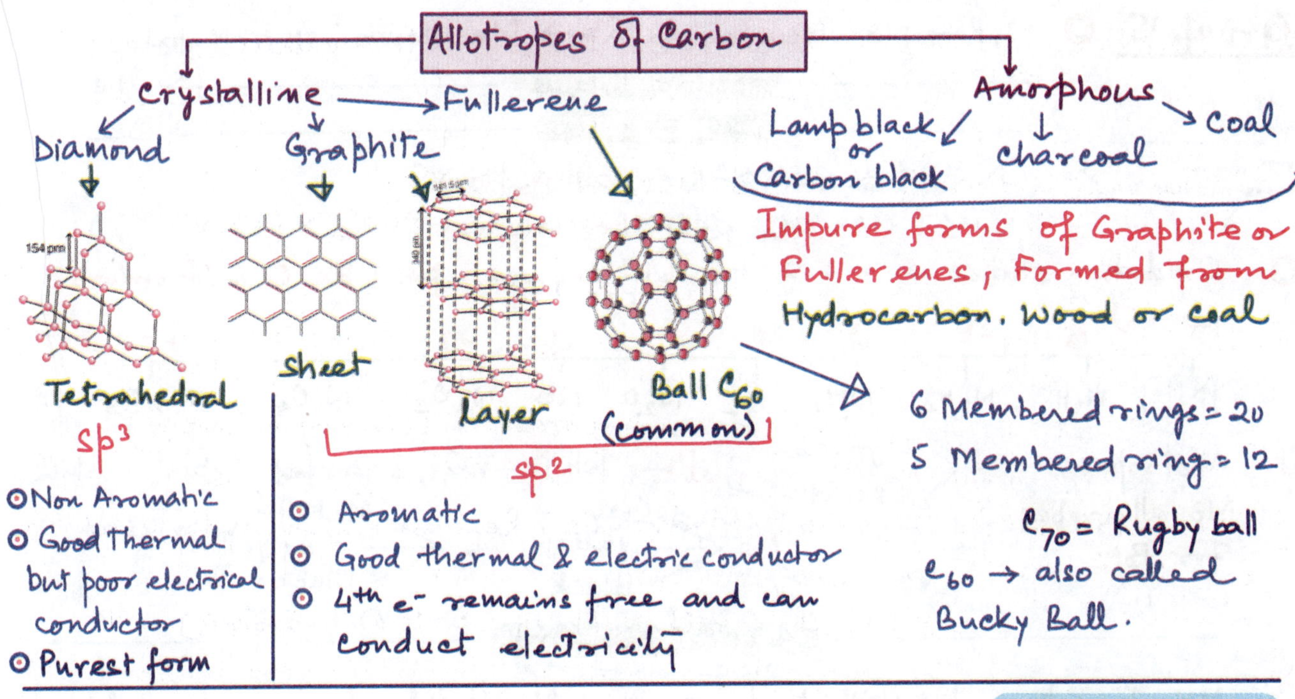

NEET concentrate

Graphite is thermodynamically more stable than Diamond. Its free energy of formation ($\Delta_f H^\circ$) is 1.9 kJ less than Diamond. However, Entropy of Graphite is more than Diamond.

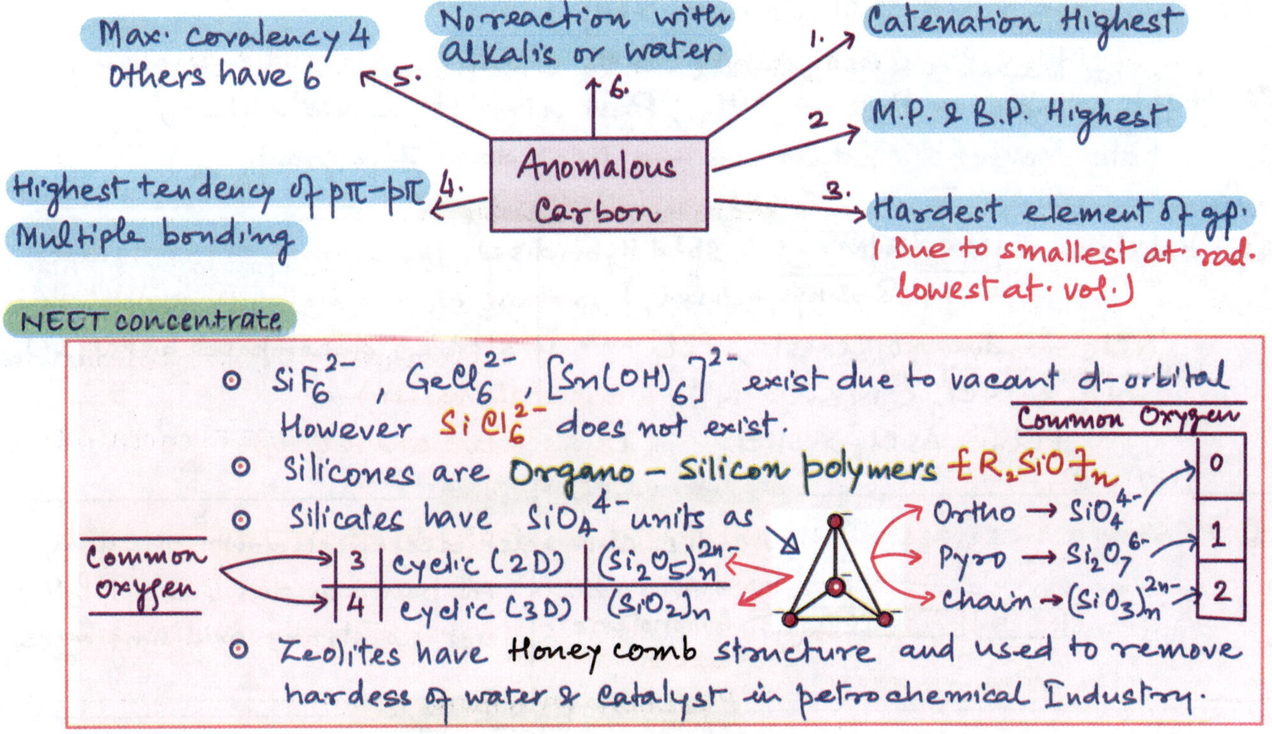

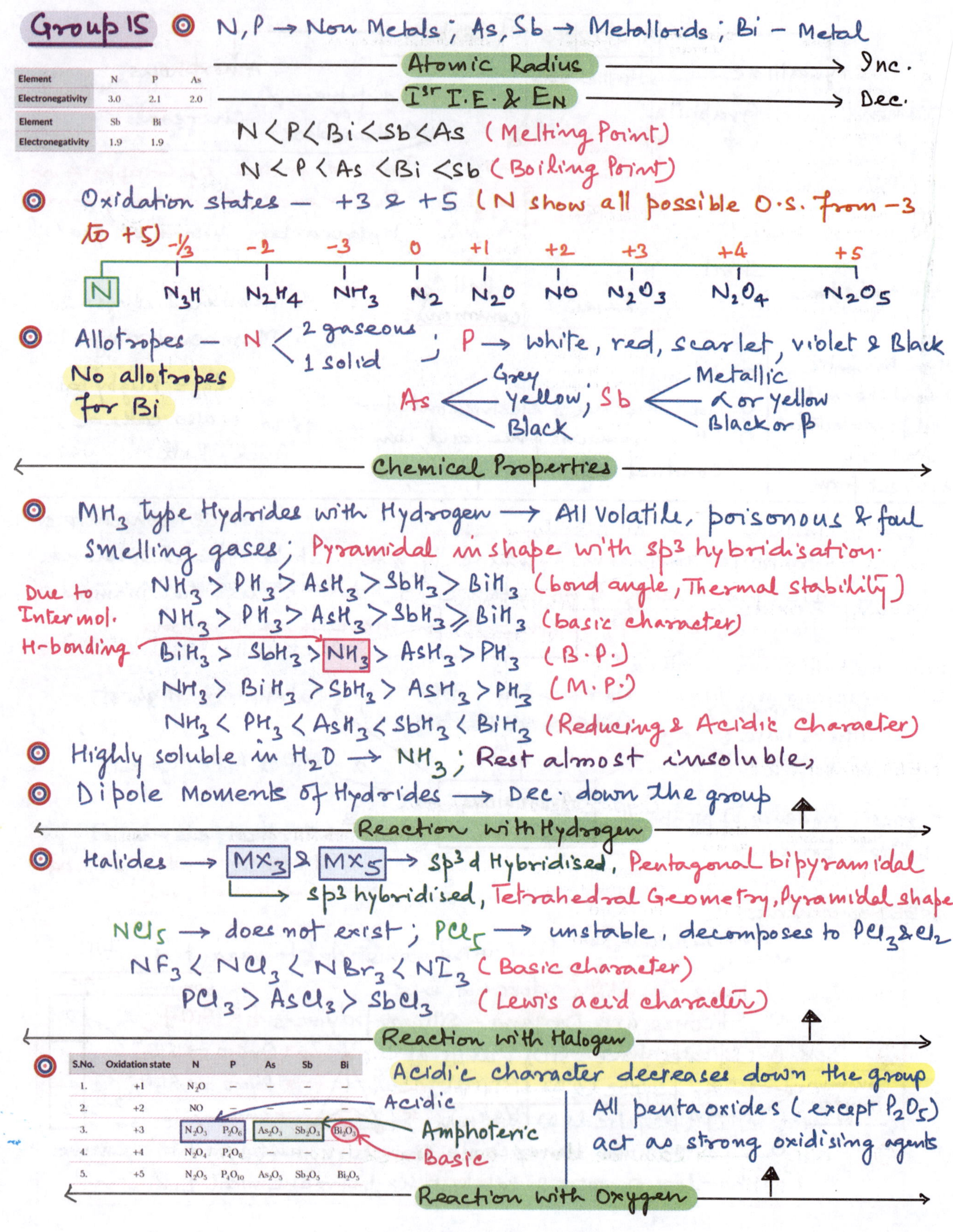

Group 15

- N, P → Non Metals; As, Sb → Metalloids; Bi – Metal

Element	N	P	As
Electronegativity	3.0	2.1	2.0

Element	Sb	Bi
Electronegativity	1.9	1.9

Atomic Radius → Inc.

1st I.E. & E_N → Dec.

N < P < Bi < Sb < As (Melting Point)

N < P < As < Bi < Sb (Boiling Point)

- Oxidation states – +3 & +5 (N show all possible O.S. from –3 to +5)

N_3H	N_2H_4	NH_3	N_2	N_2O	NO	N_2O_3	N_2O_4	N_2O_5
–1/3	–2	–3	0	+1	+2	+3	+4	+5

- Allotropes – N < 2 gaseous, 1 solid ; P → white, red, scarlet, violet & Black

No allotropes for Bi

As < Grey, Yellow, Black ; Sb < Metallic, α or yellow, Black or β

Chemical Properties

- MH_3 type Hydrides with Hydrogen → All volatile, poisonous & foul smelling gases; Pyramidal in shape with sp^3 hybridisation.

$NH_3 > PH_3 > AsH_3 > SbH_3 > BiH_3$ (bond angle, Thermal stability)

$NH_3 > PH_3 > AsH_3 > SbH_3 \geq BiH_3$ (basic character)

$BiH_3 > SbH_3 > NH_3 > AsH_3 > PH_3$ (B.P.) — Due to Intermol. H-bonding (NH_3)

$NH_3 > BiH_3 > SbH_3 > AsH_3 > PH_3$ (M.P.)

$NH_3 < PH_3 < AsH_3 < SbH_3 < BiH_3$ (Reducing & Acidic character)

- Highly soluble in H_2O → NH_3 ; Rest almost insoluble,
- Dipole Moments of Hydrides → Dec. down the group

Reaction with Hydrogen

- Halides → MX_3 & MX_5 → sp^3d Hybridised, Pentagonal bipyramidal

  MX_3 → sp^3 hybridised, Tetrahedral Geometry, Pyramidal shape

NCl_5 → does not exist ; PCl_5 → unstable, decomposes to PCl_3 & Cl_2

$NF_3 < NCl_3 < NBr_3 < NI_3$ (Basic character)

$PCl_3 > AsCl_3 > SbCl_3$ (Lewis acid character)

Reaction with Halogen

S.No.	Oxidation state	N	P	As	Sb	Bi
1.	+1	N_2O	–	–	–	–
2.	+2	NO	–	–	–	–
3.	+3	N_2O_3	P_2O_6	As_2O_3	Sb_2O_3	Bi_2O_3
4.	+4	N_2O_4	P_4O_8	–	–	–
5.	+5	N_2O_5	P_4O_{10}	As_2O_5	Sb_2O_5	Bi_2O_5

Acidic (N_2O_3, P_2O_6); Amphoteric (As_2O_3, Sb_2O_3); Basic (Bi_2O_3)

Acidic character decreases down the group

All pentaoxides (except P_2O_5) act as strong oxidising agents

Reaction with Oxygen

OXIDES OF NITROGEN

Name	Oxidation state of nitrogen	Properties	Resonance structure (Lewis dot form)
Dinitrogen monoxide or dinitrogen oxide or nitrous oxide [Nitrogen (I) oxide] (N_2O) (Laughing gas)	+1	Colourless gas, neutral	$N=N=O \longleftrightarrow N\equiv N-O$ — N 113 pm N 119 pm O, Linear Molecule
Nitrogen monoxide or nitric oxide [Nitrogen (II) oxide] (NO)	+2	Colourless gas, neutral, paramagnetic in gaseous state	$N=O$ — N 115 pm O, Linear molecule
Dinitrogen trioxide [Nitrogen (III) oxide] (N_2O_3)	+3	Blue solid, acidic	(Unsymmetrical) — 105°, 114 pm, 186 pm, 121 pm, 130°, 117°, Planar
Nitrogen dioxide [Nitrogen (IV) oxide] (NO_2)	+4	Brown gas, reactive, paramagnetic, acidic	120 pm, 134°
Dinitrogen tetraoxide [Nitrogen (IV) oxide] (N_2O_4)	+4	Colourless exists both in solid and liquid state with NO_2 in equilibrium, acidic.	121 pm, 175 pm, 135°, Planar
Dinitrogen pentaoxide [Nitrogen (V) oxide] (N_2O_5)	+5	Unstable as gas. In the solid state exists as $[NO_2]^+[NO_3]^-$, colourless, acidic.	119 pm, 151 pm, 112°, 134°, Planar

Anomalous Nitrogen

1. Gas while others solid
2. Diatomic molecule with 2π bonds.
3. Chemically Inert while others reactive (due to high Bond Dissociation En.)
4. NCl_3 exist but NCl_5 Not (due to absence of d-orbitals)
5. Non metallic while others either metalloid or Metals
6. variety of oxides
7. NH_3 Most stable & forms H-bonds
8. All O.S. from −3 to +5

NEET concentrate

Oxoacids of Nitrogen

Name of oxoacid	Molecular formula	Structure	Oxidation state of N	Basicity	Nature
Hyponitrous acid	$H_2N_2O_2$	HO—N=N—OH exists as *trans*-isomer dipole moment being zero	+1	2(dibasic)	Highly explosive
Nitrous acid	HNO_2	HO—N=O	+3	1(monobasic)	Unstable weak acid
Nitric acid	HNO_3	H—O—N=O, N→O	+5	1(monobasic)	Stable, strong acid
Pernitric acid	HNO_4	O=N—O—O—H, N→O	+5	1(monobasic)	Unstable and explosive

- Solid PCl_5 exists as $\longrightarrow [PCl_4]^+[PCl_6]^- \longleftrightarrow [sp^3]^+[sp^3d^2]^-$
  Solid PBr_5 exists as $\longrightarrow [PBr_4]^+Br^- \longleftrightarrow [sp^3]^+$
  Solid N_2O_5 exists as $\longrightarrow [NO_2^+][NO_3^-] \longleftrightarrow [sp][sp^2]$
- $NH_3 \longrightarrow$ Can be dried over Quick Lime (CaO)

Group 16

◎ O, S, Se, Te → Non Metals; Po → Radio active
Chalcogens → Ore forming (form −ve part of ore)

I^{st} I.E.
Gp.15 > Gp.16

——— Atomic Radius, MP, BP & Density ———→ Inc.
——— I.E. & EN ———→ Dec.

Element	Oxidation state
O	-2, -1, $-\frac{1}{2}$
S	-2, +2, +4, +6
Se	-2, +2, +4, +6
Te	-2, +2, +4, +6
Po	+2, +4

◎ $O \rightarrow O_2$; S & Se → S_8, Se_8; All show allotropy. Oxygen < O_2, O_3 ; S → Rhombic (α), monoclinic (β), plastic (γ), colloidal (δ) (all non metallic) Se < Red (Non metallic), Grey (Metallic)
Te < Non-metallic, Metallic (More stable) Po → α & β (Both Metallic)

NEET concentrate

Oxygen show other O.S. as well i.e., $+\frac{1}{2} \rightarrow O_2^+[AsF_6]^-$; $+1 \rightarrow O_2F_2$
$+2 \rightarrow OF_2$; $-\frac{1}{3} \rightarrow KO_3$
Dhyan Rakho! Oxygen ki (+)ve oxidation states sirf aur sirf Fluorine ke saath hi possible hai

←——— Chemical Properties ———→

◎ $M + H_2 \longrightarrow MH_2$ or H_2M ; H_2O → Liquid at room temp. rest gases (Due to its ability to form Hydrogen bonds)

$H_2O > H_2S > H_2Se > H_2Te$ (Bond Angle, Thermal stability)
$H_2O < H_2S < H_2Se < H_2Te$ (Acidic & Reducing character)
$H_2S < H_2Se < H_2Te < H_2Po < H_2O$ (MP and B.P.)

←——— Reaction with Hydrogen ———→

◎ With Oxygen MO, MO_2 & MO_3 type Oxides are formed →

Type of oxide	O	S	Se	Te	Po
Monoxide	–	SO	–	TeO	PoO
Dioxide	O_2	SO_2	SeO_2	TeO_2	PoO_2
Trioxide	O_3	SO_3	SeO_3	TeO_3	PoO_3
Heptoxide	–	S_2O_7	–	–	–

$MO_3 > MO_2$ (Oxidising power)
$SO_3 > SeO_3 > TeO_3$ (Acidic Nature)

←——— Reaction with Oxygen ———→

◎ MX_2, MX_4 & MX type halides
$M + 3F_2 \longrightarrow MF_6$
$2M + Cl_2 \longrightarrow M_2Cl_2 \xrightarrow{Cl_2} 2MCl_2$
$M + 2Cl_2 \longrightarrow MCl_4$
Oxygen forms halides only with F

Oxidation States in Halides → +1, +2, +4 & +6
F > Cl > Br > I (Stability for same M)
SF_6 → Thermodynamically inert, non toxic gas, used in High Voltage gen.

←——— Reaction with Halogens ———→

Oxoacids of S

NEET concentrate

Sulphurous Acid Series

	Formula	O.S.	Name	Structure
(a)	H_2SO_3	S (+ 4)	Sulphurous acid	$(HO)_2S{=}O$
(b)	$H_2S_2O_5$	S (+ 5) *S (+ 3)	Disulphurous acid or Pyrosulphurous acid	$H{-}O{-}S(=O)_2{-}S^*(=O){-}OH$
(c)	$H_2S_2O_4$	S (+ 3)	Dithionous acid	$HO{-}S(=O){-}S(=O){-}OH$

Sulphuric Acid Series

	Formula	O.S.	Name	Structure
(a)	H_2SO_4	S (+ 6)	Sulphuric acid	$HO{-}S(=O)_2{-}OH$
(b)	$H_2S_2O_3$	S (+ 4) *S(0)	Thiosulphuric acid	$HO{-}S(=S^*)(=O){-}OH$
(c)	$H_2S_2O_7$	S (+ 6)	Pyrosulphuric acid (oleum)	$HO{-}S(=O)_2{-}O{-}S(=O)_2{-}OH$

Peroxo Acid Series

	Formula	O.S.	Name	Structure
(a)	H_2SO_5	S (+ 6)	Peroxomonosulphuric acid (Caro's acid)	$HO{-}S(=O)_2{-}O{-}OH$
(b)	$H_2S_2O_8$	S (+ 6)	Peroxodisulphuric acid (Marshall's acid)	$HO{-}S(=O)_2{-}O{-}O{-}S(=O)_2{-}OH$

Thionic Acid Series

	Formula	O.S.	Name	Structure
(a)	$H_2S_2O_6$	S (+5)	Dithionic acid	$HO{-}S(=O)_2{-}S(=O)_2{-}OH$
(b)	$H_2S_nO_6$	S (+5) S* (0)	Polythionic acid	$HO{-}S(=O)_2{-}(S^*)_n{-}S(=O)_2{-}OH$

Anomalous Oxygen

1. Diatomic gas while others are solid
2. Highest EN (Hence form ionic and polar compounds largely)
3. Hydride (H_2O) Non poisonous while others have poisonous hydrides
4. Only pπ – pπ bonds while S → pπ – dπ bond
5. Only O_2 & S_2 are paramagnetic while others not
6. O.S. → usually (–)ve while others show usually (+)ve

Dhyan Rakha | SO_2 Bhi CO_2 ki tarah hi lime water ko milky Kar deti hai aur Yeh milkiness SO_2 ki excess mein dissolve ho jati hai.

$$SO_2 + Ca(OH)_2 \longrightarrow \underset{\text{milky}}{CaSO_3} \xrightarrow{\text{Excess } SO_2 + H_2O} Ca(HSO_3)_2 \text{ (soluble)}$$

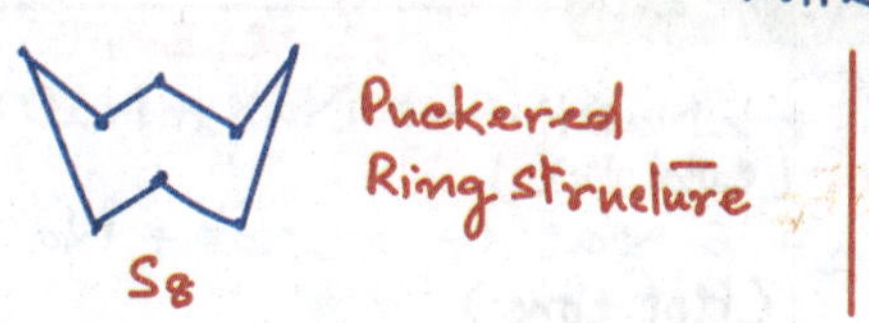

Chair form

S6

OF_6 does not exist due to absence of d orbitals in oxygen

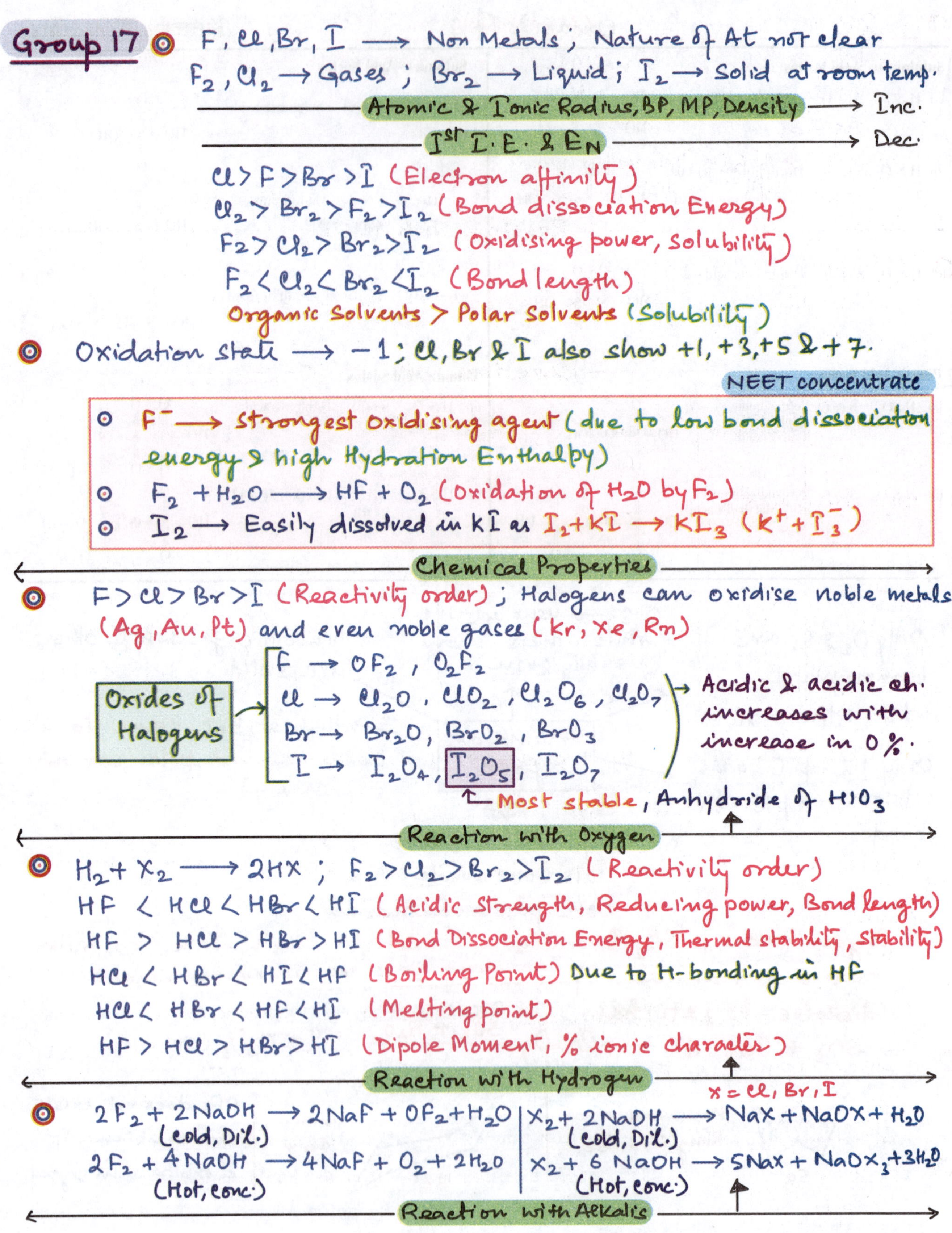

Group 17

- F, Cl, Br, I ⟶ Non Metals; Nature of At not clear

  F_2, Cl_2 ⟶ Gases; Br_2 ⟶ Liquid; I_2 ⟶ Solid at room temp.

  ⟵ Atomic & Ionic Radius, BP, MP, Density ⟶ Inc.

  ⟵ I^{st} I.E. & E_N ⟶ Dec.

  Cl > F > Br > I (Electron affinity)

  $Cl_2 > Br_2 > F_2 > I_2$ (Bond dissociation Energy)

  $F_2 > Cl_2 > Br_2 > I_2$ (Oxidising power, solubility)

  $F_2 < Cl_2 < Br_2 < I_2$ (Bond length)

  Organic Solvents > Polar Solvents (Solubility)

- Oxidation state ⟶ −1; Cl, Br & I also show +1, +3, +5 & +7.

NEET concentrate

- F^- ⟶ strongest oxidising agent (due to low bond dissociation energy & high Hydration Enthalpy)
- $F_2 + H_2O \longrightarrow HF + O_2$ (Oxidation of H_2O by F_2)
- I_2 ⟶ Easily dissolved in KI as $I_2 + KI \rightarrow KI_3$ $(K^+ + I_3^-)$

⟵ **Chemical Properties** ⟶

- F > Cl > Br > I (Reactivity order); Halogens can oxidise noble metals (Ag, Au, Pt) and even noble gases (Kr, Xe, Rn)

Oxides of Halogens ⟶

- F ⟶ OF_2, O_2F_2
- Cl ⟶ Cl_2O, ClO_2, Cl_2O_6, Cl_2O_7
- Br ⟶ Br_2O, BrO_2, BrO_3
- I ⟶ I_2O_4, I_2O_5, I_2O_7

⟶ Acidic & acidic ch. increases with increase in O%.

I_2O_5 ⟵ Most stable, Anhydride of HIO_3

⟵ **Reaction with Oxygen** ⟶

- $H_2 + X_2 \longrightarrow 2HX$; $F_2 > Cl_2 > Br_2 > I_2$ (Reactivity order)

  HF < HCl < HBr < HI (Acidic Strength, Reducing power, Bond length)

  HF > HCl > HBr > HI (Bond Dissociation Energy, Thermal stability, Stability)

  HCl < HBr < HI < HF (Boiling Point) Due to H-bonding in HF

  HCl < HBr < HF < HI (Melting point)

  HF > HCl > HBr > HI (Dipole Moment, % ionic character)

⟵ **Reaction with Hydrogen** ⟶

- $2F_2 + 2NaOH$ (cold, Dil.) $\longrightarrow 2NaF + OF_2 + H_2O$

  $2F_2 + 4NaOH$ (Hot, conc.) $\longrightarrow 4NaF + O_2 + 2H_2O$

  $X_2 + 2NaOH$ (cold, Dil.) $\longrightarrow NaX + NaOX + H_2O$ (X = Cl, Br, I)

  $X_2 + 6NaOH$ (Hot, conc.) $\longrightarrow 5NaX + NaOX_3 + 3H_2O$

⟵ **Reaction with Alkalis** ⟶

- $2M + nX_2 \longrightarrow 2MX_n$ (M → Metal; n → Oxidation state of Metal)
  $MF_n > MCl_n > MBr_n > MI_n$ (Ionic character → Different halides)
  $MCl > MCl_2 > MCl_3 > MCl_4$ (Ionic character → same halogen)
  $AgF > AgCl > AgBr > AgI$ (solubility of silver halides)
  AgCl: white ppt; AgBr: pale yellow ppt; AgI: yellow ppt

Reaction with Metals

- $F_2 + 2H_2O \longrightarrow 4HF + O_2$
  $X_2 + H_2O \longrightarrow HX + HOX$ (x = Cl, Br)
  I_2 does not reacts with water spontaneouly.

Reaction with water

Properties	HOX Hypohalous acid	HXO_2 Halous acid	HXO_3 Halic acid	HXO_4 Perhalic acid
	HOF	–	–	–
	HOCl	$HClO_2$	$HClO_3$	$HClO_4$
	HOBr	–	$HBrO_3$	$HBrO_4$
	HOI	–	HIO_3	HIO_4
Anhydride	X_2O	X_2O_3	X_2O_5	X_2O_7
Oxidation state of X	+I	+III	+V	+VII
Oxidising power	strong	←	←	weak
Acid strength*	weak	→	→	strong
Thermal stability	weak	→	→	good
Hydrolysis of anion	maximum	←	←	minimum
Structure of anion	(OCl^-) linear	(ClO_2^-) angular	(ClO_3^-) trigonal pyramidal	(ClO_4^-) tetrahedral

- Acid strength of oxo acids increases as the size of Halogen atom decreases.

HClO → Angular
$HClO_2$ → Angular
$HClO_3$ → Pyramidal
$HClO_4$ → Tetrahedral

Oxoacids of Halogen

XY	XY_3	XY_5	XY_7
ClF	ClF_3	ClF_5	
BrF	BrF_3	BrF_5	
ICl	ICl_3 (I_2Cl_6)	IF_5	IF_7 (only)
IBr			
BrCl			

XY: X — Y Linear
XY_3: T-shaped
XY_5: Square Pyramidal
XY_7: Pentagonal Bipyramidal

Possible Interhalogen Compounds with their shapes

- Interhalogen compounds > Halogens (Except F_2) Reactivity order.
  $ClF_3 > BrF_3 > IF_7 > ClF > BrF_5 > IF_5 > BrF > IF_3 > IF$ (Reactivity)
  Stability of interhalogen compound ∝ size of central atom.
- A polyatomic molecule with properties similar to halogens is called Pseudohalogen e.g., CN^-, Cyanate, thiocyanate, Azide etc.

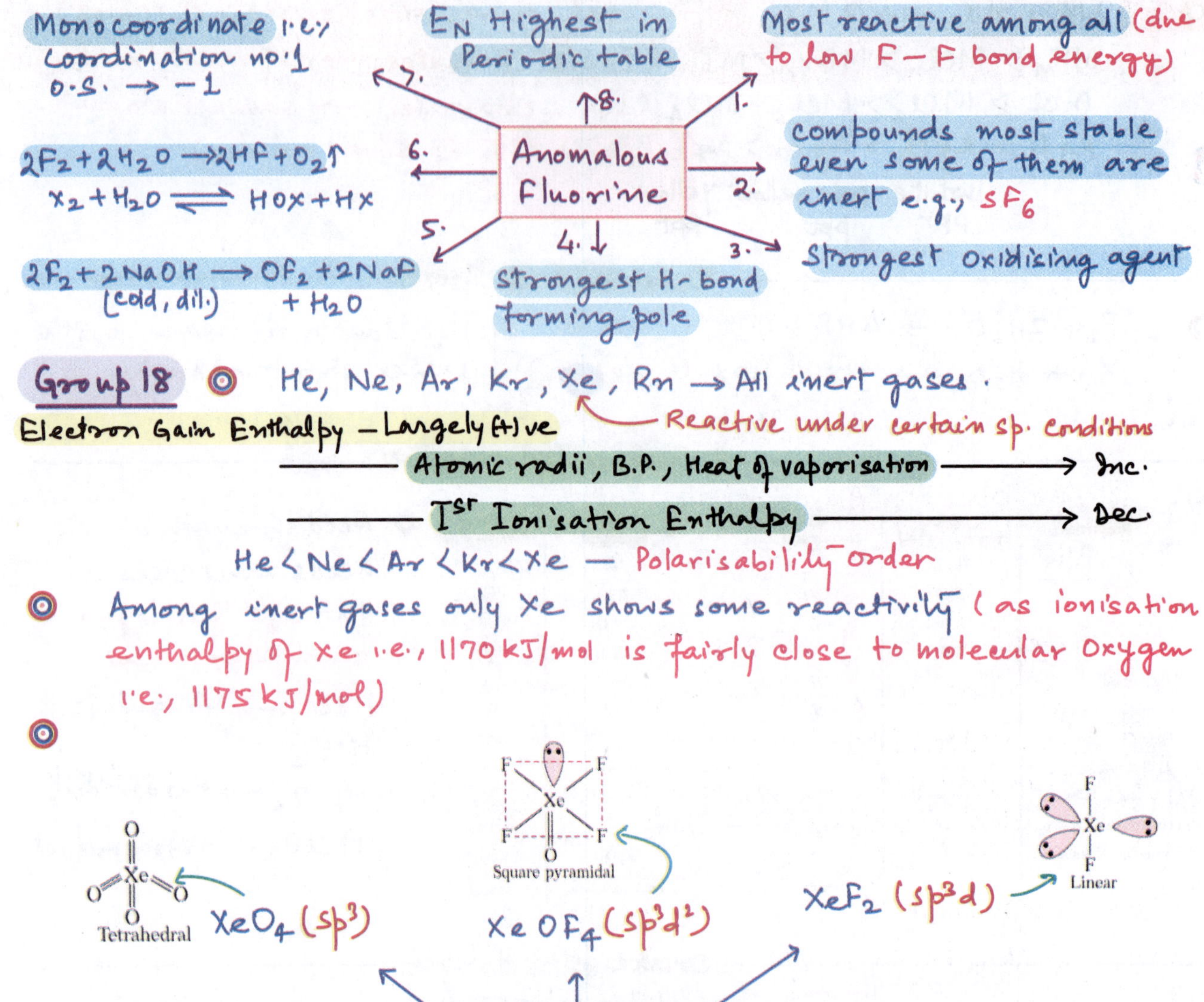

Group 18 ◎ He, Ne, Ar, Kr, Xe, Rn → All inert gases. (Xe — Reactive under certain sp. conditions)

Electron Gain Enthalpy — Largely (+)ve

——— Atomic radii, B.P., Heat of vaporisation ———→ Inc.

——— Ist Ionisation Enthalpy ———→ Dec.

He < Ne < Ar < Kr < Xe — Polarisability order

◎ Among inert gases only Xe shows some reactivity (as ionisation enthalpy of Xe i.e., 1170 kJ/mol is fairly close to molecular Oxygen i.e., 1175 kJ/mol)

◎

Compounds of Xe

- XeO_4 (sp^3) — Tetrahedral
- $XeOF_4$ (sp^3d^2) — Square pyramidal
- XeF_2 (sp^3d) — Linear
- XeF_4 (sp^3d^2) — Square planar
- XeF_6 (sp^3d^3) — Distorted octahedral
- XeO_3 (sp^3) — Pyramidal

NEET concentrate

Ar, Kr & Xe form Clathrates or Cage compounds or host-guest compounds (e.g., $Xe \cdot 6H_2O$, Quinol Clathrate). Gases are trapped in the cavities of these crystal lattices. Compound with cavities is called host and the gas trapped is called Guest.

21. Principles Related to Practical Chemistry

- These principles can be broadly categorise into –
  - (a) Principles of Qualitative salt analysis
  - (b) Preparation of inorganic compounds & chemistry involved in titration.
  - (c) Qualitative analysis of Organic compounds & principles involved in some important experiments

(a) Principles of Qualitative salt analysis

Physical Examination of Salt / Mixture

Colour
- **Blue**, whose aq. solution is also blue → Hydrated salts of Cu^{2+} (Except Cl^- & CO_3^{--})
- **Green**, whose aq. solution is also green → Salts of Ni^+
- **Yellow brown**, aq. solution is yellow → salts of Fe^{2+}
- **Dark green**, aq. solution also same → salts of Cr^{3+}
- **Yellow green**, aq. solution is light green or almost colourless → Salts of Fe^{3+}
- **Black** substance → CuO, NiO, SnO, FeS, CuS, HgS, PbS, NiS, CoS, MnO_2, Fe_3O_4, FeO, Co_3O_4, Ni_2O_3, MnO_2, Ag_2S, Cu_2S.
- **Orange** substance → $Cr_2O_7^{2-}$, Sb_2S_3
- **Violet – Pink**, aq. solution is pink → salts of cobalt.
- **Brown** substance → CdO, PbO_2, SnS, Bi_2S_3, $MnCO_3$ (pale brown)
- **Red** substance → Cu_2O, HgO, Pb_3O_4, HgI_2

Density
- Mixture of salts is heavy → Salts of Hg and Pb
- Mixture of salt is light → salts of Zn, Al, Bi, Ca, Ba, Sr, Mg etc. (Chiefly carbonates)

Odour of Substance
- Ammonical smell → NH_4^+ salts
- Vinegar like smell → Acetates
- Smell of rotten eggs → S^{2-} salts

→ Solubility of salts in water

(i) Nitrite, Nitrates & Acetates → All metal salts are soluble in H_2O

(ii) Chlorides → All soluble except $AgCl$, Hg_2Cl_2 and $PbCl_2$

(iii) Bromides & Iodides → All except AgBr, Hg_2Br_2, $HgBr_2$, $PbBr_2$, AgI, Hg_2I_2, HgI_2 & PbI_2

(iv) Sulphides → All insoluble except those of group I, II and NH_4^+

(v) Carbonates → All insoluble except those of group I & $(NH_4)_2CO_3$

(vi) Sulphates → All soluble except $PbSO_4$, Hg_2SO_4, $BaSO_4$, $CaSO_4$ and Ag_2SO_4, which are sparingly soluble

(vii) Phosphates → All insoluble in water except phosphates of group 1 and $(NH_4)_3PO_4$

(viii) Hydroxides → All insoluble except those of group I, $Ba(OH)_2$, $Ca(OH)_2$ & Sr(OH)

Analysis of Acid Radicals

- → Group I – Radicals detected by dil HCl/ H_2SO_4
  SO_3^{--}, CO_3^{--}, S^{--}, NO_2^-
- → Group II – Radicals detected by conc. H_2SO_4
  Cl^-, Br^-, I^-, NO_3^-
- → Group III – Radicals which don't give any characteristic gas with dil/conc H_2SO_4
  SO_4^{--}, PO_4^{---}, BO_3^{--}, F^-

Wet Tests

Analysis of basic Radicals

Group	Radicals	Group Reagent
Group I	Ag^+, Hg_2^{+2}(I), Pb^{2+}	Dil. HCl (cold)
Group II	Cu^{2+}, Cd^{2+}, Pb^{2+}, Hg(II) Bi^{3+}, Sb^{3+}, Sn^{2+}, As^{3+}	H_2S gas in dil. HCl
Group III	Al^{3+}, Cr^{3+}, Fe^{3+}	NH_4OH in NH_4Cl
Group IV	Zn^{2+}, Ni^{2+}, Mn^{2+}, Co^{2+}	H_2S in Amm. medium
Group V	Ca^{2+}, Sr^{2+}, Ba^{2+}	$(NH_4)_2CO_3$ + NH_4Cl
Group VI	Mg^{2+}, (Na^+, K^+ also)	NH_4OH + Na_2HPO_4
Group 0	NH_4^+	Dil. NaOH/Δ

NEET concentrate

Dhyan Rakhna | jin groups mein ek se zyada reagents hain un sabhi groups mein correct ion ke precipitation ke liye common ion effect ka funda use kiya jaata hai

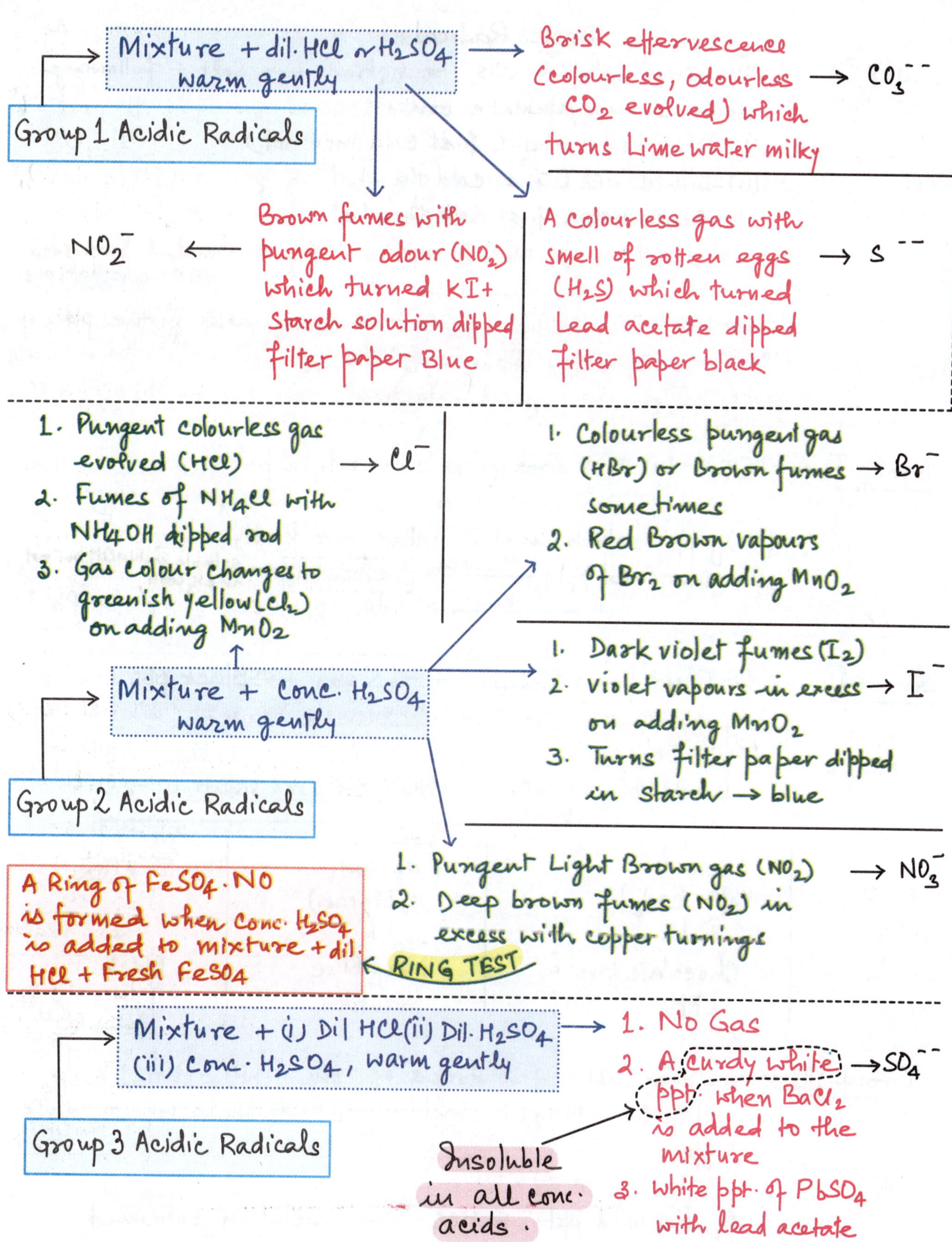
Group 1 Acidic Radicals
Mixture + dil. HCl or H_2SO_4 warm gently
Brisk effervescence (colourless, odourless CO_2 evolved) which turns Lime water milky → CO_3^{--}
Brown fumes with pungent odour (NO_2) which turned KI + Starch solution dipped filter paper Blue → NO_2^-
A colourless gas with smell of rotten eggs (H_2S) which turned Lead acetate dipped filter paper black → S^{--}
Group 2 Acidic Radicals
Mixture + Conc. H_2SO_4 warm gently
1. Pungent colourless gas evolved (HCl)
2. Fumes of NH_4Cl with NH_4OH dipped rod
3. Gas colour changes to greenish yellow (Cl_2) on adding MnO_2
→ Cl^-
1. Colourless pungent gas (HBr) or Brown fumes sometimes
2. Red Brown vapours of Br_2 on adding MnO_2
→ Br^-
1. Dark violet fumes (I_2)
2. Violet vapours in excess on adding MnO_2
3. Turns filter paper dipped in starch → blue
→ I^-
1. Pungent Light Brown gas (NO_2)
2. Deep brown fumes (NO_2) in excess with copper turnings
→ NO_3^-
RING TEST
A Ring of $FeSO_4 \cdot NO$ is formed when Conc. H_2SO_4 is added to mixture + dil. HCl + Fresh $FeSO_4$
Group 3 Acidic Radicals
Mixture + (i) Dil HCl (ii) Dil. H_2SO_4 (iii) Conc. H_2SO_4, warm gently
1. No Gas
2. A curdy white ppt. when $BaCl_2$ is added to the mixture
3. White ppt. of $PbSO_4$ with lead acetate
→ SO_4^{--}
Insoluble in all conc. acids.

Basic Radicals

Step I ⟶ Original Solution (OS) formation ⟶ Salt + following solvents in systematic order

(i) Distilled water (first cold then hot)

(ii) Dilute HCl (first cold then hot)

(iii) Conc. HCl (first cold then hot)

→ OS must be transparent & without any suspended particles.

NEET concentrate

> **Remember** | Dil. HNO_3 or H_2SO_4 can't be used in the place of HCl (as H_2SO_4 precipitates out Pb^{2+}, Ba^{2+}, Sr^{2+}, Ca^{2+} while HNO_3 gives yellow ppt. of sulphide ions.

Group I ⟶ OS + Dil. HCl drop by drop ⟶ white ppt → Gp.1 cations may be present (may be AgCl, $PbCl_2$ or Hg_2Cl_2)

(i) If ppt soluble in hot water ⟶ $PbCl_2$

(ii) Dissolved ppt. $\xrightarrow{K_2CrO_4}$ Yellow ppt ← soluble in NaOH but not in CH_3COOH

Dissolved ppt. $\xrightarrow{KI}$ yellow ppt ⟶ Pb^{2+}

Group II ⟶ OS (left from Group I) + H_2S gas ⟶ Black ppt → Any of Hg^{2+}, Pb^{2+}, Bi^{3+} or Cu^{2+} may be present (may be HgS, PbS, Bi_2S_3 or CuS)

Black ppt. + HNO_3 ⟶ Blue coloured solution ⟶ CuS

3 parts

Part 1	Part 2	Part 3
+ CH_3COOH & $K_4[Fe(CN)_6]$ ↓ Chocolate brown ppt.	+ aq. NH_3 (Excess) ↓ Deep Blue Solution	+ KSCN ↓ Black ppt ⟶ Cu^{2+}

Group III ⟶ OS or Salt + few drops of conc. HNO_3 (boil) & then NH_4Cl & NH_4OH slowly ⟶ Reddish brown or white ppt. ⟶ Fe^{3+} or Al^{3+} may be present (Reddish brown – Fe^{3+}, white – Al^{3+})

(i) Formed ppt. + HCl $\xrightarrow{\text{Dissolution}}$ Solution obtained

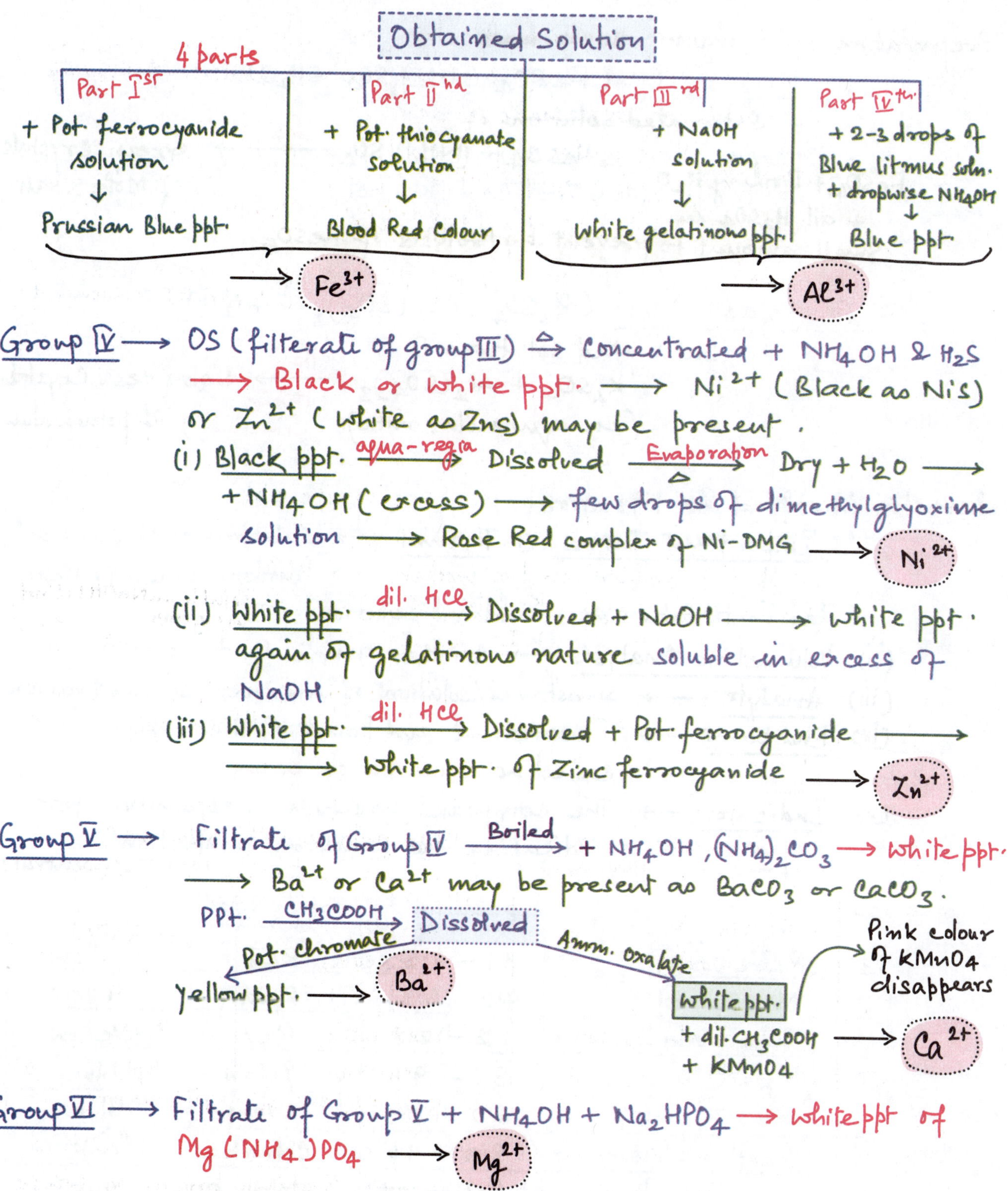

Obtained Solution

4 parts

Part I^{st}	Part IInd	Part IIIrd	Part IVth
+ Pot. ferrocyanide solution ↓ Prussian Blue ppt.	+ Pot. thiocyanate solution ↓ Blood Red Colour	+ NaOH solution ↓ White gelatinous ppt.	+ 2-3 drops of Blue litmus soln. + dropwise NH_4OH ↓ Blue ppt

Parts I and II → Fe^{3+}

Parts III and IV → Al^{3+}

Group IV → OS (filterate of group III) $\xrightarrow{\Delta}$ Concentrated + NH_4OH & H_2S → Black or white ppt. → Ni^{2+} (Black as NiS) or Zn^{2+} (White as ZnS) may be present.

(i) Black ppt. $\xrightarrow{\text{aqua-regia}}$ Dissolved $\xrightarrow[\Delta]{\text{Evaporation}}$ Dry + H_2O → + NH_4OH (excess) → few drops of dimethylglyoxime solution → Rose Red complex of Ni-DMG → Ni^{2+}

(ii) White ppt. $\xrightarrow{\text{dil. HCl}}$ Dissolved + NaOH → white ppt. again of gelatinous nature soluble in excess of NaOH

(iii) White ppt. $\xrightarrow{\text{dil. HCl}}$ Dissolved + Pot. ferrocyanide → → white ppt. of Zinc ferrocyanide → Zn^{2+}

Group V → Filtrate of Group IV $\xrightarrow{\text{Boiled}}$ + NH_4OH, $(NH_4)_2CO_3$ → white ppt. → Ba^{2+} or Ca^{2+} may be present as $BaCO_3$ or $CaCO_3$.

ppt. $\xrightarrow{CH_3COOH}$ Dissolved

Dissolved $\xrightarrow{\text{Pot. chromate}}$ Yellow ppt. → Ba^{2+}

Dissolved $\xrightarrow{\text{Amm. oxalate}}$ white ppt. + dil. CH_3COOH + $KMnO_4$ → Pink colour of $KMnO_4$ disappears → Ca^{2+}

Group VI → Filtrate of Group V + NH_4OH + Na_2HPO_4 → white ppt of $Mg(NH_4)PO_4$ → Mg^{2+}

Group Zero → Salt + 1-2 ml NaOH $\xrightarrow{\Delta}$ Smell of NH_3 + dense white fumes of NH_4Cl (when HCl wetted glass rod comes in contact with gas

Salt (aq. solution) + Nessler's reagent → red/brown ppt → NH_4^+

Preparation of inorganic compounds

(i) Mohr's Salt ($FeSO_4 \cdot (NH_4)_2SO_4 \cdot 6H_2O$)

Saturated solutions of

$FeSO_4 + (NH_4)_2SO_4 \xrightarrow[\text{& cooled}]{\text{Evaporated}}$ Green crystals of Mohr's salt.

$FeSO_4$ + Boiling H_2O + dil. H_2SO_4 in small amount to prevent hydrolysis of $FeSO_4$ → $FeSO_4$

(ii) Potash Alum ($K_2SO_4 \cdot Al_2(SO_4)_3 \cdot 24H_2O$)

Saturated solutions of

$K_2SO_4 + Al_2(SO_4)_3$ (in equimolar ratio) $\xrightarrow[H_2SO_4 \text{ (small amt.)}]{H_2O}$ Colourless Crystals of potash alum

Chemistry involved in titration

1. Important Terms (i) Titrant → substance of precisely known concentration added in titration as standard solution

(ii) Volumetric Analysis → Another name of titration

(iii) Analyte → substance/solution of unknown concentration

(iv) End point → Theoretical end point of the reaction also called as equivalence point.

(v) Indicator → The compound which is responsible for indicating the reaction completion.

Most common Acid-base Indicators

NEET concentrate

		pH Range	Colour In Acid	In Base
1.	Methyl orange	3.1 — 4.5	Red	Yellow
2.	Methyl red	4.2 — 6.3	Red	Yellow
3.	Thymol Blue	1.2 — 2.8	Red	Yellow
4.	Thymol Blue (Base)	8.1 — 9.6	Yellow	Blue
5.	Bromothymol blue	6.0 — 7.5	Orange	Blue
6.	Phenolphthalein	8.0 — 9.8	Colourless	Pink
7.	Thymophthalein	9.3 — 10.5	Colourless	Blue
8.	Phenol Red	6.4 — 8.2	Yellow	Red
9.	Bromophenol Blue	3.1 — 4.6	Yellow	Purple
10.	Alizarin yellow	10.1 — 12.1	Yellow	Lilac.

Your Important Notings

Your Important Notings